RELIGION, IDENTITY, AND GLOBAL GOVERNANCE:
IDEAS, EVIDENCE, AND PRACTICE

Edited by Patrick James

Religion, Identity, and Global Governance

Ideas, Evidence, and Practice

UNIVERSITY OF TORONTO PRESS
Toronto Buffalo London

© University of Toronto Press Incorporated 2011
Toronto Buffalo London
www.utppublishing.com
Printed in Canada

ISBN 978-1-4426-4066-5

∞

Printed on acid-free, 100% post-consumer recycled paper with vegetable-based inks.

Library and Archives Canada Cataloguing in Publication

Religion, identity, and global governance : ideas, evidence, and practice / edited by Patrick James.

Includes bibliographical references and index.
ISBN 978-1-4426-4066-5

1. Religion and international relations.   I. James, Patrick, 1957–

BL65.I55R44 2011   201'.727   C2010-905888-7

University of Toronto Press acknowledges the financial assistance to its publishing program of the Canada Council for the Arts and the Ontario Arts Council.

Canada Council for the Arts   Conseil des Arts du Canada   ONTARIO ARTS COUNCIL   CONSEIL DES ARTS DE L'ONTARIO

University of Toronto Press acknowledges the financial support of the Government of Canada through the Canada Book Fund for its publishing activities.

Contents

Figures and Tables vii

Preface ix

PART ONE: INTRODUCTION

1 Religion, Identity, and Global Governance: Setting the Agenda 3
 PATRICK JAMES

PART TWO: IDEAS

2 The Religious Challenge to International Relations Theory 19
 JOHN F. STACK JR

3 Religion and International Affairs: The State of the Art 37
 RON E. HASSNER

4 Mutual Renewal: On the Relationship of Human Rights to the Muslim World 57
 ANTHONY CHASE

PART THREE: EVIDENCE

5 State Religious Exclusivity and International Crises, 1990–2002 81
 JONATHAN FOX and NUKHET SANDAL

6 Religion, Identity, and the 'War on Terror': Insights from Religious Humanitarianism 108
 CECELIA LYNCH

7 Extremism and Military Intervention in South Asia: Indian Muslims and Sri Lankan Tamils   128
MANUS I. MIDLARSKY

8 Religion, Security Dilemma, and Conflict: The Case of Iraq   159
YASEMIN AKBABA and ZEYNEP TAYDAS

9 World Religions and Local Identities: The Case of Islamic Arbitration in Ontario, Canada   187
PATRICIA M. GOFF

PART FOUR: PRACTICE

10 John Paul II and the 'Just War' Doctrine: 'Make Peace through Justice and Forgiveness, Not War'   203
JAMES L. HEFT

11 Christian Mediation in International Conflicts   220
ROBERT B. LLOYD

12 The Role of Religious NGOs in Shaping Foreign Policy: Western Middle Powers and Reform Internationalism   244
STEVEN L. LAMY

13 Religion and Canadian Diplomacy: Promoting Pluralism on the Global Stage   271
EVAN H. POTTER

14 From Ideology to Identity: Building a Foundation for Communities of the Willing   292
CHRIS SEIPLE

PART FIVE: CONCLUSION

15 Religion, Identity, and Global Governance: What Have We Learned?   313
PATRICK JAMES

Contributors   325

Index   329

Figures and Tables

Figures
Figure 3.1   Broad, Deep, and Thick Religion   46
Figure 7.1   Changes in Authority Space over Time   130
Figure 7.2   Changes in Authority Space of Indian Muslims, Early Eighteenth Century to Present   138
Figure 7.3   Changes in Jaffna Tamil Authority Space over Time, Sixteenth Century to 1987   152

Tables
Table 5.1   Influence of State Religious Exclusivity on Crisis, 1990–2002   94
Table 5.2   Influence of State Religious Exclusivity on Crisis in Protracted Conflicts, 1990–2002   95
Table 11.1   Christian Traditions and Negotiation Types   228
Table 11.2   The Conflict Resolution Process and Third-Party Mediation   230
Table 11.3   Christian Traditions and Negotiating Goals and Levels   236
Table 12.1   Progress in Meeting MDG Goals in Developing Countries, 1990–2002   267

Preface

The University of Southern California hosted its first annual Religion, Identity, and Global Governance Conference on 18 and 19 October 2007. This volume is the legacy of that conference. Six panels and two special guest lectures comprised the two-day event during which debate and discussion of religion's role in foreign policy and political alliances throughout the world took place. Many of the papers presented during those two days have made their way into this volume and we are grateful to the Henry Luce Foundation for supporting the conference. Luce kindly conferred upon USC a major grant as part of an initiative to develop research on religion and international affairs.

With Steven L. Lamy and me as co-investigators, the Religion, Identity, and Global Governance (RIGG) Project, funded by Luce, is a major initiative on the USC campus. The following entities comprise RIGG at USC: School of International Relations (SIR), Center for International Studies (CIS), Center on Public Diplomacy, Center for Religion and Civic Culture, and the Knight Chair in Media and Religion. Participants in RIGG engage in research, teaching, and outreach. As editor of the first RIGG volume, I am grateful to all of those associated with the project for their input. The published work would not be the same without them.

I also want to thank the Center for International Studies and School of International Relations for administrative and financial support. This work benefited greatly from the support offered by Laurie Brand, director of SIR, an excellent administrator and academic colleague with whom I am privileged to work. My staff at CIS, most notably Indira Persad and our work study students, Jennifer Barrios and Daniel J. Smith, also have helped at various stages.

Some of the contributors to the volume also wish to extend their thanks or provide an acknowledgment. Anthony Chase acknowledges that some portions of his chapter are drawn from his previous work. Cecelia Lynch is grateful to the Andrew W. Mellon Foundation's New Directions Fellowship for funding to conduct interviews cited in her chapter. She also acknowledges that both the New Directions Fellowship and a previous SSRC-MacArthur Fellowship provided funding for background research. Jonathan Fox is grateful to the Israel Science Foundation (Grant 896/00) and the Sara and Simha Lainer Chair in Democracy and Civility. He also notes that the opinions expressed in this study are those of the authors and do not necessarily reflect the views of the John Templeton Foundation. Evan Potter notes that the views expressed in his chapter are those of the author and do not necessarily reflect the views of Foreign Affairs and International Trade Canada or the Government of Canada. Chris Seiple is grateful to Patrick James and Steve Lamy for leadership in the field of international relations as they work to reintroduce religion to the discipline in a manner that honours the field, its practitioners, and people of faith everywhere. Chris Seiple also thanks his family and the team at the Institute for Global Engagement, through whom he had the experiences and journey described in his chapter. He especially thanks his parents, Bob and Margaret Ann, and his wife, Alissa, and also notes that Liam and Hanan make everything worthwhile.

PART ONE

Introduction

1 Religion, Identity, and Global Governance: Setting the Agenda

PATRICK JAMES

Purpose

This volume seeks greater understanding of the connections between and among religion, identity, and global governance. Its central theme is that religion plays an important role in international relations and foreign policy. The volume pursues answers to several sets of interrelated questions:

- How is it established that religious identity is the relevant factor in explaining or understanding politics? How can it be known whether religion is 'real' versus a cover for some other factor such as ethnicity or group power?
- When and how can religion be applied to advance positive, peace-oriented agendas? What is the balance between religion as a cause of violence versus a possible source for achievement of a more peaceful world? In an overall sense, how do religion and global governance relate to each other?[1]
- How might governments in general, and especially the international system–leading United States, reconsider their foreign and domestic policies in light of religious resurgence around the world? In particular, what is the legacy of the Bush Doctrine and what should come next?

These questions obviously are worthwhile to answer in a world that continues to struggle with the legacy of 9/11 and multiple interstate and civil wars connected in some way to a 'War on Terror,' even if the rhetoric of the Obama Administration does not match that of its predecessor. Global governance, it is held here, cannot and will not improve unless a way is found to coexist with the powerful force of religion in creating and sustaining identity – even in the most technologically advanced societies.

Outline of the Volume

In some ways the current volume follows on the outstanding work of the *Fundamentalism Project*. Published in a series of high-profile volumes, the *Project* includes over one hundred case studies and provides powerful evidence that religious belief – regrettably, even its extremist incarnations – is a major part of today's world (Marty and Appleby 1993, 1994, 1995, 1996, 2004; see also Almond, Appleby, and Sivan 2003). The current study builds on that achievement. It addresses religion in a general sense as related to identity and prospects for global governance. The volume does so in three parts corresponding to ideas, evidence, and practice.

Part Two of the book, made up of chapters 2–4, features encompassing *ideas*. The chapters appear approximately in order of increasing specificity, although each is general and primarily theoretical.

Chapter 2 throws down the gauntlet regarding the ongoing relevance of religion to the discipline of international relations (IR). Stack asks a basic question: Why has religion been ignored over the course of so many decades? For too long, according to Stack, the field has bought into the catechism – please excuse the pun – from secularization theory. Standing on the shoulders of the giant figures from nineteenth- and early-twentieth-century social science, modern scholarship gradually came to the conclusion that religion, along with other manifestations of the pre-modern world, simply would wither away. People everywhere could be expected to give up their primordial beliefs in the face of modernization.

As Stack points out, nothing could be further from the truth. The 'liberal expectancy' about religion's demise is disappointed throughout the developing world in general and some parts of the developed world as well. Standard theorizing in IR, from realism through neorealism and various strains of liberalism, focuses exclusively on material processes and thereby misses the important persistence of religious beliefs. For example, models based on the distribution of capabilities, as are various incarnations of realism and neorealism, cannot help much in explaining what is observed when religious differences exacerbate conflict.

Religion's role in providing the basis for group identity is fundamental. Stack draws attention to the importance of religion as a form of *affective* motivation in accounting for the international and domestic politics of religion in today's world. He finishes on a positive note: faith-based organizations (FBOs) may provide the means to channel the enormous amount of religious energy that exists in a constructive direction.

Chapter 3 introduces the idea of 'thick religion' as a new approach that could help IR move beyond its current level of understanding. Hassner's chapter diagnoses the current scholarly situation as one that features an explosion of activity carried out largely by those with a lack of basic sympathy toward and understanding of religion itself. This comes across most directly in the vast number of post-9/11 studies that pertain in some way to Islam and violence in particular. (Hostility to religion and especially Islam has also come across in the mainstream media's storytelling since 9/11.) To Hassner this looks like a dead end. What, then, is to be done?

Hassner begins the case for his new idea of thick religion by classifying existing research under two headings: 'broad' and 'deep' religion. While valuable in many ways, each approach has limited scope. The former studies focus on religion in the international realm. They essentialize its role in terms of political or other implications. The latter emphasize context. They seek intimate familiarity with a specific religious movement or geographic region. Not surprisingly, these two strands of research tend to remain unconnected. To improve on this situation, which is inherently self-limiting, Hassner puts forward the concept of thick religion. The letters stand, respectively, for *t*heology, *h*ierarchy of religion organization, *i*conography or symbols, *c*eremony or belief, and *k*nowledge.

According to Hassner, research now should focus on (a) issue-areas in which religion intersects with international relations and (b) do so in a way that spans the five dimensions just enumerated. In this way, the best of both worlds – breadth and depth, so to speak – can be obtained. Thick religion is sensitive to religious context while also seeking generalization. Analytical chains, in ascending order of intrinsic value, can be correlative, causal, and constitutive. Existing studies generally feature the former two, but Hassner already sees evidence of the third being developed. Examples include recent research on religiously motivated terrorism and the origins of the modern state system within the Protestant Reformation. These studies tell constitutive stories in the sense that the analysis moves from religious motivations of the actors to political behaviour and stand as exemplars for further research on identity and global governance.

Chapter 4 puts forward an idea that even the author describes as 'startling,' that human rights is a useful frame of reference in seeking to understand a wide range of issues defining politics in the Islamic world. Equally startling is the fact that, by the chapter's end, the case for this idea is made in such a compelling way. Chase begins his argument by pointing out the non-monolithic nature of Islam with regard to human rights – as can be observed about any number of other matters. Through analytical treatments, along with anecdotes provided for illustration, three arguments are established. Each is important in understanding religious identity and its connection to global governance.

First, Chase observes that human rights clearly have a history in the Muslim world, which provides a basis for the position of human rights today in Islamic states. Given their experience with state-level coercion, Islamists in Egypt, for example, have engaged with other oppressed groups in dialogue about the meaning of human rights in theory and practice. A second argument is that human rights are defined in a transnational space, within which the Islamic world coexists. It is interesting to note, for example, the positive role that certain Islamic states have played in development of the international human rights regime. Third, and finally, conversations about human rights frame a wide range of issues as they have become integrated into the consciousness of Muslims around the world. Democracy, for instance, generally is regarded in a positive way, while perceptions are mixed to negative within the Islamic world when it comes to gender equality and homosexuality. Taken together, the three arguments are sufficient to establish that the Islamic world is engaged with human rights in spite of the fact that their governments generally find such measures to be threatening.

Part Three of the book conveys *evidence* about religion. Chapters 5–9 proceed from generalities to particulars. Evidence begins at a cross-national, data-based level and proceeds all the way to a sub-national case study.

Chapter 5 focuses on state religious exclusivity and involvement in international crises. This is the only data-based study in the volume. It covers the period from 1990 to 2002, for which the two essential data sets – religion and state (RAS) and international crisis behaviour (ICB)

Religion, Identity, and Global Governance 7

– are available. Fox and Sandal argue that factors converge and lead to diversionary behaviour, witnessed in involvement in an international crisis and the causes of state sponsorship of religion. Religious exclusivity provides another 'excuse' for international conflict, which is deemed especially likely in a protracted interstate conflict. From the RAS data, two variables are gleaned to represent religious exclusivity: (1) state support for religion along a six-point scale from none to an official state religion, and (2) religious legislation along thirty-two dimensions that include restrictions on dress, censorship, and mandatory education.

Fox and Sandal focus on the state-year as the unit of analysis. The regression equations include control variables that reveal the ability to predict crisis involvement in other studies. It turns out that state religion predicts crisis involvement in a protracted conflict, while religious legislation also predicts it, as well as other aspects of crisis activity. The overall conclusion is that crisis involvement can be explained at least in part by state religious exclusivity, which lends credibility to the theoretical argument put forward at the outset of the chapter as related to diversionary behaviour.

Chapter 6 focuses on religious humanitarianism. Lynch begins by asking why one would study religion, and how. Part of the answer reinforces the ideas from Part One about the importance of religion and the need to study it in proper context. Three arguments are provided about how to study religion: look at practice, understand that religion provides guidelines, and be aware that it is shaped by history.

Given that global political processes and religion affect each other, religious humanitarian groups emerge as an interesting avenue for exploration. These FBOs operate in a world defined largely by the 'War on Terror' with, according to Lynch, largely pernicious effects over the last decade. Lynch observes that religious humanitarian groups are caught up involuntarily in War on Terror discourse. Islamic FBOs in particular are confronted with the need to choose between being labelled 'good' and 'bad' Muslims while understanding that the choice is more nuanced than that dichotomy represents. In addition, the U.S. government aids and abets Christian religious humanitarian groups, in all likelihood perceiving them as an extension of national power, while blocking the same activities when proposed by Islamic groups. The chapter advocates interfaith action to counteract the divisiveness inherent in the War on Terror, with its generally negative implications for global governance.

Chapter 7 poses and answers an interesting question: Why would some ethno-religious minorities engage in violence while others do not? Midlarsky's answer takes the form of implications derived from a diachronic model and applied to cases in South Asia. Violent conflict becomes much more likely when a group experiences 'ephemeral gain.' If, after a period of subordination, there is dramatic improvement and then a decline, that is most likely to stimulate intense inter-group conflict. The most basic reason is surprise, which creates a sense of urgency and anger about the reversal of fortune. It becomes likely that the reduced 'authority space' will be challenged.

Application to South Asia provides strong support for the model. With the exception of Kashmir, India's 130 million Muslims accept their minority status without resorting to significant acts of violence. Midlarsky's historical analysis is compelling; the *absence* of an ephemeral ascendancy accounts effectively for what occurs there. While Muslim authority space contracts after respective cycles of violence initiated by Hindu neighbours, responses are relatively restrained and in line with Midlarsky's exegesis of Islamic thought in India. Less happy, however, is the story told in Sri Lanka. Jaffna Tamils had experienced an ephemeral ascendancy due to their ability to function in English during the later colonial era. Their advantageous position disappeared suddenly, however, after the 1956 Sinhalese Language Bill. It is interesting to observe that the extreme violence that escalated over subsequent decades did not have a religious basis, but certainly is consistent with the diachronic model put forward in this chapter.

Chapter 8 takes on the issue of religion's role in the Iraqi civil war. Akbaba and Taydas focus on the interconnectedness of religion, the security dilemma, and intrastate conflict. Three theories are combined to explain how religion contributes to emergence and intensification of the security dilemma, with resultant civil war: identity, religious psychology, and religious legitimacy. In Iraq, these three factors clearly come into play. Even before the U.S.-led invasion, Saddam Hussein had turned to Islam to legitimize his oppressive and violent regime. This had the effect of sensitizing both Sunnis and Shiites to their religious identities. Religious psychology came into play in that those living under Saddam's dictatorship took comfort from their worship rather than identity as Iraqi citizens. All of this created great potential for conflict after the invasion, the fall of Saddam, and the occupation. In the resultant power vacuum, it became obvious that the relatively small occupation force could not guarantee security – a problem connected not only to its size but also a lack of understanding about the role being played by religion. As a result, the dynamics of the security dilemma, intensified by the presence of religious identity among the combatants, took hold. Sectarian violence spiralled out of control. Shiite infighting, along with Sunni-Shiite attacks and counterattacks, became the unpleasant result. While some progress is evident, sectarian instincts still predominate at the expense of the Iraqi state, revealing the power of religious identity to mobilize people against each other and carry out acts of extreme violence.

Chapter 9 focuses on the sub-national level of interaction in an advanced industrial state – Canada. Goff investigates the controversy in the province of Ontario over potential use of sharia law in family law arbitration. In 1991, Ontario passed the Arbitration Act, which permitted use of voluntary faith-based arbitration as a substitute for court proceedings. Such activity continued uneventfully until 2003, when the Islamic Institute of Civil Justice announced that it intended to set up sharia-derived arbitration. Controversy ensued among the public, and the provincial government reacted by commissioning a report.

Debate in this case reveals the complications raised in even the most tolerant states in the world after 9/11. Public outcry reflected a sense that Islamic principles might be at variance with Canadian identity, most notably as manifested in the Charter of Rights and Freedoms. Advocates responded by claiming that Islam suffered from a lack of understanding and to single out sharia for exclusion would clearly – and ironically – go against the spirit of the Charter. Goff sees this debate in terms of competing 'social imaginaries' or ideas about society's practices. Arguments back and forth also included references to identity, human rights, and separation of church and state. The provincial report settled nothing and Ontario proceeded to ban all faith-based arbitration in September 2005, in an obvious effort to avert further controversy. As the chapter points out, however, the issues raised in the case go far beyond the immediate matter of faith-based arbitration and focus on the most fundamental aspects of national identity and life in a free society.

Part Four on *practice*, which includes chapters 10–14, looks at actions taken on the part of religion toward more effective global governance. It begins with a review of achievements by one actor on a global basis and finishes with an autobiographical study of religious identity formation and its connection to practice.

Chapter 10 focuses on Pope John Paul II and the 'just war' doctrine. Heft begins by tracing the evolution of the Catholic Church as a pacifist enclave during the first two centuries in the Roman Empire to a relatively permissive position on involvement in war a millennium ago, to the relatively restricted sense of just war and active role in peacemaking and peace-building that stands as a legacy of John Paul II. When John Paul II assumed the papacy in 1978, his predecessors over the previous sixty years had set the stage for the impressive role the new pontiff would play in international affairs.

John Paul II's role in the liberation of Eastern Europe from communism is the best known among his many contributions. He urged non-violent resistance and spoke out not only in favour of Poland's Solidarity movement but also labour rights in general. With regard to the Middle East, John Paul II opposed both Gulf Wars and only reluctantly approved of the war in Afghanistan, showing how far he had moved the church in restricting the conditions for just war. The pontiff instead emphasized social justice and forgiveness as the foundation for a lasting peace.

Chapter 11 explores faith-based diplomacy as practised through non-official Christian mediation. Lloyd reveals a diversity of traditions and subsequent negotiating types within Christianity. The analysis includes Roman Catholic, Reformed, Baptist, and Anabaptist traditions, which, while remaining diverse, share an emphasis on three aspects of mediation: reconciliation, a just outcome based on equality, and a role as 'communicator' rather than 'manipulator.'

What, then, are the characteristics and impact of Christian mediation? These mediators tend to focus on the earliest or 'pre-settlement' stage of a conflict, where their chances are best, because a conflict at that point may still be under government radar, while also requiring neither major resources nor coercion to achieve settlement. Each of the traditions is found to exhibit its own special traits, a result of different paths of historical development and relationships with the state, along the way. Points of emphasis include the Reformed tradition vis-à-vis religious liberty and radical reformation's preference for a pacifist and grassroots approach. One positive result includes, among others, the prominent role of the Sant Egídio Community in resolving the long conflict in Mozambique. Lloyd also warns, however, of the possibility for disappointing outcomes because Christian mediation lacks coercive power and also may tend to set unrealistic goals.

Chapter 12 focuses on Western middle powers and religious non-governmental organizations (NGOs). Reform internationalism is the goal of such actors, who work in tandem to achieve better global governance. Lamy shows how 'good Samaritan states' seek to overcome obstacles to human security such as weak and failed states and predatory aspects of globalization. These middle powers are multilateralists by disposition, share cosmopolitan norms and values, and are concerned with the welfare of people on the whole. Lamy refers to them as 'guide states' who rely on NGOs to provide them with information to facilitate the most effective action toward improved global governance.

NGOs have five sources of power and influence: information politics, symbolic politics, leverage politics, accountability politics, and the global campaign. Lamy shows how the principles enumerated by the 'Responsibility to Protect' document from the International Commission on Intervention and State Sovereignty is acted upon effectively by religious NGOs. Examples include the American Jewish World Service, My Sister's Keeper, and Project Ploughshares. While NGOs and guide states work together to implement the UN's Millennium Development Goals, much work remains to be done.

Chapter 13 focuses on religion and Canadian diplomacy. Canada is an interesting case to explore in depth because of the country's constitutional commitment to multiculturalism and its tradition of middle power internationalism. Potter notes the increasing politicization of religion in global politics as a challenge to be met by states such as Canada, which seek to manage pluralism in non-violent ways both at home and abroad. The Canadian position is that, like Canada itself, the world is made up of a 'community of communities.' Thus Canadian statecraft, in a religious context, is not engaged with the War on Terror; instead, Canada puts itself forward as an example of how to achieve 'unity through diversity.' This promotion of the Canadian 'brand,' in turn, enhances the country's soft power and pays off in any number of ways.

Potter also illustrates how pluralism is promoted in Canada's diplomacy within the context of religion. Canada's emphasis on human security dovetails with the Christian emphasis on freedom from want and freedom from fear. Coordination with faith-based organizations such as the Mennonite Central Committee plays a key role in areas like food security and peace-building. The new Global Centre for Pluralism in Ottawa is a product of collaboration with Ismaili Muslims through their spiritual head, the Aga Khan. Canada established the Muslim Communities Working Group to improve its relations with Muslim communities abroad. In sum, these and other elements of Canadian diplomacy reveal its incremental engagement with religion in world politics.

Chapter 14 is the autobiographical journey of Chris Seiple, president of the Institute for Global Engagement (IGE). Seiple begins by reiterating the long-term neglect of religion by both academe and American foreign policy and explains this by observing that, until very recently, neither made room for the 'Absolute' in its conception of the world. This disregard causes a lack of respect – a key requirement for positive engagement with Islam, and all religions for that matter – in both the academic and policy-making communities. The United States in particular suffers from a 'Cold War hangover' and needs to move away from its preoccupation with security understood exclusively in a military sense (a natural after-effect of 9/11). In other words, the Cold War created a militarized sense of national security that strongly conditioned the response to 9/11 as well as events in general. The path to respect is through dialogue that produces more mutual understanding, which in turn leads to practical and positive effects.

The IGE works for sustainable religious freedom based on mutual respect, achieved through development of 'communities of the willing' who work together with governments to create a more peaceful and respectful world of religious practice. The IGE uses 'relational diplomacy' – both top-down with governments and bottom-up with faith communities – to counteract the damaging effects of religious extremism. A prominent instance of that work is in Pakistan's Northwest Frontier.

Part Five of the volume consists of its conclusion. Chapter 15 reflects on the achievements of the volume in understanding the connections between and among religion, identity, and global governance. James offers tentative answers to the challenging questions posed at the outset of this chapter. As will become apparent, religion is real and needs to be viewed in a more balanced way by both IR as an academic discipline and policymakers. Bias against seeing the positive side of religion can lead to missed opportunities. Greater knowledge, cooperation with NGOs, and interfaith dialogue are examples of priorities that emerge in the effort to struggle with religion, identity, and global governance. This final chapter finishes with recommendations for future research.

Scope of the Volume

Two points are in order. One concerns the special role of the United States as a quasi-hegemonic power and the state that experienced the most shocking event of the new millennium: 9/11. The other relates to the range of world religions covered by the volume and implications for its general relevance.

Given the centrality of the United States to the international system, it is appropriate to pause at this point and assess the meaning of the most important idea produced by 9/11: the Bush Doctrine.[2] If one means an official policy prescription as articulated by the president or his administration, there is no such thing as the Bush Doctrine. However, the foreign policy analysis community has routinely assigned the 'doctrine' label to many administrations: (1) The Carter Doctrine amounted to Carter's post-Soviet invasion of Afghanistan (1979) statement that the United States would not tolerate any direct threats to the free flow of oil to the free world. (2) The Reagan Doctrine essentially equated to Reagan's policy of rolling back the advances made in the socialist camp over the previous two decades. (3) Extrapolated from a series of Bush's public utterances post-9/11 (the 2002 National Security Strategy of the United States and the West Point speech on 1 June 2002, among others), the Bush Doctrine asserted the U.S. policy of pre-emption that would be illustrated in Iraq. The United States would not wait until it was attacked, but instead choose to unilaterally invade countries where terrorists were lurking and, if deemed necessary, would do so without prior approval by the UN Security Council or an other entity.

As such, the Bush Doctrine as generally understood in U.S. security studies (and by practitioners) has nothing to do *explicitly* with religious doctrine. Most understand it as basically a return to a more aggressive realpolitik position that harkens back to the nineteenth century or even earlier (Buckley and Singh 2006; Kaufman 2007; see also Gaddis 2005 on President John Quincy Adams and the doctrine of pre-emption). Classic amorality of interest is a more persuasive argument. There is no empirical evidence in any of Bush's public statements that explains his policies as an agent of the divine. His political opponents have painted him with this brush, but the paint fades quickly under scrutiny.

This is not to say that religion did not influence the Bush Administration's foreign policy; after all, pre-emption would seem consistent with his evangelical world view. There is clearly a religious subtext in some of the Bush Administration's foreign policy ideas, especially as manifested by the speech-writing of Michael Gerson and the emphasis on spreading freedom as 'God's gift.' In a more general sense, the president's speechwriters often turned to phrases that had special meaning for evangelicals in particular (Suskind 2007, 295).[3] Any number of expositions attempt to understand and convey the role that President Bush's faith played in his role as president. The literature is quite polarized. Sympathetic observers, such as Kengor (2005), discuss the role of the president's faith in his 'freedom' agenda (see also Mansfield 2004). A balanced account by Bush insider David Kuo (2007) examines the faith-based initiatives of the presidency. A number of sources, however, take a quite negative view of the policy implications of pre-emption and occupation of Iraq. Prominent expositions include Woodward (2003) and Meyer (2008).

Ultimately, however, evaluations of the basis for the Bush Doctrine must be made on evidence rather than speculation. First, find if one could find a single line about God in any post-9/11 security strategy document, the circumstantial evidence would be more compelling. Perhaps wisps of smoke are visible, but not fire. Second, many of the ideas associated with the Bush Doctrine are not unique to his presidency. Third, the authors of the Bush Doctrine came from a wide variety of theological and perhaps even secular perspectives. Is it obvious that Paul Wolfowitz, Richard Perle, Joshua Muravchik, and Dick Cheney – advocates of the neoconservative roots of the Bush Doctrine – acted on the basis of Christian evangelism? Similarly, Sharansky's (2006) prominent book, *The Case for Democracy*, was reported widely to have influenced the president's thinking. When interviewed, the president claimed that the desire for freedom is universal and does not depend on one's religion (Kaplan 2008, 145). While important in how he may have assimilated a rapidly changing view toward international security through democratization, Bush's theological beliefs do not emerge as the critical factor in explaining his post-9/11 policies.

No doubt the Bush Doctrine will have a lasting legacy, for good or ill. From the evidence, it would be fair to say that the Bush Doctrine emerged as a curious admixture of realpolitik, American exceptionalism, and the rise of the neoconservatives. The Bush Doctrine, for such reasons, does not take on the character of an explicitly religious statement. However, its relevance to religion, identity, and global governance in the new millennium is undeniable, even as the Bush Administration recedes with time. As noted above, the chapters of this volume will try to answer the question of the Doctrine's impact, with the understanding that, rather than standing as a statement of faith, it contains a significant religious subtext.

Another aspect of this volume's scope that requires clarification is its primary focus on the Abrahamic religions. It is understood that practices elsewhere, most notably in China and Southeast Asia, are different from those of the religions featured in this volume. Religion tends to be eclectic there, even at the household level: no unifying religious theme or set of rituals binds people to a collective. In China, for example, it is common for some citizens to practise different parts of respective religions, taken from Christianity (perhaps reading a Bible), Buddhism (maybe visiting a temple), and Taoism (such as burning paper at the altar of a deceased relative). The same home might have a portrait of Chairman Mao for protection.

Given the fact that no volume can do everything, two responses are offered in light of the preceding observations. First, the Abrahamic religions represent approximately 3.6 billion people, so the project is hardly narrow in its immediate relevance. Second, the chapters in this volume will discuss more general implications of their findings beyond the Abrahamic religions, but with sensitivity to context based on diverse religious beliefs and practices around the world.

NOTES

1 *Global governance* is defined authoritatively by Thakur and Weiss (forthcoming; see also Thakur 2006, 233) as 'the complex of formal and informal institutions, mechanisms, relationships and processes between and among states, markets, citizens, and organizations – both intergovernmental and nongovernmental – through with collective interests are articulated, rights and obligations are established, and fundamental differences are mediated.'
2 Valuable treatments of the Bush Doctrine from a variety of perspectives include Bacevich (2006), Buckley and Singh (2006), Daalder and Lindsay (2005), and Kaufman (2007).
3 In addition, there is a significant literature on the growing influence of Christian believers in the Republican Party as a whole, along with certain decision-making centres in the Bush Administration (Phillips 2006).

REFERENCES

Adherents.com. http://www.adherents.com.
Almond, G.A., R.S. Appleby, and E. Sivan. 2003. *Strong religion: The rise of fundamentalisms around the world*. Chicago: University of Chicago Press.
Bacevich, Andrew J. 2006. *The new American militarism: How Americans are seduced by war*. New York: Oxford University Press.
Buckley, Mary, and Robert Singh. 2006. *The Bush Doctrine and the war on terrorism: Global reactions, global consequences*. New York: Routledge.
Daalder, Ivo H., and James M. Lindsay. 2005. *America unbound: The Bush revolution in foreign policy*. New York: Wiley.
Gaddis, John Lewis. 2005. *Surprise, security, and the American experience*. The

Joanna Jackson Goldman Memorial Lectures on American Civilization and Government. Cambridge: Harvard University Press.

Kaplan, Fred. 2008. *Daydream believers: How a few grand ideas wrecked American power*. New York: Wylie.

Kaufman, Robert Gordon. 2007. *In defense of the Bush Doctrine*. Lexington: University Press of Kentucky.

Kengor, Paul. 2005. *God and George W. Bush: A spiritual life*. New York: Harper Perennial.

Kuo, David. 2007. *Tempting faith: An inside story of political seduction*. New York: Free Press.

Mansfield, Stephen. 2004. *The faith of George W. Bush*. Lake Mary: Charisma House.

Marty, M.E., and R.S. Appleby. 1993. *Fundamentalisms and society: Reclaiming the sciences, the family, and education*. Urbana: University of Chicago Press.

– 1994. *Fundamentalisms observed*. Urbana: University of Chicago Press.

– 1995. *Fundamentalisms comprehended*. Urbana: University of Chicago Press.

– 1996. *Fundamentalisms and the state: Remaking polities, economies and militance*. Urbana: University of Chicago Press.

– 2004. *Accounting for fundamentalisms: The dynamic character of movements*. Urbana: University of Chicago Press.

Meyer, Jane. 2008. *The dark side: The inside story of how the war on terror turned into a war on American ideals*. New York: Doubleday.

Phillips, Kevin. 2006. *American theocracy: The perils and politics of radical religion, oil and borrowed money in the 21st century*. New York: Viking Adult.

Sharansky, Natan. 2006. *The case for democracy: The power of freedom to overcome tyranny and terror*. Green Forest: Balfour Books.

Suskind, Ron. 2007. *The one percent doctrine: Deep inside America's pursuit of its enemies since 9/11*. New York: Simon & Schuster.

Thakur, Ramesh. 2006. Enhancing global governance through regional integration. *Global Governance* 12:233–40.

Thakur, Ramesh, and Thomas G. Weiss. (forthcoming). *The UN and global governance: An idea and its prospects*. Bloomington: Indiana University Press.

Woodward, Bob. 2003. *Bush at war*. New York: Simon & Schuster.

PART TWO

Ideas

2 The Religious Challenge to International Relations Theory

JOHN F. STACK JR

The sweet dream of American political thought – reborn in each generation, it seems – is that cultural factors like religion will shrink into insignificance as blessed pragmatism finally comes into its own. After the fall of the Soviet Union, many were eager to go beyond religion and announce that even secular ideology would no longer be a cause for war. But something close to the polar opposite has occurred. *The West is confronted with an extranational, religiously self-defined entity with something ominously like a nation's power to make war.*

– Jack Miles (2004, 25; emphasis added)

The greatest assault on the United States since the end of the cold war, perhaps since its founding, had little plausible origin in the dynamics of alliances and polarity, in the rise and fall of great powers, in any state's quest for security, or even in the actions of any state at all ... *Rather, those involved in crashing planes into the World Trade Center and the Pentagon on September 11, 2001, were animated by a kind of conception, were organized around a kind of idea, and appraised the international system according to a kind of notion to which international relations scholars have paid relatively little attention: religion.*

– Daniel Philpott (2002, 66–7)

The ferocity of religious violence was brought home to me in the midst of the conflict in Northern Ireland when I received the news that a car bomb had exploded in a Belfast neighborhood I had visited the day before ... What I realized then is the same thing that all of us perceive on some level when we see pictures of terrorist events: on a different day, at a different time, perhaps on a different bus, one of the bodies torn to shreds by any of these terrorist acts could have been ours.

– Mark Juergensmeyer (2003, 4–5)

Religion and International Relations Today

In the wake of 9/11, the wars in Afghanistan and Iraq, the War on Terror, and ethno-religious terrorism around the globe, religion has been pushed to the forefront of the world stage. Long before concern and hysteria zeroed in on Islam as a principal threat to the United States, it was apparent that religion, far from having disappeared, remained a powerful global force.[1] As Kiernan documents in his history of genocide, religion served as a potent catalyst for the mass slaughter of millions throughout the ages. Writing about the waning decades of the twentieth century and the first years of the twenty-first, Kiernan makes disturbing observations as he considers the powerful impact of globalization: 'But as the century progressed, power, technology, and communications also linked diverse populations around the world and disseminated developments in more global patterns. These included postwar decolonialization, the emergence of multiple new states, and a global arms trade – but also global patterns of genocide' (2007, 571; see also Murphy 2000). Religion occupies an important place in the complex bundle of identities and values that continue to form transnational civil society relations not only in the newly democratizing states of Central Europe but across the globe (Rudolph 1997, 246–8).

Even as early as 1980, both Protestant fundamentalism and evangelicalism entered significantly into the political arena of the United States. Religious issues entered with fury on a host of constitutional and social issues including prayer in public schools, abortion, gay marriage, financial assistance to parochial and religious schools, stem cell research, and end of life. Religious extremists also emerged in the United States: 'The Christian militia, the Christian identity movement, and Christian anti-abortion activists – have brought Americans into the same uneasy position occupied by many in the rest of the world' (Juergensmeyer 2003, 4). Religion was reborn following the collapse of communism in the former Soviet Union and the states of Central and Eastern Europe (Greeley 1994, 2003). In Central America and South America, Christian evangelicals and Pentacostals made huge inroads as well in sub-Saharan Africa, the Philippines, Korea, and China. The transnational influence of Islam in religion, economics, politics, and culture in Africa, Asia, and Europe was described by Eickelman and Piscatori as a phenomenon they called Muslim politics: 'Muslim politics, like politics everywhere, thus involves a contest over the extent of state control – locating the boundaries of legitimate state and nonstate activity or what has been unhelpfully termed the "public" and "private" ... [B]oundaries are also negotiated between and among nonstate actors, such as those between religious scholars and mystical (Sufi) *shaykhs* ... [T]he boundaries between public and private are constantly shifting; family concerns can also have a "public" dimension. A notable consequence of this more diffuse process of boundary setting ... is the fragmentation of authority' (1996, 20). They understood and anticipated the power of the Muslim world in regional and international contexts well before the attack on the Pentagon and the destruction of the World Trade Center's twin towers. So the effects of religion are important. It matters even more when it is factored into domestic policy considerations of states, considerations of the legitimacy or illegitimacy of governments, prospects for human and civil rights around the world, the reach of democratic or authoritarian governments, and many other foundational questions affecting individuals around the planet. Why then has religion been so ignored as a significant influence in world politics?

The epigraphs from Miles, Philpott, and Juergensmeyer reinforce our awareness of the presence of religion in the twenty-first century. Its ubiquity is undeniable and its influence on the lives of individuals, countries, and transnational politics is obvious to even the most casual of observers. This chapter suggests first that religion poses a fundamental challenge to how international relations has been studied. This means that the conventional wisdom defining the central research questions and established research orthodoxies has failed at both empirical and conceptual levels. (As chapter 3 points out at some length, this situation may reflect an anti-religious disposition among social scientists that creates a bias toward neglect.) Second, the chapter considers why religion as a basic group identity matters. Third, it considers why religion is relevant to US foreign policy. The chapter concludes with some brief observations about the ironies of the 1648 Peace of Westphalia upon which the central orthodoxies of the study of international relations rest, along with the presumed irrelevance of religion.

The Liberal Expectancy and the Demise of Religion

The Peace of Westphalia in 1648 marks a breakpoint in the development of world politics: the formal end of the bloody Thirty Years War pitting Catholics against Protestants. It also concluded more than a century of religious wars beginning with the Protestant Reformation in the early sixteenth century. Westphalia established a system of state sovereignty. No more was the Roman Catholic Church the formal institution to which temporal rulers of regions, duchies, principalities, kingdoms, or states would turn for guidance and legitimacy. (Of course, as chapter 10 on John Paul II brings out, the church continues to influence world politics along any number of dimensions.) The Westphalia system provided for territorially based sovereignty. As such, states were recognized as the legitimate governing entities in the European political system. The Peace of Westphalia was the product of transforming forces in religion, politics, culture, learning, economics, and science as seen in the Renaissance, the Protestant Reformation, and the Enlightenment. The growth of cities, the rise of capitalism, the invention of the printing press, new political philosophies, the colonization of the New World, and European imperialism heralded the arrival of an international system fundamentally different from the pre-Westphalia world presided over by the Holy Roman Emperor and the pope. Roman Catholicism was pushed to the margins as new political doctrines and constitutions emphasized the separation of religion from politics, popular sovereignty, and secularization of state functions (Philpott 2002).

The Collapse of Religion?

Roman Catholicism, and religion more generally, came to be seen as 'false knowledge,' discredited by many of the most important thinkers and writers of the Enlightenment (Rudolph 1997, 6). From this perspective, Roman Catholicism debased free inquiry in the study of science, arts, and letters and became widely seen as the crucial linkage to a bankrupt Roman Catholic political order. Karl Marx saw religion as 'actively negative, shoring up exploitation and oppression' (ibid., 6).

The intellectual giants of the nineteenth and early twentieth centuries, Auguste Comte, Herbert Spenser, Emile Durkheim, Max Weber, and Sigmund Freud 'all believed that religion would gradually fade in importance and cease to be significant in the advent of industrial society' (Norris and Inglehart 2004, 3). As a major sociologist of religion observed, 'Most Enlightenment thinkers and most progressive-minded people ever since have tended toward the idea that secularization is a good thing, at least insofar as it does away with religious phenomena that are "backward," "superstitious," or "reactionary"' (Berger 1999, 3). Thus, these sociologists saw the great forces of nineteenth-century life – the growth of industrialization, the creation of the urban metropolis, and the rise of governmental bureaucracies along with secularization – as the transforming processes of modernity at work. The bureaucratic and rational state would gradually supplant the role played by religion in societies. Opportunities for religion to exert significant influence in either public or private spheres of modern societies therefore would decrease. Ultimately, secularization theory predicted that industrialization, urbanization, bureaucratization – the hallmarks of the modern twentieth-century welfare state – would combine to deprive religion of its role in pre-modern agrarian societies (Norris and Inglehart 2004, 3). Twentieth-century social theorist C. Wright Mills described the downfall of religion more vividly: *'Once the world was filled with the sacred – in human thought, practice, and institutional form. After the Reformation and the Renaissance, the forces of modernization swept across the globe and secularization, a corollary of the historical process, loosened the dominance of the sacred. In due course the sacred shall disappear altogether except, possibly in the private realm'* (ibid.; emphasis in original).

These powerful intellectual perspectives transformed into the twentieth-century social science disciplines of sociology, political science, and psychology, resulting in a growing body of literature that hypothesized the irrelevance of religion. That intellectual orientation, for all intents and purposes, became part of a canon almost never questioned. The consequence was unmistakable: 'Modernist social scientists cannot imagine religion as a positive force, as practice and worldview that contributes to order, provides meaning, and promotes justice' (Rudolph 1997, 6). It was easy therefore to discount religion as a holdover from a pre-modern world destined to simply fade away. This is what the sociologist Milton Gordon, writing in the early 1960s, referred to as the liberal expectancy: the inability of primordial-based affinities simply to disappear, not withstanding the certitude of social science theorizing: 'As though with a wily cunning of its own, as though there were some essential element in man's nature that demanded it – something that compelled him to merge his lonely individual identity in some ancestral group of fellows smaller by far than the whole human race, smaller often than the nation – the sense of ethnic belonging has survived. *It has survived in various forms and with various names, but it has not perished, and twentieth-century urban man is closer to his stone-age ancestors than he knows'* (Gordon 1964, 25; emphasis added).

Writing nearly a decade later, Glazer and Moynihan saw a totally unexpected persistence and revitalization of religion and ethnicity in the United States:

> The expectation [exists] that the kinds of features that divide one group from another would inevitably lose their weight and sharpness in modern and modernizing societies. There would be increasing emphasis on achievement rather than ascription, that common systems of education and communication would level differences, that nationally uniform economic and political systems would have the same effect. Under these circumstances the 'primordial' (or in any case the antecedent) differences between groups would be expected to become of lesser significance. The 'liberal expectancy' flows into the 'radical expectancy' – that class circumstances would become the main line of division between people, erasing the earlier lines of tribe, language, religion, national origin, and that thereafter these class divisions would themselves, after revolution, disappear ... *Interest should guide rational men – or drive them – in social action; and interest was determined by economic position.* (Glazer and Moynihan 1975; emphasis added)

For mainstream sociologists, however, the death of religion was a near certainty (Berger 1967; 1999, 2–3). Secularization theory presumed that religious convictions would gradually give way to more authentic forms of group mobilization such as socio-economic class. The social sciences thus became predisposed to dismiss religion as a less than meaningful area of research and social inquiry (Fox 2001, 34). The continued vitality of religion in post-communist Europe, the United States, and Africa for both Christian evangelicals and Pentecostals and Islamic believers suggested that religion was not simply going to fade away (Eickelman and Piscatori 1996; Greeley 2003).

In a landmark study of religious values, beliefs, and practices, political scientists Norris and Inglehart (2004) acknowledge the limitations of secularization theory's dogmatic insistence that religion will disappear. Their cross-national assessment of seventy-six states covering nearly 80 per cent of the world's population is telling. Religious beliefs, unexpectedly, continue to remain vibrant in the United States and have increased within poor counties around the globe. 'Societies where people's daily lives are shaped by the threat of poverty, disease, and premature death remain as religious today as centuries earlier' (216). Rapid population growth is a key demographic dimension of these societies as is the case of immigration to the United States from non-advanced countries (ibid.). This contrasts markedly with affluent societies where secularization continued to erode religious beliefs and participation. Significantly, these are also the societies where fertility rates are declining and populations are shrinking (ibid.). On the basis of these trends Norris and Inglehart contend that *'rich societies are becoming more secular but the world as a whole is more religious'* (ibid. 217; emphasis in original). They also note different value systems in affluent and disadvantaged societies make 'religious differences *increasingly* salient' (ibid.).

Religion in International Relations?

Limitations of the liberal expectancy have led sociologists to rethink the importance of religion as a dimension of world politics. The persistence of religion in the lives of believers, the domestic policies of countries and in transnational and international politics is now difficult to deny. Interestingly, the dominant orthodoxies of international relations (IR) theory continue to remain on a course that dismisses the salience of religion.

More than three decades ago, Hoffmann (1977) characterized the study of international relations as a discipline dominated by scholarship based in the United States. More recent assessments confirm the biases of U.S.-based social science perspectives (Waever 1998). Noting the continuing viability of the liberal expectancy as it relates to the study of culture in IR, Waever observes, 'The difference in how – and how much – IR has developed in different countries is not just a matter of national idiosyncrasies or unnamable national character. Political institutional history explains different definitions, relationships to neighboring disciplines, and scientific ideals. Widespread American expectations that others will follow their current developments are therefore likely to be frustrated. As often pointed out by French scholars, American IR scholars are prone to thinking in universalistic categories, but they are likely to be reminded of the cultural specificity of these categories' (1998, 726). Thus religion has never been an important dimension of the U.S.-centric study of IR, focused as it was on the sovereignty of states and their relentless competition over geopolitical resources.

For Carr, the British scholar of the period between the First World War and the Second World War and an iconic figure in realist theory, religious beliefs also had little relevance in world politics as he recounted the litany of failures of British and American idealists leading to the Second World War (Carr 2001). In the case of Hans Morgenthau, the most important realist of his time, religion and personal moral beliefs were incompatible with the exercise of power in a world of states characterized by a constantly shifting balance of power (Morgenthau 1978,

3–14) The 'Six Principles of Political Realism' of this European émigré to the United States sharply distinguished between personal morality and the higher moral duties of the statesman to safeguard the state from the competing interests of other states. Development of successful foreign policies, therefore, demanded that decision-makers set personal moral and religious beliefs aside.

This resulting zero-sum character of world politics underscored the importance of the levels of analysis problem (Singer 1961; Waltz 1959). National level decision-makers could not be concerned with religion unless it aided or threatened the national security objectives of their states. For example, American foreign policy's interest in and support of the 'captive nations' of Latvia, Lithuania, and Estonia in the 1950s can be traced to realpolitik more than Christian solidarity. Thus realism's emphasis on sovereignty, military power, and control of foreign policy channels discounted the importance of religion as a factor in international relations.

With the development of neo-realism as the dominant paradigm, religion came to matter even less than it did for realists. For Waltz (1979, 88–9), in the key exposition of neo-realism, the capacity (power) of the international system absent a central governing apparatus structured interstate relations amid differential economic and political power. Religious groups, movements, and beliefs and ideas were, therefore, irrelevant. 'Neorealism ... appears ideologically to be a science at the service of big-power management of the international system.' In making that observation, Cox (1986, 248) effectively underscored in fundamental ways the continuation of the liberal expectancy. More recently, Mearsheimer (2002) offers a further twist on neo-realism in *The Tragedy of the Great Powers*. Witnessed in the relentless struggle for power based on shifting regional balances, a ferocious offensive version of realism emerges. Great powers seek domination rather than just Waltzian security.

Religious movements and actors could well play a role in the competition for resources but, like realism itself, the levels of analysis problem likely reads out less well-defined and armed actors. Realism in its various incarnations has not done well in anticipating or predicting significant shifts in world politics. For the late sociologist and U.S. senator Daniel P. Moynihan, its failure to anticipate the collapse of communism in 1989–91 was a damning indictment of the liberal expectancy's capacity to understand a complex multidimensional world: '[Realism] made no provision for the passions – the appeal of ethnic loyalty and nationalism, the demands for freedom of religious practice and cultural expression, and the feeling that the regime had simply lost its moral legitimacy.' The inability to understand religion in IR theory is also mirrored in both qualitative and scientific methodologies. Religion, according to Fox (2001, 58), is a variable not easily quantified or measured, thus creating a twofold problem. The first is the paucity of studies on religion, which hampers development of conceptual approaches necessary for empirical research. The second problem is more daunting: 'It is clear that the only truly accurate measure would involve reading the minds of political actors to discover their true motivations. Since this is not currently possible, researchers currently using quantitative methods probably choose not to measure religion at all' (ibid., 58).

Realism's continued emphasis on state power, regional subsystems, and the power of the global system continues to dominate the study of IR, albeit not without criticism from liberals, constructivists, and others. It presumes that material interests dominate and that the atavistic, parochial, ephemeral longings for authenticity, community, identity, and other spiritual values simply are not of enough weight to really matter when the chips are down. The dominant assumptions of IR theory constitute a brittle determinism, mistaking cause for effect and embodying an ideology peculiar to the context of the nineteenth- and twentieth-century state systems that is historically and culturally bounded (Stack 1997, 23–5). The liberal expectancy legitimizes the obvious while dismissing the counterfactual as Philpott's (2002, 206–45) assessment of the meaning of the Westphalia state system suggests.

This causes IR to miss out on a lot of substantive, significant activity with a religious character. Consider just a few examples from elsewhere in this volume: the activities of the pontiff in conflict management (chapter 10), Christian mediation of civil and interstate conflicts (chapter 11), and the role of religious non-governmental organizations (NGOs) in shaping foreign policy among middle powers (chapter 12). Moreover, lack of attention to instances such as these also causes a bias toward seeing religious beliefs as a negative factor to be eradicated if and when they do appear.

Why Religion Matters

One of our most basic tasks is to establish why religion is actually a relevant factor in explaining or understanding international politics. How do we know when religion is 'real' versus a cover for some other factor such as ethnicity or group power? This is a basic question and it is also a complex one. The short answer is that religion matters hugely in how people live their lives from birth to death. Religion is relevant because it is such a basic dimension of human life encompassing culture, tradition, language, world view, and the fundamental necessity of the spiritual realm. It is an essential element of life for billions of people around the globe. Religious belief may not be satisfying for Western social scientists studying the behaviour of individuals, groups, social movements, or states, but it resonates deeply in the most basic values and choices. The irony of the current configuration of global politics is that religion also survives and flourishes in the world dominated by states and other global actors, be they public, economic, or special interests.

Religion is embedded deeply in the system of world politics in the form of diverse sovereign states under international law and custom. (This property is clear from the discussion in chapter 4 of how Islamic states have violated human rights within their own borders while, in some cases, also playing key roles in shaping the international human rights regime.) So religion has been 'grandfathered' into the structure of world politics, despite the progressive growth of secular institutions of government and the separation of church and state (Philpott 2000). This does not mean, however, that religion is fading away. As Rudolph observed, religion 'refers to practice more often than belief. Although guided and sustained by the meanings of systems of transcendent realms, religion as practiced is embedded in everyday life' (1997, 5).

Religion is important because it serves as a fundamental marker of individual and group identity. The journalist/sociologist Isaacs (1975a, 1975b) saw religion as one of six fundamental dimensions that shapes individual identity. Conceptualizing identity as a series of concentric circles radiating from an individual at birth, Isaacs looked first at the family into which the child is born, in other words, the inheritance defined by a child's phenotype and genotype, a family's name, language, history, religion, and nationality. The outward progression from an infant to increasingly broader levels of group inclusiveness offers a glimpse at the formation of a basic collective identity (Isaacs 1975b). This means that religion, along with language, culture, and ethnicity provides a basic orientation about the world for an individual as a part of a community whose identity does not easily melt away.

Underscoring the dynamic tension among individual believers and larger collectivities, Isaacs noted, 'In all but very rare varieties of religious experience, the individual and social aspects of the matter interlock.' He saw, as well, power in religious belief and affiliation for the individual as religion has formed an underpinning 'in the social and political history of every society' (1975a, 148–9). This is not to say that religion is somehow apolitical. As communities of believers living in the world and affected by it, respective religions interact with politics throughout history as a 'force to mobilize opposing political and military forces and to command ... [their] popular support or submission in a cause. Often it serves to identify the contestants' (ibid. 160–1). Across the world, religions have served as basis for group conflict as in the Biafra civil war, 1960–70, initiated when Muslim Hausas murdered thousands of Catholic Ibos; conflict in Cyprus pitting Turkish Muslims against Orthodox Greeks; the Arab-Israeli conflict placing Jews and Muslims in a seemingly endless conflict; and the bitter decades-long conflict among Sunni Muslims and Shiite Muslims in Iraq. Prolonged conflicts in Malaysia, Burma, Sri Lanka, and the Philippines include significant religious dimensions, as do ongoing conflicts in the Balkans and many former Soviet republics, to cite merely a few examples.

The Authenticity of Religious Beliefs

Central to an understanding of why religion matters is this question: How do we know when religion is 'real' versus a cover for some other factor such as ethnicity or group power? Religion taps into a powerful sense of identity that often follows a person through life in one form or another. It is most often manifested in group behaviour. Thus religion shares important similarities with ethnicity. It is difficult and probably impossible to isolate religion entirely from the other basic social markers identified by Isaacs – ethnicity, language, culture, and race. But religion is analytically different from ethnicity; it comes from the Latin noun *ligare* meaning 'to bind, to tie, to fasten' (Isaacs 1975a). A religion is a community of believers rooted in tradition and received learning, scripture, and other sacred teachings. It ties the believer to a concept of God or the supernatural; it is expressed in terms of language and culture (ibid.). Thus religious belief is not easily expressed in isolated and hermetically sealed systems of beliefs. It is messy and spills over into ethnic and racial identity on many occasions.

Given that religious sentiments are most often expressed in a community of believers, the potential for social or political mobilization is clearly present. Thus, religion responds to change and evolves over time. This observation, however, does not reach the more elusive question of how religious identity forms. Connor reminds us of the elusive nature of identity and offers an important caveat: 'Ethnic strife is too often superficially discerned as principally predicated upon language, religion, customs, economic inequality, or some other intangible element. But what is fundamentally involved in such a conflict is the divergence of basic identity which manifests itself in the "us-them" syndrome. And the ultimate answer to the question of whether a person is one of us, or one of them, seldom hinges on adherence to overt aspects of culture ... Cultural assimilation need not mean psychological assimilation' (1972, 341–2). Chapter 14, with its autobiographical character, provides an example of how religious identity is formed in the case of one individual. It brings to life Connor's preceding observations about the complexity of both identity and inter-group conflict.

The Nature of the Religious Community

There is no simple answer to the question of what defines a religious community. Religious communities have much in common with ethnic communities based on the continuing relevance of affective ties sufficient to mobilize individuals to work for group goals. The power of the affective, emotive, and sometimes seemingly non-rational side of religious practice illustrates its continuing relevance in a world that for many in the West clearly has outgrown whatever it has to offer. A number of works highlight the power of affective dimensions of group mobilization within world politics (Connor 1972; Croucher 2004; Kaufman 2001). Pioneering works by Isaacs (1975a, 1975b) and Geertz (1973) defined a primordial approach to the understanding of identity. They posited that a deep need to belong and a fear of loneliness tethers individuals and groups to religions, ethnicities, and cultural communities not easily understood or explainable in terms of modern social science concepts. 'An individual belongs to his basic group in the deepest and most literal sense that he is not alone, which is what all but a few human brings fear to be' (Isaacs 1975b, 42–3). For Clifford Geertz, the pioneering anthropologist and social thinker, 'the assumed givens of social existence' are expressed in shared religion, language, and manifestations of kinship binding people together. But Geertz paused to consider the significance of hugely important personal and spiritual longings and noted the power of such affinities: 'These congruities of blood, speech, custom ... are seen to have ineffable, and at times overpowering coerciveness in and of themselves' (1973, 259). The emergence of these communities of affect transcend simple individual self-aggrandizement. He saw in these needs a good deal more than 'practical necessity, common interest, or incurred obligation,' concluding that they originate *'at least in great part by virtue of some accountable absolute import attributed to the very tie itself'* (ibid.; emphasis added). America's poet laureate, Robert Frost, put it more simply but no less profoundly when he described home as the place, when you go there, they have to take you in (Isaacs 1975b, 43).

Religious belief and practice also may include periods of latency but their significance derives from an ability to tap into powerful needs for which adherents will fight and die. Congruities of blood, speech, and custom, to put them in Geertz's nomenclature, challenge the easy assumptions of the liberal expectancy. This observation foreshadows the emphasis in chapter 3 on the constitutive role played by religion, which cannot be reduced to a mere epiphenomenon.

Islam and the Bush Doctrine

The terrorist attacks of 11 September 2001 forced many Americans to grapple with the complexity of a distant and unfamiliar faith for the first time. The Bush Administration's ensuing declaration of a 'global war on terrorism' ignited a vigorous and often contentious public debate in the United States about the Islamic faith, in particular, and more generally about the influence of religion in international politics. This debate has shaped the evolution of American views toward Islam and religion's role in politics ever since. As chapter 3 will bring out forcefully, discussion in and out of academe features much superficiality and misunderstanding of the role of religion in the contemporary world.

Promulgation of the Bush Doctrine complicated U.S. perceptions of Islam, as many of the following chapters illustrate. As a statement of geo-strategic policy, the Bush Doctrine is difficult to apply with consistency. It embraces a view of American uniqueness heightened by a sense of national and global insecurity in the wake of the 11 September 2001 attacks on the United States. As a policy prescription it aimed to justify regime change in the Middle East and the invasion of Iraq in particular. It formed a justification for war based on what turned out to be non-existent weapons of mass destruction and later for American occupation of Iraq based on the global War on Terror, thereby dramatically energizing al-Qaida's presence in Iraq and the Middle East. 'By invading Iraq, the Bush administration created a self-fulfilling prophecy: Iraq has now replaced Afghanistan as a magnet, training ground, and operational base for jihadist terrorists, with plenty of American targets to shoot at' (Fukuyama 2006, 181).

The Bush Doctrine successfully linked Islam and terrorism in the mind of the American public following the 11 September 2001 attacks, and justified the war in Iraq and the necessity of occupation as a way to stop future terrorist attacks on the United States. As chapter 1 points out, it represented something more than an abstract geo-strategic doctrine. Just as the war effort in the Pacific following the attack on Pearl Harbor (7 December 1941) led the U.S. Supreme Court to defer to the U.S. Army's order interning U.S. Japanese citizens, so too did the Bush Doctrine introduce a religious subtext into the War on Terror at home and abroad. Parallels to the American military and cultural mobilization against Japan and Japanese-American citizens following the Pearl Harbor attack are striking. The linkage between Islam and terrorism became a subtext of the Bush Doctrine. Shortly after the 9/11 attacks, only a quarter of Americans believed Islam encouraged violence. Just 18 per cent maintained 'all or most' Muslims were anti-American. A year later however, almost half (44 per cent) confirmed Islam's affinity for violence while nearly half (49 per cent) thought 'about half, most, or all' Muslims were anti–United States (Pew 2003, paras. 1, 22). This widespread shift in public perception occurred across genders, education levels, regions, religious denominations, political affiliations, and levels of knowledge about Islam. At the same time, in terms of religion and politics, more than half (62 per cent) of Americans in 2003 were comfortable with religious influence on policymaking, while almost half (41 per cent) believed American politicians voiced their religious beliefs 'too little' (Pew 2003, para. 4).

While American attitudes toward Islam have become increasingly unfavourable in the last few years, many Americans claimed to understand very little or nothing about the Islamic faith. Almost half (45 per cent) of Americans in 2007 considered Islam to fuel violence as opposed to 36 per cent surveyed in 2005; this shift in perception also occurred across education levels, religious denominations, and political affiliations (Pew 2007, para. 5). When asked what they respected most and least about the Islamic faith, one-third of Americans identified extremism and radicalism as Islam's 'least admired' feature while more than half (57 per cent) could not or did not mention any favourable aspect of Islam (Gallup 2006, 1).

Although Americans generally favour religious influence in public life, a majority do not believe religious *doctrine* should govern politics.

Of those Americans who considered religious influence on government to be decreasing (45 per cent), 80 per cent (that is, 36 per cent overall) believe this trend is a 'bad thing.' In contrast, more than half (63 per cent) of Americans surveyed agree 'the will of the American people' should have more influence in public life than the Bible (Pew 2006, paras. 6–7). Attitudes expressed by the American public suggest both vulnerability and uncertainty and are likely reinforced by images of the daily carnage reported by news outlets covering the fighting in Iraq and Afghanistan in particular.

Barack Obama's election in 2008 may illustrate an important shift in the strategic assumptions that defined the Bush Doctrine, along with a commitment to multilateral diplomatic initiatives. But the global economic crisis of 2008/2009, continuing violence in Iraq, and the intensifying conflict in Afghanistan are daily reminders that Islam and U.S. diplomatic and military initiatives will be linked for years to President Obama's popularity throughout the world. And part of that legacy is the fear that terrorism and Islam are inextricably linked as adversaries of the United States and other Western secular democracies.

Westphalia's Continuing Legacy

Religion remains a major factor in the world of the twenty-first century. It is ironic, therefore, that the Peace of Westphalia in 1648 created political and legal structures out of which the national secular national state emerged. It rose out of the ashes of the unrelenting religious hatreds that had burned through Europe. A desperate new consensus was born of exhaustion and self-interest. The long and destructive religious wars in Europe finally came to an end. While the post-Westphalia concept of sovereignty expressed the triumph of Protestantism over Catholicism, its territorial base in the end protected religion from external interference, especially as the state system spread across the globe in the centuries following the treaty of 1648 (Philpott 2002, 76–7). This is the Westphalia synthesis as assessed by Philpott (ibid.) carrying sovereignty to the four corners of the globe and with it religion as well. Just like the state system itself, religion is unlikely to wither away.

NOTES

1 Religion is a multidimensional phenomenon embracing belief and practice

and shaped by history (real and imagined), politics, culture, customs, and traditions. Religion also locates the believer along a spectrum in which the past, present, and future may converge. Because religion has been held in such disrepute it is important to examine its relevance to world politics. This chapter does so in broad strokes, given limitations of space. The intent, however, is to demonstrate its relevance to contemporary international studies.

REFERENCES

Berger, P.L. 1967. *The sacred canopy: Elements of a sociological theory of religion.* New York: Anchor Books

Berger, P.L. 1999. The desecularization of the world: A global overview. In *The desecularization of the world: Resurgent religion and world politics*, ed. A.A. Ahmad Naim, P.L. Berger, G. Davie, D. Martin, J. Sacks, G. Weigel, and T. Weiming, 1–18. Grand Rapids, MI: Eerdmans.

Carr, E.H. 2001. *Twenty years' crisis 1919–1939: An introduction to the study of international relations.* London: Palgrave Macmillan.

Connor, W. 1972. Nation-building or nation-destroying? *World Politics* 24:319–55.

Cox, R.W. 1986. Social forces, states and world orders: Beyond international relations theory. In *Neorealism and its critics*, ed. R.O. Keohane, 204–54. New York: Columbia University Press.

Croucher, S. 2004. *The politics of belonging.* Lanham, MD: Rowman & Littlefield.

Eickelmann D.F., and J. Piscatori. 1996. *Muslim politics.* Princeton: Princeton University Press.

Fox, J. 2001. Religion as an overlooked dimension of international relations. *International Studies Review* 3:53–73.

Fukuyama, F. 2006. *America at the crossroads: Democracy, power, and the neoconservative legacy.* New Haven, CT: Yale University Press.

Gallup Poll News Service. 2006. Americans' views of the Islamic world. http://media.gallup.com/WorldPoll/PDF/AmericansViewsIslam2806.pdf.

Geertz, C. 1973. *Interpretation of cultures.* New York: Basic Books.

Glazer, N., and D.P. Moynihan. 1970. *Beyond the melting pot.* Rev. ed. Cambridge, MA: Harvard University and MIT Press.

– 1975. Introduction. In *Ethnicity: Theory and experience*, ed. N. Glazer and D.P. Moynihan, 1–26. Cambridge, MA: Harvard University Press.

Gordon, M.M. 1964. *Assimilation in American life: The role of race, religion, and national origins.* New York: Oxford University Press.

Greeley, A.M. 1995. The persistence of religion. *Cross Currents* 45:24–41.
– 2003. *Religion in Europe at the end of the second millennium.* New Brunswick, NJ: Transaction.
Hoffmann, S. 1977. An American social science: International Relations. *Daedalus* 106:41–60.
Isaacs, H.R. 1975a. Basic group identity: The idols of the tribe. In Glazer and Moynihan, 29–52.
– 1975b. *Idols of the tribe, group identity and political change.* New York: Harper Collins.
Juergensmeyer, M. 2003. *Terror in the mind of God: The global rise of religious violence.* Berkeley: University of California Press.
Kaufman, S. 2001. *Ancient hatreds: The symbolic politic of modern war.* Ithaca, NY: Cornell University Press.
Kiernan, B. 2007. *Blood and soil: A world history of genocide and extermination from Sparta to Darfur.* New Haven, CT: Yale University Press.
Mearsheimer, J. 2002. *The tragedy of the great powers.* New York: Norton.
Miles, J. 2004. Religion and American foreign policy, *Survival* 46:23–37.
Morgenthau, H.J. 1978. *Politics among nations.* New York: Knopf.
Moynihan, D.P. 1993. *Pandemonium: Ethnicity in international politics.* New York: Oxford University Press.
Murphy, C.N. 2000. Global governance: Poorly done and poorly understood. *International Affairs* 76:789–803.
Norris, P., and R. Inglehart. 2004. *Sacred and secular: Religion and politics worldwide.* Cambridge: Cambridge University Press.
Pew Forum on Religion and Public Life. 2006. Many Americans uneasy with mix of religion and politics. http://pewforum.org/docs/index.php?DocID=153.
– 2007. Public expresses mixed views of Islam, Mormonism. http://pewforum.org/surveys/religionviews07.
Pew Research Center for the People and the Press. 2003. Religion and politics: Contention and consensus. http://people-press.org/reports/display.php3?ReportID=189.
Philpott, D. 2000. The religious roots of modern international relations. *World Politics* 52:206–45.
– 2002. The challenge of September 11 to secularism in international relations. *World Politics* 55:66–95.
Rudolph, S.H. 1997. Introduction: Religion, states, and transnational civil society. In Rudolph and Piscatori, 1–24.
Rudolph, S.H., and J. Piscatori, eds. 1997. *Transnational religion and fading states.* Boulder, CO: Westview.

Singer, J.D. 1961. The level of analysis problem in international relations. *World Politics* 14:77–92.
Stack, J.F. Jr. 1997. The ethnic challenge to international relations theory. In *Wars in the midst of peace*, ed. D. Carment and P. James, 11–25. Pittsburgh, PA: Pittsburgh University Press.
Waever, O. 1998. American and European developments in international relations. *International Organizations* 52:687–727.
Waltz, K.N. 1959. *Man, the state and war: A theoretical analysis*. New York: Columbia University Press.
– 1979. *Theory of international politics*. New York: McGraw-Hill.

3 Religion and International Affairs: The State of the Art

RON E. HASSNER

Introduction

The aftermath of 9/11 has seen a veritable explosion in publications about religion and international studies. More books on Islam and war have been published since 9/11 than ever before, from the invention of the printing press up to September 2001, whereas references to Islam in the *New York Times* have tripled, on average. Many of these sources betray a deep suspicion of religion in general (particularly recent best-sellers written from a secularist perspective) and an antagonism toward Islam in particular.

We are members of a generation of Americans that derives its information about religion from sources that display a strong bias against religious belief. Our reasons for doing so, in the shadow of 9/11, are understandable but the costs of this secular, foaming-at-the-mouth backlash are prohibitive. Dismissing religion as a dangerous form of group dementia is not only unreasonable, it also is unhelpful because one cannot both reject and expect to understand religion. As chapter 2 points out, the liberal expectancy about the demise of religion already has been challenged by socio-political processes around the globe.

This bias in the popular press in mirrored, to some extent, in academia. Opinion surveys among academics reveal a systematic secular bias. Academic texts on religion and international affairs go one of two routes: The *broad* route, in which the focus is placed on the international level of analysis and religion is essentialized, reduced to economics, politics, or some parallel sphere; or the *deep* route, in which the political impact of a particular religious movement or the impact of religion in a particular region is examined at depth without offering generalizations for the international sphere.

The complementary approach I propose here, *thick religion*, requires sensitivity to theology, religious organization, iconography, ceremony, and belief but also a willingness to generalize from particular religious movements, regions, or instances to arrive at broader conclusions for international relations (IR). This implies an issue-area approach, in which the focus of analysis is a particular area of concern in which religion and international affairs interact. I examine several texts in the *broad* and *deep* traditions, exemplify *thick religion* by means of two prominent texts – Mark Juergensmeyer's *Terror in the Mind of God* and Daniel Philpott's *Revolutions in Sovereignty* – and suggest an agenda for future research. This agenda builds on the compelling case made in chapter 2 that religion was and remains relevant to IR concerns.

Religion and IR in the Popular Literature and the Media

Events on 11 September 2001 caused a rapid surge in demand for information on religion and conflict. A basic search of the Library of Congress online catalogue confirms that authors and publishers responded rapidly to this need. The catalogue lists five books under the subject headings 'religion' and 'politics' before 1970.[1] Of the three hundred–odd books published under this heading since 1970, a full third appeared after 9/11. The data on books discussing religion and international affairs are even more striking: the catalogue lists no books at all, in any language, before 1973. Half the books on these subjects that appear in the catalogue were published since 9/11.[2]

The average yearly output of books on religion and international affairs has thus sextupled, from about a book a year in the 1970s, 1980s, and 1990s to approximately 6 books per year since 2002. The figures for volumes on religion and war are even more startling: publication has expanded from 2 or 3 books a year in the last three decades to an average of 14 books a year since 2001. The publication record on Islam and war, however, dwarfs all these achievements. More books have been published on Islam and war since 9/11 than ever before, if the online catalogue of the Library of Congress is to be believed. From the 1430s, when Johann Guttenberg first experimented with his printing press, until the end of 2001, only 154 books appeared under the subject headings 'Islam' and 'war' that would later take up space on the shelves of the Library. An additional 155 volumes have appeared since then (not counting publications after December 2006), thus raising the yearly average from just over 4 books a year in recent decades to a whopping 30 books per average year since 2001.

This spike in supply raises troubling questions regarding authorship. Writers who enjoyed an expertise on religion and international relations before 9/11 might have increased their output after 2001 but they are unlikely to have increased it six-fold. More often than not, then, popular books on religion and international affairs are being written by scholars of opportunity who have little to no substantive knowledge of the topic. Three recent best-sellers, all of which touch on the topics of religion, international politics, and conflict in one way or another, exemplify this trend: Richard Dawkins's *The God Delusion* (2006), Sam Harris's *The End of Faith* (2006), and Christopher Hitchens's *God Is Not Great* (2007).[3]

Popular texts such as these display an anti-religious bias aimed primarily at Islam, coupled with a startling disinterest in conversing with, or drawing upon, the rich intellectual tradition in the study of religion, secularism, and politics. By refusing to evaluate evidence carefully, these texts espouse a gross double standard. Wherever religion is associated with war, the authors emphasize and elaborate the correlation and characterize it as substantial and causal. Yet at the same time they dismiss as spurious any association of religion with the promotion of morality, science, or art, suggesting instead that such progress is driven by culture and civilization (Dawkins 2006, 86–7, 270; Hitchens 2007, 254). The reader learns that wars ostensibly fought in the name of religion do in fact reveal the true hatred and divisiveness that is at the core of all religious belief. Yet wars fought in the name of fascism and communism are no evidence for the wickedness of atheism; rather, they suggest that even fascism and communism may be religious at their core (Dawkins 2006, 275, 278). Religiously motivated pacifists, we learn from Hitchens, are either not truly religious, as is said to have been the case with Martin Luther King, or not truly pacifists, as was allegedly the case with Gandhi (2007, 176, 182–4).

Newspaper editors were as quick as their colleagues in the publishing world to realize the sudden salience of religion and politics after September 2001. Since 1999 the number of *New York Times* articles referencing Islam, for example, has undergone a dramatic shift: one is three times as likely to find an article about Islam in the *New York Times* in 2007 compared to 2001.[4] The *Washington Post* rose to the challenge of covering religion and contemporary affairs by launching On Faith, an online forum for discussions 'about faith and its implications' (Meacham and Quinn, 2006). A year into the initiative, the online discussion of Islam and violence overshadowed in volume all other topics of conversation combined.[5] Given the diversity within

Islam that emerges in chapter 4 on the international human rights regime, for example, this one-dimensional, violence-oriented dialogue is particularly disappointing.

Coverage of religion and politics is not merely comprehensive. It also is biased. Articles in English-speaking papers worldwide that contain keywords related to religion – such as *holy, Allah,* or *Islam* – are highly likely to be articles that also reference political violence. In 1999, I found that a quarter of the articles that contained the word *holy* also contained terms such as *terror/ism/ist, fundamentalism/ist, war,* or *violence*.[6] This strikes me as a very high figure, considering the fact that articles about *holy* might discuss holy cows, holy week, or the Holy See. Instead, nearly a quarter were about holy war. The figures for *Allah* and *Islam* were even higher. In 1999, one in three articles referencing Allah was an article about violence, and these odds rose to one in two if the article contained the word *Islam*. The numbers for 2006 are even more staggering: half of the articles containing *holy* or *Allah* were associated with political violence as were 60 per cent of the articles on Islam!

Americans today are not deriving information about religion from even-handed sources. Bias is particularly worrisome, given evidence of how ill-informed the American public is in matters of religion. In Gallup polls from the 1950s, three-quarters of Catholics or Protestants questioned could not name a single Hebrew prophet, more than two-thirds did not know who preached the Sermon on the Mount, and a substantial number listed Moses among the twelve apostles (Dawkins 2006; Hinde 1999, 341). Stephen Prothero, chairman of the religion department at Brown University, who regularly tests his students on basic 'religious literacy,' only to see 87 per cent fail, has suggested that this ignorance leads Americans to be 'too easily swayed by demagogues' (2007). In particular, as chapter 14 will reveal, it bodes poorly for the ability of the United States to engage positively with societies outside the Christian West.

Social Scientists, Political Scientists, and Religion

Religion has garnered similar attention from social scientists. Political science was among the first academic disciplines to realize the growing salience of religion in contemporary society in the late twentieth century and to respond with invigorated research programs, increased publication in scholarly journals, and higher enrolment in academic organizations focused on religion and politics (Clayton 2002). This pattern is also apparent in the subfield of international relations: the average number of articles on religion in leading international relations journals has shot up from about fifteen a year before 9/11 to nearly 60 articles a year thereafter.[7] Coverage of religion in IR journals between 2001 and 2006 accounts for over 70 per cent of all the articles published on this subject in these journals before 2006. Indeed, the subfield of IR has outpaced by far the coverage of religion in the discipline as a whole (Wald and Wilcox 2006).

Sadly, the bias in the popular press is also mirrored, to some extent, in academia. Opinion surveys among academics reveal a systematic secular bias among academics, particularly social scientists. Some studies explain this tendency by suggesting an inverse relationship between IQ and religiosity (Terman and Oden, 1959). Others show an inverse link between self-definition as an intellectual, positive attitudes towards creativity, intellectual freedom, and scholarly perspectives, on the one hand, and religious observance, on the other (Beit-Hallahmi 2007). Universities dominated by religious organizations suffer a lower reputation, and student religiosity tends to decline in proportion to a university's ranking (Goldsen et al. 1960).[8]

Researchers focusing on science, religion, and academia in the first half of the twentieth century, such as James L. Leuba and Anne Roe, found consistently low rates of believers among eminent scientists and Nobel laureates (Leuba 1916). A more recent study by Larson and Witham showed that the rate of belief in a personal God among eminent scientists in the United States had fallen from 27.7 per cent in 1914 to a mere 7 per cent in 1998 (1998, 213). This figure is more striking yet if one takes into account that, outside academia, 72 per cent of Americans are said to believe in angels and 83 per cent of Americans believe the Bible to be the word of God (Gottlieb 2007, 79).

Yet even among these relatively secular scientists, social scientists stand out as particularly unlikely to define themselves as religious (Leuba 1916). Survey data from the 1960s by Fred Thalheimer that compared religiosity across six academic fields found that social scientists scored lowest in professing an affiliation with a religion, lowest in church attendance, lowest in conducting private prayer, and highest in disbelief in God (1973, 183–202). The author concluded, 'The social scientists' lowest ranking in religiosity is a result of *both* the tendency of persons who are non-religious in high school to go into the social sciences and remain non-religious and the tendency for individuals in the social sciences to abandon traditional beliefs and practices *after entering* college' (ibid., 194–5). Alarmingly, whereas the majority of religiously *active* social scientists in Thalheimer's survey expressed some concern about the relationship between their belief and their professional knowledge, most of those who *did not* believe felt no such compunction: 69 per cent claimed that they were not concerned at all about the relationship between their professional knowledge and their religious convictions (ibid. 200).

Several recent surveys have offered more specific information on the religious attitudes of political scientists. In a 1984 survey of college faculty sponsored by the Carnegie Foundation for the Advancement of Teaching, only 6 per cent of political scientists reported being deeply religious, compared to 12 per cent who reported being hostile to religion (Wald and Wilcox 2006, 526). As Wald and Wilcox, who analysed these results, report, both deeply religious and hostile political scientists might be inclined to investigate the impact of religion on politics, whereas those who reported an indifference to religion, 41 per cent in all, were likely to simply ignore the role of religion in politics (ibid.). A 2005 survey of 225 political scientists at elite research universities in the United States backed this statistic: only 34 per cent of political scientists surveyed expressed a belief in God and only 25.7 per cent attended religious services with any regularity (Ecklund and Scheitle 2007, 296). The 1984 Carnegie survey also confirmed findings from previous polls on the inverse relationship between professional vigour and religiosity: the political scientists who attended the most professional meetings, who published the most articles and books, who taught at the top-ranked universities – in sum, those who set the research agenda for the profession – were more likely to be secular than other political scientists (Wald and Wilcox 2006, 526).

Proponents of the 'new secularism' in the popular literature have used data such as these to intimate that religion is a form of feeble-mindedness, common among the less educated and those gullible and prone to superstition. Irrespective of whether this condescending presumption has some truth in it, these figures bear a different implication altogether: the data suggest that many political scientists might be ill-suited for conducting unbiased research on the topic of religion and politics. If the survey data are to be believed, political scientists are extraordinarily secular yet fundamentally uninterested in the impact of their secularity on their research. This disregard for religious belief not only places the social scientist out of touch with the religiously motivated actors and societies he or she may be studying, it also creates significant obstacles in maintaining neutrality in research. Indeed, some have gone so far as to argue that social scientists purposefully adopt a secular stance in order to distance themselves from the general public.[9]

Deep and Broad Religion

It is because of these proclivities, as well as the methodological challenges that I discuss below, that analyses of religion and international relations have experienced a bifurcation, diverging into a *broad* route and a *deep* route. In the former case, authors focus their attention on the international arena at the cost of examining religion at depth. Their analyses tend to essentialize religion and reduce it to its social, economic, or political implications. Authors espousing the *deep* route place their emphasis on an intimate familiarity with a particular religious movement or a particular geographical region, without offering generalizations for the international sphere.

This state of affairs, in which authors choose between generalizability and interdisciplinary rigour, is the exception to the norm in IR, an interdisciplinary field par excellence. International relations scholars habitually borrow insights, themes, and even methods from disciplines as far afield as geography, psychology, and anthropology. Yet IR scholars who rely on geographical explanations located on the sub-global level, for example, have taken great care to expand and link these accounts to the international outcome they are trying to explain. They do not simply assert that regional or state geography, for example, has immediate implications for global geography, nor are they content to conclude their analyses with findings at the sub-global level and leave it at that.

Similarly, scholars who seek insight into international affairs from psychology or anthropology have eschewed treating these fields of inquiry as mere metaphors for international affairs. Instead, they have linked findings at the individual level of analysis (for psychology) or the societal level of analysis (for social psychology and anthropology) to the international level of analysis of carefully traced causal chains. Studies of psychology and IR have inquired, for example, into the relationship between the perceptions of the individual leader and global outcomes by analysing individual leaders at crucial decision-making junctures that affect global politics. Students of anthropology and IR have extracted observations about cooperation and conflict at the tribal level to arguments about cooperation and conflict at the international level by establishing the causal chain with an appropriate methodology at each intervening level of analysis – an ethnographic approach to sociology, for example, for the tribal or regional levels, a positivist approach to politics for the state level, and a positivist approach to international politics for global level of analysis.

Few IR scholars have extended this courtesy to religion. The most cited text on religion and international affairs, Huntington's *Clash of Civilizations and the Remaking of World Order*, for example, offers one of the clearest examples for the *broad* approach. Although Huntington's argument is ostensibly about clashes between civilizations, it is, in essence, an argument about conflicts between large religious blocks (Huntington 1993, 32). Nonetheless, *The Clash* offers no insight into civilizational identity, not to mention religious identity. Relying explicitly on distinctiveness theory, Huntington presents a billiard-ball theory of religious conflict in which all cultural disagreements are zero-sum, all religious blocks in contact are also at war, and all clashes are uniform in kind and degree, irrespective of what particular religions happen to be involved (ibid. 67–8, 129–30, 245, 292). Religions clash not because of what they are but because of what they are not: a religious identity serves merely as a tag to differentiate one side of a conflict from the other. There is little about Islam or Christianity, for example, that explains conflict between these two civilizations other than the fact that Islam is not Christianity.

The mechanisms driving Huntington's global clash of religions are primarily demographic, economic, technological, and political, not religious. In the 360 pages in his volume, only four paragraphs discuss the religious causes of this clash and these offer a sophomoric analysis at best: Huntington asserts that Christianity is distinct from Islam because it recognizes the separation of church and state; Islam is an absolutist religion of the sword; both Christianity and Islam are monotheistic (so they 'cannot easily assimilate additional deities'), universalistic, missionary, and teleological religions that espouse crusades and jihad respectively (1996, 70, 210–11, 263–4). These superficial observations are not linked to the outcome explained: Huntington does not tell us why teleology, for example, should lead these two movements into conflict.

The disconnect between the explanatory outcome, at the international level of analysis, and the underlying religious cause does not invalidate Huntington's claim or detract from the value of his analysis but it does suggest that, while Huntington is writing *on* religion, he is not writing *about* religion. In contrast, Martin Marty and Scott Appleby's Fundamentalism Project exemplifies the *deep* approach to religion and international affairs. In over one hundred case studies spread over five volumes, some of the foremost scholars of comparative religion, experts on extremist movements, and country specialists examine the problem of fundamentalism, using either the religious movement or the geographical region as their unit of analysis.[10] The analysis, throughout, is sensitive to religious practices and beliefs, the content of scripture, exegesis and interpretation, rituals and symbols, religious hierarchies and leadership structures. Together, these volumes offer the most meticulous and comprehensive survey of fundamentalism available.

The multiple contributions in the Fundamentalism Project do not, however, amount to an international theory of fundamentalism. The disparate chapters remain distinct case studies and their findings are not generalized beyond the particular region or religion each discusses, despite introductory chapters that emphasize similarities and differences across cases. Because the project offers no generalized system-level explanation, it remains a text in comparative politics, not a contribution to international relations theory, no matter how thorough its coverage of the globe.[11]

Vali Nasr's study of Shi'ism and its growing influence across the Middle East, *The Shia Revival*, offers yet another example for the *deep religion* approach (2006). It has been celebrated as the most important and most accessible contribution to the study of this religious movement in recent decades, and quite rightly so. Nasr bases his analysis of contemporary Shia politics in a reading of Shia history, theology, and religious hierarchy; he is as interested in the political significance of *ashura* rituals and the symbolism of the Battle of Karbala as he is in the demographic or economic underpinnings of the spread of Shi'ism (ibid. 31–77, 93–8, 130–6). His analysis thus extends from religion almost to the very top of the level of analysis ladder: he stops short of applying his conclusions to global Shi'ism and he does not develop his argument about this particular branch of Islam in a manner that would facilitate its extension to other religions or regions.

The two approaches exemplified by Huntington, on the one hand, and Marty and Appleby or Nasr, on the other, as well as the vast majority of texts on religion and IR currently available, can be located in a two-dimensional space that represents the relationship between an argument's level of analysis and its methodology. In this two-dimensional space (see figure 3.1), the horizontal axis forms a continuum ranging from the domestic to the international. This represents the level of analysis on which research of religious behaviour focuses. The vertical axis captures the degree to which research engages religion in a positivist or reflectivist manner. A positivist approach rationalizes

Figure 3.1: Broad, deep, and thick religion

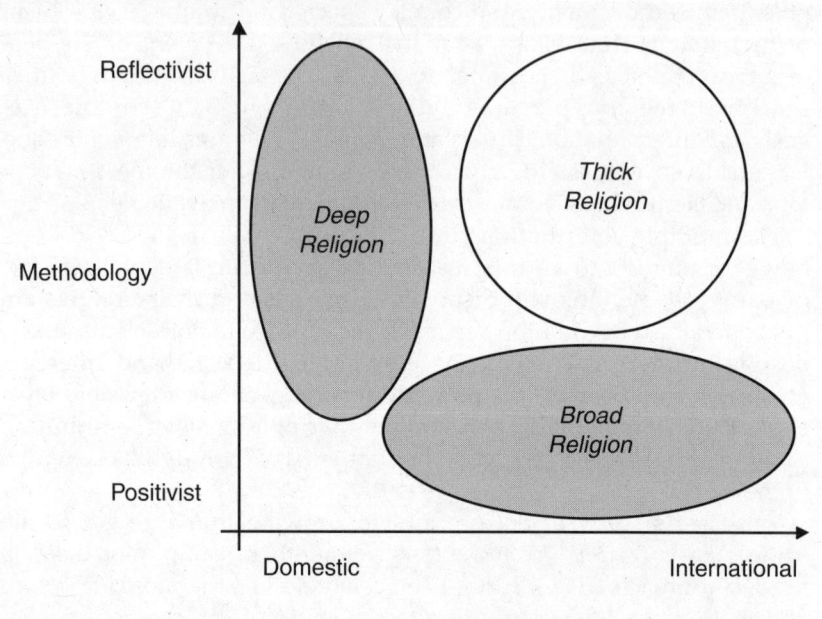

[Figure: A two-dimensional plot with "Methodology" on the vertical axis (ranging from Positivist at the bottom to Reflectivist at the top) and "Level of Analysis" on the horizontal axis (ranging from Domestic on the left to International on the right). Three overlapping shapes are shown: a vertical shaded ellipse labeled "Deep Religion" on the left spanning most of the methodology range; a circle labeled "Thick Religion" in the upper right; and a horizontal shaded ellipse labeled "Broad Religion" in the lower right.]

religion by measuring its empirical effects in some parallel sphere, be it demography, ethnic identity, trade and so forth, whereas a reflectivist approach attempts to understand religious behaviour by describing religious beliefs and practices (Adler 1997).

Research in the *broad religion* category falls towards the international end of the level of analysis continuum because it tends to emphasize the effects of religious behaviour on the international sphere. At the same time, this research, so far, tends to restrict its methodology to positivism. These authors are interested in the effects of religion on international conflict and cooperation, diplomacy, or globalization, but they have been hesitant to trace these effects to their origins in religion itself.

Research in the *deep religion* category, on the other hand, has adopted a reflectivist stance on religion and politics by using a religious context to understand religious behaviour. At the same time, this research has, so far, restricted itself to operating at or below the domestic level of analysis. These authors study a single religious movement or religion in depth, often revealing insights regarding ritual practice, the meaning of symbols and language, the implications of theology and exegesis, and the role of beliefs in local political practices. However, they seldom if ever extend these conclusions to the international sphere.

Thick Religion

Figure 3.1 reveals a significant gap in the literature. What is lacking is an approach that combines an international relations focus with an interpretivist methodology. This is the approach I have labelled *thick religion*. It is not designed as a critique of or substitute for its alternatives but as a complementary method that ties a deep understanding of religion to broad-ranging effects at the international level. The challenge facing this approach is thus twofold: it must bridge the levels of analysis separating religion from international relations and it must adapt a reflectivist methodology, useful for gaining insight into religious beliefs and practices, to a discipline with a positivist orientation.

Given this formidable methodological challenge, the decision by most international relations scholars to opt for a *broad* or *deep* approach is understandable. Linking an explanation from outside the political realm to an outcome in IR necessitates shifts in both levels of analysis and epistemology. Whereas international relations works its immediate effects at the very top of the level of analysis ladder, religion affects the individual and group levels most directly. Scholars can approach either discipline with any of a variety of available epistemologies. Yet should they choose to employ a different epistemology for religion, on the one hand, and IR, on the other, then connecting the various levels of analysis that separate the individual or group level from the international level will also require 'translating' one epistemology to the other, possibly using an intermediary epistemology to bridge the two. Connecting religion and IR thus requires ascending the level of analysis ladder while presenting arguments with the appropriate methodology for each rung.

The resulting analytic chains connecting religion to IR come in different strengths: correlative, causal, and constitutive. At their weakest, these chains employ the language of *correlation*, suggesting that religious and political phenomena are merely associated with one another in time or space. Chains that succeed in establishing a *causal* link between observations about religion and outcomes regarding IR are of stronger analytic quality. A causal chain suggests that religious variables contribute directly to the production of international outcomes.

The strongest possible connection is established by a *constitutive* argument. By espousing a constitutive logic, the author asserts that the religious phenomenon observed gives not just existence but meaning and identity to the phenomena observed at the IR level.

The differences among these three modes of explanation can be discerned in one of the most ambitious book series on religion and IR, the Praeger series, Culture and Religion in International Relations, edited by Yosef Lapid. Authors in this series have focused their attention on the international relations level of analysis and have employed a positivist epistemology to do so. They rarely 'dip' more than one level of analysis below the international level towards the religious phenomena they are relying on as explanatory variables, thus exemplifying the *broad religion* approach.

Most often, the authors in this series link the international level of analysis to the level immediate below it by means of a correlative claim. In *Bringing Religion into International Relations* (2004), for example, Jonathan Fox and Shmuel Sandler rely on the religious identities of states to explain patterns of conflict and cooperation. Yet, as in Huntington's *Clash*, the identities assigned to states by these authors are religious in name only: the analysis does not go beyond the state level to examine where this religious label comes from or how the presence of dominant religious groups in a state, a religiously influenced constitution, or high levels of piety among leaders, which must have given rise to this label in the first place, shape the outcome they are trying to explain. There is, in sum, no causal or constitutive link between the independent variable (the religious identity label attached to a state) and the dependent variable (conflict or cooperation). A similar *broad religion* approach employing correlative logic can be discerned in Pippa Norris and Ronald Inglehart's *Sacred and Secular* (2004), in which statistical analyses of survey data provide the sole input on religion.

Scott M. Thomas in his contribution to the Palgrave project, *The Global Resurgence of Religion and the Transformation of International Relations* (2005), takes the analysis further by providing a causal underpinning for the link between the international and religious levels of analysis. This remains a text in the *broad religion* tradition: Thomas does not venture into the specifics of religious belief or practice. But he does investigate the causal pathways through which religious identities shape religious alliances, transnational religious actors exert influence on states, and religious ideas act as ideological motivators for state action.

Thick religion offers an alternative approach to the study of religion and international relations that is both *deep*, in that it traces the pathways by which religion affects international affairs to their origins in the content and meaning of religion, and *broad*, in that it offers generalizable implications across states and regions. A *thick religion* approach to the study of religion and international politics requires an understanding of religious detail but also a willingness to generalize from particular religious movements, regions, or instances to arrive at broader conclusions.

The term I have chosen for this approach is an obvious nod to Clifford Geertz's seminal text on the study of culture as well as a useful mnemonic for those aspects of religion in which studies of religion and international relations should be grounded: theology, religious organization (hierarchy), symbol (iconography), ceremony, and belief (or knowledge – hence 't.h.i.c.k'). A *thick religion* analysis should thus be anchored in answers to one or more of the following questions:

- *Theology*: What are the tenets of this religious movement? What do its most important texts and scholars propose?
- *Hierarchy*: How is the religious movement organized, socially and politically? Who rules and makes decisions? How are these individuals chosen and ranked?
- *Iconography*: How does this religious movement use symbols, myths, images, words, or sounds to convey its ideas? How do believers treat these icons?
- *Ceremony*: How do believers act out the theology, hierarchy, and iconography of this religious movement? What are their rituals, practices, feasts, and commemorations?
- *Belief*: What do members of this religious community believe in? What are the foundations of their faith?

We need to know at least some of this before we can proceed to critically examine the role religion plays in current affairs, notably as related to global governance.

Thick religion implies an issue-area approach that focuses analysis on a particular topic of concern in which religion and international affairs interact. Instead of identifying mere correlations, this method traces a comprehensive logical chain, from the content of specific religious ideas to particular outcomes in international politics, and thus identifies causal or even constitutive relationships between religious ideas and political behaviour. *Thick religion* starts its investigation with the religious micro-foundations of a political phenomenon and then constructs successive layers of explanation, each more removed from the religious and closer to the political, until it reaches the outcome to be explained. By encouraging the analysis of a broad range of religious belief and practices, this approach is as suitable to studying the monotheistic religious movements of the West as it is to studying religions of the East. This distinguishes *thick religion* from prevailing Christian-centric approaches that privilege theology over practice, conflate scripture with theology, and marginalize the impact of heterodox beliefs, figurative art, and religious ceremony.

Thick religion rests on the assumption that the study of religion and international politics is necessarily an interdisciplinary exercise. Viewing religion merely through a political lens will not do. In addition to politics, we ought to also study religion directly, be it through the sociology of religion, comparative religious analysis, or theology.

One of the most successful texts in the *thick religion* tradition is Mark Juergensmeyer's (1998) analysis of religiously motivated terrorism. The first half of the book consists of five case studies, examining distinct fundamentalist religious movements in five locations around the globe. Juergensmeyer focuses on how particular sets of religious beliefs and practices drive the history, identity, and motivation of each unique movement. The second half of the book identifies commonalities among these cases and expands the case studies into a generalized argument about religious violence worldwide, thus translating the *deep religion* of the first half of the book into a *thick religion* argument at the international level of analysis. The author then relies on an argument from the sociology of religion – Rene Girard's theory of religious ceremony as ritualized violence – to translate the disparate findings from the case studies into a unified theory of fundamentalist terrorism as performance in which theology supplies both script and justification. Juergensmeyer translates this interpretivist theory into a set of empirical hypotheses that predict the location, timing, and audience for the 'performances' of terrorism, based on the cosmology and eschatology of a given religious movement.

Juergensmeyer constructs his *thick religion* argument in a progression of detailed and gradual steps. Yet *thick religion* does not require protracted analyses or exhaustive description. In *Revolutions in Sovereignty* (2001), Daniel Philpott succeeds in linking the religious underpinnings of the Protestant Reformation – indeed, the theological foundations of that Reformation – to the ensuing revolution in the structure of international relations in less than four pages. He begins this segment of his volume with a discussion of Martin Luther and John Calvin's theology, tracing their argument from their interpretation of the Fall of Man and the Original Sin to the doctrine of *Sola Fide* (104–5). This provides the background for the Reformation's critique of the papacy, its practices, wealth, and temporal powers (105–6). Here the analysis shifts gradually from the religious motivation of the reformers to their political aspirations. These, in turn, provide the explanation for the political and military support provided to the reformers by the princes of Europe, a support that results in the creation of sovereign states ruled by secular rulers (106–8).

Having spanned the gap between theology and the structure of the international system at lightning speed, Philpott pauses briefly to consider the implications of his argument: 'In none of Luther's tracts, nor in Calvin's *Institutes*, do we explicitly find mention of sovereignty, or still less, a Westphalian system of sovereign states. But what their political theology prescribed was the substance of sovereignty ... The point is crucial: sovereignty, in substance if not in name, comes directly out of the very propositions of Protestant theology in all its variants' (2001, 107–8). Philpott concludes this *coup de main* by contrasting Protestant theology to the theology of other 'heresies' of the period to demonstrate why the particular ideas at the core of the Protestant Reformation unleashed political effects that other theologies did not. This is *thick religion* at its finest.

Conclusion

Thick religion proposes to trace international phenomena to their religious origins while identifying generalizable patterns across states and regions. If successfully implemented, this methodology can provide the impetus for investigations into a wide variety of areas at the confluence of religion and international affairs. Two broad categories suggest themselves: issues linked to fundamental concepts in international affairs and issues related to contemporary international concerns.

Research in the first category might shed light on core themes in international relations theory, from sovereignty and identity to legitimacy, leadership, power, and global governance. Philpott's work on the religious roots of sovereignty in the West exemplifies this research agenda. Further research might investigate the religious foundations of the sovereignty concept outside the Western hemisphere, trace the identities and interests of international actors to their roots in religious beliefs and practices, uncover the religious foundations of international legitimacy and leadership, or establish the religious sources of power in the international sphere.

How do theology and religious hierarchy, for example, inform notions of hierarchy and law in international affairs? The investigation in chapter 11 of Christian mediation in international conflict answers some of the preceding questions in one significant context. By adopting thick religion as an implicit approach, Lloyd finds that theology and hierarchy affect the negotiating styles of respective Christian traditions. Other questions might follow: How do religious rituals, beliefs, and symbols underpin international institutions and organizations, foster cooperation, and bolster alliances? How can religious communities contribute to the spread and institutionalization of international taboos and norms? How might religion as a transnational authority contribute to global governance that is more 'ethical and moral'? (Murphy 2000, 789). The concepts have preoccupied IR scholars for decades but the religious dimension of answers to most of these questions have eluded us so far.

A second avenue for fruitful research encompasses issues of current concern, from weapons proliferation and war to underdevelopment and state collapse. Juergensmeyer's work on terrorism fits into this category. Research projects might seek to reveal the link between religious ideas and military doctrine, uncover how faith informs key aspects of war (the willingness to fight, how and when to fight, what weapons are considered legitimate), and establish links between religious power structures and the rise of militant fundamentalism. What role do religious leaders play in exacerbating or restraining the costs of civil and ethnic wars? How do believers employ the sacred, be it sacred land, ritual, language, or icons, to justify, motivate, or constrain violence? An example of thick religion in action is provided by chapter 4, which investigates directly the roles of Islamist and Islamic states in relation to human rights. Another instance is the connection in chapter 7 of Islamic thought in India to the relative dearth of violent protest by Muslims in that state. In sum, by engaging some of the preceding questions with a sensitivity to religious context and detail, students of faith and politics can begin the rewarding task of shifting the research agenda in religion and international relations towards more fruitful directions in the quest for improved global governance.

NOTES

1 These findings are based on a Boolean search for the subject keywords *religion* and *politics* in the online catalogue of the Library of Congress for books published on or before 2006. The search was not limited to books in English. The search for texts using these two keywords presumably includes as many books strictly irrelevant to the topic of religion and politics as it excludes relevant volumes. It should nonetheless provide a rough metric for the supply of books related to politics and religion.
2 Twenty-two books on religion and international affairs appear in the catalogue as having been published before or during 2001 compared to twenty-four books on *religion* and *international affairs* published between 2002 and 2006. Similar results apply for the subject headings *religion* and *international relations*, with thirty-five books up to 2001 and thirty-one books since.
3 These volumes were accompanied by other publications, somewhat less popular, that shared their anti-religious fervour, such as Daniel Dennett's *Breaking the Spell* and Sam Harris's *Letter to a Christian Nation*. For a brief critique of this literature, see Gottlieb (2007).
4 I searched the Lexis-Nexis online database for *New York Times* articles that included the words *Islam, Islamic, Muslim,* or *Muslims*. An average of 1.9 articles per day mentioned these terms prior to the end of September 2001 and 5.8 articles per day on average did so between October 2001 and the end of 2006.
5 As of October 2007, the homepage of the On Faith initiative (http://newsweek.washingtonpost.com/onfaith/) listed 659 comments on Islam and violence, 117 comments on Middle East politics, 121 comments on life after death, and lower figures for discussions of clergy sexuality, religious tolerance, etc.
6 To arrive at these figures, I conducted a Lexis-Nexis search of articles in the first nine months of 1999 and the first nine months of 2006 that included the terms *holy, Allah,* and *Islam*. I searched major newspapers in English worldwide. I then conducted searches for articles that included each of these terms in addition to one of the political violence keywords listed above. Since the first set of searches necessarily subsumes the second set of searches, I was able to establish the ratio of articles with religious keywords that include political violence keywords as well. Needless to say, the presence of any of these keywords in an article cannot reflect the actual content of the article or its position on religion and violence. Presumably

this sample includes as many irrelevant articles (that mention religion and violence keywords in passing) as it excludes relevant articles.
7 These data are based on a search of the Academic Universe Citation Index, which includes only articles cited in journal articles. I searched for articles with the words *religion/religious* and then limited the results to IR journals.
8 For a more nuanced analysis of this claim, see Mixon, Lyon, and Beaty (2004, 400–19).
9 This argument about the 'boundary posturing mechanism' among social scientists was proposed in Wuthnow (1985, 187–203).
10 In order of publication, these volumes, all edited by Martin E. Marty and R. Scott Appleby and published by the University of Chicago Press, are *Fundamentalisms and Society: Reclaiming the Sciences, the Family, and Education* (1993); *Fundamentalisms Observed* (1994); *Fundamentalisms Comprehended* (1995); *Fundamentalisms and the State: Remaking Polities, Economies and Militance* (1996); and *Accounting for Fundamentalisms: The Dynamic Character of Movements* (2004).
11 The authors amend this, to some extent, in a separate text that functions as a summary of the Fundamentalism Project: Almond, Appleby, and Sivan (2003).

REFERENCES

Adler, E. 1997. Seizing the middle ground: Constructivism in world politics. *European Journal of International Relations* 3 (3): 319–63.
Almond, G.A., R.S. Appleby, and E. Sivan. 2003. *Strong religion: The rise of fundamentalisms around the world*. Chicago: University of Chicago Press.
Beit-Hallahmi, B. 2007. Atheists: A psychological profile. In *Cambridge Companion to Atheism*, ed. M. Martin, 300–18. New York: Cambridge University Press.
Clayton, M. 2002. Scholars get religion: More academics are starting to see the 'religion factor' as key to understanding forces in economics, politics and society. *Christian Science Monitor*, 26 February.
Dawkins, R. 2006. *The God delusion*. Boston: Houghton Mifflin.
Ecklund, E.H., and C.P. Scheitle. 2007. Religion among academic scientists: Distinctions, disciplines, and demographics. *Social Problems* 54 (2): 297–9.
Fox, J., and S. Sandler. 2004. *Bringing religion into international relations*. New York: Palgrave Macmillan.
Goldsen, R.K., M. Rosenberg, R.M. Williams, and E.A. Suchman. 1960. *What college students think*. Princeton, NJ: Van Nostrand.
Gottlieb, A. 2007. Atheists with attitude. *New Yorker*, 21 May, 77–80.

Harris, S. 2006. *Letter to a Christian nation*. New York: Knopf.
Hinde, Robert. 1999. *Why gods persist: A scientific approach*. New York: Routledge.
Hitchens, C. 2007. *God is not great: How religion poisons everything*. New York: Hachette Book Group USA.
Huntington, S.P. 1993. The clash of civilizations. *Foreign Affairs* 72 (3): 22–50.
Juergensmeyer, M. 1998. *Terror in the mind of God: The global rise of religious violence*. Berkeley, CA: University of California Press.
Larson, E.J., and L. Witham. 1998. Leading scientists still reject God. *Nature* 394 (6691): 313.
Leuba, J.H. 1916. *Belief in God and immortality: A psychological, anthropological and statistical study*. Boston: Sherman and French.
Marty, M.E., and R.S. Appleby. 1993. *Fundamentalisms and society: Reclaiming the sciences, the family, and education*. Urbana: University of Chicago Press.
– 1994. *Fundamentalisms observed*. Urbana: University of Chicago Press.
– 1995. *Fundamentalisms comprehended*. Urbana: University of Chicago Press.
– 1996. *Fundamentalisms and the state: Remaking polities, economies and militance*. Urbana: University of Chicago Press.
– 2004. *Accounting for fundamentalisms: The dynamic character of movements*. Urbana: University of Chicago Press.
Meacham, J., and S. Quinn. 2006. About on faith, *Washington Post*, 9 November. http://newsweek.washingtonpost.com/onfaith/2006/11/about_on_faith/comments.html.
Mixon, S.L., L. Lyon, and M. Beaty. 2004. Secularization and national universities: The effect of religious identity on academic reputation. *Journal of Higher Education* 75 (4): 400–19.
Murphy, Craig N. 2000. Global governance: Poorly done and poorly understood. *International Affairs* 76:789–803.
Nasr, V. 2006. *The Shia revival: How conflicts within Islam will shape the future*. New York: Norton.
Norris, P., and R. Inglehart. 2004. *Sacred and secular: Religion and politics worldwide*. Cambridge, MA: Cambridge University Press.
Philpott, D. 2001. *Revolutions in sovereignty: How ideas shaped modern international relations*. Princeton, NJ: Princeton University Press.
Prothero, S. 2007. Worshipping in ignorance. *Chronicle of Higher Education* 53 (28): B6.
Quinn, Sally, and Jon Meacham. On faith. *Washington Post*. 9 November 2006. http://newsweek.washingtonpost.com/onfaith/2006/11/about_on_faith/comments.html.
Roe, A. 1952. *The making of a scientist*. New York: Dodd.

Terman, L.M., and M.H. Oden. 1959. *The gifted group at mid-life, thirty-five years follow-up of the superior child: Genetic studies of genius.* Vol. 2. Stanford, CA: Stanford University Press.

Thalheimer, F. 1973. Religiosity and secularization in the academic professions. *Sociology of Education* 46 (2):183–202.

Thomas, S.M. 2005. *The global resurgence of religion and the transformation of international relations: The struggle for the soul of the twenty-first century.* New York: Palgrave Macmillan.

Wald, K., and C. Wilcox. 2006. Getting religion: Has political science rediscovered the faith factor? *American Political Science Review* 100 (4): 523–29.

Wuthnow, R. 1985. Science and the sacred. In *The sacred in a secular age*, ed. P.E. Hammond, 187–203. Berkeley, CA: University of California Press.

4 Mutual Renewal: On the Relationship of Human Rights to the Muslim World

ANTHONY CHASE

Islam and Human Rights

The issue of compatibility of the Muslim world with human rights is often posed as if the question is whether or not a monolithic bloc of Muslims cares about human rights. Indeed, the Bush Administration showed a sort of split personality on this issue during its eight years in office, at times demonizing the Muslim world as a global outlier standing outside the human rights regime and, at other times, using rhetoric suggesting that human rights are not ideologically contested within predominantly Muslim states, but rather are blocked solely by unrepresentative governments. This framing obscures the diversity within Muslim societies and their definition in the context of interconnections with a wide variety of local, regional, transnational, and international forces. There, the issue is not the relationship of human rights to a disconnected 'Muslim world' or an unchanging religious-cultural entity called 'Islam,' but rather to individuals and societies that cross regional borders, exist within differing political systems and shifting ethnic configurations, share commonalities across oceans, and experience intense local differences.

'Do Muslims care about human rights?' and 'Are Muslim societies compatible with human rights?' are, therefore, questions that are as irrelevant as asking analogous questions of Catholic Chileans, Hindu Indians, or practitioners of diverse (and often syncrectic) religions in countries such as China or Vietnam. These queries reflect the anti-religious and especially – given their prevalence regarding the Muslim world – anti-Islamic biases that chapter 3 identifies as regrettably ascendant since 9/11. Instead, the essential question is this one: Do *some* Muslims care or, more precisely, does some significant subsection of Muslims find human rights relevant to their political stances or to the political context in which they function? Despite all the ink and emotion spilled over this question, it is actually rather straightforward. It does not require Qur'anic exegesis examining different schools of Islamic law for a definitive statement on the compatibility or incompatibility of Islamic and human rights law.

You can probably easily guess that Islamic sources are elusive and conflicting on this front. Some read Islamic sources as contradictory, others as complementary, and yet others as supportive or as essentially irrelevant (truth be told, I am in this last category, but do not claim the last word on the topic). It does not require a cultural anthropologist to definitively survey Muslim societies and determine whether, collectively, Muslim societies do or do not find human rights norms relevant. Again, as you can probably guess, the evidence will be ambiguous and contradictory. Some Muslims passionately argue human rights are absolutely necessary, others the opposite, and both positions can be put forth for very different reasons (and, of course, other Muslims will not much care one way or the other, or will care only sometimes and in some contexts). Such is the case in all parts of the world, among all peoples.

Human rights cannot be and do not have to be proven relevant to all Muslim societies, always and everywhere – just to some Muslims, sometimes, in some political contexts and in some important ways (again, the same as in other parts of the world). That would be enough to say there is empirical proof that Muslims and human rights are not incompatible – that some Muslims can and do care about human rights and one cannot, therefore, impose a notion of incompatibility from the outside, as has too often been done. This conclusion is in line with the general argument in favour of 'thick religion' from chapter 3. The issue-area of human rights in relation to Islam will be pursued with sensitivity to context, as chapter 3 advocated.

So, finally, do significant numbers of Muslims find human rights relevant? The short answer is, in fact, there have been significant movements for human rights in many parts of the Muslim world. A familiar narrative sees the Great Other in the Muslim world standing eternally opposed to human rights. What upsets this narrative is that, decades ago, states in the Muslim world helped construct the UN declaration and early treaties that are the foundation of human rights (Waltz 2004). Granted, these states have never been enthusiastic about actually implementing those rights, but in this they are simply kin to virtually all other states (human rights may or may not be universal, but government resistance to respecting human rights is absolutely universal!).

In addition – policies aside – the role of Muslim states in building the rights regime and formally accepting its validity has, perhaps unwittingly, sustained human rights movements outside their governmental control. Over the last quarter-century a strong movement to implement substantive human rights has been institutionalized in human rights non-governmental organizations (NGOs) in virtually all parts of the Muslim world (Chase 2009). These organizations uncomfortably straddle both civil society and domestic governments, and international organizations and transnational networks concerned with similar issues.

Contrary to stereotype, even in the Arab world – the region in the larger Muslim world with seemingly the most difficult relationship with international norms – there are these same sorts of state and non-state connections with the human rights regime. Its human rights NGOs epitomize the way that human rights play a central role in civil societies around the globe. Arab human rights NGOs have placed themselves firmly on the political map despite state repression and being plagued by a rhetorical association (perhaps unfair, but an effective tactic for human rights opponents, all the same) with an unpopular West (Pratt 2005). Within that difficult political context, they represent a current that is vulnerable to foundations that are more principled than populist – in this sense more akin, from a US perspective, to the American Civil Liberties Union: influential but not claiming to lead a mass movement. They also are vulnerable, frankly, because they reject violence as a tactic, though violence is often the only way to gain attention in oppressive societies. Despite such structural constraints, they are the only serious centre of non-Islamist opposition to the Arab world's status quo – albeit of considerably less force than Islamists.

Beyond state engagement and the birth of civil society human rights groups, perhaps most surprisingly Islamists can often also be found invoking the taboo language of human rights – in their own ways and to their own benefit. In Islamist political and ideological platforms there are sometimes demands for human rights (just as, of course, there are also sometimes denunciations of human rights – there is no argument for uniformity here) and affirmations that human rights do not conflict with Islam. For example, Kamal Kharazi – a former foreign minister of Iran, the Muslim world's only long-standing Islamist regime

– affirmed that human rights are 'a universal concept independent of any conditions' and called for the 'strengthening of civil society and encouragement of toleration.'[1] In this, Kharazi was following the line of Iran's president, Mohammad Khatami, who was a vocal exponent of civil society and often spoke publicly about the validity of human rights. It is worth noting, however, that Kharazi had previously been ambassador to the UN well before Khatami's term in office, and can effectively be called a man of the Iranian establishment that represents one particular strand within the larger universe of political Islam.

Aside from this rhetoric, in political practice Islamist groups also sometimes work with human rights lawyers (particularly when their members are in jail) and cooperate with human rights institutions against the status quo. Bahey el-Din Hassan, for example, tells of being a part of a group of Nasserist (leftist Arab nationalist) political prisoners held in the same Egyptian jail as groups of Islamists (Hassan 2006). In the hierarchy of political prisoners, authorities 'privileged' Nasserists over Islamists, but the Nasserists insisted on using this marginal level of privilege to make common cause with Islamists and representing their demands (for better treatment, access to prayer rugs, etc.) to the prison administration. The irony that Hassan notes is that Islamists took advantage of this cooperation and yet, when a moment came after the release of some Nasserists that gave the Islamists a numerical advantage among prisoners, still savagely beat their erstwhile Nasserist allies. So much for collaboration, it would seem.

Once released from prison, however, one segment of the Nasserists migrated toward human rights and became founding members of the Egyptian Organization of Human Rights (EOHR). The EOHR immediately faced a strategic conundrum: would they advocate for the rights of Islamists subject to rights violations, even after having had the experience of cooperation based on common ground and a common antagonist being met with violence at the first opportunity? The EOHR under Hassan's leadership – he became the organization's secretary-general in 1988 – made the ethical, strategic choice to represent claims on behalf of Islamists just as for other political and social segments (just as EOHR has also critiqued Islamist actions). Perhaps it was an odd choice, given the past prison history Hassan recounts.

EOHR's decision resulted in further alliances of convenience between human rights groups and Islamists. These were, in some sense, short-term, as there is both an ideological opposition – rhetorical and substantive – between them and, as the prison story illustrates, even a history of opportunistic cooperation followed by violence. At the same time, this type of principled representation has opened the door for interaction by EOHR and other human rights groups with Egyptian Islamists and given Islamists a chance to use the language of human rights to their own benefit. This takes place despite the obvious irony that Islamists and human rights activists clearly have different (if not opposing) political agendas. Yet, all the same, the relevance of human rights to Islamists is clarified: Islamists exist on the political margins of society, subject to brutal rights violations and struggling (some violently and some not) for political space and, even, democracy – human rights principles are supportive to those in that position. This is part of the foundation for the degree of cross-fertilization that has taken place between Islamism and human rights language.

Hassan's implicit lesson is that even-handed, non-ideological representation is a matter of principle by which human rights groups maintain their bona fides, but also a step toward signalling the relevance of human rights to Islamists. It may not co-opt them, but it can indicate that cooperation can lead to productive intermingling and ultimately result in conversations that help break apart an overly stark opposition between human rights and Islamism. Indeed, the story simultaneously demonstrates two intersecting lines in the history of human rights in the region: the increasing contemporary relevance of human rights and the importance of transnational networks and norms in framing and informing this sort of cross-fertilization.

So, many Muslims in many different sectors do find human rights relevant. Human rights have had a terrible record of implementation in many parts of the Muslim world, particularly in the Arab region. But empirical realities do not justify historical determinism. The realities of human rights violations are harsh, but this makes all the more remarkable the resilience of a human rights discourse in the Muslim world. This stubborn presence indicates the relevance of human rights to individual Muslims and to social groups within the Muslim world, historically and currently. This is enough to justify saying that Muslims care about rights and care enough to justify beginning our exploration into how rights have come to frame many issues in the Muslim world.

The Relevance of Human Rights to the Muslim World

The real question regarding the relevance of human rights is not if Muslims care, but which populations care – why, how, and with what impacts. Because, yes, it is an important question – not just in a normative sense, because more rights protections would be good for people in the region (though, in my opinion, they would) – because rights frame so many key questions under debate globally and it is significant if they do the same in the Muslim world. The assumption that human rights comprise a useful frame for understanding a broad range of issues defining the Muslim world's politics may be a startling point of departure. As I hope to have indicated, however, it is not as optimistic a starting point as it may seem at first blush. It is not to say that human rights are widely implemented, on the verge of being widely implemented, or even the foundation of political attitudes in this region. That would, indeed, be foolhardy. As chapter 6 on religious humanitarianism points out, it is important to take a balanced view. Oppressive governments and religious extremists hardly speak for anything close to Muslims in general – an easy point to overlook in the face of a virtual phalanx of negative media coverage.

The assumption regarding human rights as a relevant frame rests on three specific arguments. One is that human rights have a history in the Muslim world that undergirds their current presence. A second argument is that these discussions are defined in a transnational space in which human rights have become quite present and of which the Muslim world is a part. Third is the argument that, through these conversations, human rights have come to frame a broad range of issues as they have been integrated into the consciousness of peoples both globally and in the Muslim world.

The first argument – that human rights have a substantive history and are a topic of serious discussion both within and outside the Muslim world – is primarily historical, but can be first illustrated with some anecdotal and empirical examples. Anecdotally, I began seriously studying human rights in the Muslim world because Arab human rights NGOs hit me over the head with their relevance once I was already in the region as a PhD student, not because I arrived with them as part of my research agenda. My academic assumptions were that human rights are Western, and anyone talking about advancing human rights in the Muslim world was either a Westerner trying to impose his views or some sort of upper-class fellow traveller who was not really an 'authentic' Muslim. It turned out, however, that my original dissertation topic (on apostasy in Islamic and international law) kept leading me to Egyptian human rights NGOs and there I found a network of public intellectuals who insisted on raising human rights issues, despite their governments, Western governments, and academics turning away from their claims. It was at this point that I began to sense that human rights were taken much more seriously than I had assumed and that one should not mistake the resistance by powerful institutions and discourses to human rights for a lack of local relevance.

Obvious or not, if you stop at a tea shop in Damascus or Sana'a or Peshawar (or, extrapolating from my own experiences in those and other cities, many other places in the Muslim world), the topic of conversation will quickly turn to politics and, from there, seemingly inevitably, to a reference (positive or not!) to human rights. A typical example, in my experience, comes from my first extended stint in the Muslim world – in Syria, studying Arabic. On my way to Palmyra, where some historic ruins (and a prison notorious for torture) are located, I missed my bus stop and ended up in the village just past the ruins. Asking directions, I was not so much directed as gradually led – as seems to happen in the Arab world – to my destination. Along the way I drank tea in a few households where the topic of conversation, of course, was politics, and quickly passed to questions about human rights. This raised an eyebrow, as it was certainly the last topic I expected to be discussed in Syria. Arabs, I had imbibed from my properly cultural relativist academic training, did not know or care much about human rights. To the contrary, however, I soon found that, whether in this brief sojourn into people's houses in Palmyra, or in tea houses, television, and think tanks, human rights are a recurring topic in public discourse.

I should add, however, that during this anecdotal experience in Palymra the *Syrian* regime's human rights record was not mentioned even in passing (it was only later I would learn of the nearby prison that made this a particularly unlikely place for Syria's human rights record to be raised, not that it was much different in other parts of the country). The point as well as the irony is obvious. Human rights may be broadly recognized as a key issue, even if what is meant by that is subject to some serious argument, and even if the limits of what can be safely discussed are severely circumscribed.

Empirical data are not necessarily more decisive than anecdotes, but can be indicative. While we lack good data on attitudes toward human rights, there are data sets such as the World Values Survey (WVS) that show what opinions are on democracy and the status of groups traditionally discriminated against in different regions, including predominantly Muslim countries. These can serve as viable proxy data giving indications on attitudes toward human rights, particularly as many would define substantive democratization as the implementation of a broad range of human rights (Marks and Clapham 2005). The WVS shows that in the Islamic world there are mixed views on gender equality and negative views on whether or not homosexuality is 'justifiable.' On the WVS's scale, the Islamic world scores 55 per cent in positive attitudes toward gender equality and just 12 per cent in positive attitudes toward the permissibility of homosexuality. This is not, however, necessarily due to a 'Muslim' attitude – China, for example, scores a similar number in attitudes toward gender equality, and 92 per cent of Chinese reject homosexuality.

The commonality in resistance to gender and sexuality rights is something that Inglehart and Norris link to a lack of democracy rather than religion. Beyond the specific numbers from countries such as China, they point out more generally that 'in every stable democracy, a majority of the public disagrees with the statement that "men make better political leaders than women." None of the societies in which less than 30 percent of the public rejects this statement (such as Jordan, Nigeria, and Belarus) is a true democracy' (Inglehart and Norris 2003, 71, 73). It need not be added that relatively few countries in the Muslim world – and none in the Arab world – are democracies.

This points to a larger issue in human rights. If democracy is appropriately and inclusively defined as the substantive implementation of the broad range of human rights, it is interesting to balance the Muslim world's views on gender equality and homosexuality against attitudes toward democracy and the broad panoply of rights it implies. In this regard, Muslims differ very little from those in the rest of the world. Despite their authoritarian circumstances (or perhaps because of them), those in Muslim countries believe that democracies perform well (68 per cent, the same as in the West) and have a higher approval for democratic ideals than those in other regions (87 per cent, virtually the same as the 86 per cent in the West).

Together, this points to obvious conclusions: generalized support for democracy and, implicitly, the rights that constitute a functioning democracy coupled with degrees of resistance to social equality for women and homosexuals. These are the clearest empirical data that exist on such issues and do, indeed, indicate that human rights are relevant, are broadly supported, and face challenges and resistance. This pattern is interesting to ponder in the context of the investigation in chapter 9 of would-be sharia arbitration in the Canadian province of Ontario. Advocates and at least some opponents of Islamic law as an alternative to the standard court system seemed aware of the nuanced character of human rights as conceived of among Muslims regardless of location.

Ongoing internal but transnationally informed discussion was in some sense furthered and in some sense distorted by the Bush Administration's invocation of human rights to justify invading Iraq. While no doubt this high-profile event accentuated these discussions on human rights, it also cut them off by making a widely distrusted Western superpower their conveyer. In the long term, by distorting discussion of human rights in the Arab and broader Muslim world into a discussion of U.S. foreign policy, the job of human rights advocates in focusing on the internal reasons that greater human rights implementation makes sense for their societies was undermined. Nonetheless, even if the co-optation of human rights language to serve the foreign policy agenda of a superpower is regrettable, for our purposes it does not negate the broader relevance of human rights to conversations regarding this region at the local, regional, transnational, and international level.

Despite such anecdotes and empirical evidence, the cliché that human rights have no foundation in the Muslim world has, like most clichés, some basis. There is, first, the institutional resistance of the region's states. Out of pure survival instinct, if nothing else, they have reason to be wary of a human rights regime that would empower their societies and hold states to standards of accountability. Various sorts of ideological resistance have emerged in nationalist and, particularly, religious nationalist discourse: the rights regime is contested and controversial at all levels. There also are the mixed empirical measures of support for human rights just cited, not to mention that the anecdotal stories can no doubt be met with contradictory anecdotes.

Beyond anecdotes that can be contested and empirical data that are mixed, history gives the best guide to the variable place of human rights in the Muslim world. The historic touchstone for the questionable assumption that the Muslim world has always been on the outside of the rights regime is twofold. One, in an era during which decolonization was just underway, it is widely assumed that many Muslim states simply did not have a seat at the table when the rights regime was elaborated. The sceptics point out that the United Nations General Assembly (as well as the committees in which human rights declarations and treaties were drafted) was dominated to a much greater degree by Western states than it would be a few decades later, after decolonization had led to the formation of the non-aligned bloc. Two, a prominent Muslim state that was at the table during that era, Saudi Arabia, notably abstained when the Universal Declaration of Human Rights (UDHR) was approved by the United Nations General Assembly in 1948. It is assumed that this set the pattern for Muslim abstention, at best, during the following two decades during which negotiations took place to convert the principles of the UDHR – a so-called soft law, non-binding declaration[2] – into hard law human rights treaties, as binding on states upon their signature and ratification as any other treaty obligation.

Nonetheless, scholars – most prominently Susan Waltz – have documented how misleading this standard account of Muslim abstention is. Waltz records the substantial contributions of Muslim state diplomats from the mid-1940s to the mid-1960s in the construction of the international human rights regime and how Western accounts have systematically overstated the roles of Eleanor Roosevelt, Rene Cassin, and other representatives of Western states. In essence, there has been a lazy conspiracy of assumptions in which those from both Western and non-Western states take for granted the primacy of Westerners in human rights, without consulting the historic record.

In addition to the lead taken on many issues by the countries of the non-aligned movement as a whole, specific to the Muslim world Waltz's work shows how the engagement of states like Pakistan, Iraq, Lebanon, and even Saudi Arabia resulted in significant impacts at the international level. Some of this was in line with the priorities of the non-aligned movement in general. A right to self-determination – in essence, the right to self-rule within formerly colonized territories – did not exist in the UDHR. Egypt had proposed such an article for the UDHR and was vigorously supported in this by Lebanon's Charles Malik in the General Assembly's Third Committee, where it was debated. In the end, however, the Western colonial powers won the day and beat back attempts to include such a right for the colonized in the UDHR. In Third Committee considerations of draft human rights treaties, however, in Waltz's words, 'Afghanistan, Saudi Arabia, Syria, and Egypt led and shaped the debate' on this issue (2004, 831). This was key to the eventual insertion in the two founding human rights treaties – the International Covenant on Civil and Political Rights (ICCPR) and the International Covenant on Economic, Social, and Cultural Rights (ICESCR) – of their Article 1, which affirms a right to self-determination.[3] This is a right that has been particularly instrumental to grounding South African and Palestinian struggles for self-determination in international law. It should be noted – for those who assume that the rights regime is simply a Western-imposed template – that both the United Kingdom and France were fiercely opposed to the inclusion of a right to self-determination in the human rights treaties.

The presence of Muslim state delegations at a figurative negotiating table (in fact, these treaties were drafted over decades in a long, drawn out process) affected many other debates. Let me select two additional examples, the first because it contradicts in a particularly interesting way common expectations and the second because it connects to a larger point about the historic continuities in human rights concerns in the Muslim world. Regarding the first, given current assumptions about the Muslim world, it is startling that the proposal for a specific article affirming gender equality in the draft human rights treaties came from a Muslim state delegation. Concerned by the covenants' silence on gender equality when the Human Rights Commission draft treaties were sent to the Third Committee, it was the Iraqi delegate who insisted on the insertion of a new, generic article recognizing gender equality. With the support of countries including Pakistan (and despite the opposition of other predominantly Muslim states – again, there is no argument here for uniformity), this resulted in the creation of what is now Article 3 in both the ICCPR and ICESCR, instructing state parties to ensure the equal right of men and women to the rights set forth in both covenants (Waltz 2004). This is a remarkable example of a substantial impact due to Muslim state delegations' participation in these negotiations. Gender equality is now one of the animating themes of the work of international organizations due, in part, to how it came to be firmly embedded in international human rights law during this process.

Among the various impacts of Muslim state delegations, Waltz documents a second example during this period. It had no immediate impact but is all the more significant for the way in which it presaged eventual changes in the human rights regime. One enduring controversy in human rights is over the decision to divide the UDHR into two treaties, one focused on political-civil rights and the other socio-economic rights. Muslim states led opposition to the isolation of socio-economic rights into a separate covenant, with the statement of Saudi Arabia on the topic remarkably prescient in terms of later criticisms of the decision to divide human rights into separate categories: 'We still maintain that human rights and freedoms, whether civil and political on the one hand or economic, social and cultural, on the other hand, are so interconnected and interdependent that their separation into two documents would be artificial and arbitrary' (Waltz 2004, 827).

This battle was lost in the short term, as we know. In the long term, however, advocates of the indivisibility of rights would win the day. The division of human rights into separate categories came under increasingly bitter criticism as the human rights regime accelerated its global spread. The language of this criticism echoed in a remarkable manner the criticisms made by Muslim state delegations. Indeed, the quote from the Saudi Arabian delegate sounds as if it were plagiarized verbatim in arguments used during global human rights conferences in the 1980s and 1990s when the indivisibility of rights debate came to a head. By the 1993 Vienna conference, the notion of separate categories of rights had been firmly rejected and replaced with the notion of rights as indivisible and interdependent. This conceptualization of human rights now dominates the field, indicating the relevance of the arguments first made in the 1950s by Muslim and non-aligned state delegations. This continuity not only shows how human rights have a history with sinews in the Muslim world; it also demonstrates the continuing dynamism of rights as globalization forces it to redefine itself under the impact of voices from a globalized constituency.

So, without further belabouring specific examples, Muslim world delegations were at the table(s) at which the human rights regime was constructed and reconstructed, and they were far from passive – to the contrary, they helped shape outcomes in significant ways.[4] This is not to mention the history of human rights NGOs in the Muslim world, which is grounded in over a century of intellectual discourse on human rights in many parts of the Muslim world and a more recent history of attempts to institutionalize civil society organizations as defenders of human rights, often within difficult political constraints.

This history connects to the current presence of human rights in discourse in the Muslim world. An insistence on self-determination, for example, has never gone away, but rather continued with focus on the Palestinian right to self-determination articulated, consistently, in the language of human rights. Human rights, in others words, have foundations and continuity in the region that helps make it a frame relevant to contemporary debates.

Transnational Context for Human Rights

So, if human rights are relevant to everyday political life in the Muslim world and human rights invoked by many, including Islamists, it is in part because this historical background gives sinews to present human rights discourse. But, of course, human rights as a frame relevant to Muslim world politics is about more than just historical antecedents. Why else would human rights be relevant? Well, in practice human rights often resonate with the political, economic, and social needs of societies' most vulnerable populations, giving a basis for legal and political claims to those usually found at the bottom of the status barrel. Human rights are often invoked as a barren abstraction – whether by cultural relativist opponents who decry human rights as an imperialist imposition, or by supporters who, nonetheless, do not engage with its tangible specifics. Human rights as an abstract shell is meaningless; it takes on relevance in the very real obligations it imposes on states to respect rights such as the right not to be tortured, to protect rights such as the right to non-discrimination, and to fulfil rights such as the right to equal status to work. When conversation focuses on specifics, its resonance is advanced on a substantive basis that grapples with what the rights regime actually proposes, not abstract projections.

More than just useful, there has been a real dynamism to human rights norms as they have evolved in transnational dialogues about their implementation. In other words, it is not simply that human rights as defined on high by Geneva-based treaty bodies are useful, but rather that – as human rights have entered into political discussions via transnational networks and local activists – they have been redefined in ways that make them even more apt locally. Without this flexible dynamism to be remade, human rights would not have the global resonance it has found in recent years.

This leads into my second claim regarding human rights relevance: conversations about human rights take place in what can be called a transnational space. Whether it be human rights, economic development, political ideology, or social belief, in even the world's most out-of-the-way locales conversations about these issues use language and frames of reference that are recognizable everywhere. To give a rather extreme example, representatives of indigenous tribes from around the world are always notable at United Nations–sponsored conferences in which human rights for indigenous peoples are discussed. They do not agree to attend to serve as decoration; rather, they connect to these conferences because the legal and political language defined there is relevant to their local politics. That is the essence of transnationalism's impact. Even isolated locales are plugged into transnational networks (connections among non-state actors that freely cross national borders), transnational dialogues (satellite television, the Internet, a globalized mass media), and transnational diasporas (economic and political migrants, as well as communities that have long crossed national borders) that have increasing impact on local and global politics. An example of religious transnationalism in action is provided by the review in chapter 12 of the significant partnership between FBOs and middle-power states in pursuit of the UN's Millennium Development Goals.

A curious romanticism likes to imagine that the absence of McDonald's arches somehow places foreign sites out of place and out of time – beyond globalization. But reality is different. Even in a country like post-revolutionary Iran that should be insular and inward-looking – anti-Western ideologically, with laws enforcing this anti-Westernism, minimal foreign investment, no official relations with the U.S. government, a U.S. government ban on U.S. companies trading with Iran, and certainly no golden arches – the public sphere is remarkably filled by transnational connections. These include connections to satellite television and the Internet (Persian is the fourth most heavily used blogger language, for example), diaspora populations (and the television stations and Internet feeds that the Iranian diaspora supports), and transnational networks dealing with issues as diverse (and intersecting) as sport, human rights, music, and Islam. Images, ideas, and currents that flow from these connections manifest themselves daily in Iran. The increasing weight of transnationalism in defining the language of local politics is a distinctive characteristic in contemporary politics.

Bahey el-Din Hassan's story is, again, illustrative, this time of the impact of the globalization of the modern state system and the increasingly transnational movement of ideas and norms. Nasserists and Islamists first made common cause in Egypt because both were subject to political persecution. In other words, despite their ideological differences, in jail they each faced the power of the modern nation state to massively violate human rights. This common structural position made human rights relevant to both groups, as each could use rights as a shield (admittedly thin) against the power of the state to dominate.

The relevance of rights goes beyond the branch it extends to those subject to the modern state's ability to infiltrate all aspects of daily life. The EOHR was formed in the wake of the Egyptian state's acknowledgement – via international treaty – of human rights applicability. These international treaties spawned the creation of transnational networks – governmental and non-governmental – and with the rise of human rights concerns in the Arab world, Middle East, and broader Muslim world led to the founding of domestic human rights organizations like the EOHR in Egypt or Kowani in Indonesia, or regional organizations such as the Arab Organization for Human Rights. These groups and networks did not arise out of thin air, but rather reflect the increasing transnationalism of global politics that took the language of human rights from the treaty bodies of Geneva into discussions in dank Egyptian prisons, fledging human rights groups, and the consciousness of those whom these organizations represented, including Islamists.

Islamist interest in human rights is unsurprising not just because invoking rights has legal and political benefits, but because human rights have become part of a global lingua franca for advancing claims. Islamists invoke human rights because they are every bit as much a part of a transnationally defined world as the rest of us. As such, they naturally imbibe the language of human rights that takes up so much space in transnational discussions. It is for this reason that one finds everyone from human rights NGOs, to Islamists in Egypt, to Iranian foreign ministers dealing with – and hence recognizing – human rights.

This fact contradicts the caricature of Islamists oozing out of the primordial mud. The stereotype is to be expected, given the observations in chapter 2 about the view that religion is destined for the dustbin of history, along with other 'primitive' manifestations of the past. By contrast, Islamism has always been an innovative, modernist movement, whether as established among Sunnis by Hassan al-Banna at the height of Egyptian anti-colonial tumult in the 1920s, or among Shia by the Ayatollah Khomeini in the midst of diaspora politics and distinctly affected by strains of French political philosophy in the 1970s. Both of these 'fundamentalist' movements – and their offshoots and variants – are deeply distorted if they are viewed as projections of an insular, primordial Islamic world. To the contrary, each is an expression of a particularly intense transnational moment. Specifically, each felt the impact of global political currents (imperialism and Third World anti-colonialism, most notably), changes in global political structures (the globalization of the modern state), and the transnational movement of ideas that underpinned their novel reconfigurations of the place of Islam in politics.

Regarding the Muslim Brotherhood, the Egyptian novelist Naguib Mahfouz describes in his *Cairo Trilogy* better than any historian how it emerged in the 1920s at the nexus of ideologies running in contradictory directions during the most dynamic period in Egypt's anti-colonial struggle. Mahfouz interweaves the politics of this era with a family history. Liberals were ascendant in Egypt's anti-colonial drive, but after the First World War Egyptian anti-colonialism became a populist movement with many overlapping and intersecting elements. Family members in the *Cairo Trilogy* represent political trends from liberal nationalism, to socialism, to the birth of contemporary political Islam in Hassan al-Banna's Muslim Brotherhood. The three novels beautifully evoke the era's ideological diversity but also, literally and figuratively, the family resemblances within this diversity. These ideologies shared an anti-colonial foundation and a search for a new basis of political community. It is this search and interactions with others within the same 'family' that inform political Islam's dynamism.

In the Shia world, Khomeini's 'barefoot Islam' is an even more obvious example of how dynamic and globalized these 'fundamentalist' ideologies are. The institutionalization of an Islamic republic (just the combination of 'Islamic' with 'republic' indicates its hybrid origins) in Iran came out of a creative ideological mixture of Marxist-influenced philosophy, Third World rhetoric, and Shia Islamic motifs – much of it brewed by Iranian exiles influenced by French intellectual currents. The pairing in Iran of Islam with constitutional republicanism (and with talk of Islamic socialism in economics) should put to rest any notion that such an ideology comes from some return to a pure Islam or represents a rejection of modernity. To the contrary, it epitomizes the hybrid, transnationally informed nature of the ideological movements that characterize contemporary global politics. Human rights comprise just one wave among the currents that have affected such accelerating reconfigurations.

This can be seen all the more with today's Islamists. They are as plugged in and transnationally networked as anyone and determined to radically redefine the role of Islam in politics. Indeed, it is Muslims trained in classical methods, steeped in Sufism or more pious and mystical traditions in Islam (Tessler 2002),[5] or simply isolated (geographically or otherwise) and therefore insulated from transnational ideological currents that tend to be the most distant from the political Islam in theory and in practice. A group like al-Qa'ida, on the other hand, is made up of a multi-ethnic membership without a specific nation-state base but rather organized transnationally, communicates with members via the Internet (Kohlmann 2006), has a particularly strong base in second- and third-generation diaspora populations disconnected from traditional sources of authority (Mekhennet, Sautter, and Hanfeld 2006), and markets its image via dramatically planned manipulations of satellite television (Alterman 2004; Lynch 2005).

To take this full circle, for the same reasons that al-Qa'ida is a typical example of the accelerating pace of transnational politics, we should not be surprised by Islamists referencing human rights. This is not as paradoxical as it may sound. Human rights are part of the same transnational currents on which Islamism floats and, thus, plugging into one transnational source and its media (Internet, satellite television, diaspora politics, etc.) almost inevitably leads to exposure to a range of views far from those that dominate local and domestic politics.

This does not mean, of course, that Islamism and human rights will somehow magically merge. To the contrary, there are sharp conflicts and contradictions between them. It does mean, however, that Islamists are being forced to confront human rights in varied ways as they engage in a transnationalized world in which debates inevitably brush up against and are engulfed in human rights language. This has resulted in a range of responses, from virulent attacks against rights to various ways of implicitly or explicitly adopting rights-based language. While disconcerting in the sense that there are some fundamental contradictions between rights and religion as the basis of politics, the integration of human rights motifs into Islamist politics should not be a shock. Such integration can be, at times, in their self-interest. Human rights are also part of global political dialogues of which Islamists are a part, so naturally become a part of their own political language. The same is true, by the way, regarding human rights discourse in the Muslim world. It is heavily affected by 'reformist' attempts to base human rights *in* Islam. It is, in other words, the transnationalism of contemporary political dialogues that explains the overlap and hybridity of human rights and Islamic discourses. It also shows how human rights have become such a prevalent frame within the Muslim world.

Human Rights as a Normative Frame for Contemporary Debates in the Muslim World

My third claim is that these transnational conversations about human rights have become integrated into the frame of a broad range of issues and so are increasingly part of normative consciousness in the region. This is what gives human rights such importance, even in places where their actual implementation is minimal. I mentioned economic development, political ideology, and religious belief previously, and, in fact, discussions on all three topics consistently intersect with human rights. Cutting-edge development work, for example, increasingly revolves upon questions of whether or not equitable development is based on implementing human rights. Ideologies and belief systems also often justify themselves as advancing human rights or are de-legitimized by opponents as being antithetical to rights. In the Muslim world, for example, there are constant polemics about whether or not Islam and human rights conflict or correspond.

Beyond the specifics of this debate, just its intensity signifies how important human rights can be as a frame. The ability to coexist with human rights is increasingly important to the legitimacy of those from any number of ideological perspectives; it is increasingly rare that human rights are explicitly rejected. This is all the more obvious when one considers the intensity of emotion regarding calls for protecting the human right to self-determination for Palestinians, the right not to be tortured (as in Abu Ghraib), the polemics around issues of women's rights, the lack of legitimacy for authoritarian regimes (and authoritarianism, more generally, as seen in the World Values Survey), and the sort of intellectual and policy diagnoses one finds in reports such as the Arab Human Development Report (AHDR) that trace lags in the predominantly Muslim Arab world's development to respect a broad range of human rights.

Bahey el-Din Hassan's story of EOHR's work with Islamists gives a specific illustration of human rights normative relevance and how it has come to frame politics. When that sort of legal representation – based on human rights principles – is helpful, it will naturally be welcomed, and it has also led to changes in how human rights are articulated in Egypt and the broader Muslim world. Intersections between human rights groups and Islamists, in other words, are not a one-way street – how human rights are conceptualized and applied is transformed in such intersections. Whether this is a risk or an opportunity, or both, is a key question, but in any case it points to how human rights utility is essential to its impact. This utility is why human rights have moved from a vague abstraction into being a part of everyday consciousness. When legal representation, political legitimacy, and social justice can all be advanced – out of principle or expediency – by invoking rights, they become less abstract and more real. When headlines invoke human rights violations as a reason for condemnation and those suffering such violations as worthy of political support, rights become less abstract and more real. And when governments, international organizations, non-state actors, and powerful transnational networks that connect them all speak the language of rights in their rhetoric, programming, and demands, then rights become less abstract and more real. All of this is part of how human rights have moved from abstract natural law into tangible positive law and, from there, increasingly into local policy discussions.

But, for now, let us stay with the question posed earlier: why do so many, including Islamists, insist on appealing to human rights? All three arguments I have traced – the history of human rights in the region, their existence in a shared transnational space, and their practical integration into everyday political and normative consciousness – make it unsurprising that Islamists would, therefore, find it useful to invoke the language of human rights in their legal defences and to gain political sympathy. If you or your colleagues were being tortured, would you not do the same?

Such appeals indicate more than just short-term self-interest, but instead a real change in mental attitudes and expectations – a normative shift. In other eras it would not have occurred to most people – particularly an Islamist in a Cairo jail – to invoke an expectation that a human right should be respected. Such a change in expectations can be expected to arise only to the degree that they refer to real positive law obligations that have some prospect, however loose, of enforcement. So the utility and concrete impacts of human rights have led to increasing reference being made to rights in contemporary global politics, even by those – like Islamists – who pursue aims that contradict rights. This may be hypocritical on their part, but it also indicates broader trends. Six decades ago, authoritarian ideologues would either ignore rights or discount them off-handedly. This need to justify political stances in human rights terms is important as an example of how integrated rights have become into political expectations in the Muslim world. If human rights are tangibly relevant to the issues and groups that define politics, this leads directly to their becoming part of the mental frames through which the political world is conceptualized.

Human rights have a history in the region and are constantly invoked in regional debates, these debates are informed by a transnational context, and, beyond attention to specific human rights issues, human rights increasingly frame broad conceptual debates that have an impact on the region and the normative expectations of the region's inhabitants. I am wary of overstating or understating the importance of human rights. They fall someplace between being much less than the basis of mass political mobilization and much more than just a discrete issue of interest to an isolated stratum of human rights campaigners. In short, human rights are an important frame through which peoples increasingly analyse, understand, and judge a range of issues.

As chapter 6 points out, all of that might progress more effectively if not held back by the confrontational discourse imposed by the War on Terror. In the Muslim world, as it is elsewhere, human rights are part of the collective conversation and have just as many variations. The Bush Doctrine's sometimes Manichean world view informed and distorted U.S. foreign policy, with harmful impacts in the short term and (likely) in the long term as well. Time will tell whether the Obama Administration, which remains militarily engaged in both Afghanistan and Iraq, will fare better. If the pernicious after-effects of actions taken by the United States after 9/11 (most notably the Iraq War) are to be superseded, it can be done only in a context that moves beyond monolithic understandings of the Muslim world having a collective view on issues such as human rights and, instead, engages with the shifting and often fragmentary currents that inform politics in all parts of the world, including different parts of the Muslim world.

NOTES

1 *Al-Hayat*, 1 March 1998 (my translation from the Arabic, *Al-Hayat*'s translation from the Persian).
2 Some argue that this declaration now has the status of binding customary law, but that is another issue.
3 International Covenant on Civil and Political Rights, *adopted* 16 December 1966, GA Res. 2200 (XXI), U.N. GAOR 21st Sess., Supp. No 16, U.N. Doc A/6316 (1966), 999 U.N.T.S. 171 (*entered into force* 23 March 1976); International Covenant on Economic, Social, and Cultural Rights, *adopted* 16 December 1966, GA Res. 2200 (XXI), U.N. GAOR 21st Sess., Supp. No 16, U.N. Doc A/6316 (1966), 993 U.N.T.S. 3 (*entered into force* 3 Jan 1976).
4 Of course these states were far from democratic but, at the same time, the American Eleanor Roosevelt represented a country with apartheid-like Jim Crow in effect, and France's Rene Cassin represented a state still determined to hold onto its colonial possessions – perhaps the site of the twentieth century's most brutal rights violations outside of the Axis powers in the Second World War and a few of the worst communist dictatorships.
5 Indeed, Tessler's surveys show political Islamists are *less* religious – in

the sense of self-reported piety and mosque attendance – than non-Islamist Muslims.

REFERENCES

Alterman, J. 2004. Made for television events. *Transnational Broadcasting Studies* 13. http://www.tbsjournal.com/Archives/Fall04/alterman.html.
Chase, A. 2009. Arab human rights NGOs. In *Encyclopedia of Human Rights*, ed.-in-chief D.P. Forsythe. New York: Oxford University Press.
Chase, A., and A. Hamzawy, eds. 2006. *Human rights in the Arab world: Independent voices*. Philadelphia: University of Pennsylvania Press.
Hassan, B. 2006. A question of human rights ethics: Defending the Islamists. In Chase and Hamzawy, 37–48.
Inglehart, R., and P. Norris. 2003. The true clash of civilizations. *Foreign Policy* 135:62–70.
Kohlman, E. 2006. The real on-line terrorist threat. *Foreign Affairs* 85 (5): 115–24.
Lynch, M. 2005. *Voice of the new Arab public: Iraq, al-Jazeera, and Middle East politics today*. New York: Columbia University Press.
Marks, S., and A. Clapham. 2005. *International human rights lexicon*. New York: Oxford University Press.
Mekhennet, S., C. Sautter, and M. Hanfeld. 2006. *The children of jihad: The new generation of Islamist terror in Europe*. Munich: Piper Verlag.
Pratt, N. 2005. Human rights NGOs and the 'foreign funding debate' in Egypt. In Chase and Hamzawy, 114–26.
Tessler, M. 2002. Islam and democracy in the Middle East: The impact of religious orientations on attitudes toward democracy in four Arab countries. *Comparative Politics* 34:337–54.
Waltz, S. 2004. Universal human rights: The contribution of Muslim states. *Human Rights Quarterly* 26 (4): 799–844.

PART THREE

Evidence

5 State Religious Exclusivity and International Crises, 1990–2002

JONATHAN FOX and NUKHET SANDAL

Introduction

The role of religion in foreign policy has, until recently, been neglected in scholarly work. Prior to the twenty-first century, major international relations (IR) journals rarely published articles that described religion as a major factor in international relations (Philpott 2002, 69). When addressed, religion was generally subsumed into another category such as culture, civilization, or terrorism (Laustsen and Waever 2000). This was part of a larger trend in the social sciences of marginalizing religion that ebbed quite recently. As chapter 2 established, this pattern of neglect was a product of secularization theory's hegemonic status throughout the social sciences over several decades. With its generally state-centric character, IR is perhaps the last of the social sciences to begin to reintegrate religion into its paradigms (Fox and Sandler 2004).

This observation also is true of the study of international crises. In this area of research, structural accounts have been emphasized at the expense of primordial ethnic and religious ties (Carment and James 1997, 16). Accordingly, this chapter attempts to fill part of that gap in the literature by examining the influence of state religious exclusivity, as measured by the religion and state (RAS) data set, on crisis, as measured by the international crisis behaviour (ICB) data set.[1] The findings show that while structural explanations remain important, religious factors also influence crisis behaviour.

This chapter first discusses the general literature on crisis. It examines how theories of religion can be integrated into the crisis literature and what influence religion is likely to have in a crisis. It then discusses the nature and expected impact of state religious exclusivity on crisis.

The research design for the empirical portion of the chapter then is presented, followed by the data analysis. Finally, the concluding section integrates the findings into the general themes of this volume.

Crisis

This chapter takes 'international crisis' as the unit of analysis. The defining conditions of an international crisis are (a) a change in type and/or an increase in intensity of disruptive interactions between two or more states with an increased probability of military hostilities, and (b) destabilization in those states' relationship resulting in a challenge to the structure of the international system (Brecher and Wilkenfeld 1997b, 3–6). It is important to bear in mind that international crisis and international conflict – albeit closely related – are not synonymous. The focus of crisis is a set of issues within a specific period. A crisis can be part of a protracted conflict, but such strife requires hostile interactions that extend over a long period of time (Azar, Jureidini, and McLaurin 1978, 50). In this chapter, however, to be able to come up with a more comprehensive account, we also control for the variables that have been employed mostly in the conflict literature as a whole.[2]

Involvement in international crises has been investigated frequently within the framework of diversionary theory, which focuses on links between domestic politics and foreign policy behaviour. It assumes that political actors attempt to divert attention from problems related to domestic politics by getting involved in international crises that will help to mobilize the support of the constituency. Thus leaders in struggling governments can be expected to resort to diversionary force (Miller 1999; Morgan and Anderson 1999). A struggling economy (Fordham 2002; Hess and Orphanides 2001; James and Oneal 1991) and regime type can also determine the frequency of involvement in crises, although findings differ for the latter. Bueno de Mesquita and Lalman (1992), Enterline and Gleditsch (2000), and Miller (1995, 1999), demonstrate that democracies tend to use diversionary force less often than their authoritarian counterparts, whereas Davies (2002) and Gelpi (1997) reach an opposite conclusion. In a theoretical synthesis, Keller (2005, 206) states that leaders respond differently to domestic constraints: 'Democracies led by constraint respecters stand out as extraordinarily pacific in their crisis responses, while democracies led by constraint challengers and autocracies led by both types of leaders are demonstrably more aggressive.' Despite having developed rapidly in recent years, diversionary theory remains confined largely to studies on the United States and Britain, with a few exceptions (Dassel and Reinhardt 1999; Heldt 1999; Miller 1999). That being said, it is important to emphasize that idiosyncrasies of specific leaders and their views of foreign policy can be important. For example, George W. Bush's 'Bush Doctrine' stands out clearly as a 'constraint challenger' that would lead to a higher propensity for crisis participation.

Religion has not been investigated as a factor in diversionary behaviour. Other studies focused on crisis involvement have not included religion-state interaction. The closest hypothesis investigated in the framework of crisis dynamics is related to the role of ethnicity in the degree of violence and outcomes of crises (Brecher and Wilkenfeld 1997a). Studies that use the most comprehensive database on international crises – ICB – focus mostly on crisis escalation (Lai 2004), crisis responses (Keller 2005; DeRouen Jr and Goldfinch 2005) and crisis outcomes (Ben Yehuda and Mishali-Ram 2006).[3] Our investigation, in this respect, contributes to the relevant literature on crisis by linking crisis involvement and state-religion interaction.

Religion and Crisis: A Theoretical and Empirical Framework

While the role of religion in crisis has not been examined, both the theoretical and quantitative literature on religion and conflict imply that religion should influence crisis. For one, both of these literatures link religion to conflict; therefore, religion also should be linked to crisis. Space considerations make it impossible to fully explore the links between religion and conflict described in the literature in this context. Accordingly, this review is intended to provide a brief summary of the theorized links between religion and strife, with a specific emphasis on those aspects that are particularly relevant to the crisis literature.

A growing number of quantitative studies link aspects of religion to conflict. Studies link religious differences – when two groups belong to different religions – with higher levels of domestic conflict (Fox 2004; Roeder 2003), international conflict (Henderson 1997, 1998; Lai 2006), and international intervention (Fox 2004; Khosla 1999, 1152). Several studies connect religious diversity and conflict (Reynal-Querol 2002; Rummel 1997; Sambanis 2001; Vanhanen 1999). Fox (2002, 2004) links numerous religious factors including religious legitimacy, religious institutions and religious discrimination to ethnic conflict. A series of studies on terrorism found that the majority of terrorist acts and new terrorist groups in the past few decades have been religious ones (Weinberg and Eubank 1998; Weinberg, Eubank, and Pedahzur 2002), but others argue that even so, this terrorism is primarily motivated by nationalism (Pape 2003). Ben-Dor and Pedahzur (2003) link Islam with a higher propensity toward terrorism between 1988 and 2002. Fox (2004) and Toft (2007) similarly link Islam with higher levels of domestic conflict. Religion also is connected to conflict mediation, though there is no agreement on whether it has a positive or negative influence (Bercovitch and DeRouen 2005; Leng and Regan 2002; Mollov and Lavie 2002; Svensson 2007; Toft 2007).[4]

A number of survey-based studies also link aspects of religion to individual propensities for tolerance and violence. These examples are part of a much larger literature but are sufficient to demonstrate this connection. The nature of one's religiosity is linked to one's propensity for conflict and authoritarianism (Leak and Randall 1995; Nielson and Fultz 1995). Religious extremism is linked with prejudice against various groups including blacks, homosexuals, and communists (Kirkpatrick 1993). Laythe, Finkel, and Kirkpatrick (2002) show that among U.S. college students Christian beliefs are negatively correlated with racial prejudice but positively correlated with prejudice against homosexuals. Miller (1996) found that one's religious denomination influences one's attitude toward lifestyle and tolerance of diversity. Eisenstein (2006) found that higher doctrinal orthodoxy led to decreased levels of tolerance.[5]

The link between religion and conflict also is well documented in the theoretical literature. Some even argue that violence is an inseparable and intrinsic element of religion (Girard 1977; Juergensmeyer 1991). It is linked to numerous specific types of conflict and violence including terrorism (Hoffman 1995; Rapoport 1988), ethnic conflict (Fox 2002, 2004), civil wars (Fox 2004), and international wars (Henderson 1997). Others link religious world views to conflict, especially when those world views are perceived to be in danger (Little 1996; Wentz 1987). This viewpoint reflects the primordialist approach as expressed by Hasenclever and Rittberger (2000) and its most ardent proponent is Samuel Huntington, with his 'Clash of Civilizations' thesis (1996). Huntington divides the world into eight civilizations, which reflect major religions; he states, 'Religion is a central characteristic in defining civilizations' (Huntington 1996, 47) and with the end of the Cold War, even without a rallying attempt by the political elite, mass-led movements towards a more 'religious' order will become more plausible. Given the absolutist nature of 'religion' and usually unconditional demands of its adherents, it is not surprising that a political structure based on religious precepts will be more likely to pursue inflexible and less tolerant policies.

Many link religious legitimacy to conflict. Religion can legitimize otherwise unacceptable political behaviour. This argument has been presented under 'instrumentalist' approaches in the analysis of the impact of faith on political behaviour (Hasenclever and Rittberger 2003). Legitimacy is a key concern of political leaders, whose interest is to stay in power in a relatively stable environment. Regimes that lack legitimacy are more prone to collapse in periods of economic and social distress (Diamond, Linz, and Lipset 1990, 10). In fact, lack of legitimacy has been linked to the rise of religious opposition groups (Juergensmeyer 1993). This need for legitimacy is no less – if not more – important for the governing elites of the states that support a particular religion. With the failure of modernization, especially in developing countries, people have turned to religious leaders as sources of authority (Haynes 1994, 12; Juergensmeyer 1993). Modernization in these countries alienated the masses who could not take part in the process effectively. With a breakdown of traditional values, 'religion' as a governing value has been embraced easily by the frustrated mass public (ibid. 34; Sahliyeh 1990, 9).

Beyond these general links between religion and conflict, aspects of religion are more directly connected to the incidence of crisis. For example, religion can be linked to diversionary theories, which are common explanations for crisis. Specifically, the same conditions that can lead to leaders' desire to divert their population's attention also can lead to politicization of religion. Politicization of religious traditions is especially likely during times of economic and social distress. Power-seeking elites exploit these tendencies for their own interests (Brown and Oudraat 1997, 254–5). Religious leaders are usually vested with traditional or charismatic authority, instead of rational-legal power. Religion, therefore, has been an important factor in legitimizing government policies by creating an 'other' in a way quite different from secular, modern justifications; it has the power to render extreme measures possible, even if it means taking the lives of innocent people or systematic destruction of rival groups (see Hoffman 1995; Osiander 2000; Rapoport 1988). The 'other' or rival group need not be members of another religion; interdenominational, even intra-denominational violence can be well justified by religion, on the grounds that the members of the other group do not live up to expectations of the supported religion.

Moral authority exercised by political groups that define themselves by their religious identity will be acknowledged often even by those who are not religious (Williams 1994, 792–6). Because of their protected status in society, religious motivations and organizations, especially when supported officially by the state, can achieve what other organizations cannot (Harris 1994, 46; Johnston and Figa 1988, 35). Religion unifies society by answering the needs and questions of human psychology, even to the extent of providing answers regarding death (Geertz 1973; Greely 1982; Turner 1991; Wilson 1982), and it has access to a long tradition of myths about rebirth and reawakening (Douglass 1988, 201; Kaufman 2001). Seul (1999, 558) argues, 'No other repositories of cultural meaning have historically offered so much in response to the human need to develop a secure identity. Consequently, religion often is at the core of individual and group identity.' When seeking to oppose a policy elite with easy access to religious discourse, institutional checks and balances are ineffective; consequently, we expect that it is easier to justify involvement in a crisis in a religious state than in a state that is not. However, it is also important to note that this does not have an institutional implication for our purposes; religion and state separation does not imply democracy and vice versa (Fox 2007, 2008).

Another direct link between religion and crisis involves the nature of religious motivations. Individuals, including policymakers, can become more intractable when religious issues are at stake. This is due to the non-negotiable nature of religious ideologies. Wentz (1987) calls this phenomenon the 'walls of religion.' People build walls around their belief systems and defend them at all costs. This is because religion has to do with one's place in the world and the manner in which the world is meaningfully put together, and it is difficult, at best, to get someone to negotiate issues that fall into this category. Laustsen and Waever (2000, 719) similarly argue that 'religion deals with the constitution of being as such. Hence, one cannot be pragmatic on concerns challenging this being.' Thus, if one or both sides of a dispute are guided by faith and not power gains, compromise is unlikely. This can result in intractable positions that easily lead to crisis.

It is important to note that other types of motivations, particularly national and ethnic motivations, also can cause similar intractability (Carment and James 1998, 68). This is recognized indirectly in the literature's concept formation, which includes threat to basic values as one of the conditions for crisis. For example, in the case of Iran's desire to develop nuclear arms, a power-based perspective would indicate that there is room for compromise. However, if this policy is seen by its instigators as a reflection of divine will or necessity to defend their religion, compromise seems less likely. If so, this policy, combined with the desire of Western policymakers to limit proliferation, creates a clash of interests that is unlikely to be solved peacefully. Accordingly, this dispute may escalate to the level of crisis and, perhaps, open conflict.

State Religious Exclusivity and Crisis

This chapter focuses specifically on the link between state religious exclusivity and crisis. For present purposes, state religious exclusivity is defined as the propensity of a state to support a single religion to the exclusion of all others. It is measured here by two variables that focus on whether the state officially endorses a single religion and the extent to which a state legislates religion as law. While data-based, the analysis is in line with the call in chapter 3 for 'thick religion' because it connects the role of theology in public policy to a state's propensity for involvement in interstate strife. Put differently, knowledge about religious doctrine itself plays a role in shaping the data analysis.

Findings from the Religion and State (RAS) project – the source of the religious exclusivity variables used in this chapter – show a wide variety of patterns of relationships between religion and state. However, one of the most striking findings is that most states do *not* separate religion and state and most states favour some religions over others. Of the 175 states in the study, almost 67 per cent favour some religions over others and almost 75 per cent restrict the religious practices of minority religions. Taking overlap into account, about 85 per cent of states do one, the other, or both. Also, all states other than the United States legislate at least some aspects of religion as law (Fox 2008). Given these results, most governments can be said to support at least low levels of religious exclusivity and some support even very high levels. Nevertheless, there is substantial variation in state religious exclusivity across states, so it is possible to assess the impact of religious exclusivity on a state's propensity to be involved in crisis.

State religious exclusivity can be linked to crisis through all of the direct links between religion and crisis noted above. First, the presence of state religious exclusivity is prima facie evidence that religion has been politicized. To the extent a state is religiously exclusive, its political institutions directly support religion and presumably draw legitimacy from doing so. This also links the collective national identity to a specific religion and, to the extent that the religion is legislated into law, to its precepts. As noted above, this politicization of religion often occurs under the same conditions that can lead to the creation of crises to divert public attention from a government's shortcomings.

Second, to the extent that a state supports a religious ideology – another element of state religious exclusivity – it is better able to justify a crisis. The presence of an official ideology creates a situation where it is more difficult to question government decisions connected to that ideology, including the decision to confront another state. Finally, the reliance on a religious ideology creates a situation where some policies, including those that can lead to crisis, are intractable. If a policy is based on perceptions of divine will, it is unlikely to be subject to compromise. If such a policy is an element of international tension, this makes a crisis over the policy considerably more likely.

On the basis of this reasoning we can expect that crises will be more common among states that are more religiously exclusive.

It is also important to note that the link between state religious exclusivity and crisis is also a natural one based on another aspect of the crisis literature – regime. As noted above, aspects of regime, such as whether the state is a democracy or autocracy, influence state involvement in crisis. This is also true of government stability and regime duration. Accordingly it is logical to argue that another aspect of regime – religious exclusivity – also may be linked to crisis.

This chapter focuses on state religious exclusivity rather than the religious identity variables used in most studies because we argue that state religious exclusivity is a superior variable in this context. A link between religious identity and crisis, while suggestive, cannot definitively connect religion to crisis. This is because religious identity is a very general cultural trait that is both theoretically and empirically correlated with other cultural traits. For example, studies have shown that Muslim states are strongly correlated with non-democratic regimes (Fisch 2002; Midlarsky 1998). As regime type has been shown to influence crisis, it would be difficult to sort out whether religious identity or regime is the true causal factor.

In contrast, state religious exclusivity is a much more specific variable. It focuses on an aspect of a regime that, while correlated with a number of other social and political factors (Fox 2008), is much more distinct than religious identity. The causal relationship between state religious exclusivity and crisis is more defined and distinct than the relationship between state religious exclusivity and identity. Put differently, the influence of government structure and policy in one area (religion) is related more clearly to its policy behaviour in another (crisis) than is a general cultural trait of society.

The reason so many previous studies use religious identity variables is likely to have been data availability. It is time-consuming and expensive to collect data sets such as RAS. Until recently the more easily and cheaply collected religious identity and demography variables were the only ones available to researchers who wished to include more than a limited number of states in their studies. This lack of developed data is likely due to the neglect of the topic of religion in the social sciences, which we describe briefly above – a trend that has begun only recently to abate in the empirical branches of the social sciences (Fox 2008). The RAS data set is relatively new and allows studies based on its more developed and sophisticated set of measures.

That being said, it is important to emphasize that state religious exclusivity varies considerably across religious traditions. On the religious legislation variable described below, Muslim majority states average almost 13 of the 33 laws measured by the RAS project.[6] In contrast, Christian majority states average 4.8 of these laws. States with Asian religions (eight Buddhist majority states and two Hindu majority states) average 6.7 of these laws. Despite this link between religious identity and state religious exclusivity, if it is a religiously exclusive state, the reasoning behind the link between state religious exclusivity and crisis should hold, whatever its religious tradition. This is true even if the state's population is less religious, more diverse, or more religiously eclectic than would be indicated by the level of state religious exclusivity, because state religious exclusivity indicates attitudes among government decision-makers, the same people who make foreign policy decisions.

Research Design

This chapter uses the religion and state (RAS) and international crisis behaviour (ICB) data sets as well as data from other sources to examine the impact of state religion on state participation in international crisis. We focus on 1990 to 2002, the period in which the two data sets overlap. The unit of analysis is a state-year. That is, each state included in this analysis is coded thirteen times, once for each year between 1990 and 2002.

Only the dependent variables from this chapter are taken directly from the ICB data set. The unit of analysis in ICB is an international crisis. In order to code the dependent variable we went over all crises included in ICB and measured whether a state participated in a crisis in a given year. We also coded in a separate variable whether a state participated in a crisis that was part of a protracted conflict. Both of these variables are coded as 1 if the state participated in the designated type of crisis and 0 if it did not. Of the 2249 units of analysis in this problem set, 137 are coded as participating in a crisis and 86 as in a crisis within a protracted conflict.[7]

This chapter uses logistic regression to assess the influence of the independent and control variables on the two dependent variables. The variables that measure state support for religion are taken from the RAS data set. The first measures whether the state has an official religion and, if not, the extent of official support for religion on the following scale:

1. No religions given preference.
2. Supportive: The state supports all religions more or less equally.
3. Cooperation: The state falls short of endorsing a particular religion but certain religions benefit from state support more than others. (Such support can be monetary or legal.)
4. Civil religion: While the state does not officially endorse a religion, one religion serves unofficially as the state's civil religion.
5. The state has more than one official religion.
6. The state has one official religion.

The second variable measures religious legislation. The types of religious legislation included in this variable are:

- Dietary laws (restrictions on producing, importing, selling, or consuming specific foods)
- Restrictions or prohibitions on the sale of alcoholic beverages
- Personal status defined by clergy
- Laws of inheritance defined by religion
- Restrictions on conversions away from the dominant religion
- Restrictions on interfaith marriages
- Restrictions on public dress
- Blasphemy laws or any other restriction on speech about religion or religious figures
- Censorship of press or other publications on grounds of being antireligious

- Mandatory closing of some or all businesses during religious holidays, including the Sabbath or its equivalent
- Other restrictions on activities during religious holidays including the Sabbath or its equivalent ('blue laws')
- Standard but optional religious education in public schools
- Mandatory religious education in public schools
- Government funding of religious schools or religious educational programs in secular schools
- Government funding of religious charitable organizations
- Taxes collected by government on behalf of religious organizations (religious taxes)
- Official government positions, salaries, or other funding for clergy
- Funding for religious organizations or activities other than those listed above
- Clergy and/or speeches in places of worship require government approval
- Some official clerical positions made by government appointment
- Presence of an official government ministry or department dealing with religious affairs
- Certain government officials also given an official position in the state church by virtue of their political office
- Certain religious officials become government officials by virtue of their religious position
- Some or all government officials must meet certain religious requirements in order to hold office
- Presence of religious courts that have jurisdiction over some matters of law
- Seats in legislative branch and/or Cabinet are by law or custom granted, at least in part, along religious lines
- Prohibitive restrictions on abortion
- Presence of religious symbols on the state's flag
- Religion listed on state identity cards
- Religious organizations must register with government in order to obtain official status
- Presence of an official government body that monitors 'sects' or minority religions
- Restrictions on women other than those listed above
- Other religious prohibitions or practices that are mandatory

These components are added to create a scale. While there are thirty-three components to this variable, the optional and mandatory religious education components are mutually exclusive. Thus, when totalled, this measure ranges from 0 to 32.

The regressions also include a number of control variables: *Log-population* is based on the population figures from the CIA World Factbook (2002).

Time measures change in time in crisis behaviour by subtracting 1990 from the year.

The *polity* variable measures democracy on a scale ranging from -10 (the most autocratic) to 10 (the most democratic). The variable is based on the regulation, openness, and competitiveness of executive recruitment, constraints on the executive, and regulation and competitiveness of political participation.[8] The version used here is lagged by one year. *Stability* is another variable based on the polity data set and measures the number of years since the last change in the polity variable. These variables help us to see any links between the regime type and crisis involvement. Thus, it enables us to test the regime-related aspects of diversionary behaviour as well as a possible 'democratic peace' argument in crises.

We have added 'age of the state' to the existing variables in order to see whether the tradition of holding status as a state has any effect on crisis involvement, regardless of its regime or stability. We also employ the change in inflation (International Monetary Fund), real gross national product (U.S. Department of Agriculture), and social unrest (Political Instability Task Force-Consolidated Events Data), which are the other variables (in addition to regime type and stability) that have been used by proponents of diversionary theory to explain involvement in crises (Davies 2002; Fordham 2002; James and Oneal 1991; James and Rioux 1998; Miller 1999; Morgan and Bickers 1992).

Power status and bordering major powers are coded in accordance with the ICB data set. In addition to power status and bordering major powers, we also took into account military exports (Stockholm International Peace Research Institute military expenditure data set) to test the realist variants of possible conflict and crisis involvement theories. We use 'past protracted conflicts' from the ICB data set to determine the effect of the 'conflict' involvement on 'crisis' involvement. Finally, the export–import variable (which is tested both as an individual variable and separately as exports and imports) is based on United Nations Conference on Trade and Development data. It allows us to see whether trade has a positive or negative effect on crisis involvement, which is also a test of neo-liberal strands of international relations theory (Barbieri 1996; Keohane and Nye 1977; Mansfield 1994; Pollins 1989).

Data Analysis and Discussion

The results in tables 5.1 and 5.2 show that state religion has a significant impact on both crisis and the subset of crises that are part of protracted conflicts.[9] The religious legislation variable is associated significantly with crisis and protracted crisis in all four tests. The official religion variable is significantly associated only with whether the state is involved in a crisis that is part of a protracted conflict. This clearly supports the contention that religious states are more likely to be involved in crises. It is also important to note that GDP, existence of a social unrest, power status, polity, and commercial ties (as demonstrated by exports and imports) all play a role in involvement in crises, but among those, only GDP helps us to predict crises that are part of a protracted conflict. As expected, the presence of a conflict history contributes significantly to involvement in crises as part of a protracted conflict. The significance of social unrest shows especially that instrumental explanations for the relatively frequent involvement of religious states in crises are as convincing as – if not more than – the primordial ones.

A few more details are in order about the overall performance of the models. While the percentage of cases predicted correctly is high, the pseudo-R^2 is low. This disparity is likely because very few of the cases are coded as having crises: only 7.4 per cent, along with 4.6 per cent coded as having experienced protracted crises. When so few cases are coded positively in logistic regressions, the pseudo-R^2 is rarely high. Despite this finding, the fact that the religion variables are strongly significant gives us confidence that they represent a real influence of religion on crisis.

Conclusions

The literature on religion and all aspects of conflict, both theoretical and empirical, is a relatively new one. Events since the late 1970s have made it increasingly apparent that past assumptions about religion moving from the public sphere to the private sphere have been misguided.[10] These events include 9/11, decades of violence in Afghanistan, the Iranian revolution, and violent Islamic opposition movements

Table 5.1
Influence of state religious exclusivity on crisis, 1990–2002

	Model 1	Model 2	Model 3	Model 4
Log of real GDP	0.484**	0.384	0.576**	0.469**
Social unrest	0.621**	0.573**	0.597**	0.544**
Power status	0.546	0.774	0.893**	1.115**
Bordering states	-0.051	-0.055	-0.061	-0.064
Bordering major powers	0.016	0.043	0.021	0.052
Age	0.043	0.060	0.049	0.067
Military expenditures	0.030	0.028	0.030	0.027
Past protracted conflict	0.420*	0.370	0.406	0.356
Δ inflation	0.000	0.000	0.000	0.000
Log-population	0.298	.359	0.280	0.348
Time	-0.033	-0.037	-0.029	-0.033
Polity	-0.038**	-0.022	-0.038**	-0.022
Stability	-0.003	-0.003	-0.002	-0.003
Imports	0.000**	0.000***	–	–
Exports	0.000*	0 .000*	–	–
Exports and imports	–	–	0.000***	0.000***
Official religion	0.061	–	0.047	–
Religious legislation	–	0.041**	–	0.040**
Constant	-5.109****	-5.452****	-5.092****	-5.484****
N	1863	1863	1863	1863
Cox & Snell R^2	.065	.066	.064	.066
Nagelkerke R^2	.175	.180	.174	.178
Percentage correctly predicted	94.2	94.2	94.2	94.2

* Significance < .1
** Significance < .05
*** Significance < .01
**** Significance < .001

that appeared in its wake. Other destructive events with a religious dimension include the sarin gas attack on Tokyo's subway by the Aum Shrinkyo sect on 20 March 1995, the fifty-one-day standoff between U.S. federal forces and the Branch Davidians in Waco, Texas, in 1993, numerous incidents of violent opposition to abortion in the United States (e.g., clinic bombings), and ethno-religious conflicts such as the protracted civil war between the Hindu Tamils and the Buddhist majority in Sri Lanka. To this list could be added certain aspects of the civil war in Iraq, covered by chapter 8. Less prominent but also significant are some of the more positive activities reported elsewhere in this volume. Examples include religious humanitarianism (chapter 6), efforts to

Table 5.2
Influence of state religious exclusivity on crisis in protracted conflicts, 1990–2002

	Model 1	Model 2	Model 3	Model 4
Log of real GDP	1.925***	1.789****	1.831****	1.642****
Social unrest	0.665	0.556	0.680	0.592
Power status	0.467	0.774	0.284	0.490
Bordering states	-0.103	-0.115*	-0.098	-0.109*
Bordering major powers	0.103	0.164	0.102	0.155
Age	0.182*	0.199*	0.174	0.185*
Military exports	0.013	0.015	0.014	0.016
Past protracted conflict	1.288****	1.214****	1.307****	1.236****
Δ inflation	0.000	0.000**	0.000	0.000**
Log-population	-0.449	-0.367	-0.431	-0.347
Time	-0.094**	-0.095**	-0.098**	-0.101***
Polity	-0.010	0.018	-0.010	0.019
Stability	0.001	0.001	0.001	0.000
Imports	0.000	0.000	–	–
Exports	0.000	0.000	–	–
Exports and imports	–	–	0.000	0.000
Official religion	**0.177****	–	**0.188****	–
Religious legislation	–	**0.075*****	–	**0.077*****
Constant	-5.914****	-6.266****	-5.866***	-6.115****
N	1863	1863	1863	1863
Cox & Snell R^2	.068	.069	.068	.069
Nagelkerke R^2	.268	.273	.268	.273
Percentage correctly predicted	96.7	96.7	96.7	96.7

* Significance < .1
** Significance < .05
*** Significance < .01
**** Significance < .001

avert war by the pontiff (chapter 10), Christian mediation (chapter 11), and attempts by states and religious non-governmental organizations (NGOs) to coordinate with each other to improve global governance.

While the link between religion and crisis is not overwhelming, it clearly exists. The analysis presented here shows that state religious exclusivity is linked clearly and significantly to the incidence of crisis. Given the context of a growing quantitative literature linking aspects of religion with various types of conflict, this is not surprising. However, these results constitute the first study of which we are aware that connects religion to crisis and one of very few that address the influence of religion on interstate relations. As such, it is a significant piece of a larger research agenda that is only beginning to uncover the empirical relationships between and among religion and violence, conflict, and crisis.

These results also speak to the central issues addressed in this volume. As discussed in more detail in the state religious exclusivity section of this chapter, the results presented here are specific to religion and are not attributable to other bases for identity such as ethnicity. This is because the religious variables used here do not focus on identity but rather focus on the extent to which a religion or religious ideology influences a government. This aspect of government behaviour is attributable unambiguously to religion.

That being said, it always is possible to argue that religion is really a cover for some other factor such as an elite's desire to consolidate and support its rule. In the past, Marxists and a tradition in sociology called functionalism did exactly this.[11] While this argument is no doubt true in some circumstances, it is problematic for at least two reasons. First, there are no circumstances in which it cannot be argued that religion is being used for ulterior motives. Put differently, there is no action that an individual motivated by religion might take that cannot be ascribed to other motivations including secular political and economic incentives. Yet individuals are motivated by religion – including people willing to sacrifice themselves and their personal interests to further a religious cause. Second, even assuming that religion is being used as a cover or tool to motivate others, its effectiveness shows that religion does have an influence.

Take, for example, the case of suicide bombers. It is easy to argue that those who send the suicide bombers are cynically manipulating religion in order to recruit and motivate them. It is also true that in many cases families of the suicide bombers receive large sums of money relative to their average earning potential. Yet most suicide bombers are associated with organizations that have religious ideologies (Ben-Dor and Pedahzur 2003, 85). This indicates that, even assuming their leaders and families are motivated by secular and material motives, an added element of religion makes it easier to motivate someone to become a suicide bomber. Thus, religion is clearly among the factors that influence this type of behaviour, even in the presence of political motivations and economic incentives.

We believe the same is true of crisis. Even if the motivation behind creating a religiously exclusive state has nothing to do with religion and the country's leaders are secretly sceptical of the state's religious ideology – a contention whose universal truth we find to be unlikely – religion is still an influence. Choosing an openly religious ideology to guide a state creates a situation where policymakers have little choice but to act in accordance with that ideology, even if they may not personally subscribe to it. To do otherwise would critically undermine their legitimacy (Fox and Sandler 2004). Thus, if a religious ideology guides these (supposedly) secretly secular policymakers to follow a policy that leads to crisis, it is arguably just as difficult for them to deviate from that policy, as would be the case for a true believer. Furthermore, we argue that in many, if not most, cases the policymakers are, in fact, true believers or at least significantly influenced by religious ideology.[12]

This has an important implication for foreign policy. When dealing with opponents who ascribe their policy to a religious ideology, it is likely that it will be difficult to get those opponents to change the policy in question. This is especially true if interpretation of religious doctrine is consistent with state-supported religious ideology and possesses wide legitimacy in the policymaker's constituency. If the conflict is seen as being over an issue tied to a religious ideal, compromise is difficult. Compromises generally involve dividing the issue – each side getting some of what it wants – and substituting other benefits in return for compromise on the issue. In the eyes of a believer, such an ideal cannot be traded for other economic or political benefits, and anything less than full adherence to the ideal is unacceptable.

In such cases, appeasement and negotiation are unlikely to result in a change in policy. In fact, they are potentially counterproductive in that they are likely to antagonize both the policymakers in question and their constituency. The only option that is likely to force movement away from an intractable, religiously motivated policy – at least in the short term – is confronting the instigator of that policy with a negative consequence sufficient to make compromise seem like a better alternative. Such consequences can include the potential removal of the leader from power or something that will harm a goal that is even more important to that leader.

This is not to say that religion always leads to intractable policies and crises. Religion is very much a double-edged sword that can promote both violence and peace. Consequently, there is the ability to use religion as a bridge between different groups, even in cases where those groups are in conflict. Scholars like Appleby (2000) and Gopin (2000, 2002) have argued that religion can be used for conflict management and resolution. Themes of forgiveness and reconciliation, found in most religions, can be emphasized along with commonalities between religious traditions in order to diffuse conflict. However, this approach requires the active participation of both sides. It is likely not intended to handle immediate problems caused when a religious ideology emphasizes one of its more intractable aspects. Rather, this process is intended to create a path toward long-term peace-building in cases for which both sides are at least reluctantly willing to participate.

Whether it manifests in its more peaceful or violent forms, it is clear that religion in general and religious exclusivity in particular are significant factors in modern politics. As discussed in more detail in the religious exclusivity section of this chapter, most states can be shown to support at least low levels of religious exclusivity. Furthermore, the more general findings of the RAS project show that religious exclusivity is increasing (Fox 2008). Thus, policymakers need to pay closer attention to the religious aspects of foreign policy. Religion clearly is present in most regimes and few states have a shortage of religious individuals (Norris and Inglehart 2004). Even setting aside the results presented in this chapter, that property would make it hard to argue that manifestations of religion in domestic policy are not accompanied by similar effects on foreign policy.

In the pre-9/11 era, many observers, such as Gopin (2000, 37–40), Luttwak (1994, 8–14) and Rubin (1994, 20–1), accused the United States and other Western foreign-policymakers of ignoring religion, preferring to focus on paradigms based on material power. While there seems to be a growing recognition that religion can be an important motivating force,[13] the revolutionary, paradigmatic change that is necessary to deal with this fact does not seem to have penetrated the Western foreign policy community. For example, the U.S. evangelical community had only a limited influence on the foreign policy of the George W. Bush Administration (Den Dulk 2006), even though the latter was arguably more open to influence by religion than any other in recent memory. Hurd (2004, 2007) argues that the United States and many European states consider religious states such as Iran the 'other' and projects on them a negative and violent image, thus distancing themselves from religion. The West tends to associate Islamism with fundamentalism, which, like dogmatism and fanaticism, are viewed always in negative terms.

U.S. and other Western policymakers need to begin to see religion and religiously motivated policymakers in more objective terms. Any policy that automatically projects a negative view of the religiously motivated 'other' is likely to result in suboptimal relations. Once religious motivations are not automatically considered in a negative light, it becomes possible to more accurately assess the objectives and motivations of policymakers who are influenced by religion. This, in turn, will allow Western policymakers to design more effective policies in cases where religious motivations are involved. Avoiding the tendency to automatically project political manifestations of religion in a negative light cannot help but give policymakers the ability to better understand policymakers with religious motivations.

NOTES

1 The RAS data set is available at the RAS project website at http://www.religionandstate.org; see http://www.cidcm.umd.edu/icb for the ICB data set.
2 Several variables have been used to investigate the dynamics of international conflict and crisis. These variables include relative military capabilities (Huth 1988; Organski and Kugler 1980), the influence of nuclear weapons (Betts 1987; Schelling 1966), interstate rivalries (Diehl and Crescenzi 1998; Goertz and Diehl 1993), state capabilities (Rummel 1968; Wright 1964), power status (Eberwein 1982), state-level arms expenditures (Kemp 1977), proximity (Bremer 1992; Hensel 2000; Senese 1996; Vasquez 1995; Wallenstein 1981, 84), number of borders (Richardson 1960, 197), trade and interdependence (Barbieri 1996; Kegley 1995; Oneal and Russett 1999) and regime type (Chernoff 2004; James, Solberg, and Wolfson 1999; Russett 1993; Spiro 1994).
3 For a more comprehensive list of the books and articles that employ ICB, refer to the database website http://www.cidcm.umd.edu/icb/references/.
4 Not all studies of religion and conflict find that religion causes conflict. Pearce (2004, 2005) found no link between religious identity and conflict; several other studies reveal no connection for religious diversity and conflict (Collier and Hoeffler 2002; Fearon and Laitin 2003; Lacina 2006).
5 It is worth noting that a number of survey-based studies link religious identity to a wide variety of political and social phenomena including, for example, domestic violence (Cunradi, Caetano, and Schafer 2002; Nason-Clark 1997, 2001), political issues including abortion, working women, capital punishment, confidence in institutions, and support for religion in politics (Hayes 1995). Religious identity also is linked to diverse political activities, such as voter turnout and choice, lobbying elected officials, engaging in collective communal action, and participating in protests (Beyerlein and Chaves 2003, 229).

6 For a full discussion of these findings, including a state-by-state description of religion-state interactions, see Fox (2008).
7 Only seven states are coded as participating in more than one crisis in a given year, so this information does not provide sufficient variation to be used to create a variable.
8 For more information in the Polity data set and a copy of the data, see Jaggers and Gurr (1995) and http://www.systemicpeace.org/polity/polity4.htm.
9 To check for multi-collinearity, we ran a correlation matrix for all dependent variables. All but five of the correlations are below .5 and the highest is .702. In addition, we ran regressions using each independent variable as a dependent variable and all of the other independent variables as independent variables. This was done separately for each of the four models for a total of sixty tests. Forty-four of the 60 R-squared are below .5. The highest adjusted R-squared was .777. As a general rule, multi-collinearity is considered a serious problem only if the R-squared is above .8. On the basis of these results, multi-collinearity is not an issue for our interpretation of the logistic regressions.
10 For more on this assertion in terms of both theory and evidence, see Fox (2002, 2008).
11 For a discussion and critique of this type of argument see Fox (2002: 65–76).
12 Svensson (2007) makes a similar argument in the context of domestic conflict and in a quantitative study finds that, if either side made explicitly religious demands, the conflict is significantly less likely to terminate in a negotiated settlement.
13 See, for example, Albright (2007).

REFERENCES

Albright, M. 2007. *The mighty and the Almighty: Reflections on America, God, and world affairs.* New York: Harper Perennial.

Appleby, R.S. 2000. *The ambivalence of the sacred: Religion, violence, and reconciliation.* New York: Rowman & Littlefield.

Azar, E.E., P. Jureidini, and R. McLaurin. 1978. Protracted social conflict: Theory and practice in the Middle East. *Journal of Palestine Studies* 8 (1): 41–60.

Barbieri, K. 1996. Economic interdependence: A path to peace or a source of interstate conflict? *Journal of Peace Research* 33 (1): 29–49.

Ben-Dor, G., and A. Pedahzur. 2003. The uniqueness of Islamic fundamentalism and the fourth wave of international terrorism. *Totalitarian Movements and Political Religions* 4 (3): 71–90.

Ben-Yehuda, H., and M. Mishali-Ram. 2006. Ethnic actors and international crises: Theory and findings, 1918–2001. *International Interactions* 32 (1): 49–78.

Bercovitch, J., and K. DeRouen Jr. 2005. Managing ethnic civil wars: Assessing the determinants of successful mediation. *Civil Wars* 7 (1): 98–116.

Betts, R. 1987. *Nuclear blackmail and nuclear balance*. Washington, DC: Brookings Institution.

Beyerlein, K., and M. Chaves. 2003. The political activities of religious congregations in the US. *Journal for the Scientific Study of Religion* 42 (2): 229–46.

Brecher, M., and J. Wilkenfeld. 1997a. The ethnic dimension of international crises. In Carment and James, 164–93.

– 1997b. *A study of crisis*. Ann Arbor: University of Michigan Press.

Bremer, S.A. 1992. Dangerous dyads: Conditions affecting the likelihood of interstate war 1816–1965. *Journal of Conflict Resolution* 36 (2): 309–41.

Brown, M.W., and C.J. Oudraat. 1997. International conflict and international action: An overview. in *Nationalism and ethnic conflict: An international security reader*, ed. M.E. Brown, O.R. Cote Jr, S.M. Jones, and S.E. Miller, 163–93. Cambridge, MA: MIT Press.

Bueno de Mesquita, B., and D. Lalman. 1992. *War and reason*. New Haven, CT: Yale University Press.

Carment, D., and P. James, eds. 1997. *Wars in the midst of peace*. Pittsburgh: University of Pittsburgh Press.

– 1998. Escalation of ethnic conflict. *International Politics* 35:65–82.

Central Intelligence Agency. 2002. The world factbook. https://www.cia.gov/library/publications/the-world-factbook/index.html

Chernoff, F. 2004. The study of democratic peace and progress in international relations. *International Studies Review* 6 (1): 49–77.

Collier, P., and A. Hoeffler. 2002. Military expenditure – threats, aid, and arms races. *Policy Research Working Paper Series* 2927. The World Bank.

Cunradi, C.B., R. Caetano, and J. Schafer. 2002. Religious affiliation, denominational homogamy, and intimate partner violence among U.S. couples. *Journal for the Scientific Study of Religion* 41 (1): 139–51.

Dassel, K., and E. Reinhardt. 1999. Domestic strife and the initiation of violence at home and abroad. *American Journal of Political Science* 43:56–85.

Davies, G.A. 2002. Domestic strife and the initiation of international conflicts. *Journal of Conflict Resolution* 46:672–92.

Den Dulk, K.R. 2006. Evangelical elites and faith-based foreign affairs. *Review of Faith and International Affairs* 4 (1): 21–9.

DeRouen, K.R. Jr, and S. Goldfinch. 2005. Putting the numbers to work: Implications for violence prevention. *Journal of Peace Research* 42 (1): 27–45.

Diamond, L., J. Linz, and S.M. Lipset, eds. 1990. *Politics in developing countries: Comparing experiences with democracy.* Boulder, CO: Rienner.

Diehl, P.F., and M. Crescenzi. 1998. Reconfiguring the arms race-war debate. *Journal of Peace Research* 35:111–18.

Douglass, W. 1988. A critique of recent trends in the analysis of ethnonationalism. *Ethnic and Racial Studies* 2 (2): 192–206.

Eberwein, W. 1982. The seduction of power: Serious international disputes and the power status of nations, 1900–1976. *International Interactions* 9:57–74.

Eisenstein, M.A. 2006. Rethinking the relationship between religion and political tolerance in the US. *Political Behavior* 28:327–48.

Enterline, A.J., and K.S. Gleditsch. 2000. Threats, opportunity, and force: Repression and diversion of domestic pressure, 1948–1982. *International Interactions* 26:21–53.

Fearon, J., and D. Laitin. 2003. Ethnicity, insurgency, and civil war. *American Political Science Review* 97 (1): 75–90.

Fisch, M.S. 2002. Islam and authoritarianism. *World Politics* 55 (1): 4–37.

Fordham, B.O. 2002. Another look at 'parties, voters and the use of force abroad.' *Journal of Conflict Resolution* 46:572–96.

Fox, J. 2002. *Ethnoreligious conflict in the late 20th century: A general theory.* Lanham, MD: Lexington Books.

– 2004. *Religion, civilization and civil war: 1945 through the new millennium.* Lanham, MD: Lexington Books.

– 2007. Do democracies have separation of religion and state? *Canadian Journal of Political Science* 40:1–25.

– 2008. *Religion and the state: A world survey of government involvement in religion.* New York: Cambridge University Press.

Fox, J., and S. Sandler. 2004. *Bringing religion into international relations.* New York: Palgrave Macmillan.

Geertz, C. 1973. *The interpretation of culture.* New York: Basic Books.

Gelpi, C. 1997. Democratic diversions: Governmental structure and the externalization of domestic conflict. *Journal of Conflict Resolution* 41:255–72.

Girard, R. 1977. *Violence and the sacred.* Baltimore: Johns Hopkins University Press.

Goertz, G., and P.F. Diehl. 1993. Enduring rivalries: Theoretical constructs and empirical patterns. *International Studies Quarterly* 37:147–71.

Gopin, M. 2000. *Between Eden and Armageddon: The future of world religions, violence, and peacemaking.* Oxford: Oxford University Press.

– 2002. *Holy war, holy peace: How religion can bring peace to the Middle East.* New York: Oxford University Press.

Greely, A.M. 1982. *Religion: A secular theory.* New York: Free Press.

Harris, F.C. 1994. Something within: Religion as a mobilizer of African-American political activism. *Journal of Politics* 56 (1): 42–68.

Hasenclever, A., and V. Rittberger. 2000. Does religion make a difference? Theoretical approaches to the impact of faith on political conflict. *Millennium* 29 (3): 641–74.

Hayes, B.C. 1995. The impact of religious identification on political attitudes: An international comparison. *Sociology of Religion* 56 (2): 177–94.

Haynes, J. 1994. *Religion in third world politics*. Boulder, CO: Rienner.

Heldt, B. 1999. Domestic politics, absolute deprivation, and the use of armed force in interstate territorial disputes, 1950–1990. *Journal of Conflict Resolution* 43:451–78.

Henderson, E.A. 1997. Culture or contiguity: Ethnic conflict, the similarity of states, and the onset of war, 1820–1989. *Journal of Conflict Resolution* 41 (5): 649–68.

– 1998. The democratic peace through the lens of culture, 1820–1989. *International Studies Quarterly* 42 (3): 461–84.

Hensel, P.R. 2000. Territory: Theory and evidence on geography and conflict. In *What do we know about war*, ed. J.A. Vasquez, 57–85. Lanham, MD: Rowman & Littlefield.

Hess, G.D., and A. Orphanides. 2001. War and democracy. *Journal of Political Economy* 109:776–810.

Hoffman, B. 1995. Holy terror: The implications of terrorism motivated by a religious imperative. *Studies in Conflict and Terrorism* 18:271–84.

Huntington, S.P. 1996. *The clash of civilizations and the remaking of the world order*. New York: Simon and Schuster.

Hurd, E.S. 2004. The international politics of secularism: US foreign policy and the Islamic republic of Iran. *Alternatives* 29 (2): 115–38.

– 2007. Political Islam and foreign policy in Europe and the United States. *Foreign Policy Analysis* 3 (4): 354–67.

Huth, P.K. 1988. *Extended deterrence and the prevention of war*. New Haven, CT: Yale University Press.

Jaggers, K., and T.R. Gurr. 1995. Tracking democracy's third wave with the Polity III data. *Journal of Peace Research* 32 (4): 469–82.

James, P., and J.R. Oneal. 1991. The influence of domestic and international politics on the president's use of force. *Journal of Conflict Resolution* 35:307–32.

James, P., and J. Rioux. 1998. International crises and linkage politics: The experiences of the United States 1953–1994. *Political Research Quarterly* 51:781–812.

James, P., E. Solberg, and M. Wolfson. 1999. An identified systemic model of the democracy-peace nexus. *Defense and Peace Economics* 10 (1): 1–37.

Johnston, H., and J. Figa. 1988. The church and the political opposition: Comparative perspective on mobilization against authoritarian regimes. *Journal for the Scientific Study of Religion* 27 (1): 32–47.

Juergensmeyer, M. 1991. Sacrifice and cosmic war. *Terrorism and Political Violence* 3 (3): 101–17.

– 1993. *The new cold war?* Berkeley: University of California Press.

Kaufman, S.J. 2001. *The symbolic politics of ethnic war.* Ithaca, NY: Cornell University Press.

Kegley, C.W. 1995. *Controversies in international relations theory: Realism and the neoliberal challenge.* New York: St Martin's.

Keller, J.W. 2005. Leadership style, regime type, and foreign policy crisis behavior: A contingent monadic peace? *International Studies Quarterly* 49 (2): 205–32.

Kemp, A. 1977. A path analytic model of international violence. *International Interactions* 4:53–85.

Keohane, R., and J. Nye. 1977. *Power and interdependence: World politics in transition.* Boston: Little Brown.

Khosla, D. 1999. Third world states as intervenors in ethnic conflicts: Implications for regional and international security. *Third World Quarterly* 20 (6): 1143–56.

Kirkpatrick, L.A. 1993. Fundamentalism, Christian orthodoxy and intrinsic religious orientation as predictors of discriminatory attitudes. *Journal for the Scientific Study of Religion* 32 (3): 256–68.

Lacina, B. 2006. Explaining the severity of civil wars. *Journal of Conflict Resolution* 50 (2): 276–89.

Lai, B. 2004. The effects of different types of military mobilization on the outcome of international crises. *Journal of Conflict Resolution* 48 (2): 211–29.

– 2006. An empirical examination of religion and conflict in the Middle East, 1950–1992. *Foreign Policy Analysis* 2 (1): 21–36.

Laustsen, C.B., and O. Waever. 2000. In defense of religion: Sacred referent objects for securitization. *Millennium* 29 (3): 705–39.

Laythe, B., D. Finkel, and L.A. Kirkpatrick. 2002. Predicting prejudice from religious fundamentalism and right wing authoritarianism: A multiple regression approach. *Journal for the Scientific Study of Religion* 40 (1): 1–10.

Leak, G.K., and B.A. Randall. 1995. Clarification of the link between right-wing authoritarianism and religiousness: The role of religious maturity. *Journal for the Scientific Study of Religion* 34 (2): 245–52.

Leng, R.J., and P.M. Regan. 2002. Social and political cultural effects on the outcome of mediation in militarized interstate disputes. *International Studies Quarterly* 47 (3): 431–52.

Little, D. 1996. Religious militancy. In *Managing global chaos: Sources of and responses to global conflict*, ed. C.A. Crocker and F.O. Hampson, 79–91. Washington, DC: United States Institute of Peace Press.

Luttwak, E. 1984. The missing dimension. In *Religion, the missing dimension of statecraft*, ed. D. Johnston and C. Sampson, 8–19. Oxford: Oxford University Press.

Mansfield, E.D. 1994. *Power, trade, and war*. Princeton, NJ: Princeton University Press.

Midlarsky, M.I. 1998. Democracy and Islam: Implications for civilizational conflict and the democratic peace. *International Studies Quarterly* 42 (3): 458–511.

Miller, A.S. 1996. The influence of religious affiliation on the clustering of social attitudes. *Review of Religious Research* 37 (3): 123–36.

Miller, R.A. 1995. Domestic structures and the diversionary use of force. *American Journal of Political Science* 39:760–85.

– 1999. Regime type, strategic interaction, and the diversionary use of force. *Journal of Conflict Resolution* 43:338–402.

Mollov, B., and C. Lavie. 2002. Culture, dialogue, and perception change in the Israeli-Palestinian conflict. *International Journal of Conflict Management* 12 (1): 69–87.

Morgan, T.C., and C.J. Anderson. 1999. Domestic support and diversionary external conflict in Great Britain, 1950–1992. *Journal of Politics* 61:799–814.

Morgan, T.C., and K.W. Bickers. 1992. Domestic discontent and the external use of force. *Journal of Conflict Resolution* 36:25–52.

Nason-Clark, N. 1997. *The battered wife: How Christians confront family violence*. Louisville, KY: Westminster/John Knox.

– 2001. Making the sacred safe: Woman abuse and communities of faith. *Sociology of Religion* 61:349–68.

Nielson, M.E., and J. Fultz. 1995. Further examination of the relationships of religious orientation to religious conflict. *Review of Religious Research* 36 (4): 369–81.

Norris, P., and R. Inglehart. 2004. *Sacred and secular: Religion and politics worldwide*. New York: Cambridge University Press.

Oneal, J.R., and B.M. Russett. 1999. Assessing the liberal peace with alternative specifications: Trade still reduces conflict. *Journal of Peace Research* 36 (4): 423–42.

Organski, A.F.K., and J. Kugler. 1980. *The war ledger*. Chicago: University of Chicago Press.

Osiander, A. 2000. Religion and politics in Western civilization: The ancient world as matrix and mirror of the modern. *Millennium* 29 (3): 761–90.

Pape, R.A. 2003. The strategic logic of suicide terrorism. *American Political Science Review* 97 (3): 343–61.

Pearce, S. 2004. The double-edged sword: The impact of religion on the intensity of political conflict. PhD diss., Trinity College, University of Dublin.

– 2005. Religious rage: A quantitative analysis of the intensity of religious conflicts. *Terrorism and Political Violence* 17 (3): 333–52.

Philpott, D. 2002. The challenge of September 11 to secularism in international relations. *World Politics* 55 (1): 66–95.

Pollins, B. 1989. Conflict, cooperation and commerce: The effect of international political interactions. *American Journal of Political Science* 33 (3): 737–61.

Rapoport, D.C. 1988. Messianic sanctions for terror. *Comparative Politics* 20 (2): 195–213.

Reynal-Querol, M. 2002. Ethnicity, political systems, and civil wars. *Journal of Conflict Resolution* 46 (1): 29–54.

Richardson, L.F. 1960. *Statistics of deadly quarrels*. Pacific Grove, CA: Boxwood.

Roeder, P.G. 2003. Clash of civilizations and escalation of domestic ethnopolitical conflicts. *Comparative Political Studies* 36 (5): 509–40.

Rubin, B. 1994. Religion and international affairs. In *Religion, the missing dimension of statecraft*, ed. D. Johnston and C. Sampson, 20–34. Oxford: Oxford University Press.

Rummel, R.J. 1968. The relationship between national attributes and foreign conflict behavior. In *Quantitative international politics: Insights and evidence*, ed. J.D. Singer, 187–214. New York: Free Press.

– 1997. Is collective violence correlated with social pluralism? *Journal of Peace Research* 34 (2): 163–75.

Russett, B. 1993. *Grasping the democratic peace*. New Haven: Princeton University Press.

Sahliyeh, E. 1990. *Religious resurgence and politics in the contemporary world*. New York: State University of New York Press.

Sambanis, N. 2001. Do ethnic and nonethnic civil wars have the same causes? *Journal of Conflict Resolution* 45 (3): 259–82.

Schelling, T. 1966. *Arms and influence*. New Haven, CT: Yale University Press.

Senese, P.D. 1996. Geographical proximity and issue salience. *Conflict Management and Peace Science* 15 (2): 133–61.

Seul, J.R. 1999. Ours is the way of God: Religion, identity and intergroup conflict. *Journal of Peace Research* 36 (3): 553–69.

Spiro, D.E. 1994. Give democratic peace a chance? The insignificance of the liberal peace. *International Security* 19 (2): 50–86.

Svensson, I. 2007. Fighting with faith: Religion and conflict resolution in civil wars. *Journal of Conflict Resolution* 51 (6): 930–49.

Toft, M.D. 2007. Getting religion? The puzzling case of Islam and civil war. *International Security* 31 (4): 97–131.

Turner, B.S. 1991. *Religion and social theory.* London: Sage.

Vanhanen, T. 1999. Domestic ethnic conflict and ethnic nepotism: A comparative analysis. *Journal of Peace Research* 36 (1): 55–73.

Vasquez, J.A. 1995. Why do neighbors fight? Proximity, interaction, or territoriality. *Journal of Peace Research* 32:277–93.

Wallensteen, P. 1981. Incompatibility, confrontation and war: Four models and three historical systems, 1816–1976. *Journal of Peace Research* 18 (1): 57–90.

Weede, E. 1970. Conflict behavior of nation-states. *Journal of Peace Research* 7:229–37.

Weinberg, L.B., and W.L. Eubank. 1998. Terrorism and democracy: What recent events disclose. *Terrorism and Political Violence* 10 (1): 108–18.

Weinberg, L., W. Eubank, and A. Pedahzur. 2002. Characteristics of terrorist organizations 1910–2000. Presented at the 25th Annual Meeting of the International Society of Political Psychology, Berlin, 2002.

Wentz, R. 1987. *Why people do bad things in the name of religion.* Macon, GA: Mercer.

Williams, R.H. 1994. Movement dynamics and social change: Transforming fundamentalist ideologies and organizations. In *Accounting for fundamentalisms: The dynamic character of movements,* ed. M.E. Marty and R.S. Appleby, 785–833. Chicago: University of Chicago Press.

Wilson, B.R. 1982. *Religion in sociological perspective.* Oxford: Oxford University Press.

Wright, Q. 1964. *A study of war.* Chicago: University of Chicago Press.

6 Religion, Identity, and the 'War on Terror': Insights from Religious Humanitarianism

CECELIA LYNCH

Introduction

Why and how should we think about religion in international relations? Why should we think about religion now, in particular? In this chapter I focus on the first of these two questions. The second question assumes that there is some reason for analysing religion now that was not present before, such as the often-quoted assertion of a resurgence of religion in world politics, or the belief that the world is plagued by an increase in new and dangerous forms of religious extremism. However, we do not have enough evidence to argue that there is a resurgence of religion in world politics today compared to some mythical past, and religiously affiliated forms of extremism have waxed and waned for centuries in world politics.

I assert, however, that there is a resurgence of *interest* in religion among academics, especially those in fields such as international relations that have ignored it for too long. I argue, further, that while religion has never disappeared from world politics, more people in both the West and the Middle East are openly expressing religious sentiments in the public sphere and explicitly using guidelines they identify as religious to make decisions about political, economic, social, and cultural concerns. It remains an open question, nevertheless, whether these expressions represent a resurgence of religion itself, or rather changes in the relationship between public and private, and religious and secular, spheres of action.

Given these observations, I argue that we should *always* be interested in the ways in which religious belief intersects with political, economic, and social practices in the world, and that our perceptions regarding the strength, value, and purpose of religious ethics are also worthy of study. In this chapter, therefore, I first emphasize *how* we should study religion, in order to probe the relationship between religious identities and processes of global governance. I then focus on *why* we should study religion *writ large* and why we should pay attention to religious humanitarianism more specifically. In doing so I analyse the impact of the alleged global 'War on Terror' on perceptions of Islam among the transnational community of faith-based humanitarians.

How Should We Study Religion?

In this era of renewed fascination with religious identities, an incident in June 2007 brought home to me once again the importance of resisting the urge to reify others. While conducting interviews with Muslim human rights activists in Mombasa, Kenya, I needed to get from one interview to another in a different part of the city before the start of Friday prayers, so I searched for an available tuk-tuk (a three-wheeled taxi more common in South Asia but increasingly seen in East Africa). A driver pulled over with two women seated in the back wearing black garments that fully covered their bodies, heads, and faces, except for their eyes (terms used to describe such clothing – abaya, burka, veil, niqab – vary depending on the society). Thinking that the women might be uncomfortable sitting next to me, I suggested to the driver that his taxi was already full. But he said there was room, *hakuna matata* (no problem), the women moved over, and I clambered in. The woman seated next to me began chatting, asking me as we bounced around how I liked Mombasa, where I was from, and whether I had any children. As we talked, I took off my sunglasses, and she said, 'You have nice eyes – why do you cover them?'

This incident indicates to me that we must always be prepared to jettison preformed ideas about the ethics and practices of the religious 'other.' I am not Muslim, but even as someone who likes to think of herself as open to new and unexpected interpretations of religious identities, I was nonplussed. It had never occurred to me that a fully covered woman might consider my wearing sunglasses to be too self-effacing. I found myself thinking about Lila Abu-Lughod's article, 'Do Muslim Women Really Need Saving?' (2001), which I had used in teaching several times, to reflect on my ongoing responsibility to resist the meanings too-often assigned to the imagery of 'the Muslim woman.'[1] In the context of lamenting the superimposed rationale of 'saving' burka-clad women as a reason for invading Afghanistan in 2001, Abu-Lughod also discusses the increasing number of women wearing veils and other coverings (a trend also apparent at my Southern California campus). This trend can incorporate a political statement, an expression of comfort in demonstrations of Islamic ethics and practices, or both. Abu-Lughod, however, had not prepared me for understanding covering everything but the eyes as an expression of feminine individuality, though I soon realized that if I had paid more attention to her central point about rejecting dominant inferences, I would not have been so surprised.

This chapter brings together aspects of my research on Islamic, Christian, and interfaith religious humanitarians in Africa, the Middle East, and the United States, along with previous work on religion, to flesh out an explanation of the relationship between religion and identity to help analyse this incident as well as many other contemporary situations and trends. In doing so, I make three interrelated arguments about the religion–identity relationship, and hence about *how* we should think about religion in international relations. These arguments are consistent with the concept of thick religion, as put forward in chapter 3.

First, we should think about and analyse religion by looking at its *practice:* this is as important, if not more so, than equating religion with doctrine. 'Religions of the book' – Judaism, Christianity, and Islam – can be interpreted in different ways, giving rise to pacifist or 'just war' traditions, social justice, or self-help theologies, etc. The doctrines of these and other religious traditions evolve over time in a constitutive manner with practice, influenced by external events. Consequently, it is not possible to equate any given religion with a single doctrine that has consistent implications for political, economic, or social action.

Second, we should understand religion as providing *ethical guidelines* for action, but always with gaps that leave openings for interpretation – in other words, guidelines that always leave room for situations that need to be morally interpreted and assessed. Religious doctrines and traditions can never cover all eventualities in prescribing behaviour, and religious ethics must always be rethought, given the specifics of particular situations. Moreover, religious identity acts today as one among others (e.g., identities of nationhood, ethnicity, language, race, gender, sexual orientation, age, and class), and one person may also have a hybrid religious identity, made up of more than one religious tradition.[2] As a result, religious identity may relate to other identities in several different ways: it may overtake other identities, compete with them, or take a back seat to them (and this hierarchy of relationships may change over time). Religious identity may also be interpreted *through* other identities. For example, right-wing Christians in the United States interpret their religious tradition through the lens of nationhood and American exceptionalism. Consequently, what appears to them to be a strong, *religiously constituted* identity (with important ramifications for action) strikes others – Christians and non-Christians – as privileging national identity and filtering a selective interpretation of the Christian faith through an overarching nationalist commitment. Likewise, Jewish or Islamic 'extremists' who adhere to religious interpretations that justify violent action are criticized by others of the same faith who believe that such interpretations incorrectly and selectively subsume spiritual tenets to political grievances.

Third, we should view religious belief and actions as *shaped by* historical circumstances and traditions as well as contemporary political, economic, social, and cultural factors. A large part of our current fascination with religion in international relations comes from fears that religion is causally related to violence. I argue in this chapter that the security framework of the War on Terror influences religious identity as much as religious identity influences security. Likewise, dominant discourses associated with liberalism, the Enlightenment, feudal hierarchy under the Catholic Church, or empire under Islam also shape or shaped communal as well as individual beliefs and actions (Lynch 2009).

These three arguments provide the basis for theological distinctions among religious identities that I have employed in other work. Religious adherents may be *exclusivist* in the operationalization of their religious identities, believing that their religion is not only superior to others, but that they must do all in their power to spread their faith and ensure that believers and non-believers alike follow their interpretation of its dictates. Believers may also be *inclusivist*, acting from the conviction that their faith is superior but that others can also contain a glimmer of truth. Or religious adherents may be *pluralist* in their religious outlook. Pluralism, some argue, is in practice difficult to sustain, because it requires a strong belief in one's own religious tradition, but it also holds to the conviction that other religious traditions are equally valid. Religious pluralism, in other words, goes beyond tolerance to accept the idea that other faith traditions have an equal claim to believers' fidelity and any central 'truths,' and that which tradition one follows is based at least in part on historical, geographic, and cultural circumstances (Eck 1994; see also Lynch 2000b). Yet a fourth ethical possibility is that of religious syncretism. Given the massive movements of peoples, ideas, and cultural practices in the world, many people of faith actively draw on more than one religious tradition (Lynch 2000b).[3] Whether religious believers take one or another of these ethical stances depends in part on their historical, political, and social context, how they practise their faith traditions, and how they interpret doctrine, texts, and traditions. Whether believers 'fit' one or another of these stances (or fall through the cracks, fitting none of them comfortably) has major implications for how we should think about the effects of their religious identities on action.

These arguments, taken together, also challenge our current obsession with the relationship between religion and violence in international relations. Focusing almost exclusively on this relationship, I argue elsewhere, assumes that religious belief is inevitably exclusivist. This assumption impoverishes our understanding of religion and paradoxically diminishes our ability to explain any actual connections between religion and violence (Lynch 2007).[4] This is because such a focus prevents us from seeing the variety of interpretations and courses of action that exists. It channels our analytical focus and, in other words, forces us to 'select on the dependent variable.'

Why Should We Study Religion?

So ... *why* should we study religion?

Studying religion enriches our understanding of the relationship between culture and knowledge, deepens our capacity to analyse how people act and the ethical meanings they assign to their actions, and raises interesting questions about our supposedly secular experience in the West since the Renaissance. A first step in appreciating the richness of the relationship between religious identities, culture and knowledge, and ethical possibility is to dissect and demolish the mythical narrative that portrays secularism as a historic triumph of reason over religiously based irrationality in global governance, and ties the creation of the nation-state system in the West to the emergence of secular values. José Casanova incisively recounts the story as follows:

> Once upon a time in medieval Europe there was, as is typical of pre-modern societies, a fusion of religion and politics. But this fusion, under the new conditions of religious diversity, extreme sectarianism, and conflict created by the Protestant Reformation, led to the nasty, brutish, and long-lasting religious wars of the early modern era that left European socie-

ties in ruin. The secularization of the state was the felicitous response to this catastrophic experience, which apparently has indelibly marked the collective memory of European societies. The Enlightenment did the rest. Modern Europeans learned to separate religion, politics, and science. Most importantly, they learned to tame the religious passions and to dissipate obscurantist fanaticism by banishing religion to a protected private sphere, while establishing an open, liberal, secular public sphere where freedom of expression and public reason dominate.

Casanova soon demolishes this mythical story, even though, he argues, it is still one of the foundational myths of both European identity and international political theory.

The religious wars of Early Modern Europe and particularly the Thirty Years' War (1618–1648) did not ensue, at least not immediately, into the secular state but rather into the confessional one. The principle *cuius region eius religio*, which served as one of the foundations of the Treaty of Westphalia, is not the formative principle of the modern secular democratic state, but rather that of the modern confessional territorial absolutist state. Nowhere in Europe did religious conflict lead to secularization, but rather to the confessionalization of the state and to the territorialization of religions and peoples.

Casanova points out, moreover, that a 'logical consequence' of this state formation was ethno-religious cleansing, such as of Jews and Muslims by Spanish Catholics (Casanova 2007, 4). Lest we think that the problem of violence still lies with the *religious* character of the early modern absolutist state, and that this remaining issue was resolved with the 'secular' Enlightenment, however, all we need look at are the examples of the brutality of colonialism, the purges of secular communism in the Soviet Union, the ethno-religious cleansing brought about by national socialist fascism, and the two world wars. The thesis that the modern secular state has excised fanaticism from international politics, therefore, runs into numerous empirical problems.

Complementing and yet differing from Casanova's work, Talal Asad (1993) points out that the very category of 'religion' became possible only with the Enlightenment's new (at the time) distinctions between what was appropriately 'public' and what was to be confined to the 'private' sphere, with attendant implications for interstate and intrastate relations. Asad's argument shows how these distinctions came about more specifically as the absolutist and Christian state put stringent limits on the practice of Islam.

One of the ironies of the imposition of public/secular versus private/religious categories, however, is that 'religion,' through the actions of its adherents, never remained complacently within private sphere domains, resulting in multiple definitions of secularity as well as fluid borders between public and private. Moreover, religion continues to erupt out of the private sphere today. A major debate concerns to what degree the public/private delineation can account for forms of participation, order, and power prevalent in non-Western societies, as well as (increasingly) the West itself. Salvatore and LeVine (2005), for example, argue that public spheres are conceptualized and actualized in multiple ways in Muslim-majority societies, but that for the most part these ways do not reflect Western notions of secular public sphere dominance over privatized religious expression. Increasing numbers of scholars argue, moreover, that secularism itself is not a singular phenomenon, but rather takes multiple forms, including laicism, Judeo-Christian secularism, etc. (Shakman Hurd 2007). And debates over whether women and girls can wear headscarves in public schools in France and Turkey (Elver 2008; Göle 1997), as well as debates in the United States about the proper role and interpretation of Christian tenets in state practice, demonstrate the uncertainties about public/private delineations that also arise in the West. Taken together, these studies point to the necessity of studying not only religion, but also the ways in which global processes influence the very construction of religious and secular identities and political formations, and vice versa.

One significant area of international politics in which religious adherents play an increasing – but relatively neglected – role is that of humanitarianism. I focus in the remainder of this chapter on the phenomenon of religious humanitarianism: the explosion of religious groups all over the world concerned with refugees, famine, HIV/AIDS and other health issues, human rights, environmental degradation, and war. We should think about and study religion because these faith-based groups are an indispensable component of governance in the world today (Berger 2003), and they influence both ethical and policy debates about how we should address major world problems.

Religious Humanitarianism: Muslim, Christian, and Interfaith Manifestations

Religious humanitarians include activists of every faith – Christianity, Islam, Judaism, Hinduism, Buddhism, and others. Since the end of the Cold War, humanitarian activists (both religious and secular) have been witting or unwitting partners in privatizing welfare and foreign aid functions around the world.

The rise of post–Cold War humanitarianism was part of a move from anti-state to less politicized activism by many civil society actors. Rather than the critiques of state militarism, intervention, and the arms race so prevalent during the Cold War, humanitarian activists (often but not always from the West) working in Eastern Europe, Africa, and parts of Asia after 1991 often agitated *in favour of* state intervention to stem ethnic cleansing, stop genocide, and provide relief aid (Lynch 1998). This new humanitarian activism attempted to cope with civil wars occurring in tandem with the break-up of empires and nation-states. Because some of these conflicts occurred in multi-religious and Muslim-majority societies, Christian humanitarian activists increasingly began to work with their Islamic confrères to bring relief. Religious humanitarian non-governmental organization (NGO) umbrella groups, such as the Geneva-based International Council of Voluntary Agencies, included groups such as the international Islamic Relief Organization and the Islamic African Relief Agency in their networks (Lynch 2000a, 91–2).

Moreover, both religious (predominantly Christian) and secular groups attempted to come to grips with the fact of religious pluralism in the world, including the fact that they often operated in Muslim-majority societies, by adopting the Code of Conduct for the International Red Cross and Red Crescent Movement and Non-Governmental Organizations (NGOs) in Disaster Relief in 1994. Alex de Waal criticizes the Code of Conduct for mandating an apolitical stance that, he argues, humanitarian organizations almost never can attain in practice (de Waal 1997). But adhering to the Code also requires NGOs to respect the cultures and customs, including religious beliefs, of aid recipients: 'We will not tie the promise, delivery, or distribution of assistance to the embracing or acceptance of a particular political or religious creed.'[5]

However, after 1998 and especially 2001, some of these relationships have been disrupted; others have stalled, as many Western and some Third World states have cast suspicion on Islamic humanitarian aid groups as part of the 'War on Terror.' Still others may have been hindered. For example, many Islamic assistance groups work on the local level and have not have developed either the reach or the contacts to enable them to make alliances with transnational NGOs (Petersen 2008; Sparre 2008; Sparre and Petersen 2007). As a result, we need to ask not merely whether religion 'causes' violence, but also whether and how the heightened securitization of identity promulgated through the War on Terror constitutes religious humanitarianism and shapes religious identities and actions.

Interviews with representatives of Middle Eastern and African humanitarian organizations (including groups operating in Cameroon, Kenya, and Somalia), as well as statements by representatives of Muslim organizations in Southern California, together provide a picture of how Islamic humanitarian activism is influenced by the War on Terror.[6] The War on Terror discourse shapes humanitarian identities by affecting the distribution and donor funding of Islamic groups, and putting Muslim groups on the defensive and influencing non-Muslim perceptions of them. Just as the mythical narrative of the secular state created the 'reasonable' secularist opposed to the 'fanatical' religious believer, contemporary security discourses produce a dichotomy between 'good' and 'bad' Muslims (Mamdani 2004). In both cases, however, these identities are impossible to determine with any confidence and lead, therefore, to problematic policies.

War on Terror Discourses and Religious Identities

In the aftermath of the 1998 U.S. Embassy bombings in East Africa (Nairobi and Dar Es Salaam), the U.S. government, with the support of European counterparts, began a campaign to stop funding of terror-related Islamic networks. This campaign was intensified after the 11 September 2001 attacks and extended into all areas of U.S. policy, including humanitarian relief. The 2002 National Security Strategy included a two-pronged approach affecting aid organizations: it elevated 'development' as a 'third pillar' of U.S. foreign policy, 'along with defense and diplomacy,' and it brought U.S. efforts to combat the financing of terrorist organizations directly into the policy purview of U.S. foreign aid (USAID Summer Seminar Series 2004). The comprehensiveness of the campaign, including the publicity surrounding it and the secretive charges against individual Muslims and Islamic groups, created dissension within the NGO humanitarian community and put Islamic aid groups on the defensive.

Two post-9/11 U.S. laws, in particular, affect the distribution of relief and the identity construction of religious humanitarians: Executive Order 13224, which designates individuals and groups as supporting terrorism, and the USA Patriot Act, which greatly expands the scope of U.S. law-enforcement capabilities to prosecute those labelled terrorists or their supporters. As part of the procedures stemming from these laws, the United States Agency for International Development (USAID), which channelled large amounts of its funding through NGOs after the end of the Cold War, began a 'vetting program in which grantees applying for grants with USAID are required to first be screened through the intelligence community.'[7] Edwin Hullander, senior policy advisor to USAID, acknowledges that these laws represent a significant change for humanitarian groups. 'Terrorist activity is targeted toward civilians and that's the group that NGOs are trying to serve. On the other side, there has traditionally been a separation between the development community and the security community. Development and security are coming together' (USAID Summer Seminar Series 2004).

Bringing development and security together, vetting USAID grants through the U.S. intelligence community, and labelling and prosecuting some groups as terrorist supporters has had important ramifications for faith-based humanitarians. On one hand, Islamic group representatives know that their activities may be viewed with suspicion.[8] On the other hand, U.S. Muslims who wish to donate to Islamic charities are wary lest their donations be seen as evidence of material support to terrorists. As one commentator put it, 'For American Muslims ... the "material support" for terrorists rap presents a real dilemma. One of the most fundamental tenets of Islam is charitable giving. But giving to whom?' (Fisher 2008).[9] Surveillance puts groups and potential donors in the awkward position of wanting to avoid the charge of providing material support to terrorist suspects while challenging simplistic definitions of 'good' versus 'bad' Muslims. Moreover, the secrecy surrounding Executive Order 13224 and the US Patriot Act mean that definitions of good and bad can change rapidly, with serious implications for groups and individuals concerned.[10]

As a result, Islamic humanitarians in the United States are on the defensive vis-à-vis the U.S. government in order to demonstrate that they are good Muslims, and vis-à-vis their own communities in order to demonstrate that they will not be cowed by what is perceived as government-sponsored racial and religious profiling.

Most Islamic charities and NGOs under surveillance in the United States have close ties to the Middle East. Their members are often immigrants from Palestine, Lebanon, Syria, or Iran, or descendants of nationals from those countries, and their central purpose often is to provide medical relief or educational assistance. However, similar dynamics are also at play in Africa, though these receive less attention in the United

States. In interviews with faith-based activists in both Central and East Africa, for example, people expressed pride in accepting a variety of faith traditions (Protestant, Catholic, Muslim, traditional) as a normal part of life (in Cameroon and Kenya), and also an awareness that governments and the West had increased their surveillance of Muslims.

African Muslim women involved in a 2004 dialogue with Christians asserted that the media breed suspicion of Muslims and that 'the general misapprehension that all Muslims are terrorists has always played a part in the way Muslims are treated all over the world' (Odhiiambo 2004, 21). In Cameroon, this was expressed during interviews in vague terms as an additional concern in a context in which an authoritarian government keeps watch on all its citizens. In Kenya, however, the practices of surveillance are more public and openly discussed. The Kenyan government's collaboration with the U.S. government's anti-terrorism policies, including the operations of the East African Counter-Terrorism Initiative (set up in 2003) and the funding and training of the Kenyan Anti-Terrorist Police, are well known (Hammer 2007). Muslim NGOs in Kenya have been viewed with suspicion since the bombing of the U.S. embassy in Nairobi in 1998 (Hirsch 2006). Sometime between 1998 and the aftermath of the 11 September 2001 attacks in New York and Washington, many Islamic groups were forced out of the country (as a result of collaboration between the Kenyan and U.S. governments). Some of these no longer operate in the Nairobi slum of Kibera (the largest slum in sub-Saharan Africa), even though Muslims until recently made up the majority of this religiously mixed area of up to 1 million people. Several Kenyan interviewees told me that the government regularly deports Muslim activists thought to be stirring up Islamist sentiment, particularly in the Muslim areas of the coast and the northeastern regions bordering Somalia. While some Christian NGO representatives felt that their Muslim counterparts should do more to denounce potential radical infiltration and distance themselves from deportees, coastal Muslims felt unfairly stigmatized and pressured to differentiate themselves from people they either did not know or believed to be harmless.

These dynamics shape fear and suspicion that influence Muslim identities and the perception of Muslim identities by non-Muslims. As one analyst reported in an analysis of a pre-December 2007 parliamentary election campaign in the north between a Muslim convert and a Western-educated Christian, both 'gave the impression of being caught up, not unlike Kenya itself, in a political narrative that didn't entirely make sense to them or fit their reality but that they were nonetheless unable to escape' (Hammer 2007).

Similarly, good/bad Muslim identity distinctions affect humanitarianism in neighbouring Somalia. Somali NGOs (all established during the past fifteen years) are frustrated by their inability to be taken seriously by Western governments, donors, and non-Muslim transnational NGOs. The UN office in Nairobi brokers discussions between these groups (Nairobi is a major centre for organizing aid to Somalia), but better-funded Western aid groups suspect many Somali NGOs of being 'briefcase NGOs' – a term widely used to describe either foreign or domestic front groups led by unscrupulous entrepreneurs who pocket donor money without enacting promised projects. Somali group efforts also are hampered by the fact that transnational Islamic humanitarian organizations have not been allowed to operate in Kenya, where a major UN office as well as many transnational NGO offices are located. For example, the U.K.-based Muslim Aid was granted a temporary licence to operate in Kenya in 2008. Nevertheless, Muslim Aid is one of a handful of transnational organizations that provide essential channels into Somali communities for the humanitarian aid that does reach the country. Conversely, transnational Christian evangelical organizations such as World Vision and World Concern, which expressed the desire to operate in Somalia during interviews, possess sufficient funding and Western government support, but do not have adequate contacts or means of access inside the country.

The experiences of Islamic humanitarians in the War on Terror differ considerably from those of evangelical Christians, who frequently have been supported officially and unofficially in both their humanitarian and their missionizing functions. The U.S. Congress passed the International Religious Freedom Act of 1998, in order to protect the right to religious freedom worldwide. The Act, inspired by previous Senate and House resolutions concerned with the persecution of Christians, interprets religious freedom as including the right of transnational Christian groups to proselytize in non-Christian majority societies, and seeks 'to channel United States security and development assistance to governments other than those found to be engaged in gross violations of the right to freedom of religion' (USCIRF 1998). Moreover, the language of the 1998 Act appears to target Muslim-majority societies and governments in its description of where religious persecution is found: 'Though not confined to a particular region or regime, religious persecution is often particularly widespread, systematic, and heinous under totalitarian governments and in countries with militant, politicized religious majorities' (Sect. 2 (a)(6)).

The Act, therefore, can work in opposition to the Code of Conduct signed by many religious as well as secular humanitarian organizations. Whereas the Code affirms a right to practise one's religion, it also counsels against compelling others to share or advocate the same beliefs in order to receive assistance. The International Religious Freedom Act, passed four years after the Code of Conduct, affirms the goal of directing U.S.-funded assistance to those countries that do not penalize or hinder transnational (Christian) evangelism.

Despite the shaping of religious identities by the War on Terror discourse, some religious humanitarians themselves have acted to blunt the good versus bad Muslim monikers, in part through interfaith arenas for dialogue and action. Activists in Mombasa described how, in response to the 1998 bombing, Islamic groups organized interfaith efforts such as the Coast Interfaith Council of Clerics (CICC) to demonstrate that 'the coastal people' – Muslims and Christians – worked together and possessed a strong inclusive identity. Whenever there is a deportation or other government action that is perceived as unjustly dividing the community according to religion, the interfaith organizations on the coast organize peaceful protests and renew their commitment to unity.

Across Africa, interfaith groups have long been active. The Programme for Christian-Muslim Relations in Africa (PROCMURA) was founded by Christians in 1961, before decolonization was completed in many African nations, to 'promote within the churches in Africa 1) faithful Christian witness to the Gospel in an interfaith environment of Christians and Muslims, 2) constructive engagement with Muslims for peace and peaceful co-existence for the holistic development of the human person' (PROCMURA 2007). According to PROCMURA's general advisor, Johnson Mbillah, the post–11 September period 'has seen a great move and a proliferation of movements all working towards the promotion of peace and peaceful coexistence among people of religions' (Mbillah 2004, 2). This situation differs from that before 1970, when 'Christian-Muslim relations was more of a situation of "mind-your-own-business,"' that of the late 1980s and early 1990s characterized by 'several experiences of violent confrontations precipitated by a combination of political, ethnic, economic, social and religious factors,' and that of the late 1990s, when there was a 'gradual but concerted effort ... to work towards understanding Islam for the purpose of Christian witness and building bridges of understanding between adherents of the two faiths' (ibid.).

The World Conference of Religions for Peace began as an actual conference held in 1970 in Kyoto, Japan, and is now an established interfaith nongovernmental organization with strong ties to the UN and regional organizations (Religions for Peace 2004–5). It works to develop interfaith networks that represent the religious organizations of societies in countries all over the world, and brings together Muslims, Christians, Jews, Hindus, Buddhists, and others to work on conflict resolution, health (HIV/AIDS), and women's empowerment. Religions for Peace operates 'interreligious councils' in sixty-one countries, including each of the countries where I conducted interviews, and seeks to bring religious leaders together in war zones such as Iraq to resolve conflict. Another pan-African offshoot is Inter-Faith Action for Peace in Africa (IFAPA), which formed a separate organization in Johannesburg in 2002 in order to focus on peace. IFAPA brings together the 'seven major faith traditions working for peace and human rights on the African continent: African Traditional Religions, the Baha'i Faith, Buddhism, Christianity Hinduism, Islam, and Judaism,' and intentionally 'builds on African values and good practices' (IFAPA 2007, 1).

In the United States, many longstanding interfaith groups have become more active and work not only on issues of mutual understanding, but also on education, human rights, and social justice. In Southern California, for example, several interfaith organizations are active within overlapping geographical boundaries, holding educational seminars on spiritual issues, organizing youth group discussions and activities, arranging interfaith tours to the Middle East, and coalescing on immigration issues.[11]

One strategy employed increasingly by interfaith groups in the Middle East, who focus on bringing together Jews, Christians, and Muslims, is to study the similarities and differences in the narratives and interpretation of the sacred texts of the three monotheistic religions. For example, the Palestinian Academic Society for the Study of International Affairs (PASSIA), began a Religious Studies Unit in 1999, which engages in a wide variety of interfaith and multi-faith studies addressing both hermeneutical issues and contemporary political positions, making sure that a wide range of views are represented. Recent publications include a series of Jewish, Christian, and Muslim 'Statements and Positions' in its Documents on Jerusalem series, and short books on Abraham, Joseph, and Moses 'in the Three Monotheistic Faiths' that are co-authored by rabbis, imams, and priests (Rosen, Hazboun and Sway 2003; Salem, Milgrom and Neuhaus 2002; Shinan, Lahham and Sway 1999). The Interreligious Coordinating Council in Israel (affiliated with World Religions for Peace) also published *Women of the Book*, a compilation of experiences of faith and interpretations of sacred texts by Jewish, Christian, and Muslim women in East and West Jerusalem, and translated into English, Hebrew, and Arabic (ICCI 2005).

Interfaith organizations and dialogue may replicate the good versus bad Muslim dichotomy by differentiating between acceptable and unacceptable partners for dialogue based on criteria informed by the War on Terror discourse, or they may confront and attempt to break down the dichotomy by a willingness to challenge media perceptions and government policies. The coastal Kenyan interfaith organizations and PASSIA in Jerusalem are some of the most active in confronting state and public policies and perceptions, the former by reacting publicly in a unified manner to deportations, and the latter by calling into question a wide range of interpretations of each religion through its scholarly work.

Conclusions

What does the War on Terror discourse mean for religious humanitarianism? In the introduction, I make three interrelated recommendations regarding how we should assess the relationship between religion and identity: analyse religious practice (instead of simply doctrine), understand religion as providing meaningful but always incomplete ethical guidelines for action, and situate religious belief in its socio-historical and politico-economic context. Given these arguments, several conclusions obtain.

First, the political and military context produced by the War on Terror discourse tends to reify the identities of religious actors, including humanitarians, in the United States and abroad. Muslim activists, especially, chafe under the imposition of good versus bad identities that the global War on Terror attempts to create but can never support credibly. The vagaries of the terrorist appellation are constantly brought forward by Muslim activists in the United States and abroad as potentially stigmatizing all adherents of Islam. The existence of multiple and overlapping identities, as well as the fluidity of the categories used in the War on Terror discourse, mean that government policies are unable to affix reliable labels on humanitarian activists and groups. The resulting policies are indeterminate at best, and destructive at worst.

Second, the context produced by the War on Terror also shapes the organizational component of contemporary religious humanitarianism. The discourse of the War on Terror has a global reach, although it was articulated by a core of Western governments, led by the United States, and is reproduced in collaboration with selected allies in Africa, Asia, Latin America, and the Middle East. This global reach affects the distribution of religious humanitarian groups and their ability to operate. Implications for global governance are far from positive.

Specifically, policies of the U.S. government and its allies concerning humanitarian NGOs have too often equated an Islamic orientation with suspicious activities. As scholars have demonstrated, groups of any faith can promote and carry out violent acts (Juergensmeyer 2000), but in the contemporary, securitized global context, the actual practices followed and ethical guidelines promoted by Islamic as well as Christian humanitarians are often overlooked. Instead, government policies act from assumptions that link political affinities to rigid religious doctrines. When such affinities and doctrines are in accord with official perceptions of state interests, they are encouraged, as in the case of Christian evangelical organizations; when they are perceived to conflict, as in support of Muslim organizations concerned with Palestine, East Africa, or elsewhere, they are viewed with suspicion, blocked, or investigated. Consequently, in addition to unsupported accusations against individuals, we need to probe whether mutually beneficial relationships between humanitarian organizations of different faith traditions are being prevented, as well as ask what kinds of critical assistance to refugees and other endangered populations are being thwarted by this discourse.

Nevertheless, discourses such as the War on Terror, despite their global reach, are not the sole determinants of religious identities. Counter-discourses within Islamic and interfaith humanitarian and human rights communities attempt to provide alternative interpretations to constructions of good versus bad Muslims. Moreover, the imperative to address localized conflicts within the organizational frameworks provided by interfaith organizations can bring faith-based leaders together, reinforcing perceptions of the value of religious pluralism. Future research should pay attention to whether groups within the burgeoning interfaith movement merely reflect the contemporary security discourse, or whether they move the discourse towards a more nuanced analysis of Islamic as well as other types of faith-based humanitarianism.

NOTES

1 Abu-Lughod (2006) also dissects the contradictions in Western policies towards Muslim women's rights and women's rights writ large in this piece; see especially pp. 784–5.
2 Religious hybridity is a common, though under-evaluated, phenomenon, challenging essentialist understandings. Many of my students, for example, claim multiple religious identities, including Christian/Muslim, Buddhist/Christian, and many other variations. See also Lynch (2009).
3 Feminist liberation theologian Chung Hyun-Kyung (1996) describes her own syncretic identity, while Jeffrey Carlson (1994, 35–6) asserts that all religious identities, past and present, are syncretic.
4 A similar argument can be made for our secondary focus on whether religious regimes can be democratic, in that it reveals an allegedly 'secular' vision for world politics that is as teleological as any religious one.
5 The Code of Conduct was sponsored by Caritas International, Catholic Relief Services, the International Federation of Red Cross and Red Crescent Societies, the International Save the Children Alliance, the Lutheran World Federation, and Oxfam, and was taken up by organizations such as Action by Churches Together (1996). See also Lynch (2000a).
6 Interviews in Cameroon were conducted in early January 2007; in Nairobi and Kenya, from 16 June to 1 July 2007 and from 20 August to 3 September 2008; in the Middle East from 4 to 16 December 2007.
7 'Executive order 13224 and the Patriot Act maintain that grantees have default obligation to ensure that their subcontractors are not terrorists ... [T]here is no dollar threshold for mandatory vetting because any small increment of money may add up' (USAID Summer Seminar Series 2004).
8 Informal comments by Ahmad El Bendary of Islamic Relief, Workshop on Religion and International Affairs: Challenges for International NGOs, UCSB, 19 January 2008.
9 This wariness has also become evident in Web traffic on the Arab Forum listserve.
10 The U.S. government (USG) has not had success in prosecuting Islamic charities. Its case against the Holy Land Foundation, a charity created

in 1989 that was shut down by the USG in 2001, ended in a mistrial in October 2007, with allegations that the USG had engaged in a witch-hunt. See, for example, Mohder (2007). The USG has also investigated, but not brought charges against, the Palestine Children's Welfare Fund (PCWF), the Middle East Children's Alliance, and Kinder USA.

11 I counted over forty-five interfaith organizations on the Web in Southern California alone. Each city has at least one, and additional councils are based on issue-areas such as HIV/AIDS, the environment, GLBT issues, etc. The Islamic Center of Southern California, based in Los Angeles, organizes interfaith tours to the Middle East. The New Sanctuary Movement is a national movement created in the spring of 2007 to organize churches, temples, and mosques to support immigrants who face deportation and have family members living legally in the United States.

REFERENCES

Abu-Lughod, L. 2001. Do Muslim women really need saving? Anthropological reflections on cultural relativism and its others. *American Anthropology* 104:783–90.

Action by Churches Together. 1996. Mission statement. http://act-intl.org/media/documents/8115-GlobalActions2008web.pdf.

Asad, T. 1993. *Genealogies of religion: Discipline and reasons of power in Christianity and Islam.* Baltimore, MD: Johns Hopkins University Press.

Berger, J. 2003. Religious non-governmental organizations: An exploratory analysis. International Society for Third-Sector Research and the Johns Hopkins University. Unpublished.

Carlson, J. 1994. Crossan's Jesus and Christian Identity. In *Jesus and faith: A conversation on the work of John Dominic Crossan*, ed. Jeffrey Carlson and Robert A. Ludwig, 31–43. Maryknoll, NY: Orbis Books.

Casanova, J. 1994. *Public religions in the modern world.* Chicago: University of Chicago Press.

– 2007. The problem of religion and the anxieties of European secular democracy. Paper presented at the 25th Jubilee Conference on Religion and European Democracy. Jerusalem, September 2007.

de Waal, A. 1998. *Famine crimes: Politics and disaster relief in Africa.* Bloomington, IN: Indiana University Press.

Eck, D. 1994. *Encountering God: A spiritual journey from Boseman to Banares.* Boston: Beacon.

Elver, H. 2008. Secularism, human rights, and Muslim women's headscarves. Unpublished paper.

Fisher, W. 2008. Muslim charities, guilty until proven innocent? *InFocus News*. http://www.infocusnews.net/content/view/20066/484/.

Göle, N. 1997. Secularism and Islamism: The making of elites and counter-elites. *Middle East Journal* 51 (1): 46–58.

Hammer, J. 2007. The African front: Have aggressive post-9/11 policies fomented the very sectarianism they were meant to fight? *New York Times Magazine*, 23 December.

Hirsch, S. 2006. *In the moment of greatest calamity: Terrorism, grief, and a victim's quest for justice*. Princeton: Princeton University Press.

Hyun-Kyung, C. 1996. *The wisdom of mothers knows no boundaries*. Women's perspectives: Gospel and cultures. Pamphlet 14. Geneva: World Council of Churches.

Inter-Faith Action for Peace in Africa (IFAPA). 2007. Geneva.

Interreligious Coordinating Council in Israel (ICCI). 2005. *Women of the book: A Jerusalem collage*. Jerusalem: Interreligious Coordinating Council in Israel.

Juergensmeyer, M. 2000. *Terror in the mind of God: The global rise of religious violence*. Berkeley: University of California Press.

Lynch, C. 1998. Security of the people, for the people, by the people? *Northwestern Review of International Affairs* 1.

– 2000a. Acting on belief: Christian perspectives on suffering and violence. *Ethics & International Affairs* 14 (1): 83–97.

– 2000b. Dogma, praxis, and religious perspectives on multiculturalism. *Millennium: Journal of International Studies* 29:741–59.

– 2009. A neo-Weberian approach to religion in international politics. *International Theory* 1 (3): 381–408.

Mamdani, Mahmood. 2004. *Good Muslim, bad Muslim: America, the Cold War, and the roots of terror*. New York: Doubleday.

Mbillah, J. 2004. Christian–Muslim relations in Africa: Where we have come from, where we are and where we go from here. *PROCMURA PRICA* 61/62:2.

Mohder, G. 2007. Holy Land Foundation trial spells defeat for government. *InFocus News*, 6 November. http://www.infocusnews.net/content/view/17443/135.

Odhiambo, E. 2004. What we can do together, let us not do it differently from each other: Christian and Muslim women speak out. *PROCMURA PRICA* 61/62:21–2.

Petersen, M.J. 2008. *Social welfare activism in Jordan: Democratisation in disguise?* Copenhagen: Danish Institute for International Studies.

PROCMURA. 2007. Programme for Christian–Muslim Relations in Africa (brochure). Nairobi.

Religions for Peace. 2004–5. *Annual report.* http://religionsforpeace.org/resources/reports/rfp-2005.html.

Rosen, D., L. Hazboun, and M. Abu Sway. 2003. *Moses in the three monotheistic faiths.* Jerusalem: Palestinian Academic Society for the Study of International Affairs.

Salem, I.A., J. Milgrom, and D. Neuhaus. 2002. *Joseph in the three monotheistic faiths.* PASSIA: Jerusalem.

Salvatore, A., and M. LeVine, eds. 2005. *Religion, social practice, and contested hegemonies: Reconstructing the public sphere in Muslim majority societies.* New York: Palgrave Macmillan.

Shakman Hurd, E. 2007. *The politics of secularism in international relations.* Princeton: Princeton University Press.

Shinan, A., M. Lahham, and M. Abu Sway. 1999. *Abraham in the three monotheistic faiths.* Jerusalem: Palestinian Academic Society for the Study of International Affairs.

Sparre, S.L. 2008. *Muslim youth organisations in Egypt: Actors of reform and development?* Copenhagen: Danish Institute for International Studies.

Sparre, S.L., and M.J. Petersen. 2007. Islam and civil society: Case studies from Jordan and Egypt. DIIS Report 13. City: Publisher.

USAID. 2004. USAID's role in the war on terrorism. Summer Seminar Series. Comments by Jeff Denale. http://www.usaid.gov/km/seminars/2004/0810.html.

USCIRF. 1998. Response to query: United States Commission on International Religious Freedom. International Religious Freedom Act of 1998. http://www.uscirf.gov/about-uscirf/authorizing-legislation.html.

World Conference of Religions for Peace. 2004–2005. *Annual report.* New York: World Conference of Religions for Peace.

7 Extremism and Military Intervention in South Asia: Indian Muslims and Sri Lankan Tamils

MANUS I. MIDLARSKY

Introduction

Why is it that, on the one hand, for all the communal violence that has plagued Hindu-Muslim relations in India, that violence had virtually no influence on international conflict? On the other hand, the Sinhalese-Tamil disturbances yielded an Indian intervention in Sri Lanka, ultimately resulting in the suicide terror assassination of the Indian leader Rajiv Gandhi by a Sri Lankan Tamil militant. The Indian intervention was not motivated by a political doctrine such as that of George W. Bush, but represented a direct response to the escalating violence in Sri Lanka and the domestic reaction to that violence within the Indian state of Tamil Nadu. Realpolitik of a traditional sort entailing interstate relations and attention to public opinion within a functioning democracy lay at the root of that intervention.

Significant here is the absence of any religious motivation for the suicide attack on Rajiv Ghandi; both perpetrator and victim were Hindus. Also notable is the fact that a large Muslim population has not engaged in widespread terrorist activity, while a predominantly Hindu population in neighbouring Sri Lanka has done so, even when the targets were Hindus. A major conclusion of this study is that in understanding the etiology of South Asian terror, religion plays at most a minor role, and as we shall see, given certain benign interpretations, can even play a positive role in fostering communal cooperation. Thus, this chapter suggests an important limitation on the use of religion as an explanation of terrorist activity. While many acts of violence have been cloaked in the language of religion, confessional faith itself may be irrelevant when the force of historical trajectories and psychological reactions to them take hold. Understanding these processes will require an examination of the historical trajectories of both India and Sri Lanka, especially in regard to their contending communities.

The explanation of political extremism in South Asia is a goal of this inquiry. To that end, both the presence and absence of extremism need to be analysed. Accordingly, political extremism is understood as the will to power by a social movement in the service of a political program typically at variance with that supported by existing state authorities, and for which individual liberties are to be curtailed in the name of collective goals, including the mass killing of those who would actually or potentially disagree with that program. Restrictions on individual freedom in the interests of the collectivity and the willingness to kill massively are central to this definition; note also the importance of the state.

First, I will present the model of ephemeral gains or ascendancies that has been used to explain the origins of political extremism across a wide variety of cases (Midlarsky 2011). Second, the Indian historical record is reviewed, suggesting the nonconformity of the Indian Muslim population to that model. I also include the potential influence of Indian Muslim thinkers. They are important, for in the relative absence of extremist violence, we also need to understand ideational sources of that absence. Concrete instances of communal cooperation between Hindus and Muslims are given, based in part on principles suggested by these thinkers. Next, I turn to the historical trajectory of Sri Lanka, emphasizing the Jaffna Tamil community that has given rise to the Liberation Tigers of Tamil Eelam (LTTE), an extremist group liberally utilizing suicide terrorism. Reinforcing ephemera are found that indicate the theory's applicability. Finally, the danger to regional – even international – stability in the form of military intervention is suggested by these ephemera, especially if they are reinforcing.

An ephemeral gain occurs when a severe loss (territory, population, livelihood), typically perceived as a catastrophe, is preceded by a period of societal gain, which in turn is preceded by a period of subordination. Ephemeral gains are reinforced when they occur in successive time periods.

Surprise, Vividness, and a Diachronic Model

Emotional reactions to a sudden loss or the threat of imminent loss can yield extremist consequences. As shown in figure 7.1, the diachronic model is based on a loss (often territorial and almost always surprising)

Figure 7.1: Changes in authority space over time

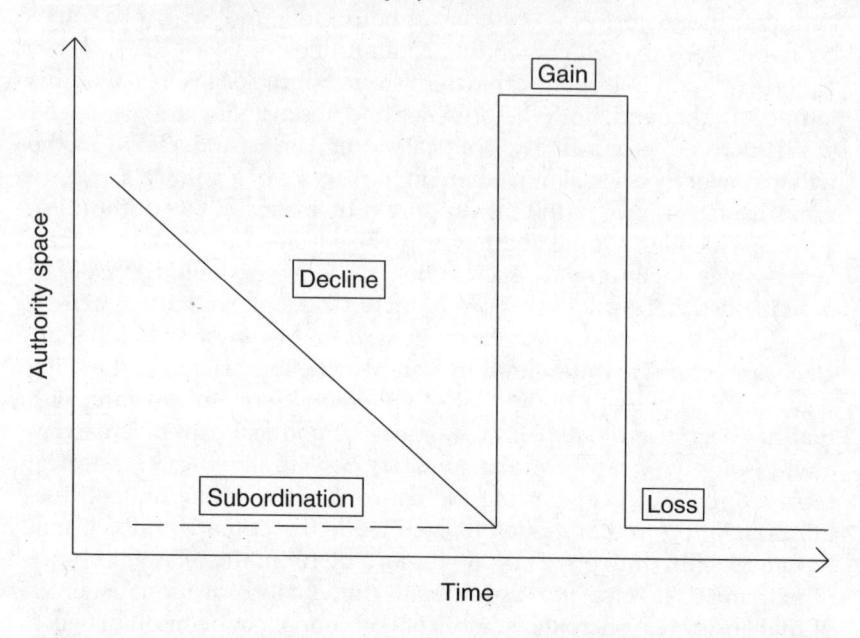

[Figure: A graph with "Authority space" on the y-axis and "Time" on the x-axis. A line labeled "Decline" slopes downward from upper left to a low point, with "Subordination" marked along the bottom dashed line. Then a vertical rise labeled "Gain" leads to a high plateau, followed by a vertical drop labeled "Loss".]

that is preceded by a gain, which followed a still earlier period of subordination. Territorially based authority spaces are frequently encountered, as in the distance from a central (capital) city that its authority extends. However, there are also other forms of authority, especially in colonial contexts that do not allow indigenously organized territorially based authority.

A stark contrast and surprise at the sudden change in fortune is important because of their vividness. Both emotional pain and satisfaction can be multiplied substantially by the experience of surprise (Elster 2004, 160). Or, as Loewenstein and Lerner (2003, 624) suggest, 'People respond with greater emotional intensity to outcomes that are surprising – that is, unexpected.' The emotional intensity associated with surprise therefore can lead to vivid information – which is most likely to be acted upon rapidly (Mele 2003, 165). Because of the emotional intensity and consequent vividness, a sense of urgency is imparted, or as Nico Frijda (1986, 206) puts it, 'Urgency is the irreflexive counterpart of felt emotional intensity.' Urgency is demanded without the contemplation and introspection associated with reflexivity (ibid. 186–7). Anger can also independently lead to a sense of urgency (Elster 2004, 154).

In the case of a previous loss prior to the existing one, an individual can explain the current circumstance by referring to the earlier one – perhaps a syndrome of loss stemming from episodic battles against overwhelming odds. Effectively, nothing different had really happened in the second instance that requires explanation. But in the case of an earlier gain prior to the current loss, especially if substantial, the present loss becomes puzzling, even frightening and then angering, for there must be a special reason for its occurrence. Urgent action is then required against the putative offender to redress the loss, or at least to act quickly to prevent further loss.

Figure 7.1 maps the changes in authority space, both increase and decrease, over time. Authority space is understood as the proportion of society over which governmental influence legitimately extends. Most spectacular were the contractions of authority space occurring after the First World War when the Austro-Hungarian and Ottoman empires disintegrated and imperial Germany was truncated. But there are important varieties of authority space in which societal groups have 'captured' a particular governmental authority space, and on the basis of custom, expect to continue occupying an authoritative position within a governmental sector. As we shall see, the traditional increased Tamil dominance of the Ceylonese British civil service is a case in point, and its loss constituted a major contraction of that authority space.

Equally telling in its ultimate impact is the period prior to the increase in authority space. This period is not frequently considered but is nevertheless important. If the period before the increase consists of a long decline or remains at a consistently small or nonexistent national authority space, then reversion to that condition may be a major fear. The subsequent ascendant portion of the trajectory can then be seen to be an exceptional blip in national history, if in turn followed by the downturn. Note that the figure here is not a smooth one, in order to signify that the increases or decreases in authority space take place abruptly at a war's end or independence of a colony, and not as the result of a continuous process of change. The dashed line represents a constant period of subordination that can have the same consequence as a steady decline. The figure does not show small changes in authority space that indeed can occur but are dwarfed by the changes in authority space resulting from expansions or contractions of territorial domains, or changes in sovereignty.

Finally, an important buttressing of the diachronic model emerges from prospect theory. This theory tells us that losses are more highly valued than gains, or put another way, that the lost entity is psychologically more valued than an entirely identical entity that is gained (Kahneman and Tversky 1979, 2000; Levy 2000). Experimental evidence has consistently demonstrated the asymmetry between losses and gains, even to the extent that, in contrast to gains, losses can generate extreme responses. Losses as the result of a shrinking spatial environment, therefore, may have a magnified role in human consciousness, out of all proportion to their real-world consequences. When we add this asymmetry between gains and losses originating in prospect theory alone to the surprise, vividness, and emotional intensity stemming from the contrast between earlier gains and later losses, these losses can be deeply consequential. Losses also are associated with risky behaviour, often associated with extremist movements.

The Salience of Loss

Anger has been found to be associated with loss (Stein, Trabasso, and Liwag 1993). Equally important, anger has been shown to be a significant emotional response to injustice (Haidt 2003). Aristotle in his *Rhetoric* (2.2) defined anger as 'an impulse, accompanied by pain, to a conspicuous revenge for a conspicuous slight directed without justification towards what concerns oneself or toward what concerns one's friends.' Commenting on Aristotle's definition, Haidt notes that 'anger is not just a response to insults, in which case it would be just a guardian of self-esteem. Anger is a response to *unjustified* insults, and anger can be triggered on behalf of one's friends, as well as oneself' (856). Thus, anger is categorized by Haidt as one of the 'moral emotions,' those 'that are linked to the interests or welfare either of society as a whole or at least of persons other than the judge or agent' (853).

People in a state of anger are 'more apt to blame others for mishaps that occurred' (Berkowitz 2003, 816). Further, persons of an ethnicity different from one's own are more likely to be targeted (Bodenhausen, Sheppard, and Kramer 1994; DeSteno et al. 2004). Anger in response to loss also has been associated with the desire to obtain restitution or compensation (Stein, Trabasso, and Liwag 1993) or revenge (Frijda 1994; Nisbett and Cohen 1996).

Following this normative theme, Frijda (1986) amplifies: anger is provoked by a violation of what 'ought to be' in the agent's view. Thus, a normative order has been violated and thus justifies a challenge to this changing of the rules by the offending party. That normative order could be based on religion in which, for example, Osama bin Laden and his followers perceive a gross violation of Islam in the presence of Christians and Jews in proximity to the holy sites of Mecca and Medina at the time of the 1991 Gulf War.

'Anger implies nonacceptance of the present event as necessary or inevitable; and it implies that the event is amenable to being changed' (Frijda 1986, 199). Or, as a consequence of loss, 'anger often carries with it a desire not only to reinstate the goal, but also to remove or change the conditions that lead to goal blockage in the first place' (Stein, Trabasso, and Liwag 1993: 291–4). Thus, loss (or the threat of imminent loss) generates anger at the injustice of the loss, which in turn can be mobilized by extremist groups that seek not only to redress the loss (or counter the threat) but also can direct their anger at helpless civilian targets who are somehow implicated, often in the most indirect fashion, in the origins of the loss (Midlarsky 2005a, 2005b). Recent findings indicate that even routine partisan activity, as in an American presidential election, can generate emotional responses. When subjects were confronted with information that was inconsistent with their partisan leanings, MRI scanners indicated that the 'cold reason' regions of the cortex were relatively quiet. Instead, emotions guided their reactions (Westen et al. 2006).

An additional element suggests near universality for an authoritarian response to normative threat. Defining an authoritarian predisposition as a human characteristic akin to a personality trait, and an authoritarian response as an expression of the intolerance of difference, Stenner (2005) finds that normative threats to the unity of a collectivity activate the authoritarian predisposition.

Among all of the variables she considered, authoritarianism was found to explain by far the largest percentage of the variance in intolerance of difference (Stenner 2005, 131). More generally, Stenner concludes that 'much intolerance of different races, beliefs, and behaviors is driven … by a fundamental and overwhelming desire to establish and defend *some* collective order of oneness and sameness. In short, the entire defensive arsenal is fueled by the need to identify, glorify, privilege, and reward "us," and whatever beliefs and behaviors make us "us," and to differentiate, denigrate, disadvantage and punish "them," and whatever beliefs and behaviors make them "them"' (277–8).

Fear can easily be generated by loss. Following Witte (1992, 331), fear is understood as 'a negatively-valenced emotion, accompanied by a high level of arousal, and is elicited by a threat that is perceived to be significant and personally relevant.' When the loss and consequent fear entail a likely reversion to an earlier period of subordination, then they can be even more consequential.

India

Let us now examine the tendencies toward extremism, or lack of same, among the upward of 130 million Muslims of India, the third-largest population of Muslims after those of Indonesia and Pakistan. A question immediately arises: excluding the unique circumstances of Kashmir, why has this Muslim population not engaged in terrorism as have those from Saudi Arabia (al Qaeda), Egypt (Muslim Brotherhood and Egyptian Islamic Group), Algeria (Salafist Group for Preaching and Combat), or even Britain (al Muhajiroun)?

An immediate answer lies in the obvious nonconformity of Indian Muslim history to the pattern of figure 7.1. The Muslim population, although subordinate under the British, has continued in a minority status, in certain respects (e.g., economically) also subordinate to the majority Hindus after Indian independence in 1947. Certainly there has been no Muslim ascendancy, ephemeral or otherwise, and losses have been incurred but sporadically, such as the 1984 intrusion of the Indian Supreme Court in Islamic personal law, the riots and Muslim deaths after the destruction of the Babri Mosque in 1992 (Sikand 2004, 41–2), or the rise to power of the Hindu nationalist Bharatiya Janata Party (BJP). The workings of Indian democracy have mostly reversed these losses, as in the limits imposed on the government's ability to regulate personal Islamic law, the prevention of additional attacks on Muslim holy places, and the decline in the political fortunes of the BJP. There is still communal strife (Varshney 2002), but it is generally local and does not reflect state policy – the most dangerous condition for threatened minorities.

Certainly all is not well in the political and especially economic circumstances of Indian Muslims, but there is little or no evidence for ephemeral gains in the recent past. The closest intimation of such a condition was found in the somewhat greater proportion of Muslims relative to Hindus in the early colonial Indian civil service. But after the great mutiny-rebellion of 1857 instigated in part by Muslim sepoys, quotas were established in the governmental service that began eliminating that disproportion (Robb 2002, 189). By the turn of the twentieth century that disproportion had largely disappeared. Thus, there is little memory of this more than century-old small advantage over Hindus. Even more important, there were no later such advantages for Muslims that could call to mind that earlier condition.

Pre-Independence

The roots of the relative passivity of the Muslim community go deeper still and suggest two different paths for the Hindu and Muslim communities. The first of these is state-centred. While Mughal (essentially Muslim, while strictly meaning Mongol) power was in rapid decline beginning in the early eighteenth century, the Maratha (Hindu) kingdom was in its ascendancy. The last of the great Mughal leaders, Aurangzeb (ruled 1658–1707), expanded the empire and imposed a much more stringent Islam than had his predecessors, but some of his conquests were transitory (Assam), and his brutality as well as attempts to convert large numbers of Hindus led to insurgencies that would sap the imperial power. By the end of his reign, the Mughal empire was on the verge of a long and steady decline. By 1739, the government was so weak that it was virtually powerless to prevent the invasion by Nader Shah, an Iranian adventurer (Kulke and Rothermund 2004, 214). He inflicted defeat after defeat on the Mughals, sacked Delhi, massacring thirty thousand in the process, and annexed Kabul province to Iran. Ultimately, the much-diminished Mughal successor of Oudh in northern India succumbed to British power in 1801.

While the Mughal empire was being humiliated by Iranians, the Marathas were reaching the zenith of their ascendancy. The Maratha hero Shiivaji (1627–80) waged successful war against the Mughals, among others, establishing the basis of Maratha power in western India (Kulke and Rothermund 2004, 208–14). By 1740 and the death of Baji Rao, the last of the great Maratha leaders, the kingdom had spread all over India. In 1785, the Marathas even captured the Mughal capital, Delhi, which with a small territory surrounding it was all that remained of the once extensive empire. Ultimately, the Marathas also were too weak to successfully oppose British military force and finally succumbed in 1818, but only after two wars that taxed the limits of the British army in India.

This differential trajectory between Hindu and Muslim communities is reflected in the second of our two paths, the formation of organized political action under the British Raj. The Indian National Congress had its first meeting in 1885 in Bombay, significantly a principal city of the old Maratha lands (McLeod 2002, 76–99). Also significant, perhaps much more so, was the predominance of Hindu delegates. While fifty-four of the delegates were Hindu, only two were Muslim, the remainder mainly Parsi and Jain. In the Muslim view, Hindu dominance of the Congress movement would continue even after strenuous efforts of Hindus such as Gandhi to eliminate or at least attenuate that perception. Gandhi even adopted as his own the All-India Khilafat movement (Minault 1982; Niemeijer 1972, 83–4), a Muslim effort to revive the caliphate that was eliminated in 1924 by Kemal Atatürk, but to no avail. This initial perception of Hindu dominance was to yield the formation of the All-India Muslim League in 1906 (McLeod 2002, 97–8). Of course, the Congress movement was to result in the formation of a secular Indian government that would later have strong Hindu overtones, while the Muslim League would eventuate in the formation of a nominally Muslim Pakistan under Mohammad Ali Jinnah, which would later become increasingly fundamentalist under his successors.

Crucial here is the relatively powerless state of Muslims within India beginning at the end of the eighteenth century and continuing throughout the British Raj. The formation of Pakistan was intended to ameliorate that subordinate condition and was partially successful within the borders of Pakistan, despite the lost wars with India. But within the borders of India, notwithstanding the striking accomplishments of individual Indian Muslims (some of the richest men in India, leading movie stars), communal subordination persists to this day.

One could leave it at that and assert that the absence of a principal antecedent of political extremism, an ephemeral gain, explains the absence of that extremism. But that would be too cavalier an approach, for we also need to understand why any sort of generalized extremism is not expected even among Islamist elements of the Indian population. As a first cut, we must note a key difference between Indian Muslims who collectively do not govern a state, and others such as Arabs or Persians who do. Indeed the origins of Islamic theology that claims no distinction between politics and religion are coterminous with the rise of Arab (or Arab/Persian) states in the form of the Umayyad and Abbasid empires (Hodgson 1974). Islamic jurisprudence was developed mostly within the context of Muslim political supremacy. Thus, according to Zaki Badawi, a leading Muslim scholar residing in Britain, "'Muslim theology offers, up to the present, no systematic formulations of the status of being in a minority'" (qtd in Sikand 2004, 8).

Clearly, British Muslim extremist groups such as al Muhajiroun had set as their goal the Islamization of Britain, or at least the conversion to Islam of the Queen and royal family (Wiktorowicz 2005), but they have been a tiny minority of British Muslims, without widespread support. For most Muslims in the relatively recent status of minorities without direct political power, the expectation of Islamic governance is virtually nonexistent. India offers up a wide range of potential responses to this minority status, all of them short of governmental domination. And here lies the crux of the matter. Without the realistic expectation of state governance, there is little connection with one of the principal tenets of current Islamic radicalism – restoration of the caliphate, dissolved in 1924 by Kemal Atatürk (Habeck 2006, 151). Once, as we have seen, the caliphate or Khilafat movement was strong in India, but that was before establishment of an Islamic state in the region, Pakistan, and the independence of India. With these emergent states, one of them explicitly Islamic, the Khilafat movement, already in decline, virtually disappeared. Removing 'apostate' Muslim rulers in predominantly Islamic countries like Egypt or Saudi Arabia is another goal of these Islamist movements, but again has little salience for the majority of India's Muslims.

Figure 7.2 depicts the contraction of authority space during the Mughal decline of the eighteenth century, and the subsequent relatively powerless condition of India's Muslims during the period of the British Raj and contemporary India.

Indian Muslim Thinkers

What does concern the majority of India's Muslim thinkers and writers? This is exactly the kind of question, as pointed out in the exegesis of 'thick religion' in chapter 3, that is overlooked time and again in attempting to identify the role of faith in inter-group relations. As might be expected, the confrontation between tradition and modernity is of major importance today, as it once was at the time of the nineteenth-century writings of Sayyed Ahmad Khan, who attempted to reconcile Islam with the demands of contemporary life. He argued that Islam was compatible with reason and with 'nature.' Khan was very much an advocate of science and positivism. In 1877, he created a Westernizing Muslim College at Aligarh, now the Aligarh Muslim University (Brown 2000, 94–5).

A contemporary Indian public intellectual is Asghar 'Ali Engineer, who interprets the Qur'an in liberal ways. He understands the Qur'an

Figure 7.2: Changes in authority space of Indian Muslims, early eighteenth century to present*

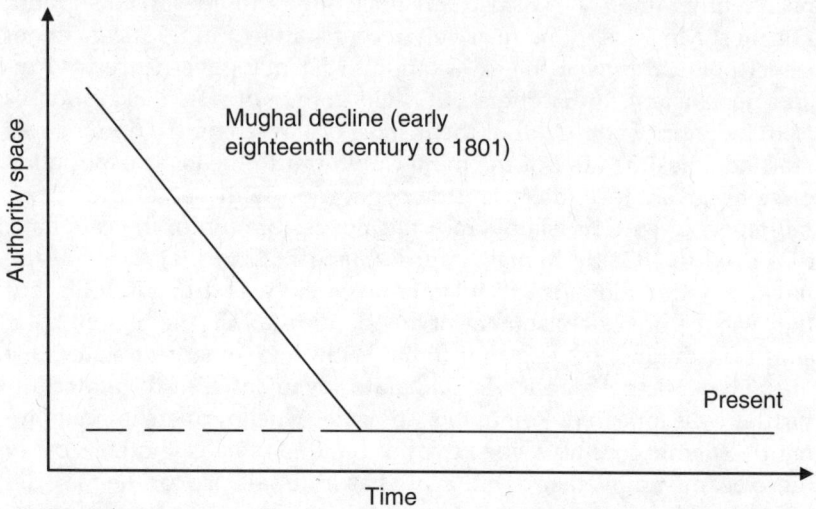

[Figure: graph with Authority space on y-axis and Time on x-axis, showing a steep declining line labeled "Mughal decline (early eighteenth century to 1801)" and a low dashed horizontal line labeled "Present"]

*Not to scale

not to be a book of specific laws, but 'above all, a call for a just social order based on a new value system, and the institutional forms that express these values can, and indeed must, radically differ across space and time' (Sikand 2004, 15). Engineer understands that the fundamental values of the Qur'an are eternally valid, but specific laws do not possess that validity, for they are more than anything a reflection of societal need at a given point in space and time. Legal context-specificity is a cornerstone of his approach. Hence, the pronouncements of the traditional 'ulama (Islamic legal scholars) or fiqh (Islamic legal rulings) represent a 'fossilized religion' and have given rise to a 'feudalized Islam' incapable of dealing with modernity. These observations recall one of the principal arguments from chapter 6, which asserted that religious beliefs should be understood in terms of guidelines rather than rigid rules of order.

A significant component of modernity is pluralism, especially in the Indian context. Instead of the monochromatic Islam of the Arabian peninsula as Islam rose to power, and which gave rise to much of the body of Islamic law, the religious diversity of the contemporary period must be addressed. (This observation follows on the complex portrayal in chapter 4 of human rights in the Islamic world.) Hence, interpretive dialogue is essential. Moreover, all religions are to be addressed as equals, for the Qur'an is clear on the lack of 'compulsion in religion' and that people vie with each other 'in virtuous deeds' (qtd in Sikand 2004, 21). The fact that religious diversity exists must be part of God's plan and must be respected, for he must have ordained its presence on this Earth. Accordingly, 'he [Engineer] writes that, while Islam stresses justice, Buddhism stresses non-violence and Christianity love. By dialoguing with Buddhists and Christians, then, Muslims can gain new insights that can be used to evolve new interpretations and understanding of their own religion' (ibid., 22).

Engineer even argues that Hinduism, although polytheistic and filled with statues and images (and therefore utterly opposed to Islam's rigorous monotheism and prohibition of idolatry), nevertheless has theistic cores that must be respected by Muslims. An emphasis on peace, justice, and equality can provide a common framework for dialogue among all major faiths of the Indian subcontinent. The idea of an Islamic state, however, has no place in this dialogue, for it is a product of another time and another place. The best that Muslims in India can hope for is a state, nominally secular, that is neutral toward all religions. Although reviled by many Islamists, democracy is the best protector for any religion that potentially can be mistreated by the state. Engineer points to the Treaty of Medina between the Prophet and his followers on the one hand, and Jews and pagan Arabs on the other, that defined all of them as part of one 'umma. The idea of a single Muslim 'nationality' (a more restricted meaning of 'umma) therefore is unacceptable, for people of many different faiths can be part of the same nation, as in the Qur'an. Clearly, Engineer has an interpretation of Islam very different from that of Islamists, especially of the radical variety.

Another addition to this corpus of writing comes from the prolific pen of Sayyed Abul Hasan 'Ali Nadwi. He was descended from a line of Islamic scholars; even his mother had memorized the entire Qur'an. Writing in the colonial period, he analysed the state of Islam in the Arab world, exhorting Arabs to return to their Islamic roots. He also criticized pan-Arabism, communism, and nationalism as false ideologies seeking to displace the pre-eminence of Islam. 'However, he stood apart from most Islamists by arguing that the Islamic political order could come about in India only in some remotely distant future. Rather than directly struggling for it at the present, he believed that the Muslims of the country should focus their energies in trying to build what he saw as a truly Islamic society, on the basis of which alone could an ideal Islamic political order come into being' (Sikand 2004, 33).

Nadwi also opposed the creation of Pakistan as a separate state for Muslims. Only in a united India could Muslims continue their required missionary activity. Although initially active in the Jama'at-i Islami founded by Maulana Sayyed Abul 'Ala Maududi, Nadwi became disillusioned with its emphasis on the struggle to found an Islamic state and with the apparent 'cult of personality' that grew up around Maududi. 'At Maududi's hands, he [Nadwi] says, "God" (ilah), "the Sustainer" (rabb), "Religion" (din) and "Worship" (ibadat) have all been reduced to political concepts, suggesting that Islam is simply about political power and that the relationship between God and human beings is only that between an All-Powerful King and His subjects. However, Nadwi says, this relationship is also one of "love" and "realization of the Truth," which is far more comprehensive than what Maududi envisages' (Sikand 2004, 36). Instead of this preoccupation with politics, 'love' and 'the realization of Truth' are to be emphasized. Only a 'silent revolution' is conceivable in order to 'prepare people's minds' for a genuinely Islamic government in the distant future.

After Indian independence, in contrast to most Islamists, Nadwi was willing to accept democracy and secularism in the face of potential Hindu extremism that could deprive Indian Muslims of their civil rights, including freedom of worship. He feared 'cultural genocide' of the Muslim population in which Islam would disappear. Cooperation with Hindus was a means of preventing this outcome. He became active politically, proclaiming that Muslims were indeed the khair ummat (the best community) on the basis of their beliefs and rigorous observance. For this purpose, Nadwi, along with other leading Muslim figures, established the All-India Muslim Consultative Assembly in 1964. Only in a climate of peace and cooperation could Muslims best make their religion inviting to the potential Hindu or Christian convert. When the Babri mosque controversy erupted in the early 1990s, Nadwi counselled restraint and dialogue, instead of retaliation and conflict. When Hindu temples were attacked after the destruction of the Babri mosque, he bitterly criticized the actions of these militants.

Summarizing his own views, Nadwi stated, 'If you make Muslims one hundred per cent mindful of their supererogatory prayers (tahajjud guzar), making them all very pious, but leave them cut off from the wider environment, ignorant of where the country is heading and of how hatred is being stirred up in the country against them, then, leave alone the supererogatory prayers, it will soon become impossible for Muslims to say even their five daily prayers. If you make Muslims strangers in their own land, blind them to social realities and cause them to remain indifferent to the radical changes taking place in the country and the new laws that are being imposed and the new ideas that are ruling people's hearts and minds, then let alone [acquiring] leadership [of the country], it will become difficult for Muslims to even ensure their own existence' (qtd in Sikand 2004, 43). At the same time, he exhorted Muslims to observe their faith rigorously and never compromise it for social or political expediency.

The last of our Islamic thinkers to react strongly to the Muslim minority status within India was Maulana Wahiduddin Khan. He, too, was influenced by Maududi and the Jama'at-i Islami. But like Nadwi, he became disillusioned. According to Khan, Maududi was more influenced by Western imperialism than by any authentic interpretation of Islam. A political understanding of Islam had emerged in his thinking to counter the spread of Western influence. Very much in agreement with the theory offered here, 'this understanding of Islam Khan now began to see as a result of *a sense of loss*, of defeat suffered by the Muslims at the hands of the West, rather than as emanating from a genuine spiritual quest' (Sikand 2004, 50–1; emphasis added).

Khan became increasingly concerned with Hindu-Muslim relations in India, advocating a personalized Islamic faith and efforts at individual reform. Accordingly, like other faiths, Islam is prepared to welcome modernity, pluralism, and inter-faith dialogue. Muslims must leave their ghettos and shed their 'persecution complex' and separatist thinking. Following the Islamic tradition, the Prophet Muhammad is said to have insisted on 'respect for every human being' and required Muslims to 'honour one of another creed' (Sikand 2004, 54). When the Muslim community was small and without much power, the Prophet sought peaceful relations with surrounding communities that would allow the propagation of the faith. The situation of Muslims in India as a minority is directly analogous.

> Khan repeatedly refers to what he calls the 'Hudaibiyah principle' as a model for Muslims to follow. In the nineteenth year of his prophethood Muhammad entered into a ten-year no-war treaty with his Meccan Qur'aish opponents at Hudaibiyah, which contained what some of his followers thought were conditions particularly humiliating for the Muslims. The Qur'an, however, announced it as a 'great victory' (fateh mubin), and

so it proved itself to be. The Qur'aish refused to allow the Prophet to sign his name as 'the Messenger of Allah' on the document of the agreement and, instead, forced him to write simply 'Muhammad, son of Abdullah.' Further, they did not allow the Muslims to enter Mecca that year to perform the 'umra, and insisted that if any Meccan Muslim was to take refuge in Medina, he would have to be returned to them. Yet the Prophet accepted these seemingly humiliating conditions, for he had, Khan says, a 'deep missionary plan' in mind. Peace with the Qur'aish opened up new possibilities of daw'ah [peaceful struggle for the propagation of Islam] work for the Muslims, as a result of which in a few years' time not just the Qur'aish alone, but, in fact, almost all of Arabia, turned Muslim. This shows, Khan argues, that 'the power of peace is stronger than the power of violence,' a valuable lesson for the Muslims of contemporary India to profit from. (Sikand 2004, 57)

Further, Khan argues for abandoning the 'Islam of pride' and recovering the 'Islam of humility and balance.' A position of modesty is desirable. In this way, like the Prophet in Mecca, Islam would turn out to be ultimately victorious. Opposed to an Islamic state like Pakistan, Khan argued that the focus of Islam should be the 'inner transformation' of the individual. Then and only then, as a gift from God, an Islamic state might come into being. To attempt to establish such a state by force is effectively to usurp a privilege for God alone. According to Khan, 'This principle of peaceful "gradualism" tempered with "pragmatism" is seen as being in complete contrast to the efforts of Islamist groups to establish an Islamic state by force. Religiously sanctified violence, Khan believes, has only given Islam a "religion of peace and mercy," a bad name, making it synonymous for many with violence and terror, thus gravely damaging the cause of Islamic da'wah' (Sikand 2004, 64). Science and scientific rationality also should be part of Islam, although revelation is always superior to reason.

Clearly, these Indian Muslim thinkers establish a paradigm for majority-minority relations when Muslims are in the minority. Even under historic Muslim rule, India 'was deemed to be *Dar-ul-Islam*, an abode of peace. According to the jurists, jihad could only be waged against a *Dar-ul-Harb*, an abode of war' (Jalal 2008, 15). Islam is to be understood as a faith, not as a form of identity associated with the state. The most important element here is the absence of a realistic expectation of state formation without some sort of cataclysmic outcome. Failing the 'Armageddon' alternative, gradualism is required. Even if this program were to fail in its ultimate purpose of converting all non-Muslims in the Indian subcontinent, still this goal would continue as a major preoccupation of the Muslim community. In the collective view of these thinkers, this alternative is vastly preferable to the mass political violence effectively advocated by radical Islamists.

Communal Violence and Cooperation

Although radical Islamism has not taken strong hold in the Indian subcontinent, with the possible exception of Kashmir, violence has occurred principally in the form of Hindu-Muslim communal rioting. This is not to say that this violence is trivial, or that political extremist tendencies in the form of the Bharatiya Janata Party (BJP), or the Jama'at-i Islami do not exist. (The August 2007 bombings in Hyderabad killing at least forty-two people were said by unnamed Indian security officials to be the work in part of Harkut-ul-Jihad-al-Islami, a Bangladeshi organization seeking to establish Islamic rule in Bangladesh. In the past, Indians have been targeted by this group [Farooq 2007]. In the radical Islamist view, these attacks are justified where Muslims had formerly ruled, as they were by the nizam of Hyderabad prior to independence [Stein 1998, 367].) Instead, even when communal violence has been on the upswing, as Varshney (2002, 95–102) chronicles in great detail, it is generally not the result of extremist tendencies but of inter-communal relations, often of a routinized political nature.

The state is crucial, not so much in daily practice, but in the imagination of the potential perpetrators of violence. In the case of al Qaeda or other radical Islamist groups, the caliphate as the sovereign political expression of authentic Islam must be recreated. And when Osama bin Laden called Mullah Omar of the Taliban a 'caliph,' it was his recognition that Taliban rule in Afghanistan was an incarnation of authentic Islamic governance that could be extended to other Muslim societies. In India, on the other hand, there is little room for Muslim speculation on the existence of a future caliphate. That expectation had already been manifested in the Khilafat movement of 1919–24 (Hasan and Pernau 2005) that petered out without significant immediate consequence. A long-term consequence may have been the movement to found Pakistan as an independent state begun in the 1930s (Niemeijer 1972, 178), but having established one such state, it was extremely unlikely that another could be founded.

More important is the common perception of Muslim neighbourhoods in India as mini-Pakistans. According to Rowena Robinson (2005, 13), 'In the north Indian plains, it is common to hear a man going to the toilet – that impure *sandas* often outside or behind the home – refer to his visit as "going to Pakistan." In the brutal communal discourses we have been made to countenance, more so over the last decades, the Indian Muslim *is* a Pakistani, a scorned being who should "go to Pakistan." Indeed, as the social geography of Indian cities manifests, the Muslim in fact *lives* in Pakistan, *many* Pakistans, *mini* Pakistans.'

And the space allotted to Muslim neighbourhoods has been contracting, especially after communal riots involving Hindus and Muslims. In many areas of India, Muslims have experienced a contraction of space, especially after the occurrence of communal strife. The following example is taken from Jogeshwari (East), where

> Muslims have been systematically pushed, over the last two decades, into a smaller and smaller settlement area at the peak of a hill, surrounded by Hindu settlements all around and having almost no access routes out of their pocket except through these Hindu areas. In the 1970s, Muslims and Hindus were interspersed throughout the area as a whole, though there were larger and smaller religion-based pockets here and there. Each riot has, however, led to the further concentration of Muslims. As Muslims tried to move inwards from the boundary line with each bout of violence, the boundary itself shifted further towards the interior, thereby reducing considerably the space available for habitation. Today Muslims are largely ghettoized in Prem Nagar which is, of course, East Jogeshwari's 'Pakistan' and the road that divides it from the Hindu area is, ironically enough, Gandhi Market road. (Robinson 2005, 51–2)

Another limitation on Muslim neighbourhoods is the heightened police presence after each riot. Thus, the area of habitation is increasingly circumscribed, and the police further limit the movement of Muslims. Given this processual loss of territory, one might expect an extremist response. However, in the absence of an ephemeral gain in the recent past and even a remote expectation of state formation for Indian Muslims, the only option is fortitude (e.g., Nadwi, see above) or the occasional act of revenge (e.g., the Gujarat train fire killing some fifty Hindus in 2002) that yields many more Muslim deaths after the subsequent more intense communal violence. 'Given the minority position and the geographical dispersion of Muslims, "devotion for political ends" has, right from the outset, very little potential of fulfillment regardless of the ambitions of individual persons or particular subgroups' (Robinson 2005, 156).

Constructive approaches have included proactive networks of cooperation between Hindus and Muslims in locations where riots have been largely absent (e.g., Calicut in Kerala in southern India), in contrast to the absence of such networks where riots have typically occurred (e.g., Aligarh in Uttar Pradesh in northern India; Varshney 2002, 122–5). The presence of the AMU in that city may be thought to heighten Muslim consciousness, thereby increasing the probability of violence. However, Calicut also has its respected Muslim institutions. According to Varshney,

> Although they restrain politicians in the short and medium run, the intercommunal civic networks in Calicut were *politically* constructed in the long run. Caste injustice within Hindu society rather than communal antagonism between Hindus and Muslims has historically formed the master narrative of Kerala politics. Caste was more central to the ascriptive hierarchy in Kerala than was religion. Hence ethnic conflict historically took the idiom of caste. Hindu-Muslim politics functioned within a larger context of intra-Hindu caste differences. In Aligarh, the reverse has been true. Communalism has been the dominant political narrative for a century, and caste politics within Hinduism has historically functioned within the larger framework of Hindu-Muslim antagonisms. (2002, 122; emphasis in original)

Inter-communal dependence exists in Calicut but not in Aligarh, where violence has been endemic (Varshney 2002, 128). Lest geography appear to be compelling – as in the proximity of Aligarh to Pakistan, but the remoteness of Calicut from Pakistan – the case of Ajmer in central Rajasthan, close to Pakistan, but peaceful in its relations between Hindus and Muslims, belies this assumption. 'Over time it became a major nucleus for Hindu and Muslim pilgrimage and for the activity of numerous tribes, castes, and sects that have been classified as Hindu, Muslim, Jain, Christian, Sikh, Parsi, and others' (Mayaram 2005, 150).

Among the sources of ethnic coexistence are a shared mythico-religious space. A Sufi shrine, for example, has served as a locus for the expected healing of the sick of virtually all sects in Ajmer. Historically, both Mughal and Hindu princes patronized the shrine (Mayaram 2005,

154). This example shows the potential inherent in interfaith cooperation, as advocated in chapter 6 in light of the achievements made by FBOs under very difficult circumstances.

Everyday life reinforces the significance of this essentially multicultural shrine. The market near the shrine has both Hindu and Muslim traders, the prosperity of both hinging on the steady flow of pilgrims. According to Shail Mayaram, 'The Sindhi-Muslim interface derives from the activity centred on the shrine. Sindhi traders dominate the Dargah Bazar and benefit considerably from the annual Urs turnover of something like Rs 80–100 million. Their post-Independence economic prosperity is, hence, dependent on the continuous flow of pilgrims' (2005, 159). Thus, the rapid settlement of disputes is in the interests of both Sindhis (local Hindu population) and Muslims. Further, it is the 'unheroic quality of everyday life' that reinforces pluralism (D.R. Nagaraj, qtd in Mayaram 2005, 159). And 'Muslims remark on the marked absence of ideas of purity – pollution among Sindhis' (ibid.) that further sustains these cooperative relationships, as one might expect, given the emphasis on purity as a major accelerant of political extremism (Midlarsky 2011).

Sri Lanka

A stark contrast with that of Indian Muslims is the trajectory of Jaffna Tamils in the neighbouring island state of Sri Lanka. Since the passage of the Language Bill of 1956 designating Sinhalese as the official language of Sri Lanka, thereby relegating Tamil to the limbo of official non-existence, communal relations between the two principal ethnicities have deteriorated. According to Peebles (2006, 5), the Liberation Tigers of Tamil Eelam (LTTE) 'created an authoritarian quasi-state in the northeast. It governs under permanent wartime conditions with heavy-handed propaganda, universal conscription (even of children and elderly people), and ruthless suppression of dissent.'

How did this extremist, terrorist organization evolve to the point of governing a portion of Sri Lanka under these conditions? In particular, the resort to suicide bombing by the LTTE with its potential for mass murder requires explanation. The theory of ephemeral gains, especially the fear of merely a transitory governance, will go far to explain this extremist behaviour. To do this effectively, the political histories of the two communities need to be addressed, even in pre-colonial times. As we shall see, a political substitutability (Most and Starr 1989) during the colonial period will be encountered that will set the stage for Sinhalese nationalism and Tamil extremism.

Pre-Independence

The history of the earliest periods prior to the arrival of the Europeans is murky, but certain basic facts are known. During this time, there were indigenous Sinhalese and Tamil kingdoms vying for control of the island. This process settled into a Tamil-governed kingdom in Jaffna in the northern portion, and one governed by the Sinhalese in the southern sector and especially the interior of the island. But the Portuguese arrived in 1505 and displaced Muslim merchants who had earlier dominated regional trade. Through gradual expansion, the Portuguese began to dominate the northern region and expanded beyond it. By 1519, the Jaffna kingdom, although still independent, was substantially reduced in strength. In 1591, after a Portuguese invasion of the Jaffna Peninsula, a local puppet monarch was installed under their tutelage. After a revolt of Christian subjects and an attempted suppression of that rebellion by the Tamil authorities, in 1619 the Portuguese annexed the kingdom outright (Peebles 2006, 36). This kingdom now lost its independence, never to be revived until some facsimile of that earlier condition was restored after 2000.

After 1621, the only surviving indigenous polity was that of Kandy, situated in the interior. Earlier, in 1581, upon an invasion by a neighbouring indigenous opponent, the kingdom lost its sovereignty for a decade. After independence was re-established, the Portuguese attempted to conquer the Kandyan kingdom, weakening it. It was the British arrival in the nineteenth century (after the Dutch expulsion of the Portuguese) that would end the independence of Kandy for good. They raided Kandy in 1803 but were unsuccessful. In 1815, however, a convention was signed between the British and the Kandyans that preserved local autonomy for Kandy while recognizing British sovereignty. A rebellion of highland Sinhalese (the backbone of Kandy) in 1818 was suppressed, leading to limitations on Kandyan self-governance, and 'the suppression of the Kandyan Rebellion unified the entire island under a single government [for a long period] for the first time in its history' (Peebles 2006, 53).

As De Silva (1995, 75–6) suggests, 'There had been a long and successful tradition of Sinhalese resistance to Western colonial powers, Portugal first, then Holland and Britain itself. The years 1815–18 when the British established their control over the whole island constitute, in every way, a decisive turning point in the country's history. This time was the first since the early and mid-fifteenth century, when a Sri Lankan (Sinhalese) ruler had effective control over the whole island for about fifty years, that the process of unification had been successfully introduced.'

A reorganization of the island colony in 1832 that effectively ended a Buddhist religious hegemony also allowed Christian missionary activity. American missionaries were to be critical in this effort and 'the best schools in the island – some say the best schools in Asia – were in the Jaffna Peninsula. American missionaries supported education as means to convert students; the people of Jaffna responded enthusiastically to the opportunity. Jaffna Tamils used education to move into the English-speaking occupations in government, the private sector, and the professions. Many Tamils migrated to the southern and central regions for employment, leading to Sinhalese protests and the British favored Tamils over the majority Sinhalese' (Peebles 2006, 63). Hereafter, English-language education was controlled largely by Christian missionaries. 'The gap in prestige and income between the English-educated and the swabasha-educated was immense' (ibid.), and 'the biggest beneficiaries of British colonialism were those who speak English' (ibid., 65).

In addition to the Dutch burghers, left over from the colonial period, missionary-educated Jaffna Tamils were to constitute an administrative elite. One consequence was the study of Jaffna history and culture by English-speaking Tamils; the sense of a unique Jaffna Tamil identity was enhanced. Although, as of 1938, Indian civil servants comprised a quarter of all government workers in Ceylon (as the colony was called under the British), by 1941 they were reduced by more than half. Correspondingly there was a net emigration of some 65,000 people of Indian origin to India. Increasingly, the English-speaking Jaffna Tamils assumed many of these vacated positions so that by 1957, when the effects of the 1956 Language Bill had not yet been felt, about half the government employees were identifiably Jaffna Tamil (DeVotta 2004, 120). This figure is out of all proportion to the 12.71 per cent (as of 1981; Fair 2004, 19) of this Sri Lankan population that was Jaffna Tamil. Not having been granted citizenship, the Indian (so-called Plantation) Tamils comprising 5.51 per cent of the population were not eligible for these positions.

Peebles, probably calculating on a different database, indicates that

30 per cent of the jobs in the 'administrative services' at that time were occupied by Jaffna Tamils; 'by 1975, that number had fallen to 5%' (2006, 113), a substantial reduction, whatever the initial estimate.

Here we see the trajectory of an initial Jaffna Tamil subordination to colonial powers after 1619 (two centuries before the demise of the Sinhalese Kandyan state), followed by a growing ascendancy of Jaffna Tamils within the colonial civil service during the nineteenth and twentieth centuries. Effectively, a substitution of civil service authority – the only kind allowed indigenous peoples within a colonial setting – for political power in an independent state had been achieved by the Jaffna Tamils. Confronted with the widespread English proficiency of the Jaffna Tamils, most Sinhalese could not aspire to that status. But after 1956, when this authority was removed from the Tamils by the Sinhalese-only Language Bill, the descent was rapid. As we shall see, economic dominance by Tamils in major cities like Colombo and Trincomalee also would prove to be transitory.

Rise of the LTTE

Initially, inter-communal conflict was the protest norm. The Sinhalese character Sri was defaced on licence plates; in response, Tamil language signs were painted over. But soon, in 1958, violence took the form of 'rape, beating, arson, and murder directed at Tamils, but Tamils soon retaliated against Sinhalese' (Peebles 2006, 111). By 26 May, attacks had become an ethnic war. A state of emergency was finally declared and law and order resumed, especially after a Tamil Language Special Provisions Bill was enacted.

Along with the 'nationalization' of language in favour of Sinhala, many Tamil-owned industries were nationalized. For example, shipping companies owned by Tamils were displaced in 1967 when the port of Trincomalee in the eastern sector was nationalized (Peebles 2006, 116). At around this time, communal pressure for an independent Tamil state began to grow. Additionally only militarized pressure was deemed to have any chance of success.

In part to palliate Sinhalese nationalists who were dissatisfied with the (minimal) alleviation of Tamil grievances, the 1972 Constitution of the First Republic of Sri Lanka 'declared Sri Lanka "a Unitary State," gave "Buddhism the foremost place" and made it the state's duty "to protect and foster Buddhism," instituted Sinhala as the "Official Language of Sri Lanka," and mandated that the regulations drafted under the Tamil Language Act of 1958 were "subordinate legislation"' (DeVotta 2004, 134).

By the late 1970s and early 1980s, several insurgent organizations were formed. The most important were the Tamil Eelam Liberation Organization, the People's Liberation Organization for Tamil Eelam, the Eelam People's Revolution Liberation Front, and last but certainly not least, the Liberation Tigers of Tamil Eelam (LTTE), the only one of these organizations to survive. Founded by Velupillai Prabhakaran in Jaffna in the mid-1970s, it became among the most brutal of the Tamil nationalist groups, ultimately assassinating members of other such groups until the LTTE was the only one remaining (Fair 2004, 18).

Slowly increasing violence became a standard part of the Sri Lankan landscape, but after 1983 it escalated dramatically. (For a graph of violence occurring between 1948 and 1990, see Richardson 2004, 42.) Earlier, in 1977, anti-government activity by Tamil youths sparked riots that were inflamed by the police and armed forces. In May 1978, the government proscribed the LTTE, and in July 1982, the Prevention of Terrorism Act that had been enacted temporarily in 1979 now became permanent throughout the island. Essentially, this bill empowered the police and other security forces to violate the civil rights of virtually all persons suspected of committing terrorist acts or simply harbouring separatist sympathies. 'The new law explicitly contravened the International Covenant on Civil and Political Rights, to which the country was a signatory, and led to many young Tamils being abused and tortured, which merely deepened their determination to secede. With the police and security forces in the Jaffna Peninsula also continuing to harass, beat, and rape Tamils with impunity, Tamil rebels stepped up their violent acts' (DeVotta 2004, 149).

Violence during a period of contentious elections to District Development Councils in Jaffna led to the destruction of the Jaffna Municipal Library by government forces in 1981. The library contained approximately one hundred thousand ancient and irreplaceable documents pertaining to that community; virtually all were destroyed in the fire. Sporadic anti-Tamil riots followed the library fire, many sparked by government agents. Inescapably, many if not most Tamils came to the conclusion that in the name of Sinhala nationalism, the Sinhalese government intended to annihilate their cultural heritage, even their very lives.

But in 1983, riots broke out that transformed the ethnic conflict into civil war. In July 1983, the LTTE ambushed a patrol in Jaffna, killing thirteen soldiers. After the bodies were flown to Colombo for a mass funeral, an anti-Tamil rampage ensued. Shops and businesses owned by Tamils were targeted. According to the *Economist* in 1983, 'Two weeks ago Tamils owned 60 percent of the wholesale trade and 80 percent of the retail trade in the capital. Today that trade is gone' (qtd in DeVotta 2004, 151). The death toll was officially estimated at 367, but unofficial estimates ran as high as 3,000. In addition, 53 Tamil prisoners were murdered in Welikada Prison and 135,000 Tamil refugees were generated, 30,000 of them immigrating to the Indian state of Tamil Nadu (Peebles 2006, 135–6).

Gradually and ruthlessly, the LTTE established its control over Jaffna. A major fillip to their efforts actually came from the Sinhalese-dominated government. Reacting to the riots of 1983, the majority Sinhalese party effectively banned members of the Tamil United Liberation Front (TULF) from the legislature. The sixth amendment to the Constitution read, 'No person shall directly, or indirectly, in or outside Sri Lanka, support, espouse, promote, finance, encourage or advocate the establishment of a separate State within the territory of Sri Lanka' (qtd in Bush 2003, 137). Since the TULF was formally committed to the establishment of a separate Tamil state, its members could not stand for office. Thus, the only non-violent avenue for the expression of Tamil grievances was now closed to them. Tamil youth now flocked to the paramilitary organizations, thereby clearing the path for paramilitary rule in the North (86 per cent Tamil in 1981), and attempted such rule in the East (40 per cent Tamil, 32 per cent Muslim, 25 per cent Sinhalese in 1981; ibid. 41).

Between 1 March 1985 and 31 January 1986, Amnesty International confirmed 2,578 murders, 12,105 arrests, and 547 disappearances. Approximately 55,000 people including 30,000 mainly Muslims from Trincomalee in the Eastern Province were displaced. In November 1984, the LTTE massacred over 80 Sinhalese men, women, and children in the Kent and Dollar Farms in the Eastern Province. Another LTTE massacre, this time of 70–75 Sinhalese (including women and children) occurred in Anuradhapura, presumably in response to the earlier murder of 43 Tamil males in Jaffna. In Vavuniya in August 1985 nearly 100 Tamils were murdered after an army patrol narrowly escaped a land mine explosion (Bush 2003, 139).

By 1986, the LTTE had established effective military control of most of the Tamil areas of northern Sri Lanka by silencing or co-opting the competing paramilitaries and effectively opposing the Sri Lankan Army

Figure 7.3: Changes in Jaffna Tamil authority space over time, sixteenth century to 1987*

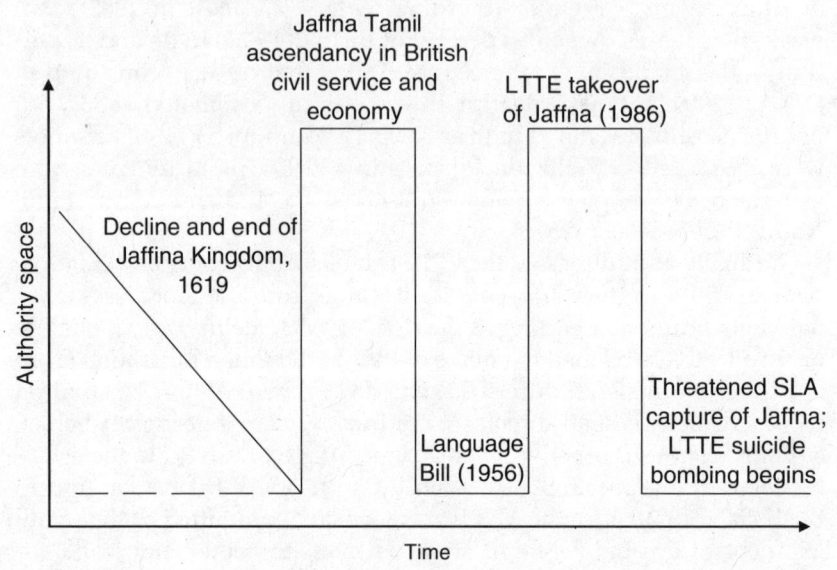

[Figure: plot of Authority space vs. Time, not to scale, with labels: "Decline and end of Jaffina Kingdom, 1619"; "Jaffna Tamil ascendancy in British civil service and economy"; "Language Bill (1956)"; "LTTE takeover of Jaffna (1986)"; "Threatened SLA capture of Jaffna; LTTE suicide bombing begins"]

*Not to scale

(SLA). The final stages of this process began in January 1983 when the Sri Lankan government reacted to increasing paramilitary activity by imposing a fuel and economic blockade on all of these Tamil areas. Simultaneously, the SLA began a campaign of air raids and artillery shelling of the Jaffna Peninsula. An LTTE response in April 1987 was to stop vehicles on the Colombo-Trincomalee Road and massacre over one hundred Sinhalese passengers. Shortly thereafter, the Colombo bus station was bombed, killing between two and three hundred people and injuring hundreds more (Bush 2003, 141). The SLA campaign continued with military thrusts into the region. And on 5 July, with its power over Jaffna increasingly in jeopardy, the LTTE carried out its first suicide bombing in which forty SLA troops were killed in the Nelliyadi army camp. Figure 7.3 illustrates this historical trajectory.

Note the increasing willingness to kill civilians by the LTTE and its first use of suicide terrorism only after the possibility of a major loss appeared on the horizon. The stiffening military opposition of the SLA and the willingness of the Sri Lankan government to establish a blockade of the Jaffna region suggested that the LTTE might be defeated and perhaps even destroyed if many of its cadres could not escape into the jungle. At the very least, the loss of Jaffna, 'the symbol of LTTE power and authority, one that had weathered all SLA attempts to capture' (Fair 2004, 21), would be a crucial defeat. The LTTE had now entered the camp of authoritarian extremism, permitting no Tamil rivals and engaging in deadly violence against civilians and military alike. When the threat of loss (of Jaffna) followed an earlier ephemeral gain (vast but temporary overrepresentation in the civil service and economy), extremism became much more likely to occur. The earlier ephemeral gain had now been reinforced by the threat of a later one.

Striking in its implications is the absence of any religious or even ideological motivation to the suicide attacks of the LTTE. And suicide bombing had been a much-used tactic of the Tigers. Between 1980 and 2000 when the LTTE was most active in its terror campaigns, its 168 suicide attacks comprised the preponderance of all such events (Gunaratna 2000; cited in Fair 2004, 41). Since that time, the Palestinian Intifada II and the Iraq insurgency have added many new suicide bombings (Pape 2005, 253–64), but the LTTE still stands prominent in this activity. According to Fair (37), 'In some ways, the entire LTTE could arguably be declared a suicide force of sorts. Each cadre is required to wear a cyanide capsule, which is distributed by the local commando leader in the celebration that follows the completion of training. LTTE cadres have shown little hesitation in consuming the capsule if their mission is compromised.'

But the elite of all of the cadres were the Black Tigers, the suicide arm of the LTTE. They were the most honoured of the Tigers. After applying for admission, they were selected for the Black Tigers only after the most thorough vetting; many applicants were rejected. Every year their sacrifices were honoured in a major celebration called Great Heroes Day (often incorrectly translated as 'Martyr's Day'). Black Tiger elite status was signified in their access to Prabhakaran, the LTTE leader, who hosted a meal with them before their final mission. It was not a religion or a specific ideology that motivated the Black Tigers. 'Instead, the mythology and reverence attached to the sacrifice of the Black Tigers serve[d] to motivate the cadres' (Fair 2004, 47).

Indian Intervention

Given the large Tamil population in the Indian state of Tamil Nadu across the Palk Strait from the Jaffna Peninsula, it might seem inevitable that India eventually would intervene in the Sri Lankan violence. Actually, it was the Indian external intelligence agency, the Research and Analysis Wing, that began training the LTTE and other Tamil rebel groups from Sri Lanka. The Indian government strongly opposed the post-1977 pro-Western policies of the Sri Lankan government and sought to undermine it (DeVotta 2004, 171). The Indian decision to intervene diplomatically, if not yet militarily, was made in the wake of the July 1983 riots between the Sinhalese and Tamil communities (Carment, James, and Taydas 2006, 50).

Training camps were set up in Tamil Nadu, but as hostility to the LTTE increased in India, the Tigers began moving their bases to the Jaffna Peninsula. In the midst of the SLA offensive (begun in February 1987) against the LTTE in Jaffna, the Indian Air Force began dropping food and medicine to the rebels, after the Sri Lankan government refused to allow such shipments by sea. In July, an agreement to allow Indian forces to enter Sri Lanka essentially was imposed upon the Sri Lankan government; soon 6,000 Indian troops of the Indian Peace Keeping Force (IPKF) were in the Jaffna region (Peebles 2006, 157). Almost immediately, the IPKF and LTTE came into conflict as the former tried to disarm the Tamil rebels, and the violence quickly escalated.

By the time the IPKF withdrew from Sri Lanka in 1990, it had lost 1,157 troops in combat and nearly three thousand wounded in India's longest war (DeVotta 2004, 173). Clearly, the initial decision to arm the Jaffna Tamil rebels had become a 'blowback' for the Indian government, as had the CIA's strategy to arm Islamic militants in fighting the Soviets in Afghanistan during the mid-1980s. The role of suicide bombing in the Indian decision to ultimately withdraw all support from the LTTE should not be minimized, for in March 1991 Rajiv Ghandi was assassinated by an LTTE suicide bomber.

The first suicide bombing by the LTTE occurred just prior to the Indian intervention; LTTE suicide bombing would also put an exclamation point to the end of that action. And the successive reinforcing ephemera experienced by the Jaffna Tamils would set the stage for that unfortunate intervention. Nothing of that sort has happened within India (again excluding Kashmir); violence at this level involving government forces has been avoided. Religion has not been a major factor in Sri Lanka's violence, as in India religion has not inspired suicide terrorism or other manifestations of extremist behaviour beyond communal acts of revenge.

Conclusion

Why are ephemeral gains, especially successive reinforcing ephemera, so dangerous for international stability, at least at the regional level, even beyond? Anger associated with these ephemera is intense. As a consequence, the violence that erupts tends to be severe and long lasting in the absence of the massive external force needed to quell the violence. If the ephemera are reinforced, as in the Sri Lankan case, the intensity of the ethnic conflict is increased to the point that external intervention becomes more likely. The histories, literature, folk tales, and legends of earlier ephemeral ascendancies are drawn upon by both politicians and citizens, intensifying the feelings of loss and anger. Another classic instance of this phenomenon is the Serbian aggression after 1991 resulting from three reinforcing ephemera that yielded massive conflict within the former Yugoslavia, including genocide at Srebrenica – the only case of this kind in Europe after 1945 (Midlarsky 2011). Western – especially American – intervention was required to end the violence. Alas, the size of the Indian force needed to decisively defeat the LTTE, and the political will to continue the IPKF mission in Sri Lanka, were absent, and so the violence persisted.

Reinforcing ephemera in the historical trajectory of Sri Lankan Jaffna Tamils distinguish this case from that of Indian Muslims. The expectation, whether realistic or not, of state formation (or at least significant autonomy) by the LTTE also demarks this instance from that of Indian Muslims. The presence of an existing Islamic state – Pakistan – precludes the possibility of another such state coming into existence in the Indian subcontinent.

REFERENCES

Berkowitz, L. 2003. Affect, aggression, and antisocial behavior. In *Handbook of affective sciences*, ed. R.J. Davidson, K.R. Scherer, and H.H. Goldsmith, 804–23. Oxford: Oxford University Press.

Bodenhausen, G.V., L.A. Sheppard, and G.P. Kramer. 1994. Negative affect and social judgment: The differential impact of anger and sadness. *European Journal of Social Psychology* 24:45–62.

Brown, L.C. 2000. *Religion and state: The Muslim approach to politics*. New York: Columbia University Press.

Bush, K.D. 2003. *The intra-group dimensions of ethnic conflict in Sri Lanka: Learning to read between the lines*. New York: Palgrave Macmillan.

Carment, D., P. James, and Z. Taydas. 2006. *Who intervenes? Ethnic conflict and interstate crisis*. Columbus: Ohio State University Press.

De Silva, K.M. 1995. *Regional powers and small state security: India and Sri Lanka, 1977–90*. Washington, DC: Woodrow Wilson Center Press.

DeSteno, D. N., N. Dassgupta, M.Y. Bartlett, and A. Cajddric. 2004. Prejudice from thin air: The effect of emotion on automatic intergroup attitudes. *Psychological Science* 15:319–24.

DeVotta, N. 2004. *Blowback: Linguistic nationalism, institutional decay, and ethnic conflict in Sri Lanka*. Stanford, CA: Stanford University Press.

Elster, J. 2004. Emotion and Action. In *Thinking about feeling: Contemporary philosophers on emotions*, ed. R.C. Solomon, 151–62. Oxford: Oxford University Press.

Fair, C.C. 2004. *Urban battle fields of South Asia: Lessons learned from Sri Lanka, India, and Pakistan*. Santa Monica, CA: Rand.

Farooq, O. 2007. Hyderabad back to normal after bombings. Associated Press 28 August.

Frijda, N.H. 1986. *The emotions*. Cambridge: Cambridge University Press.

– 1994. The Lex Talionis: On vengeance. In *Emotions: Essays on emotion theory*, ed. S.H.M. Van Goozen, N.E. Van De Poll, and J.A. Sergeant, 263–89. Hillsdale, NJ: Erlbaum.

Habeck, M.R. 2006. *Knowing the enemy: Jihadist ideology and the war on terror*. New Haven, CT: Yale University Press.

Haidt, J. 2003. The moral emotions. In *Handbook of affective sciences*, ed. R.J. Davidson, K.R. Scherer, and H.H. Goldsmith, 852–70. Oxford: Oxford University Press.

Hasan, M., and M. Pernau, eds. 2005. *Regionalizing pan-Islamism: Documents on the Khilafat movement*. New Delhi: Manohar.

Hodgson, M G. 1974. *The venture of Islam: Conscience and history in a world civilization*. Chicago: University of Chicago Press.

Jalal, A. 2008. *Partisans of Allah: Jihad in South Asia*. Cambridge, MA: Harvard University Press.

Kahneman, D., and A. Tversky. 1979. Prospect theory: An analysis of decision under risk. *Econometrica* 47:263–92.

– eds. 2000. *Choices, values, and frames*. Cambridge: Cambridge University Press.

Kulke, H., and D. Rothermund. 2004. *A history of India*. 4th ed. London: Routledge.

Levy, J.S. 2000. Loss aversion, framing effects, and international conflict. In *Handbook of war studies II*, ed. M.I. Midlarsky, 193–221. Ann Arbor: University of Michigan Press.

Lowenstein, G., and J.S. Lerner. 2003. The role of affect in decision making. In *Handbook of affective sciences*, ed. R.J. Davidson, K.R. Schere, and H.H. Goldsmith, 619–42. Oxford: Oxford University Press.

Mayaram, S. 2005. Living together: Ajmer as a paradigm for the (South) Asian City. In *Living together separately: Cultural India in history and politics*, ed. M. Hasan and A. Roy, 145–71. New York: Oxford University Press.

McLeod, J. 2002. *The history of India*. Westport, CT: Greenwood.

Mele, A.R. 2003. Emotion and desire in self-deception. In *Philosophy and the emotions*, ed. A. Hatzimoysis, 163–79. Cambridge: Cambridge University Press.

Midlarsky, M.I. 2005a. The demographics of genocide: Refugees and territorial loss in the mass murder of European Jewry. *Journal of Peace Research* 42:375–91.

– 2005b. *The killing trap: Genocide in the twentieth century*. Cambridge: Cambridge University Press.

– 2011. *Origins of political extremism: Mass violence in the twentieth century and beyond*. Cambridge: Cambridge University Press.

Minault, G. 1982. *The Khilafat movement: Religious symbolism and political mobilization in India*. New York: Columbia University Press.

Most, B.A., and H. Starr. 1989. *Inquiry, logic, and international politics*. Columbia, SC: University of South Carolina Press.

Niemeijer, A.C. 1972. *The Khilafat movement in India: 1919–1924*. The Hague: Martinus Nijhoff.

Nisbett, R.E., and D. Cohen. 1996. *Culture of honor: The psychology of violence in the south*. Boulder, CO: Westview.

Pape, R.A. 2005. *Dying to win: The strategic logic of suicide terrorism*. New York: Random House.

Peebles, P. 2006. *The history of Sri Lanka*. Westport, CT: Greenwood.

Richardson, J.M. Jr. 2004. Violent conflict and the first half decade of open economy policies in Sri Lanka: A revisionist view. In *Economy, culture, and civil war in Sri Lanka*, ed. D. Winslow and M.D. Woost, 41–72. Bloomington: Indiana University Press.

Robb, P. 2002. *A history of India*. New York: Palgrave.

Robinson, R. 2005. *Tremors of violence: Muslim survivors of ethnic strife in Western India*. Thousand Oaks, CA: Sage.

Sikand, Y. 2004. *Muslims in India since 1947: Islamic perspectives on inter-faith relations*. London: Routledge Curzon.

Stein, B. 1998. *A history of India*. Oxford: Blackwell.

Stein, N., T. Trabasso, and M. Liwag. 1993. The representation and organization of emotional experience: Unfolding the emotion episode. In *Handbook of emotions*, ed. M. Lewis and J.M. Haviland, 279–300. New York: Guilford.

Stenner, K. 2005. *The authoritarian dynamic.* New York: Cambridge University Press.

Varshney, A. 2002. *Ethnic conflict and civic life: Hindus and Muslims in India.* New Haven: Yale University Press.

Westen, D., P.S. Blagov, K. Harenski, C. Kilts, and S. Hamann. 2006. An fMRI study of motivated reasoning: Partisan political reasoning in the U.S. presidential election. Atlanta, GA: Psychology Department, Emory University.

Wiktorowicz, Q. 2005. *Radical Islam rising: Muslim extremism in the West.* Lanham, MD: Rowman & Littlefield.

Witte, K. 1992. Putting the fear back into fear appeals: The extended parallel process model. *Communication Monographs* 59:329–49.

8 Religion, Security Dilemma, and Conflict: The Case of Iraq

YASEMIN AKBABA and ZEYNEP TAYDAS

Introduction

Internal conflicts produce economic and political devastation, and pose challenges to neighbouring states, regional security, and stability. They also have broader implications for political order and human rights. Conflict in Iraq is no exception: it led to enormous human suffering and has attracted a great deal of media attention. What differentiates this conflict from many others is the nature of U.S. involvement. The stated goal of the United States, in the wake of the intervention, was to topple Saddam Hussein and to bring democracy and stability to the country. While the first goal was achieved rather quickly, the United States had not achieved the second goal in the first six years after the intervention.

Post-invasion Iraq has been marked by violent conflict between U.S.-led military units and insurgents. Tensions between Shiite and Sunni Muslims spilled over into brutal sectarian violence and the government tried unsuccessfully to restore order until the surge of U.S. troops in late 2007. The U.S. troops tried to eliminate the resistance by pushing them out of cities and provinces they had long contested. In June 2009, U.S. troops handed security over to Iraqi forces and withdrew from Iraqi cities. U.S.-led combat operations are scheduled to end by September 2010 and all U.S. troops are due to leave Iraq by the end of 2011. However, Iraq remains volatile and the power struggle in Iraq is far from being over.

Understanding of what happened in Iraq since the 2003 intervention by the United States is an essential step that needs to be taken, if the goal is to eliminate the causes of tension and have a politically stable and secure Iraq in the future. This chapter aims to explain the developments that took place in Iraq after the U.S. invasion by focusing on two important concepts: security dilemma and religion. Our case study indicates that in addition to providing the necessary opportunity structure for action, U.S.-led invasion transformed the existing security dilemma and in this process religion played a significant role. As summed up by one observer, 'Bush's invasion of Iraq unwittingly set off a religious tsunami, which has yet to make landfall' (Cole 2006, 26).

In this chapter, first we begin with a general assessment of the role of religion in politics and conflict. Second, we provide a very brief history of Iraq with a specific emphasis on the policies of Saddam Hussein. We examine the political climate during the authoritarian regime of Saddam Hussein in order to tease out the impact of his policies on the security dilemma in today's Iraq. Third, we apply the security dilemma concept to Iraq and try to explain the underlying factors behind the conflict. We also examine the importance of ethnicity and sectarianism in the post-Saddam era and take a closer look at the role of religion. The last section is devoted to conclusions and policy implications.

Religion, Politics, and Conflict

Anybody who had argued fifty years ago that religion would be attracting a great deal of attention from policy-makers, academics, and the media would have faced major scepticism. Yet today we witness a revival of religion in politics (Barkun 1994; Casanova 1994; Fox 2004b; Hadden 1987; Hart 2001; Haynes 1997; Jelen and Wilcox 2002; Marty and Appleby 1992; Rudolph and Piscatori 1997). Real world events such as the revolution in Iran, protracted Arab-Israeli conflict, tension in the Kashmir state of India, civil war in former Yugoslavia, conflict in Sudan, and terror attacks of 11 September suggest, beyond dispute, a new political role demanded by religion. Despite prominent events in the world of politics, religion, as emphasized by chapters 2 and 3, failed to take a prominent role in twentieth-century international relations (IR) as a discipline.

Studies show that the number and intensity of religious conflicts increased between 1950 and 1996 (Fox 2004c). When civil wars from 1940 to 2000 are examined, the percentage of those in which religion became a central issue increased as well. Religious civil wars are also found to be more destructive, last longer, and have a higher reoccurrence rate (Toft 2007, 2006).[1] Furthermore, earlier studies on religion and ethnic conflict have concluded that the dynamics of conflict are altered dramatically when an ethno-religious minority (ethnic minority with a different religion) is involved (Fox 2004a). The presence of religious minorities in a state increases the extent of ethnic violence (Rummel 1997). Most of the time, ethno-religious conflicts feature higher levels of discrimination and grievances over political issues (Fox 1997). They also are more violent and tend to attract third-party support more often (Fox 2001, 2004b; Khosla 1999). Reynal-Querol (2002) reports a positive relationship between religious fragmentation and intensity of ethnic conflict.

However, this does not necessarily mean that religion unavoidably leads to religious conflict. Contrarily, the literature focusing on peaceful content of religious identities is well developed.[2] It is stated that religion can be a source of peace when it stays as a mystical or spiritual aspect of life and does not reach the point of extremism (Groff and Smoker 1996).[3]

In the last decade or so, religion also has become increasingly important in political parties. Political parties with religious rhetoric are established in many countries, including Afghanistan, Algeria, Egypt, India, Pakistan, and Sudan (Juergensmeyer 1995). Political parties either are born with a religious agenda, such as India's Bharatiya Janata Party (BJP), or become more faith-driven on the way, like the U.S. Republican Party (*Economist*, 2007a, 13). No matter how they are formed, religious parties offer alternatives to the existing options in many countries, including Turkey, Malaysia, Egypt, or Palestine, and have become serious contenders for power. Religion gives power to political parties and political parties give power to religion. This synergy does not need to turn into violence, but in some cases religion becomes pernicious and generates intolerance as well as violence.

Some scholars argue that the resurgence of religion in politics is due to the destabilizing role of modernization. Social and economic changes brought not secularization, but renewal of religious ideas (Fox 2004b; Sahliyeh 1990). This also is tied to performance of secular governments: 'Religion's political comeback started in the 1970s, when faith in government everywhere was crumbling' (*Economist*, 2007b, 15). According to Juergensmeyer (1993), people lost their faith in secular ideology because the secular framework has not lived up to its promises of political freedom, economic prosperity, and social justice. Weakening of the nation-state and disillusionment with old forms of secular nationalism, in turn, produced the opportunity for alternative sources of loyalty and, in the wake of a legitimacy crisis, religious, ethnic, and traditional values reappeared, offering an alternative form of social cohesion and new sources of national identity and loyalty (ibid.).

Some scholars highlight the power of religious institutions in facilitating political activities. Through religion, places of worship become meeting places, religious leaders become political leaders, and all of these changes increase the likelihood of political mobilization (Harris 1994; Johnston and Figa 1988). Finally, there is a 'reaction and counter-reaction' factor. Wherever religious movements become visible, they trigger a counter-religious identity, and the interaction between different religious groups, within and between states, has increased the power of religion. Shiite-dominated Iran countered the majority Sunni Middle East; Hamas increased its power as a result of protracted conflict between Arabs and Israelis, and Al-Qaeda found strength in anti-Christian rhetoric. 'Fundamentalist Islam ... has helped spur radical Judaism and Hinduism, which in turn have reinforced the mullah's fervor. Hamas owes much to Israel's settlers' (*Economist*, 2007c, 15).

Why does religion play such an important role in shaping people's behaviour? First, religion is an important part of individual and group identity. In some cases, religious values can be more influential than other sources of identity because they carry a world view or a value system that can shape perceptions of individuals on anything. Religious views are non-relativistic, meaning that believers insist that what they believe is true and hence they do not accept alternative answers. This aspect of religious identity facilitates political mobilization and conflict (Shupe 1990). Abu-Nimer (2001, 687–8) summarizes this idea: 'When religious values, norms and behaviors are an integral part of the interactions between individuals and among groups, then religion helps to construct both the individual's and the group's value system and world-view. If an individual or a group has internalized a set of religious values, these beliefs can motivate changes of attitude and action.'

In multi-religious societies, emphasis on religious identities as a source of individual or group identity eventually causes formation of transparent walls between religious groups. These groups hold the potential to separate from the rest of society and defend their own interests when necessary. In the case of Iraq, religion is a major source of identity for both Shiite and Sunni Arabs. Distinctions between perceptions of these two religious groups were amplified throughout Saddam's dictatorship and that played a significant role in identity formation.

Second, religious psychology highlights the connection between psychological needs of human beings and the framework provided by religion. Religion helps us to interpret the world and understand our own place in it. With the help of religion we know, within some range of options, how to act under different circumstances: 'It provides us with a sense of what is moral and immoral, right and wrong, and good and evil' (Fox 2004b, 18). In other words, religion creates a give-and-take relationship where a believer receives the tools to deal with challenging questions such as what happens after death, or what our place is on earth (ibid.). In return, religion exerts control over hearts and minds. These might sound like unfair terms of trade, yet it is essential to remember that religion offers an immortal dimension to our mortal lives. That, in turn, makes sacrifice for our religion a rational option – at least for some people. Toft (2007, 100) states, 'The logic is simple: the physical self is mortal, and hence temporary; the religious self, however, is potentially immortal and eternal. Thus, sacrificing the temporary and mortal to obtain the eternal and immortal is not only rational but also desirable.'

In societies where fear and injustice prevail, and trust is virtually non-existent, individuals need something that will meet their psychological needs. Religion can become useful in meeting the needs of people, and this, in turn, increases the power of religion over individuals. In Iraq, eight years of war with Iran, economic sanctions, and the merciless dictatorship of Saddam Hussein created an unhealthy psychological environment. It is possible to argue that under such circumstances religion provided one of the few options Iraqis had for psychological survival.

Third, religion can grant legitimacy. Legitimacy is 'the normative belief by an actor that a rule or institution ought to be obeyed' (Hurd 1999, 381). From this point of view, religious institutions might facilitate conflict, especially when centred on religion, because of their institutions, leadership, and power to grant legitimacy to people (Fox 2004b). It is important to note that religion has a double function. On the one hand, it can be source of change and mobilization. Religious institutions provide meeting places, leadership with organizational skills, and a natural hierarchy that smoothes the progress of organization (McAdam 1982; McCarthy and Zald 1977; Tarrow 1989). On the other hand, religion can serve the opposite function and be used to justify and continue the status quo (Billings and Scott 1994; Fox 2004b; Fox and Sandler 2004; Solle 1984). Consider Gill's (1994) study of religious competition and Catholic political strategy in Latin America. He examines the 1962–

79 period to understand the impact of competition of Catholicism with Protestantism on the relationship of the Catholic Church with dictatorships in Latin America and finds that that the growing presence of Protestantism changed the trend of support from the Catholic Church to governments. Fox (2004b, 23) states that religion can be a double-edged sword because 'religious institutions will support governments as long as they benefit from this support,' and 'when such support undermines their support within the community they will oppose the government in order to remain relevant.' Reychler (1997) follows a similar approach that reveals religion to be a major source of soft power, which can be (mis)used by organizations to pursue their interests.

Religious legitimacy theory is helpful in explaining developments in Iraq because religion gave political power to leaders such as al-Sadr and Grand Ayatollah Ali Sistani, provided opportunities to organizations such as Al-Qaeda and states such as Iran, formed movements like Shiite and Sunni awakening, and contributed to the shift in the perceived position of the United States from 'liberator' to 'invader.' Prior to the invasion, the United States had expected to find a relatively secular society, which would be distant from Iran or Al-Qaeda. However, as Operation Iraqi Freedom lasted longer than initially planned and as chaos emerged through seemingly unending war, many Islamists, both Sunni and Shiite, found opportunities to expand their circle of influence in Iraq as an alternative to the Iraqi government. Hence religion could not become a straightforward source of support for the government; contrarily, it became a cause of instability.

Security Dilemma, U.S. Intervention, and the Role of Religion

According to realist theory, international anarchy leads to security concerns for states: as each state strives to increase its own security, it poses a challenge to the others. Posen (1993) applies this concept – the security dilemma – to ethnic conflict. He claims that the collapse of an imperial power might create similar fear among groups in a domestic power vacuum. These anxieties could set in motion forces that lead to widespread ethnic violence, as observed in the break-up of Yugoslavia and the former Soviet Union (ibid.; Snyder and Jervis 1999). If groups with different ethnic, religious, or cultural identities suddenly are forced to protect themselves when the state apparatus disintegrates, their threat perception can shift dramatically. Under these circumstances, a neighbouring group can be perceived as a threat, increasing the chance of conflict. Each ethnic group tries to increase its own security, thus creating an unsettled and potentially threatening environment for the others (Posen 1993, 104).

Saideman expands the security dilemma concept by applying it to not only collapsed states, but also existing states with ethnic security problems: 'If the state cannot protect the interests of all ethnic groups, then each group will seek to control the state or secede so that they can control their own state, decreasing other groups' security and decreasing the state's ability to provide security for any group' (1998, 135). The state plays a critical role in mediating or controlling ethnic group security (ibid.). The trade-off between assurance of security for each group and deterrence of one or more groups disposed toward violence or even rebellion is a delicate balancing act that is in play even before an open ethnic conflict is realized (Saideman and Zahar 2007). In an ideal situation of mutual trust, the state monopolizes the means of violence, and minorities do not compete for security. However, if the state does not protect groups sufficiently, they might compete with each other in the quest for security, with rebellion as one possible result. If groups feel insecure because of the vicious cycle created by the security dilemma, they will tend to act in one of three different ways: seek to control the state, create a state they can control (secession), or join a state where their ethnic group is more secure (irredentism) (Saideman and Ayres 2000).

Fear and suspicion are not new to Iraqis; these unfortunate feelings have been part of their lives since the state was created. However, the problem of mistrust reached its apex under the Baathist regime, built by Al-Bakr from 1968 and consolidated under Saddam Hussein after 1979. Saddam Hussein frequently used violence to sustain his regime and favoured Sunnis over Shiites and Kurds. Rivalries and strife were exacerbated with difficulties created by the economic embargo, occupation, and destruction of the infrastructure (Mockaitis 2007).

Despite extreme levels of fear, insecurity, and grievances in society under Saddam's regime, civil war and sectarian violence did not emerge until Operation Iraqi Freedom and the collapse of the Baathist government. Given that 'communal war is the outcome of two immediate causes – increased levels of fear and perceived feasibility of addressing threats by using violence,' the missing part of the puzzle, which was the opportunity for insurgency, was completed when the U.S. decided to invade Iraq to topple Saddam and establish a stable, democratic, pro-

U.S. regime (Lischer 1998, 331–2). Insufficient troops and inability of U.S. forces to provide security and rule of law in the country right after the invasion led to a power vacuum and insurgency in Iraq. Unfortunately, the defining feature of the political reality, perhaps until the 'surge,' had been constant struggle over land, people, and resources as well as 'predominance of Islamism as the major form of discourse and political mobilization at various levels' (Sidahmed 2007, 71; Norell 2007). In the next subsection we will explore these topics in great detail. First we will focus on the Saddam era in order to convey its implications for the current situation in Iraq. Second, the U.S.-led invasion and its consequences are examined.

The Roots of Instability in Iraq: The Legacy of Saddam's Rule

Iraq is a country with deep-seated ethnic and religious divisions. It is composed of three major ethno-religious communities: Shiite Arabs, Sunni Arabs, and Sunni Kurds. There are also other small minorities including Turkomans and Assyrians (CIA World Factbook). The state has been controlled by Sunni Arabs since its creation, with other groups excluded from power through oppression, coercion, and discrimination. This is at the root of extreme mistrust between parties in today's Iraq (Chaplin 2006).

Saddam, to maintain his grip on power, relied heavily on patronage, used violence as a political tool, atomized the society, and generated hopelessness among the population. Fragile Iraqi regimes always have tried to increase their autonomy from society to ensure territorial integrity and survival of the Iraqi state. Saddam Hussein proved to be no exception. Despite the fact that Shiites constitute 60 per cent of the Iraqi population, they have been systematically underrepresented and excluded from the decision-making structures of the state. Shiite Arabs also have been disadvantaged economically and socially. The government conducted a brutal campaign of murder, execution, and arbitrary arrest against religious leaders and followers of the majority Shia Muslim population (U.S. Department of State 2001). However, because of internal divisions among the Shiite community, they have failed to unite for a common cause and challenge the Sunni domination.

In addition to systematic oppression, Saddam destroyed all sorts of independent organizational or political activity, including trade unions and civil society organizations: 'With the destruction of national civil and secular platforms, ethnic and religious structures emerged as the only viable alternatives of political mobilization' (Siyamed 2007, 74). While disenfranchised Kurds and Shiite communities fell back on their ethnic and religious strongholds, Saddam tried to reshape the society by creating an artificial collective identity, that is, above all other kinds of affiliations and allegiances. The goal was to create a new generation of Iraqis loyal to the state first and then to their religion and ethnicity. This mission was doomed to failure; if anything united Kurds and Shiites, it was collective grievances, fear, distrust, and hostility towards Saddam's regime (ibid.).

One of the worst examples of the brutality of Saddam's regime is the massacre of 1991. During the first Gulf War, the Bush Administration called on Iraqis to rebel against the regime and overthrow Saddam Hussein. Shiites responded to this call by rebelling. Yet, without U.S. support, this uprising resulted in brutal suppression of Shiites and a massacre. Many prominent Shiite clerics disappeared or were executed. Some chose to escape while others remained under surveillance by the Baath secret police (Cole 2003b).[4]

Grievances formed during and after the 1991 uprisings are important causes behind Shiite insurgency and anti-U.S. sentiments in Iraq today. Cole (2003b, 550) states, 'Iraqi Shi'ites have for the most part never forgiven the US for its callous policy of standing by during these massacres.' And according to Anderson and Stansfield (2004, 114), 'Saddam and the Ba'ath have spent most of their 30 years in power using whatever means necessary – whether coercion, co-option, or bribery – to avoid the emergence of Shi'a Islam as a powerful political force in Iraq. By the time his regime was collapsed in April 2003, this is precisely the potential he had created.' They also find it very naive to believe that 'once liberated from an evil regime, the Shi'a would choose to fit neatly into a new secular government in which all of Iraq's ethnic and religious groups would be represented' (133).

Just like Shiites, the Kurds have always resented the fact that power resided in Sunni Arabs' hands. Kurds rejected Pan-Arabism and Sunni domination and questioned the legitimacy of the state. As Kurds demanded more autonomy, Saddam perceived them as a major threat to his regime. As a result, Kurds suffered inordinately during Saddam's rule. During the Iran-Iraq war of the 1980s, Saddam resorted to ethnic cleansing and destroyed Kurdish villages in strategic zones when Kurds sought Iranian support for their insurgency. The Anfal events (1988), which resulted in the killing of approximately one hundred thousand Kurds and the destruction of more than four thousand Kurdish villages by the Iraqi government, illustrate the brutality of the regime (Cole 2003a; Roth 2004). Similarly, the Baath regime used chemical warfare against civilian Kurds and killed five thousand Kurds near the city of Halabja. After withdrawal of U.S. forces from Kuwait, the Kurdish area in the north fell under Kurdish control and operated independently from the centre. With the establishment of political institutions and armed forces, it functioned as a de facto independent state and Kurds enjoyed the status quo until 2003. With the removal of Saddam, the Kurds once again started to feel insecure, vulnerable, and uncertain about their place in the future of Iraq.

Gurr (2000) argues that greater salience of ethnocultural identity facilitates mobilization for collective action. Even though he accepts that communal identities are multidimensional, he distinguishes some traits such as race and religion from others and argues they are intrinsically more important. What makes religion specifically a salient attribute in heterogeneous societies is that, theoretically, the coexistence of two religions (or two religious sects) is not possible. One can speak two languages but one cannot be both Hindu and Muslim (ibid.). When the incompatibility of the two religions is underlined, the salience of ethnic identity increases suddenly for ethnic groups. In the case of Iraq, government policies such as banning religious practices, arbitrary arrest of religious leaders, desecration of Shia mosques and holy sites, killing of clerics, restrictions, discrimination, and other brutal policies of Saddam Hussein enhanced the salience of its ethno-religious identity among Shiites (US Department of State 2001).

People who suffer from injustice find sanctuary in religion. It can provide relief in crisis. Tough questions such as 'why us?' find calming answers with the help of religion. The Shiite community in Iraq, living under major stresses due to policies of Saddam Hussein, found comfort in their religious views. The Shiites are followers of Ali, Muhammad's son-in-law, and place significant emphasis on his guidance (Haynes 2007). Shiite tradition is based on persecution and mistreatments of believers at the hands of Sunnis. Turning points of Shiite history, such as the murder of Ali and slaughter of Hassan and Hussein, are all remembered as sacrifices necessary to protect the belief system. Shiites, suffering from discrimination and repression in Iraq, found a commonality between what Ali, Hassan, and Hussein went through and their own painful conditions under Hussein's regime. This parallel kept the community close to its Shiite identity.

Even though Saddam Hussein was a secular leader, during the last decade of the Baath rule, especially after the Iran-Iraq (1980–8) and

Gulf (1990–1) Wars, his ideology shifted toward reactivation of Islam as a political force in Iraq. Devastation caused by two wars and sanctions produced economic difficulties, inflation, malnutrition, and lack of public services. These problems further distanced Iraqis from the regime.

Saddam quickly realized that his ideology had become virtually irrelevant to Iraqis, and the regime was faltering. At the same time, an upsurge of religious sentiment in society took place. In order to sustain his regime Saddam used Islam as a legitimizing and mobilizing force. Starting from 1993, under the Faith campaign (*al-Hamlah al-Immaniyah*), Saddam put a great emphasis on the Islamic identity of the country. In sharp contrast to the original ideology of the Baath party, which was secular, socialist, and pan-Arabic, the state encouraged piety and Saddam portrayed himself as a pious person. During this period he built new mosques and imposed restrictions on alcohol consumption (Siyamed 2007). Saddam Hussein gave himself religious titles like 'the leader of all Muslims' and 'servant of God' and added quotations from the Qur'an to his speeches (Anderson and Stansfield 2004). In short, the use of Sunni Islam as a political tool starting from the 1990s generated a counter-reaction among Shiites and strengthened their religious identity. It also facilitated establishment of closer links with Iran.

In sum, thirty-five years of Baathist rule and Sunni domination not only alienated Shiites and Kurds but also deepened the ethnic and religious divisions in society. When the Baathist regime was removed from power and Sunni domination finally ended, traumatized sections of the society had 'an absolute determination to secure once and for all those rights denied so long' (Chaplin 2006, 273). Contrary to events in Yugoslavia and the Soviet Union in the 1990s, where security dilemmas followed dissolution of the state, in Iraq there was no collapse or disintegration of state authority before the invasion. Instead of a complete breakdown or lack of power to keep ethnic hostilities in control, the situation in Iraq before the war can be characterized as strong central authority, Sunni domination, extreme repression, discrimination, and the use of force. As the United States failed to impose order and stability across Iraq, a serious domestic power and security vacuum emerged. Criminal gangs, Baath party loyalists, and religious fundamentalists (Sunni and Shiite) formed the backbone of a politically motivated, self-sustaining insurgency (Dodge 2005, 2006). In addition to its role in the emergence of civil war, the United States also became a major player in the security dilemma in the aftermath of the invasion.

U.S.-Led Invasion, Security Dilemma, and Insurgency

Posen's understanding of the security dilemma (also Snyder and Jervis 1999) hinges upon the collapse of central authority (like an imperial power) and the resulting domestic power vacuum. Fear of domination or extinction is mainly due to the state's inability to protect its citizens and control society. In this frame of reference, a strong external party is perceived as a factor that can contribute to stability and even a solution to the security dilemma. A third party's assurance is expected to short-circuit the security dilemma and provide security for respective groups.

However, in Iraq the situation became quite the opposite: roots of the sectarian conflict lie in U.S. occupation because 'chaos was unleashed when the Americans arrived' (Kalyvas and Kocher 2007, 214–15). Occupation by the U.S.-led coalition forces contributed to the security dilemma and brought to life a conflict with religious dimensions. The ouster of the Baath regime in April 2003 changed the balance of power among Iraq's major communities. This huge turnover empowered the Shiite majority and marginalized the Sunni minority. While this moment stood as an opportunity to redress injustices during Sunni domination by Shiites and Kurds, Sunni Arabs became more anxious, insecure, fearful, and unsure about their place in the society (Nasr 2006). As expected by the security dilemma argument, the threatened group – Sunni Arabs – responded with violence (against U.S. troops and Shiites) with the hope that political advancement could be achieved that way (Kalyvas and Kocher 2007; Lischer 1998).

The U.S.-led coalition in the country not only set the stage for emergence of communal war, it also became part of the 'emerging entrapment' and security problem that post-Saddam Iraq had been experiencing (Fontan 2006). Carried out ineptly over several years, U.S. occupation unleashed fear and 'opened the door for a variety of ruthless entrepreneurs to use violence to reshape politics along communal lines.' The occupation also provided the opportunity for groups to address perceived threats by force (Kalyvas and Kocher 2007, 215). For such reasons, in addition to the attacks against coalition forces, a growing spiral of sectarian violence between and among religious militias took place.

Fontan (2006, 220) reports that, according to the results of a poll conducted in four different regions of Iraq, 80 per cent of Iraqis agree that it would have been impossible to topple Saddam without direct military action by U.S. and British forces. However, in the same poll, more than

80 per cent of the Iraqis interviewed in Baghdad (in both Sunni and Shiite areas) indicated that they perceive coalition forces as 'occupiers' rather than liberators. It is clear that the U.S. presence in Iraq polarized part of the Iraqi population against the coalition forces and hence 'the US occupation itself has facilitated the insurgency' (Dodge 2006, 214).

How did the United States make insurgency feasible for the communal groups? How did U.S. occupation enable the growth and maturation of the Iraqi insurgency (Sepp 2007)? Why did newly liberated Iraqis perceive the coalition forces as occupiers and engage in terrorist activities instead of feeling indebted to them for having liberated their country? One major reason, as admitted by Geoff Hoon, the former U.K. secretary of state for defence, was unexpected resistance of Iraqis: 'The Americans were thinking in terms of a relatively benign environment in the post-conflict planning ... [W]e did not take as much account as we should have done of the issues of security' (Smith 2004). Expecting Iraqis to greet American soldiers as liberators was a major miscalculation and represented naive optimism of U.S. policy-makers (Norton 2004). The coalition forces did not have a well thought-out plan for post-Saddam Iraq that included a plausible response to insurgency.

When U.S. forces failed to monopolize the use of force, establish rule of law and order, and restore public services in the immediate aftermath of the war, the Iraqi people lost confidence in the coalition. Violent politically motivated groups emerged and U.S. forces could not prevent the looting that ensued. Under those circumstances the Iraqi people had no choice but to rely on the 'self-help' principle and provide their own security: 'The growing sense of violence encouraged a deep sense of insecurity in the wider population of Iraq, in turn increasing resentment against occupation' (Dodge 2005, 12). During such difficult times 'people look to whatever grouping, militia, or identity offers them the best chance of survival' and local, ethnic, religious identities provide the basis for political organization (Dodge 2007, 26). This is exactly what happened in Iraq: the continued occupation of Iraq and failures of the United States increased nationalist and religious resentment and, in turn, strengthened the insurgency. It also contributed to further fragmentation of society along ethnic, religious, and sectarian lines (Davis 2005; Marr 2007; Sirriyeh 2007).

Dodge (2006) argues that for post–Cold War peacekeeping operations to be successful, restoration of the rule of law and order in two to six weeks after the occupation is essential. Otherwise the credibility and the legitimacy of the occupiers will be questioned by the population. In Iraq, three weeks of uncontrolled violence and looting following the war tarnished the image of the coalition forces. Iraqis started to question the capability, willingness, and motivation of the U.S. forces. Dodge states that 'the security vacuum that came to dominate Iraq ... helped turn criminal violence and looting into an organized and politically motivated insurgency' (2006, 214).

Another possible reason for polarization between occupier and the occupied is the role of humiliation. Some policies of the coalition marginalized the Sunni Arab community and created a fertile ground for ex-Baathists and foreign militants (Davis 2005; Fontan 2006). One hasty decision was to dismantle the army and initiate de-Baathification in order to remove all traces of the old regime. In May 2003 the Coalition Provisional Authority (CPA) led by Paul Bremer stripped many ex–army officers and security force personnel of their power – but did so without ordering them to surrender their weapons. This decision put approximately half a million unemployed on the street overnight. Sunni Arabs who lost income, social status, and privileges became very angry and frustrated (Baram 2005). Nationalistic Iraqis associated with the Baath party were further humiliated when they were forced to sign a form abjuring membership and promising to obey the laws of Iraq and orders of the CPA.[5] According to Fontan (2006), all of these actions victimized the 'victimizers,' the ones who used their power to terrorize the population during Saddam's regime, and eventually antagonized a major part of the Iraqi population, including the Sunni professionals and elite.

Fontan (2006) argues that the negative impact of de-Baathification is by no means limited to 'victimizer': it also antagonized the 'vulnerable.' The immediate result of dismantling of the regular army and police forces was a breakdown of law and order, widespread looting, and violent crime. Providing peace and security became the sole responsibility of the coalition forces; however, since coalition forces were insufficient[6] and incredibly busy chasing the insurgents,[7] they failed to protect the Iraqi people and their property. Lawlessness served the interests of the organized crime networks,[8] increased radicalization of Islamic groups, and strengthened anti-American sentiments (Barakat 2005; Sirriyeh 2007).

Two additional factors contributed to the negative sentiments of Iraqis: non-combatant casualties and the behaviour of American troops – most notably abuse of Iraqi prisoners in Abu Ghraib prison. As civilian casualties increased, Sunni Arabs became more antagonistic to coalition forces. Similarly, U.S. troops who were unfamiliar with the cultural context and religion offended Iraqis. Scandals regarding the treatment of Iraqis and the insulting behaviour of troops (like male soldiers conducting body searches on Iraqi women, male insurgents being handcuffed and blindfolded in public interrogations, Iraqi men being forced to the ground and having their heads stepped on in front of their families, homes being entered without knocking), fostered resentment and resistance to the coalition forces (Baram 2005; Davis 2005; Hashim 2006). 'Cultural mistreatment carried significant weight among a society where tribal honor is all' (Karam 2007, 94).

Another important factor contributing to the growth and maturation of the Iraqi insurgency was, as mentioned earlier, religion. During Saddam's years in power, ethno-religious identities were used to justify the status quo, which was Sunni Arab rule. In the post-Saddam period, 'there [was] a clear ascendancy of Islamist ideology on the Iraqi political scene' and 'Islam ... definitely emerged as the most effective source of mobilization within the various communities and groupings across the Iraqi sectarian spectrum' (Sidahmed 2007, 82). In other words, with the U.S.-led occupation, religion became a source of change and mobilization in Iraq and contributed to fragmentation of society along religious lines. Multiple religious groups and their leaders saw an opportunity to increase their legitimacy. After the occupation, 'with the collapse, destruction, or weakening of secular political structures and ideologies, religious identity emerged as the most effective catalyst for political organization in post-Saddam Iraq. In such an atmosphere, mosques – both Sunni and Shia – [became] the focal points of political mobilization and vehicles for assembly, propaganda and recruitment' (ibid.).

In addition, the physical presence of American troops on Iraqi territory unleashed both anti-American and anti-Christian sentiments. Fighting against Americans became linked to fighting against Christians. As the coalition failed to provide order in Iraq, Sunni and Shiite Islamists connected to Iran or Al-Qaeda had the opportunity to build on the already marginalized religious identities. Arrest and detention of religious leaders increased the motivation of different groups to become involved in the insurgency (Hashim 2006). As coalition forces used coercion to decrease insurgency, they were seen more as 'brutal' and 'Christian' occupiers.

In sum, after the initial stages of the occupation, Iraqis started to cluster around their ethnic and religious communities to increase their security. As the insurgency escalated in Iraq, the United States realized it did not have enough troops to provide security in Iraq. The harsh U.S military response produced civilian casualties, led to increased insurgency, and reinforced the perception of the United States as an 'occupier' rather than a 'liberator' (Hashim 2006; Papagianni 2007). 'The US invasion triggered the reactivation and sharpening of the sectarian cleavage, which [took] on a new and constantly evolving form' (Kalyvas and Kocher 2007, 188). Although the 'surge' helped the Iraqi government to restore order to some extent, the country still remains volatile. Given the complex nature of insurgency, we next will identify some of the important groups that have been influential since 2003 and identify their motivations and role in the security dilemma.

Forces of Insurgency

While the civil war that began in 2004 was mainly between Sunni and Shiite insurgents and coalition forces, it later escalated to sectarian violence between Sunnis and Shiites as well as Kurds and other communities in Northern Iraq. There was also substantial criminal gang violence (Fearon 2007; Kaufman 2006). Biddle (2006) states that the Sunni heartland, comprising four provinces, accounted for 85 per cent of all insurgent attacks. By contrast, the fourteen other provinces accounted for only 15 per cent of the violence. Therefore, likely the vast majority of insurgents were Sunni Iraqis who had ruled the country since Ottoman times.

It is a challenging task to build a profile of the anti-coalition Sunni Arab insurgency. While they all reject the idea of living under foreign occupation and fear longer-term Shiite supremacy, their loyalties as well as motivations for fighting the U.S. forces differed significantly. Some Sunni groups have a more secular outlook, as opposed to ultra-radical Salafis and Wahabis (Baram 2005). Likewise, while some are former Baath members and Saddam loyalists, others show primary adherence to Islamic principles and see Iraq as an arena for global struggle against the West. Sunni nationalists perceived U.S. troops as the protector of a Shiite- and Kurdish-dominated government and opposed establishment of permanent military bases in Iraq to control the country and the oil (Biddle 2006). Instead of treating Sunnis as a single cohesive group, we differentiate them on the basis of their motivations.

The first group comprises former Saddam loyalists – former members of the security forces (especially the republican guard, the Fedayeen

Saddam) and his clientiele network. They were known to be responsible for up to 60 per cent of the politically motivated violence in Iraq (Dodge 2006). Taking advantage of the vulnerabilities of U.S. troops and chaos in the aftermath of the invasion, they launched many hit-and-run attacks on U.S. soldiers (Dodge 2005). As mentioned earlier, former Saddam loyalists and Baath party members resented the fact that they lost all privileges that they enjoyed through patron-client networks during Saddam's rule. The de-Baathification and dissolution of the army in May 2003 hurt the economic, social, and ideological interests of pan-Arab/Sunni nationalists. The losses, humiliation of living under foreign occupation, and fear of Shiite domination motivated Sunni Arabs for an armed struggle against coalition forces and the new Iraqi state. Many ex-Baathists established underground organizations to advance the sectarian interests of the Sunnis and fight coalition forces. By raising arms against the coalition forces, they hoped to return to the position of supremacy once again and prevent Shiite and Kurdish ascendancy (Baram 2005).

A strong Islamist orientation is the defining characteristic of the Sunni insurgent groups and their discourse is a combination of Islamism with Iraqi nationalism. As mentioned earlier, in the last decade of Saddam's rule, there was a clear shift towards Islam with the goal to regain lost support from society. By the 1980s, many Sunni Arabs adopted Islam as their ideology. Given that during Saddam's regime all non-Baathist social, civil, and political institutions except mosques were eliminated, Islam served critical purposes after the removal of Saddam from power. Moderate Islamists opposed the U.S. presence and preferred Islam to play a major role in the new Iraqi state; however, they opposed the idea of becoming an Islamic republic like Iran (Baram 2005). Wahabis and Salafis, on the other hand, had a much more radical outlook and their interpretation of Islamic principles was quite different from those of the moderate Sunnis. They viewed Shiites and others who do not subscribe to their ideology as infidels (Nasr 2004). Their identity and world view were known to be rigid, fixed, and uncompromising.

In addition to opposing foreign occupation, some Sunni groups, like Zarqhawi's Tanzim al-Qa'idat al-Jihad fi Bilad al-Rafidayn, had targeted Shiite and Kurdish political figures and triggered inter-communal sectarian violence. They were well known for their brutal tactics, like beheading foreign hostages and posting pictures of them on the Internet. The initiation of a sectarian conflict was central to Al-Qaeda's strategy in Iraq. Al-Qaeda's Zarqawi, killed by a U.S. strike in June

2006, once stated that the best way to 'prolong the duration of the fight between the infidels and us is by dragging them into a sectarian war, this will awaken sleepy Sunnis who are fearful of destruction and death at hands of the Shia' (Dodge 2006, 219). Jihadists believed that as the sectarian violence escalated, Iraq would become very unstable and eventually untenable for U.S. forces.

Most powerful among the Shiite militia was the Badr brigades – the military wing of the largest Shiite party in Iraq, the SCIRI. It was established in the 1980s in Iran among Iraqi exiles and its primary goal was to overthrow Saddam's regime in favour of an Islamic state. Trained by the Iranian Revolutionary Guard, Badr Brigades carried out numerous attacks including ambushes, sabotage, and assassinations against the regime. Since the invasion they had created severe security threats to the Iraqi state, especially in places like Basra and Baghdad (Cole 2007). Badr Brigades provided the local security in some neighbourhoods in the south, including Najaf, Karbala, Nasiriyah, Diwaniyah, and some part of Basra. The United States had unable to disarm and halt their influence in these areas. Cole (2007) notes that in areas with a mixed population, like Baghdad, the Badr Brigades had participated in ethnic cleansings and organized death squads against Sunni Arabs.

Another significant militia group among the Shiite community is the Sadr movement. The Mahdi army is led by Muqtada al-Sadr, a young, radical Shiite cleric. His nationalist and radical Islamic rhetoric had mobilized many poor Shiites against U.S. troops. Mahdi fighters had staged uprisings and carried out attacks against U.S. forces. The Sadr movement had managed to control 'the major mosques, Shiite community centers, hospitals and soup kitchens in East Baghdad, Kufa and Samarra and [had] strong presence in Najaf, Karbala and Basra, as well. It [was] highly networked and its preachers [took] a strong rhetorical line against what they view[ed] as an "Anglo-American occupation"' (Cole 2003b, 564). Although it eventually participated in the political process, Sadr's movement continued to oppose the occupation and policies of the U.S. Sectarian guerrilla forces, including Badr Brigades and Mahdi Army, exacerbated the sectarian tensions; this, in turn, posed a major threat to the security of the new Iraqi state.

In sum, the goal of Shiite groups was to end foreign occupation, impose religious authority on the public, and ensure that Sunnis become a subordinated minority under religious leadership of the Shiite. They complained about U.S. treatment of Shiite leaders and believed that coalition forces were imperialists doing nothing for stability or state-building in Iraq. The Sadr movement's antagonism was not limited to coalition forces; they were also hostile to secularist Iraqis and other Shiite religious forces (rival sects) since their goal was to monopolize 'sacred space in Iraq' (Cole 2003b). According to Cole (2003b, 546), Shiites inspired by Al-Sadr and his successors were 'radicalized by the example of Iran and by the brutality of the Ba'th persecution.' The most serious danger here originates from this radicalization and marginalization. There are deep grievances against both the old regime and the West. Moreover, radical Shiites are well organized and armed and contribute significantly to the security dilemma in Iraq.

Other groups that advanced the insurgency in Iraq were criminal gangs and foreign nationals. Industrial-scale criminal gangs use techniques like kidnapping, extortion, car-jacking, and break-ins to terrorize the population (Dodge 2005, 2006). Similarly, foreign nationals from Syria, Saudi Arabia, Yemen. and Sudan contributed to the insurgency and violence. Although their role in insurgency is high profile, it is interesting to note that they accounted for less than 10 per cent of the violence.

Implications and Conclusions

According to the Bush Doctrine, pre-emptive use of force in Iraq was based on the risk of weapons of mass destruction being used against the United States. Overthrowing Saddam was considered the first step 'in the eventual regional democratization of the entire Middle East' (Schmidt and Williams 2008, 200). Contrary to expectations, strong external intervention failed to bring peace and security to Iraq, at least in the short or medium term. Instead the lack of a solid counter-insurgency strategy and adequate troop levels increased tensions, and U.S. involvement deepened and transformed the security dilemma. Many Muslims came to perceive the war against Iraq as 'an attack by the Christian world against Muslims and even an attempt by Christianity to gain a foothold in the Muslim world' (Fox 2004b, 21).

Snyder and Jervis (1999) suggest that to solve the security dilemma problem it is important to answer the question of who will rule the country as quickly and decisively as possible. More importantly, it is essential to find a satisfactory answer to how the country will be ruled. In ethnic and religious civil wars with stubborn rivalries, along with diffuse and ill-defined groups, it is always a challenge to provide leadership and control that will bring stability and order. Iraq has managed to hold elections and create a government in spite of extreme political and religious affiliations among its people. Yet the transition is far from complete.

Despite the fact that U.S. troops handed security to Iraqi forces, sectarian instincts and lack of trust continue to be strong on all sides. The old ethnic and sectarian divides and tensions – between Arab and Kurd and between Sunni and Shiite – persist. Continuous attacks occur against civilians as well as the unity government, to destabilize the government and the political process. Sectarian militias have become one of the most important problems the Iraqi state is facing today. The military 'surge' aimed to improve security in Iraq so its government could function. In January 2008, the Iraqi parliament approved an 'accountability and justice' act that reverses some of the de-Baathification policies (*Economist*, 19 January 2008). Attempts to isolate Al-Qaeda and similar groups from the bottom up have showed some success.

We believe that without a functioning state and some degree of predictability in their lives, Iraqis will continue to demand protection from various groups and maintain an emphasis on their ethnic and sectarian identity (Dodge 2007). Therefore, the best way to minimize further fragmentation in Iraq is to create stable and efficient state institutions that can ensure order and security, along with public services. It is also essential to fight the endemic corruption within the Iraqi system – including the army.

In addition, it is important to note that systems that rely on exclusion and marginalization rather than social inclusion and power sharing are at higher risk of conflict (Lischer 1998). Therefore, an institutional framework with a system of checks and balances that prevents patronage, along with a power-sharing structure that guarantees security for all parties, should be priorities for policy-makers. The political arena must be widened in Iraq to include everybody because in a fragmented society, marginalization or exclusion is only a temporary solution. These observations simply reinforce the suggestion that the Iraqi government should try to bring all Iraqis into the political process, ease sectarian tensions, and encourage reconciliation among Iraqi factions. Grievances in Iraqi society have deep historical roots, and challenges to the unity and stability of Iraq will not disappear easily. If long-term policies are not developed using the breathing space created recently,

Iraq can be expected to fall back into intense violence. Only time will tell how the security dilemma dynamics of Iraq will change when U.S. troops leave Iraq by the end of 2011.

One strategy to consider further, in line with chapter 4 on human rights in the Muslim world, chapter 6 on religious humanitarianism, and chapters 12 and 14 on non-governmental organizations, would be coordination with FBOs. This pathway may have been inhibited because of military emphasis on national security among U.S. decision-makers, as described in chapter 2. Overcoming the sectarian security dilemma, however, is a problem that suggests the potential utility of FBOs in enhancing stability in Iraq.

Although this essay is concerned with Abrahamic religions, our conclusions can be applied to other religions. Security concerns constitute a cross-religious dynamic and they are part of a much larger pattern than political Islam. While Buddhism played a limited role in justifying a holy war in Sri Lanka against Hindus (Fox 2004b; Manor 1994), Hindu nationalism triggered violence in India (see chapter 7). Baha'is in Iran have not engaged in violence, yet they suffer from high levels of religious discrimination (Fox 2004b). Numerous states consider sects or cults such as the Church of Scientology, Sung Yung Moon's Unification Church, or Jehovah's Witnesses a major threat (Fox 2008). In short, the security dilemma is hardly limited to situations involving Islam.

NOTES

1 Some have assessed the relationship between religion and violence in general (Johnson and Sampson 1994; Rudolph and Piscatori 1997) and terrorism in particular (Drake 1998; Hoffman 1995; Juergensmeyer 2001; Rapaport 1984; Stern 2003). Other studies connect religion to genocide (Fein 1990) and ethnic cleansing (Osiander 2000).
2 See Appleby (2000), Brackney (2005), Coward (2005), Coward and Smith (2004), Florida (2005), Gopin (2000), Groff and Smoker (1996), Haas (2005), Johnston (2003), Little (1996), Sampson and Lederach (2000), Smith-Christopher (1998), and Smock (2006).
3 This is evident in chapters 10–14 on religious practice, along with accounts of human rights in the Muslim world and religious humanitarianism in chapters 4 and 6, respectively.
4 Cole (2003b, 550) explains the legacy of the 1991 uprisings: 'In major

Shi'ite population centers such as Basra, Nasiriyya, and Najaf, local Shi'ite religious figures emerged as popular political leaders supplanting Ba'th authority. The leaders were aware that the uprising could succeed only if it received US support. But the request for assistance ... was rejected by the US. The Ba'th military, seeing that the US had decided to remain neutral, massacred tens of thousands ... How many persons were killed and buried in mass graves may never be known, but it certainly ran into the tens of thousands.'

5 For example, a thirty-eight-year-old police officer who claimed to have been robbed by four U.S. soldiers at an army checkpoint expressed his humiliation, shame, and anger: 'Saddam never humiliated us the way Americans do, I had a job, I was safe, and now look at me' (Fontan 2006, 221).

6 Dodge (2006, 213) states that to impose order and rule of law in Iraq, between 400,000 and 500,000 troops would have been needed. However, during the invasion the United States had fewer than 120,000 soldiers in Iraq, with 310,000 personnel in the theatre as a whole.

7 Other causes of failure are inadequate planning, insufficient troops, and miscalculations.

8 Criminality had been another major problem for the Iraqi population, especially for women (Fontan 2006).

REFERENCES

Abu-Nimer, M. 2001. Conflict resolution, culture, and religion: Toward a training model of interreligious peacebuilding. *Journal of Peace Research* 38:685–704.

Anderson, L., and G. Stansfield. 2004. *The future of Iraq: Dictatorship, democracy, or division*. New York: Palgrave Macmillan.

Appleby, R.S. 2000. *The ambivalence of the sacred: Religion, violence and reconciliation*. Lanham, MD: Rowman & Littlefield.

Ayres, R.W., and S.M. Saideman. 2000. Is separatism as contagious as the common cold or as cancer? Testing the international and domestic determinants of secessionism. *Nationalism and Ethnic Politics* 6 (3): 92–114.

Barakat, S. 2005. Post-Saddam Iraq: Deconstructing a regime, reconstructing a nation. *Third World Quarterly* 26 (4–5): 571–91.

Baram, A. 2003. Saddam's power structure: The Tikritis before, during and after the war. In *Iraq at crossroads: State and society in the shadow of regime change*, ed. T. Dodge and S. Simon. Oxford: Oxford University Press.

– 2005. *Who are the insurgents? Sunni Arab rebels in Iraq*. Special report 134. Washington, DC: United States Institute of Peace.

Barkun, M. 1994. *Religion and the racist right*. Chapel Hill, NC: University of North Carolina Press.
Biddle, S. 2006. Seeing Baghdad, thinking Saigon. *Foreign Affairs* 85 (2): 2–14.
Billings, D.B., and S.L. Scott. 1994. Religion and political legitimization. *Annual Review of Sociology* 20:173–201.
Brackney, W.H. 2005. *Human rights and the world's major religions: The Christian tradition*. Westport, CT: Praeger.
Casanova, J. 1994. *Public religions in the modern world*. Chicago: University of Chicago Press.
Chaplin, E. 2006. Iraq's new constitution: Recipe for stability of chaos. *Cambridge Review of International Affairs* 19 (2): 271–84.
CIA World Factbook. https://www.cia.gov/library/publications/the-world-factbook/index.html
Cole, J. 2003a. Did Saddam gas the Kurds? History News Network, http://hnn.us/articles/1242.html.
– 2003b. The United States and Shi'te religious factions in post Ba'thist Iraq. *Middle East Journal* 57 (4): 543–66.
– 2006. A 'Shiite crescent'? The regional impact of the Iraqi war. *Current History* January: 20–6.
– 2007. Shia militias in Iraqi politics. In *Iraq: Preventing a new generation of conflict*, ed. M. E. Boullion, D.M. Malone, and B. Rowswell. Boulder, CO: Riener.
Coward, H. 2005. *Human rights and the world's major religions: The Hindu tradition*. Westport, CT: Praeger.
Coward, H., and G.S. Smith, eds. 2004. *Religion and peacebuilding*. Albany: State University of New York Press.
Davis, E. 2005. History matters: Past as prologue in building democracy in Iraq. *Orbis* Spring: 229–44.
Dodge, T. 2005. *Iraq's future: The aftermath of regime change*. Adelphi series. New York: Routledge.
– 2006. War and resistance in Iraq: From regime change to collapsed state. In *The Iraq war: Causes and consequences*, ed. R. Fawn and R. Hinnebush. London: Riener.
– 2007. State collapse and the rise of identity politics. In *Iraq: Preventing a new generation of conflict*, ed. M.E. Boullion, D.M. Malone, and B. Rowswell. Boulder: Riener.
Drake, C.J.M. 1998. The role of ideology in terrorists' target selection. *Terrorism and Political Violence* 10 (2): 53–85.
Economist. 2007a. The new wars of religion: An old menace has returned, but in very different forms. 3 November.

- 2007b. The new wars of religion: Faith will unsettle politics everywhere this century; it will do so least when it is separated from the state. 3 November.
- 2007c. In God's name: Religion will play a big role in this century's politics. 3 November.
- 2008. A hint of political compromise at last: The passage of a long-awaited law offers a ray of hope for reconciliation. 19 January.

Fearon, J.D. 2007. Iraq's civil war. *Foreign Affairs* 86 (2): 1–13.

Fein, H. 1990. Genocide: A sociological perspective. *Current Sociology* 38 (1): 1–126.

Florida, R.E. 2005. *Human rights and the world's major religions: The Buddhist tradition.* Westport, CT: Praeger.

Fontan, V. 2006. Polarization between occupier and occupied in post-Saddam Iraq: Colonial humiliation and the formation of political violence. *Terrorism and Political Violence* 18:217–38.

Fox, J. 1997. The salience of religious issues in ethnic conflicts: A large-N study. *Nationalism and Ethnic Politics* 3 (3): 1–19.
- 2001. Religious causes of international intervention in ethnic conflicts. *International Politics* 38 (4): 515–31.
- 2004a. Correlated conflicts: The independent nature of ethnic strife. *Harvard International Review* 25 (4): 58–62.
- 2004b. *Religion, civilization and civil war.* Lanham: Lexington Books.
- 2004c. Religion and state failure: An examination of the extent and magnitude of religious conflict from 1950 to 1996. *International Political Science Review* 25 (1): 55–76.
- 2008. *A world survey of religion and the state.* New York: Cambridge University Press.

Fox, J., and S. Sandler. 2004. *Bringing religion into international relations.* New York: Palgrave Macmillan.

Gill, A.J. 1994. Rendering unto Caesar? Religious competition and Catholic political strategy in Latin America, 1962–79. *American Journal of Political Science* 38 (2): 403–25.

Gopin, M. 2000. *Between Eden and Armageddon: The future of world religions, violence and peacemaking.* New York: Oxford University Press.

Groff, L., and P. Smoker. 1996. Spirituality, religion, culture, and peace: Exploring the foundations for inner-outer peace in the twenty-first century. *International Journal of Peace Studies* 1 (1). http://www.gmu.edu/programs/icar/ijps/vol1_1/smoker.html.

Gurr, T.R. 2000. *Peoples versus states: Minorities at risk in the new century.* Washington, DC: United States Institute of Peace.

Haas, P.J. 2005. *Human rights and the world's major religions: The Jewish tradition.* Westport, CT: Praeger.
Hadden, J.K. 1987. Toward desacralizing secularization theory. *Social Forces* 65: 587–611.
Harris, F.C. 1994. Something within: Religion as a mobilizer of African-American political activism. *Journal of Politics* 56 (1): 42–68.
Hart, S. 2001. *Cultural dilemmas of progressive politics.* Chicago: University of Chicago Press.
Hashim, A.S. 2006. *Insurgency and counter-insurgency in Iraq.* Ithaca, NY: Cornell University Press.
Haynes, J. 1997. Religion, secularization and politics: A postmodern conspectus. *Third World Quarterly* 18 (4): 709–28.
– 2007. *An introduction to international relations and religion.* Harlow: Pearson/Longman
Hoffman, B. 1995. Holy terror: The implications of terrorism motivated by a religious imperative. *Studies in conflict and terrorism* 18:271–84.
Hurd, I. 1999. Legitimacy and authority in international politics. *International Organization* 53 (2): 379–408.
Jelen, T.G., and C.C. Wilcox, eds. 2002. *Religion and politics in comparative perspective: The one, the few and the many.* New York: Cambridge University Press.
Johnston, D. 2003. *Trumping realpolitik: Faith-based diplomacy.* New York: Oxford University Press.
Johnston, D., and C. Sampson, eds. 1994. *Religion, the missing dimension of statecraft.* Oxford: Oxford University Press.
Johnston, H., and J. Figa. 1988. The church and political opposition: Comparative perspectives on mobilization against authoritarian regimes. *Journal for the Scientific Study of Religion* 27 (1): 32–47.
Juergensmeyer, M. 1993. *The new cold war? Religious nationalism confronts the secular state.* Berkeley: University of California Press.
– 1995. The new religious state. *Comparative Politics* 27 (4): 379–91.
– 2001. *Terror in the mind of God: The global rise of religious violence.* Berkeley: University of California Press.
Kalyvas, S.N., and M.A. Kocher. 2007. Ethnic cleavages and irregular war: Iraq and Vietnam. *Politics and Society* 35 (2): 183–223.
Karam, S. 2007. The multi-faced Sunni insurgency: A personal reflection. *Civil Wars* 9 (1): 87–105.
Kaufmann, C. 2006. Separating Iraqis, saving Iraq. *Foreign Affairs* 85 (4): 156–60.
Khosla, D. 1999. Third world states as interveners in ethnic conflicts: Implica-

tions for regional and international security. *Third World Quarterly* 20 (6): 1143–56.

Lischer, S.K. 1998. Causes of communal war: Fear and feasibility. *Studies in conflict and terrorism* 22:331–55.

Little, D. 1996. Religious militancy. In *Managing global chaos*, ed. C.A. Crocker and F.O. Hampson, 79–91. Washington, DC: United States Institute of Peace Press.

Manor, James. 1994. Organizational weakness and the rise of Sinhalese Buddhist extremism. In *Accounting for fundamentalism: The dynamic character of movements*, ed. Martin E. Marty and R. Scott Appleby, 770–84. Chicago: University of Chicago Press.

Marr, P. 2007. Iraq's identity crisis. In *Iraq: Preventing a new generation of conflict*, ed. M.E. Boullion, D.M. Malone, and B. Rowswell. Boulder: Riener.

Marty, M.E., and R.S. Appleby. 1992. *The glory and the power: The fundamentalist challenge to the modern world*. Boston: Beacon.

McAdam, D. 1982. *Political process and the development of Black insurgency 1930–1970*. Chicago: University of Chicago Press.

McCarthy, J.D., and M.N. Zald. 1977. Resource mobilization and social movements: A partial theory. *American Journal of Sociology* 82 (6): 1212–41.

Mockaitis, T.R. 2007. *The Iraq war: Learning from the past, adapting to the present, and planning for the future*. Unpublished paper.

Nasr, V. 2004. Regional implications of Shi'a revival in Iraq. *Washington Quarterly* 27 (3): 7–24.

– 2006. When the Shiites rise. *Foreign Affairs* 85 (4): 58–74.

Norell, M. 2007. Iraq: Quo vadis? *Civil Wars* 9 (1): 1–7.

Norton, A.R. 2004. Making war, making peace: The Middle East entangles America. *Current History* January: 3–7.

Osiander, A. 2000. Religion and politics in Western civilization: The Ancient World as matrix and mirror of the Modern. *Millennium* 29 (3): 761–90.

Papagianni, K. 2007. State building and transitional politics in Iraq: The perils of a top-down transition. *International Studies Perspectives* 8:253–71.

Posen, B. 1993. The security dilemma and ethnic conflict. *Survival* 35:27–47.

Rapoport, D. C.1984. Fear and trembling: Terrorism in three religious traditions. *American Political Science Review* 78:658–77.

Reychler, L. 1997. Religion and conflict. *International Journal of Peace Studies* 2 (1): 19–38.

Reynal-Querol, M. 2002. Ethnicity, political systems, and civil wars. *Journal of Conflict Resolution* 46 (1): 29–54.

Roth, K. 2004. War in Iraq: Not a humanitarian intervention. Human Rights. Watch World Report. http://www.hrw.org/legacy/wr2k4/3.htm#_Toc58744952.

Rudolph, S.H., and J. Piscatori. 1997. *Transnational religion and fading states.* Boulder, CO: Westview.

Rummel, R.J. 1997. Is collective violence correlated with social pluralism? *Journal of Peace Research* 34 (2): 163–75.

Sahliyeh, E., ed. 1990. *Religious resurgence and politics in the contemporary world.* New York: State University of New York Press.

Saideman, S.M. 1998. Is Pandora's box half-empty or half-full? In *The international spread of ethnic conflict: Fear, diffusion, and escalation,* ed. D.A. Lake, and D. Rothchild, 127–50. Princeton: Princeton University Press

Saideman, S.M., and R.W. Ayres. 2000. Determining the sources of irredentism: Logit analyses of minorities at risk data. *Journal of Politics* 62 (4): 1126–44.

Saideman, S.M., and M. Zahar. 2007. Causing security, reducing fear: Deterring intra-state violence and assuring government restraint. Unpublished paper.

Sampson, C., and J.P. Lederach. 2000. *From the ground up: Mennonite contributions to international peacebuilding.* New York: Oxford University Press.

Schmidt, Brian C., and Michael C. Williams. 2008. The Bush doctrine and the Iraq war: Neoconservatives versus realists. *Security Studies* 17:191–220.

Sepp, K. 2007. From 'shock and awe' to 'hearts and minds': The fall and rise of US counterinsurgency capability in Iraq. *Third World Quarterly* 28 (2): 217–30.

Shupe, A. 1990. The stubborn persistence of religion in the global arena. In Sahliyeh, 17–26.

Sidahmed, A.S. 2007. Islamism, nationalism and sectarianism. In *Iraq: Preventing a new generation of conflict,* ed. M.E. Boullion, D.M. Malone, and B. Rowswell, 71–87. Boulder, CO: Riener.

Sirriyeh, H. 2007. Iraq and the region since the war of 2003. *Civil Wars* 9 (1): 106–25.

Smith, M. 2004. Hoon admits resistance came as a shock to allies. *Telegraph,* 19 March. http://www.telegraph.co.uk/news/worldnews/northamerica/usa/1457286/Hoon-admits-resistance-came-as-a-shock-to-allies.html.

Smith-Christopher, D.L. 1998. *Subverting hatred: The challenge of nonviolence in religious traditions.* Cambridge, MA: Boston Research Center for the 21st Century.

Smock, D.R. 2006, ed. Religious contributions to peacemaking: When religion brings peace, not war. United States Institute of Peace. Peaceworks 55. http://www.usip.org/resources/religious-contributions-peacemaking-when-religion-brings-peace-not-war.

Snyder, J., and R. Jervis. 1999. Civil war and the security dilemma. In *Civil wars, insecurity and intervention,* ed. B.F. Walter and J. Snyder, 15–37. Columbia University Press.

Solle, D. 1984. The Christian-Marxist debate of the 1960s. *Monthly Review* 36:20–6.

Stern, J. 2003. *Terror in the name of God: Why religious militants kill.* New York: Ecco/HarperCollins.

Tarrow, S. 1989. *Democracy and disorder: Protest and politics in Italy 1965–1975.* Oxford: Clarendon.

Toft, M.D. 2006. Religion, civil war and international order. Discussion paper no. 2006-03. Cambridge, MA: Belfer Center for Science and International Affairs, John F. Kennedy School of Government, Harvard University.

– 2007. Getting religion? The puzzling case of Islam and civil war. *International Security* 31 (4): 97–131.

U.S. Department of State. 2001. Iraq: International religious freedom report. http://www.state.gov/g/drl/rls/irf/2001/5693.htm.

9 World Religions and Local Identities: The Case of Islamic Arbitration in Ontario, Canada

PATRICIA M. GOFF

(Why) do societies that are committed to tolerance and inclusion still recoil against the religious diversity that global flows engender? What are the limits of multicultural governance? In what ways does religion represent a particularly sensitive area for policy-makers working to navigate globalizing influences? This chapter uses a case study from Canadian politics to explore these questions. From 2004 through 2005, an Ontario government review of religious arbitration practices produced a passionate public debate about the prospects of Islamic arbitration in Ontario family law. The outcome suggests that, even in societies that have made great progress toward cultural diversity and peaceful accommodation of immigrant communities, there are limits to what local identities will accommodate. This is not a straightforward case of adherents to one religious tradition lining up against adherents to another. Rather, it is a complex story of heterogeneity within religious communities and of the challenge that contemporary religious debates pose to collective understandings of who we think we are.

In this chapter, two questions at the centre of this volume receive particular attention: How does identity factor into debates about religion and global governance? And what role do religious groups play in formulating and implementing foreign policy programs? The pages that follow suggest that answers to these questions are related to each other. Recent rejection of Islamic law–based family law tribunals in the province of Ontario, Canada, is reviewed at length. Cases like this, as will become apparent, can shine a light on practical and conceptual challenges of integrating Muslim communities into Western society. Furthermore, fuller understanding of such occurrences in all likelihood requires greater appreciation of the implications for identities of politically active Muslim communities in the West. Finally, it seems that how we resolve domestic diversity challenges has implications for foreign policy. Citizens who have participated in local debates over Islam's place in Canadian civil law are the same citizens who, in turn, weigh in on Canadian foreign policies toward the Muslim world and vice versa. Each debate informs the other in a variation on the two-level game.

Constructivist theorizing teaches us that how we understand our interests and how we shape our policy depends at least partially on how we understand ourselves vis-à-vis our policy partners: 'A fundamental principle of constructivist social theory is that people act toward objects, including other actors, on the basis of the meanings that the objects have for them. States act differently toward enemies than they do toward friends because enemies are threatening and friends are not ... U.S. military power has a different significance for Canada than for Cuba' (Wendt 1992, 396). Adler makes a similar point when he says about groups, including nations, 'Where they go, how, when and why, is not entirely determined by physical forces and constraints; but neither does it depend solely on individual preferences and rational choices. It is also a matter of their shared knowledge, the collective meaning they attach to their situation, their authority and legitimacy, the rules, institutions and material resources they use to find their way, and their practices, or even, sometimes, their joint creativity' (1997, 321). The preceding discussion dovetails with an approach based on 'thick religion' as advocated by chapter 3. Religious beliefs and practices are important to understanding what is observed, though often in more complex ways than dichotomous, 'we versus they' renderings might suggest.

In contemporary foreign policy debates, the object is often another state, but it also has become 'Muslims' or 'the Muslim world.' Support for and barriers to good relations have been erected in the minds of Western publics. This point is made graphically in chapters 4 and 6, which respectively focus on human rights in the Muslim world and religious humanitarianism. Interactions with members of diaspora communities residing in our own countries at least partially inform public attitudes toward their homelands. In the other direction, acrimony about international-level occurrences can poison otherwise smoothly functioning multi-ethnic environments.

In 1991, the New Democratic Party government of Ontario's Premier Bob Rae passed the Arbitration Act. Ostensibly the product of a desire to ease pressure on the Ontario provincial court system, the Act made decisions of faith-based, private, civil arbitration arrangements binding in Ontario law. Members of religious groups – Jews, Catholics, Muslims, and Aboriginal groups, among others – could use the guiding principles of their faith to settle family disputes such as divorce, custody disputes, and inheritances outside the court system. The process is voluntary and parties to it must agree to its use. The Jewish community used the Act to arbitrate disputes according to rabbinical law, Catholics used it to annul marriages, and so on.

In 2003, the Islamic Institute of Civil Justice (IICJ) announced that it intended to set up Islamic law–based arbitration panels, sparking a controversy after thirteen years of seemingly unproblematic use of tribunals by other faith communities. There was immediate concern that Muslim law–based tribunals might leave certain people at a disadvantage, especially newcomers to Canada, who might not know their rights, and women who might feel pressured by their communities to use a faith-based mediation system that did not grant them equal status. Islam is Canada's fastest growing religion. According to the 1991 census, 579,640 Muslims live in Canada, more than twice the number counted ten years earlier. Sixty-one per cent, or 352,500, live in Ontario (Trichur 2004, 1). Some statistics put this number closer to 400,000. So this issue could not be ignored. In June 2004, at the direction of Ontario's Premier Dalton McGuinty, Attorney General Michael Bryant, and Minister Responsible for Women's Issues Sandra Pupatello appointed Marion Boyd to review the arbitration process and its impact on 'vulnerable' people in Ontario. (The word *vulnerable* is used six times in the one-page press release – it also shows up in numerous submissions to the investigating commission.)

Boyd's legal and feminist credentials are impressive. Among her qualifications, she served as attorney general and as minister responsible for women's issues, minister of education, and minister of community and social services in the government of Bob Rae, whose government had introduced the Arbitration Act. The attorney general's Terms of Reference directed Boyd to assess 'the impact that the use of arbitration may have on people who may be vulnerable including women, persons with disabilities and elderly persons. The review will include consideration of religious based arbitrations.' In addition, 'She shall consider the safeguards which are available to participants in different dispute resolution settings, and in different jurisdictions.'

Boyd invited submissions and undertook extensive consultations. In December 2004 she released a 150-page report, *Dispute Resolution in Family Law: Protecting Choice, Promoting Inclusion*. The report included forty-six recommendations, the most controversial being the second, that 'the Arbitration Act should continue to allow disputes to be arbitrated using religious law, if the safeguards currently prescribed and recommended by this review are observed.' Among the safeguards, Boyd recommended imposing a duty on arbitrators to ensure that parties understand their rights and are participating voluntarily; providing for greater oversight and accountability, including empowering courts to set aside arbitral awards if a party did not understand the nature or consequences of the arbitration agreement; and public education and community development to ensure that minority rights, and especially women's rights, would be protected (Boyd 2004).

In essence, Boyd was seen to be supporting sharia law in Ontario. Much public outcry ensued. In September 2005, Premier McGuinty banned all religious arbitration in Ontario. In February 2006, the Ontario legislature amended the Arbitration Act to allow only family arbitration based on Ontario or Canadian law. This ban does not mean that faith-based arbitration cannot continue, but it does mean that its rulings will not be binding and that there will be no provincial oversight of their activities. It bans arbitration not only for Muslims, but also for Jews, Christians, Aboriginal groups, and others. (It is interesting to note that McGuinty was re-elected with a landslide majority government in October 2007.)

For many, opposition to Islamic law in Ontario seems curious. Canada is a traditional 'country of immigration,' alongside Australia, the United States, and New Zealand. Siddiqui (2007, 45) observes that, whereas one in ten Americans is an immigrant, in Canada, one in five is. More importantly, domestic relations amid ethnic diversity have been peaceful. Rather than opting for a traditional nationalist model, Canada ostensibly is 'the world's first truly cosmopolitan, post-national state' (Ibbitson 2007, 52). It has been a model of multiculturalism in the sense that the central government made multiculturalism the law of the land in 1988. As Kymlicka (2007, 107) puts it, 'Canada was the first country to adopt an official multiculturalism policy, and as a result has played an important role in shaping international conceptions of what multiculturalism is ... Canada is widely seen around the world as a country where multiculturalism "exists" – where multiculturalism is a well-established practice, not just a rhetoric – and Canadian formulations are often studied as prototypes.' In practical terms, Canada has appeared more tolerant and inclusive than many of its peers. While Americans resist challenges to English as the predominant language of the United States, Canada adopted both English and French as official languages. While the French banned headscarves in the classroom for young Muslim women, Canada allowed Sikh-Canadians joining the Royal Canadian Mounted Police to preserve their turbans in place of the traditional Mountie hat. Many other examples of Canadian multiculturalism in action abound. So why such opposition to Muslim family law tribunals?

The easy answer is that Canadians are becoming xenophobic, anti-Islamic, or anti-Muslim. I say 'Canadians,' and not 'Ontarians,' because many who opposed Islamic arbitration were quick to point out that Quebec had already banned such practices and, indeed, the issue was taken up across the country. It would be naive to think that prejudice played no role in this outcome. But such an explanation is also not complex enough to capture the dynamics in play when immigrant groups navigate multicultural societies. Missing from the 'pandering to anti-Muslim sentiment for political expediency' explanation are the ways in which the prospect of family arbitration based on Islamic principles presents opportunities and challenges where identities are concerned. Ultimately a question of group rights, this issue strikes at the heart of who Muslim and non-Muslim Canadians think they are and highlights the diverse practices that they rely on to reinforce these understandings.[1]

Identity has become a central term in the lexicon of international relations scholars, especially for constructivists who employ it in a variety of ways (Klotz and Lynch 2007). There is an intuitive sense of what we mean when we speak of identity as an analytic category, but no consensus yet on what its many dimensions imply (Goff and Dunn, 2004). For my purposes here, I borrow from Taylor to approximate what is meant by *identity*. Taylor (2002, 91) uses the term *social imaginary*. According to Taylor, 'the social imaginary is not a set of ideas; rather it is what enables, through making sense of, the practices of a society ... It tells us something about how we ought to live together in society' (91–2) Taylor goes on to clarify: 'I am thinking rather of the ways in which people imagine their social existence, how they fit together with others, how things go on between them and their fellows, the expectations that are normally met, and the deeper normative notions and images that underlie these expectations' (106). According to Taylor, the social imaginary is 'that common understanding that makes possible common practices and a widely shared sense of legitimacy' (ibid.).

The debate over Islamic law in Ontario (and probably, too, about headscarves in France; see Bowen 2006) can be understood at least partially as a case of social imaginaries that appear incompatible, as the collision between a certain understanding of Muslim identity that challenges a certain understanding of how things are done in Canada. They are secondarily about religion per se. The link that Taylor makes between identity and practice is important. He argues that 'the relation between practices and the background understanding behind them is therefore not one-sided. If the understanding makes the practice possible, it is also true that the practice largely carries the understanding' (2002, 107). Identities are expressed in the Ontario case through sets of legal and religious practices. 'What exactly is involved when a theory penetrates and transforms the social imaginary? For the most part, people take up, improvise, or are inducted into new practices' (111). Resistance to new practices has the effect of ensuring that a transformation of the social imaginary will not take place as intended, if at all.

Analysing this set of events from the standpoint of identity requires attention to the terms in which parties to these debates express their views. How do they understand their own identity commitments? How do they suggest that these might be challenged or reinforced by the adoption of Muslim family law tribunals? Can Canadian society allow family arbitration based on Islamic law without fundamentally compromising the essence of what Canadian citizens understand as the foundation of their society? Can Muslims in Canada feel that they are fully Muslim in the absence of faith-based family arbitration procedures?

Marion Boyd received numerous submissions from interested parties during her investigation and spoke to numerous people. This evidence sheds light on just these sorts of identity concerns. In a nutshell, the debates seemed to unfold as an effort on the part of the Muslim community that supported faith-based tribunals to reassure Canadians that Muslim practices that may allow Muslims to be 'fully Muslim' need not disturb the Canadian 'social imaginary.' On the other hand, Muslims and others who opposed the tribunals often noted that faith-based alternative dispute resolution mechanisms are, in some sense, 'un-Canadian.'

Syed Mumtaz Ali, on behalf of the IICJ, suggested that adherence to Muslim family law was a religious obligation and, therefore, a practice central to 'being Muslim.' Other Muslim groups, however, avoided or rejected the language of obligation, opting instead to accentuate the synergies between Muslim and Canadian social imaginaries. For example, the Ismaili community described its conciliation and arbitration board system in terms of equity: 'Our processes are designed to operate in an equitable manner (equity being a paramount Islamic ethical value) and are thus entirely consistent with Canadian legal principles, such as natural justice' (His Highness Prince Aga Khan 2004, 1).

The Canadian office of the Council on American-Islamic Relations (CAIR-CAN) supported the tribunals in terms of rights and multiculturalism. In their submission to Boyd, they argued, 'It is our position that the Muslim community in Canada is entitled to use the alternative dispute resolution tools provided under the Arbitration Act in order to resolve civil disputes according to Islamic legal principles. Supporting the creation of Islamic family law tribunals, along with those of other faith groups, is a form of accommodating the needs of religious minorities within a multicultural society' (Council on American-Islamic Relations 2004, 4). From this perspective, allowing Muslims to engage in practices that are meaningful to them will not in any way detract from cherished Canadian values and practices. CAIR-CAN went on, 'Giving members of religious minority groups the option of resolving civil disputes according to their own religious doctrine within a framework that is respectful of both Canadian law and the *Charter of Rights and Freedoms* is consistent with the *Charter*'s own guarantee of freedom of religion contained in section 2(a).' Indeed, CAIR-CAN argued that allowing for Muslim family law tribunals would actually reinforce the values that underpin the Canadian system. Being Muslim is not incompatible with being Canadian, and respecting Muslim practices like arbitration according to Islamic legal principles strengthens the Canadian social imaginary. CAIR-CAN warned the Boyd commission against singling out the Muslim community, suggesting that such discrimination would contravene Canadian values to a greater degree than Muslim family law tribunals: 'It is appropriate that the current review of the arbitration processes being carried out by the Ministry of the Attorney General and the Ontario Women's Directorate is not confined to the proposed Muslim family law tribunals, as other faith groups also operate similar alternative dispute resolution systems. Likewise, any recommendations coming out of the present review must apply to all alternative dispute resolution mechanisms. The Ministry of the Attorney General must be vigilant not to subject one faith group to standards that are more onerous than those required of other communities, as to do so would be discriminatory and contrary to the *Charter*'s equality provision' (ibid., 4).

CAIR-CAN noted, 'It is inappropriate and misleading to use the word "shariah" to describe an arbitration tribunal that will use Islamic legal principles to resolve a very specific and limited set of civil disputes.' Recognizing the connotations that many Canadians attach to the term, CAIR-CAN noted that a faith-based tribunal 'is not a full-fledged Islamic court, as may be inferred by the use of the word "shariah," and its limited jurisdiction stems from the Act. The tribunal will, more appropriately, be a form of Muslim dispute resolution consistent with Canadian law and the *Charter* within the flexibility of Islamic normative principles.' Other supporters of faith-based arbitration echoed this view. For example, moderate Muslim cleric Ahmad Kutty noted, 'Shariah is a loaded word; it includes all of the civil, criminal and other institutions associated with the Islamic legal system. No one in his right mind would propose implementing this system of laws in Canada.'

The Islamic Society of North America (ISNA) also made an argument in favour of Islamic law–based family arbitration in terms of identities. According to its spokesperson, ISNA 'tries to promote integration without losing your Islamic identity.' She went on to say, 'The Canadian way to me is a way that accepts my religion, and makes the greatest attempt legally to accommodate religious practices including the right to pray, wear a hijab and all the rights that flow from religious accommodation ... I'm committed to a more orthodox, conservative faith, but it is not contrary to Canadian values. I see them as very much in sync. There are no monolithic Canadian values and no monolithic Muslim values' (Jimenez and El Akkad 2005).

Outside of the Muslim community, supporters of faith-based arbitration echoed these rhetorical approaches to the debate refracted through the lens of identity. An editorial in one of Canada's leading national newspapers, the *Globe and Mail*, said, 'Imposing secularism on [Muslims] is not Canada's way. "Canada is founded upon principles that recognize the supremacy of God and the rule of law," says the very first line of the Charter of Rights and Freedoms. This is a country that respects freedom of religion ... The Islamic tribunal may yet send a message that Muslims can be who they are and still be as Canadian as anyone else' (Editorial 2004).

Groups who opposed the Muslim family law also refracted their arguments through the lens of identity, engaging with the degree to which the proposed arbitration practices dovetailed with Canadian policy practices, laws, and values. Amnesty International expressed their concern about resolving family disputes with faith-based tribunals: 'Due to our experience with religious and customary laws in other countries around the world, we have reason to believe that these laws may be discriminatory and not fully compliant with international human rights standards' (Amnesty International Canada 2005, 1). Given their mandate as a human rights watchdog group, it is not surprising that Amnesty expressed their opposition in terms of human rights. Interestingly, though, they also tied this to Canadian identity. The text they proposed be sent to citizens' representatives starts, 'As a Canadian, I am proud of the leadership role Canada has played in developing international human rights standards to protect the fundamental rights of all people, including women' (ibid.).

Opposition to Muslim family law tribunals came from within the Canadian Muslim community. Many of these interventions also seemed to grapple with what it means to be Muslim versus what it means to be Canadian. For example, Homa Arjomand, coordinator of the International Campaign against Shari'a Courts in Canada, argued, 'In Canada, we uphold the separation of church and state, which means that there should be no religious determination in the laws that are applied through the courts' (n.d.). Elsewhere, Arjomand stated, 'We're living in Canada. We want Canadian secular law' (Wente 2004). Similarly, the Canadian Council of Muslim Women (CCMW) said, 'Sanctioning the use of religious laws under the Arbitration Act will provide legitimacy to practices that are abhorred by fair-minded Canadians, including Muslim women' (Canadian Council of Muslim Women 2005, 1). The CCMW worried in particular about 'refugees and immigrants who do not speak either official language – French or English – who are unaware of the Canadian Charter of Rights and Freedoms and who are most likely to be coerced by family and community pressure to submit to Sharia – like it or not' (Armstrong 2005). The CCMW went on to express very directly the compatibility of Muslim and Canadian values and practices: 'We believe that Islam's principles are for equality of women in every aspect, from religious, spiritual duties to practical daily rights and responsibilities of citizens. For us, Islam is a religion of peace, compassion, social justice and equality, and we know that many of the interpretations and practices of Muslim law do not always reflect these principles. Further, we think that these fundamentals are embodied in the Canadian Charter of Rights and Freedoms' (Canadian Council of Muslim Women 2004, 1).

After consultations with Muslim women across Canada, the CCMW proclaimed, 'We are pleased to be Canadians and to have Canadian laws for our issues' (ibid.). They went on to confirm the compatibility of Muslim values with the Canadian system, noting that Islam 'teaches social justice, compassion, community consciousness and equality of all peoples, and that these should be the values of any land. Canada has these values as articulated in the Charter of Rights and this is as Islamic as any document governing any country' (ibid.). The CCMW expressed their strong belief 'in Canada's Multiculturalism policy, for it celebrates our differences and allows groups such as ours to be proud of our multiple identities ... The Multiculturalism Act works within a larger framework, which includes the Constitution and Human Rights legislation. The argument being put forward is an abuse of a great Canadian value' (ibid.).

When Ontario's Premier Dalton McGuinty ordered a review of faith-based family arbitration, he echoed ongoing debates about how to reconcile what it means to be Canadian with what it means to be a Muslim in Canada. 'We welcome different cultures and different communities to find for themselves here in Ontario a new home, but at the same time we're saying that there is something that takes precedence over all practices in cultures and those are Canadian values as enshrined in human rights codes and in our Charter of Rights' (Lindgren 2004).

The debate about family law arbitration based on Islamic law principles did not take place solely in terms of identities. Of course, central arguments turned on what the faith-based tribunals might mean for Muslim women's rights. It also proceeded in terms of the separation of church and state in an ostensibly secular, rights-based, Western society. These arguments were peppered with concern about more extremist strains of Islam in Canada that might promote the kind of practices considered unacceptable in the West.

Interestingly, in many instances, these arguments were linked back to whether one could be Muslim and Canadian and whether engaging in practices meaningful to many Muslims might compromise beliefs and practices valued in Canada. Some argued that the outcome protected Muslim women's interests; others suggested they may be left worse off without government oversight of faith-based arbitration that would almost certainly continue inside Muslim and other religious communities. In terms of ethnocultural group rights, some suggested the outcome was a defeat for Muslim Canadians; others suggested it was a victory that preserved the social imaginary in which Canadian practices unfold. Still others worried that negative stereotypes about Muslims had been reinforced as evidence from the worst abuses of sharia law were invoked to oppose tribunals based on Islamic law principles. What might this debate tell us about the ongoing need to devise ways to live together in our cultural and religious diversity?

Paradoxically, though some framed this issue in terms of religion, it often seemed to be more about who we think we are and the limits of what we should be allowed to do. As many commentators pointed out, no objections to faith-based arbitration were raised before the IICJ raised the spectre of Islamic tribunals. There was no opposition to Catholic or Jewish panels. This would suggest that the debate was about Islamic tribunals specifically and not about faith-based arbitration more generally. To the degree that it is about religion, then, it is about often-uninformed perceptions of a religion, in this case Islam. But it is also about the limits of local identities in the face of globalization and diversity.

Likewise, the fact that the Muslim community was not united around a cohesive position casts doubt on the degree to which this debate is singularly about religion. Many in the Muslim community opposed family arbitration based on Islamic law. However, this opposition did not come from a rejection of their faith. Many Muslim opponents to the arbitration tribunals indicated that they were devout in their private lives, but supported secular institutions. Perhaps one of the most interesting features of this Islam-centred debate is the resonance it has with debates about Christianity. Just as many current debates about the prominence of religion in the United States question the compatibility of religion and liberalism, so is the Islamic family law debate, at bottom, about this apparent tension.

The issue of liberalism is also relevant to multicultural policy. As Kymlicka (2007) has shown, multiculturalism as it exists in places like Canada is *liberal* multiculturalism. Multicultural policies 'go beyond the protection of the basic civil and political rights guaranteed to all individuals in a liberal-democratic state, to also extend some level of public recognition and support for ethnocultural minorities to maintain and express their distinct identities and practices' (16). Nonetheless, at bottom, they spring from an impulse to protect and promote the civil, political, and social rights at the heart of liberal democracy. As such, multicultural policies do not seek to create atomized groups and affirm unique practices; rather, they seek to integrate groups into the larger society. This poses a challenge both to the 'majority' and 'minority' groups. As Kymlicka puts it, 'The liberal view of multiculturalism is inevitably, intentionally, and unapologetically transformational of people's cultural traditions. It demands both dominant and historically subordinated groups to engage in new practices, to enter new relationships, and to embrace new concepts and discourses, all of which profoundly transform people's identities and practices' (99).

Kymlicka (2007, 100) goes on to note, 'Much has been written about the transformations in majority identities and practices this [multiculturalism] has required, and the backlash it can create. But liberal multiculturalism is equally transformative of the identities and practices of minority groups.' According to Kymlicka, the challenge that (liberal) multicultural experiments pose to identities imposes limits on them, limits that were laid bare in the Ontario Islamic arbitration debate.

The process of integrating minority communities, especially Muslim ones, into Western society likely requires much more conversation and understanding than we have had to date. The outcome in the Ontario case may be satisfying to some and it may even be the 'right' outcome for Canada. But it barely scratched the surface of inquiry into how we will live together in our (religious) diversity in globalized societies. In Taylor's theorizing of the social imaginary, he thinks about transformation in terms of a long march: 'What I'm calling the "long march" is a process whereby new practices, or modifications of old ones, either developed through improvisation among certain groups and strata of the population ... or were launched by elites in such a way as to recruit a larger base ... Or alternatively, a set of practices in the course of their slow development and ramification gradually acquired a new meaning for people and hence helped to constitute a new social imaginary' (2002, 111).

The Ontario decision reinforced the liberal multiculturalist model. However, it is debatable how far along on the 'long march' toward creative accommodation of diversity it took us. Muslim migration is significant. Islam is the fastest growing religion in Canada (and is playing an increasingly visible role in places like France, the United Kingdom, and elsewhere). How we interact at the domestic level is providing Western publics with ideas about how we should conduct our foreign policy and it is sending signals to immigrant communities about the degree to which they 'belong.' There is a perception that Muslim communities present Western societies with new challenges at nation-building. Our societies are facing some serious new tensions and it is not clear that we have thought deeply about how to confront them and about the new policy solutions they may require. This is true in spite of the positive story told in chapter 13 about the role of religious pluralism in Canadian diplomacy.

In some ways, the Ontario case is unique, reflecting a specific constellation of factors in a certain place at a certain time. These include the growth of the Muslim population within the particular experiment with multiculturalism that is contemporary Canada, influenced by the policies and actions of Canada's powerful neighbour to the south in the wake of September 11.

On the other hand, the debate over faith-based alternative dispute-settlement mechanisms in Ontario reflects similar challenges that all dynamic societies face as they evolve alongside new influences. Great Britain has had a similar debate, sparked in part by the statement of Rowan Williams, archbishop of Canterbury, in 2008 that British law would unavoidably have to introduce elements of sharia to accommodate Muslim communities and ensure broader social cohesion. Nor are such debates limited to Western societies seeking to integrate Muslim communities. Anywhere societies founded on a particular social imaginary find themselves negotiating with groups partial to an alternative social imaginary, similar challenges arise. Worth remembering in these situations is that peoples' very understandings of who they are – their identities – are at stake. Strategies that reduce these developments to reductionist religious debates miss a crucial piece of the puzzle.

NOTES

1 Not unlike debates in the United States about Mexican immigration. See Huntington (2004) and also Bowen (2006) on France.

REFERENCES

Adler, E. 1997. Seizing the middle ground: Constructivism in world politics. *European Journal of International Relations* 3:319–63.

Amnesty International Canada. 2005. Canada: Ontario Arbitration Act – High risk of discrimination. 8 September. http://www.amnesty.ca/take_action/actions/canada_ont_arbitration_act.php

Arjomand, H. n.d. A meeting to discuss shari'a court in Ontario. http://www.butterfliesandwheels.com/articleprint.php?num=66.

Armstrong, S. 2005. *International Herald Tribune*, 11 February.

Bowen, J.R. 2006. *Why the French don't like headscarves*. Princeton, NJ: Princeton University Press.

Boyd, M. 2004. Dispute resolution in family law: Protecting choice, promoting inclusion. http://www.attorneygeneral.jus.gov.on.ca/english/about/pubs/boyd/.

Canadian Council of Muslim Women. 2004. Submission to Ms Marion Boyd:

Review of the Ontario Arbitration Act and arbitration processes, specifically in matters of family law. 23 July. http://www.ccmw.com/MuslimFamilyLaw/Boyd%20presentation%200723.doc.
– 2005. Letter to Dalton McGuinty, Premier, and Michael Bryant, Attorney General of Ontario, from Alia Hogben, Executive Director of Canadian Council of Muslim Women (14 January 2005) online: http://www.ccmw.com/ShariainCanada/Letter%20to%20Ontario%20Premier%20Attorney%20General.htm.
Council on American-Islamic Relations Canada. 2004. Review of Ontario's arbitration process and Arbitration Act: Written submissions to Marion Boyd. http://www.ccmw.com/activities/act_arb_Submission_Marion_Boyd.html.
Editorial. 2004. *Globe and Mail* 28 August.
Goff, P., and K. Dunn, eds. 2004. *Identity and global politics: Empirical and theoretical elaborations.* New York: Palgrave.
His Highness Prince Aga Khan Shia Imami Ismaili National Conciliation and Arbitration Board for Canada. 2004. Submission to Ontario Arbitration Review. http://www.cba.org/cba/newsletters/pdf/ADR-NCAB_Canada.pdf.
Huntington, S. 2004. *Who we are: The challenges to American's national identity.* New York: Simon and Schuster.
Ibbitson, J. 2007. Let sleeping dogs lie. In Stein, 49–70.
Jimenez, M., and O. El Akkad. 2005. Values at heart of Islamic tensions. *Globe and Mail* 8 November.
Klotz, A., and C. Lynch. 2007. *Strategies for research in constructivist international relations.* Armonk, NY: Sharpe.
Kymlicka, W. 2007. *Multicultural odysseys.* New York: Oxford University Press.
Lindgren, A. 2004. McGuinty orders review of plan for shariah law. *National Post* 10 June.
Siddiqui, H. 2007. Don't blame multiculturalism. In Stein, 23–48.
Stein, Janet Gross, ed. *Uneasy partners: Multiculturalism and rights in Canada.* Waterloo, ON: Wilfrid Laurier University Press.
Taylor, C. 2002. Modern social imaginaries. *Public Culture* 14 (10): 91–124.
Trichur, R. 2004. Muslims divided over whether shariah belongs in Ontario arbitration law. Canadian Press Canada.com News, 22 August. http://www.muslimcanadiancongress.org/20040822.pdf.
Wendt, A. 1992. Anarchy is what states make of it. *International Organization* 46 (2): 391–425.
Wente, M. 2004. Life under sharia, in Canada? *Globe and Mail* 29 May.

PART FOUR

Practice

10 John Paul II and the 'Just War' Doctrine: 'Make Peace through Justice and Forgiveness, Not War'

JAMES L. HEFT

Introduction: Religion, Peace, and War

From its founding to the present, Christianity has taken many positions on the legitimacy of war. No one, however, has done more to rethink the traditional 'just war' theory than John Paul II (pontiff, 1978–2005). Having lived the better part of his life in Poland under a Communist regime, he was acutely aware of the destructive power of atheistic socialism. In his own teaching, especially toward the end of his pontificate, he developed an understanding of the just war teaching that made it not only more difficult to justify war, but also placed the theory within a larger normative theological and ethical framework that underscored the crucial importance of non-violent means for the resolution of conflict. As will become apparent, the story of John Paul II's papacy provides powerful confirmation for the observation in chapter 2 that religion can and does matter in both the theory and practice of international relations.

The chief rabbi of Israel since 2003, Yona Metzger (2003, 13) told a Jewish parable about a young Jew who was on a long hike. It was the custom then to mark one's progress by looking at signposts that appeared regularly at crossroads, pointing to destinations and the direction to them. At one crossroads, the sign had fallen to the ground and the young man had no idea in what direction he should continue. An old man who was passing by gave him some advice: 'If you want to know in which direction to continue, stand the signpost up with the name of the place you have come from pointing in the direction from which you have come.'

In other words, there is a real value in knowing where one is coming from. And on the subject of the Catholic Church's practice and teaching on war, the church has come, since the time of Jesus, from some very different places. This article will describe the pacifist position of the earliest Christians, draw a very different picture of the church at the end of the first millennium, and then turn to the extraordinary papacy of John Paul II. His attention to the aftermath of war and the Gospel imperatives to establish justice and offer forgiveness has made the traditional criteria for meeting the standards of a just war harder to meet. The significance of his various statements throughout his long pontificate will be made clearer by placing them in their historical contexts. Moreover, this agenda is in line with the advocacy in chapter 3 of 'thick religion'; the present chapter will focus directly on theology and religious knowledge as related to the theory and practice of international relations.

Christians started out as a persecuted minority almost invisible within the greatest empire of the times. The earliest Christians emphasized the non-violent nature of the teachings and example of Jesus. In fact, there is no evidence before about the year 170 that Christians participated in the military. According to an early church code of laws called the Apostolic Tradition, those baptized Christians or persons preparing for baptism, known as catechumens, who joined the military were to 'be dismissed [from the church], for they have despised God.' If a man already in the military converted to Christianity, he was to refuse all orders to kill anyone. Origen (185–254), a great theologian and interpreter of Scripture, wrote, 'We [Christians] no longer take up the sword against nations, nor do we learn war anymore, having become children of peace for the sake of Jesus, who is our leader' (qtd in Sniegocki 2006, 225). The fact that Christianity, in its first three centuries of existence, never even faced a temptation to become a theocracy proved significant, especially in the Catholic Church's late but significant embrace at Vatican Council II (1962–5) of the separation of church and state and affirmation of religious freedom.

But in the fourth and fifth centuries, when the Roman Empire first allowed Christianity to exist and then a few decades later made it the official religion of the Empire, church thinkers effected huge changes in its teaching on the legitimacy of war. This change has sometimes been called the Constantinian Revolution, a period lasting about one hundred years during which the just war theory, developed by Augustine (354–430) and other great Christian thinkers after him, replaced the non-violent message of the early Christian church. By the Middle Ages, popes helped to launch crusades.

In order to place in stark relief the contribution of John Paul II, whose long papacy led the church into the twenty-first century, it is instructive to go back about a thousand years when a certain John XVIII was pope (1003–9). He owed his appointment to Crescentius, the most powerful political figure in Rome at that time (Kelly 1986). When John learned that some bishops wanted the abbot of a monastery in their region to burn papal documents that ensured the monastery's independence from the local bishops, he 'peremptorily summoned [the bishops] to Rome on pain of excommunication, and even threatened King Robert II of France that he would place his entire kingdom under a ban if they failed to appear' (Kelly 1986, 138). One of John's successors, Benedict VIII (1012–24), not only used armed forces to crush some political leadership in Rome that he opposed, but he himself participated in a sea battle in north Italy to defeat Muslim invaders. It was only a little later in that same century that the College of Cardinals was created, in part to wrest from powerful secular rulers their control of papal appointments.

Nevertheless, popes continued to exercise force to protect their interests and enforce their policies, both spiritual and temporal, until they were no longer able to do so – that is, until Italian nationalists stripped Pius IX (1846–78) of the use of military force in 1870. Before 1870, the Papal States divided Italy in half. A good case can be made that after 1870, more and more popes began to exercise their spiritual authority, and to exercise it over an ever-widening arena of concerns. In speaking to the General Assembly of the United Nations in 1982, John Paul II described himself in these words: 'This is the voice of one who has no interests nor political power, nor, even less, military force' (Portier 1996, 62).

To return to this brief history of where the Catholic Church has come from on matters of war and peace, the papacy, no longer able to defend by force its own political rights, actually found itself more free to defend the rights of others. At that same time, a little more than a decade after the U.S. Civil War, one of the first modern wars, the popes began to see more clearly that it made more and more sense to oppose war. We know that Benedict XV (1914–22) made a valiant but unsuccessful effort to end the First World War and by 1920 had already called for the creation of an international alliance among the nations of the world.[1] In 1944, the influential American Jesuit moral theologian John Ford condemned obliteration bombing. But it was especially with Pope John XXIII's (1958–63) encyclical, *Pacem in terris*, published in 1963, that seeds were sown for a new way to bring about peace in the international order: the vigorous defence of human rights.

On 4 October 1965, his successor, Pope Paul VI (1963–78), gave a famous speech at the United Nations in which he declared, 'No more war, war never again!' The very next day, 2,500 Catholic bishops gathered in Rome for the fourth and last session of Vatican II in order to begin their discussion of war and peace. The conclusions of that discussion would be included in the Council document *Gaudium et spes* (Flannery 1996), which two months later they finally approved. That document flatly condemned total war (the only condemnation solemnly uttered in all sixteen Vatican II documents), and called all people of good will, especially political leaders, to approach war 'with a whole new attitude.' Paragraph 80 of *Gaudium et spes* states forthrightly, 'Any act of war aimed indiscriminately at the destruction of entire cities or of extensive areas along with their population is a crime against God and man himself. It merits unequivocal and unhesitating condemnation.' That encyclical also endorsed non-violent resistance.

These signposts indicate a long and circuitous journey that the Catholic Church took over the past two thousand years. Over the last sixty years, and especially during the papacy of John Paul II, significant changes have been introduced into the Catholic Church's teaching on just war. John Paul II's papacy erected new signposts for the church's official understanding of the just war doctrine.

Enter John Paul II

Mainly on account of his speeches on the Council floor at Vatican II on key council documents dealing with the church (*Lumen gentium*), the church in the modern world (*Gaudium et spes*), and especially religious freedom (*Dignitatis humanae*), Archbishop Karol Wojtyla, who enjoyed a fine command of Latin, came to the attention of Pope Paul VI. In 1967, Pope Paul made Wojtyla, then age forty-seven, a cardinal. In 1968, when the pope rejected the majority vote on contraception, Cardinal Wojtyla was one of his strongest supporters. In 1976, Pope Paul chose him to give the papal Lenten retreat, which Wojtyla devoted to the theme of Christ as a 'sign of contradiction.' Two years later, after the thirty-three-day pontificate of John Paul I, Wojtyla at the age of fifty-eight was elected the first non-Italian pope in 450 years. He showed extraordinary vigour, both as a writer of encyclicals and as a global spiritual leader who defended human rights and opposed war. At the time of his death in April 2005, some twenty-seven years later, the third-longest term of service for any pope in history, a *Time* editorial (Gibbs 2005) gave a stirring summary of his extraordinary achievements:

> He was the first Pope ever to visit a mosque, or launch a website, or commemorate the Holocaust at Auschwitz or find in a broken world so many saints of the Church – more saints, in fact, than all his predecessors combined. Master of a dozen languages, he was the first modern Pope to visit Egypt, Spain, Canada, Cuba, Ireland or Brazil, the equivalent of circling the globe 31 times. To half the world's people, he was the only Pope they have ever known, or mourned. Thus the prayers came not just from the Catholic faithful but also from Muslims in France and Jews at Jerusalem's Western Wall and from believers across Eastern Europe who before his crusade against tyranny would have had to mourn him in secret. Even those who disagreed with his goals were touched by his goodness and came out to honor the man who made history itself kneel down.

The Liberation of Eastern Europe

This chapter focuses on John Paul II's impact on Catholicism's understanding of the legitimacy of war, his impact on Eastern Europe and the Middle East, especially his opposition to the Persian Gulf and Iraq wars, and finally, his understanding of the importance of humanitarian intervention. Again, the focus is on John Paul's teaching on war, not on issues mainly internal to the Catholic Church, issues such as the role of women, matters of sexual morality and sexual abuse, the appointment of bishops, or the exercise of papal authority. As important and as interesting as such matters are, their discussion belongs to another essay. However, the Jesuit moral theologian Richard McCormick (2005) contrasted John Paul II's impact on internal church life with his effect on the world scene:

> In the eyes of millions of people, John Paul II was the most credible and powerful moral voice of the second half of the twentieth century. This is most evident in the areas of peace, human rights, international relations and economic justice. His impact on the world was incalculable. When we turn to the more 'domestic' dimensions of his moral teaching, the record seems far more ambiguous. The pope was unable to persuade large numbers of Catholics on key issues. When persuasion failed, various forms of enforcement followed. This led in the Catholic Church to a severe problem

of authority that makes one question whether the Pope was a true *pontifex* (bridge-builder) within his own believing community. (31)

All of John Paul's teachings on the social order, especially as they evolved over the length of his unusually long papacy, have reshaped the way in which the traditional just war doctrine is now officially understood in the Catholic Church. The core of his international vision rested on a set of theological and philosophical affirmations about human freedom and the dignity of the human person. When John Paul addressed political issues directly, he exercised a certain restraint and emphasized a fundamentally religious and Gospel-based approach – an approach that nonetheless had political ramifications. Already in 1968, having lived under the oppression of the Communist government for much of his adult life, Wojtyla wrote to the great Jesuit theologian Henri de Lubac, 'I devote my very rare free moments to a work that is close to my heart and devoted to the metaphysical sense and mystery of the PERSON. It seems to be that the debate today is being played on that level. The evil of our times consists in the first place in a kind of degradation, indeed in a pulverization, of the fundamental uniqueness of each human person. This evil is even much more of the metaphysical order than of the moral order. To this disintegration, planned at times by atheistic ideologies, we must oppose, rather than sterile polemics, a kind of "recapitulation" of the inviolable mystery of the person' (de Lubac 1993, 171–2).

There can be little doubt that he wrote his 1981 encyclical, *Laborem exercens*, in defence of human rights. It was released on the ninetieth anniversary of Pope Leo XIII's (1878–1903) first social encyclical, *Rerum novarum* (1891), which defended labour rights. While *Laborens exercens* clearly supported the Solidarity movement of his native Poland, it also endorsed all movements that supported the rights of labourers. In that sense, it was non-partisan. In essence, he supported paragraph 41 of *Gaudium et spes*, which declared, 'By virtue of the Gospel committed to her, the Church proclaims the rights of man. She acknowledges and greatly esteems the dynamic movements of today by which these rights are everywhere fostered' (Flannery 1996, 209). For John Paul, philosophical and theological affirmations grounded human rights.

A critically important part of John Paul's legacy includes the promotion of non-violent methods to bring about political and social change. Some of his conservative American Catholic critics, such as Michael Novak and George Weigel, wondered aloud whether John Paul had 'gone pacifist.' Actually, the pope had not gone pacifist since he still allowed for the use of force, but in very limited and carefully circumscribed ways. At the same time, however, he increasingly endorsed the use of non-violent methods. Political observers do not dispute the claim that John Paul played a key role in the fall of Communism in Poland. But just what role he played is not clear.

Jesuit Drew Christiansen, editor of *America* magazine, a national publication of the American Jesuits, related how in 1995 Tad Sulcz, a former *New York Times* correspondent and a biographer of John Paul, believed that, on account of a relationship with Polish president Wojciech Jaruzelski, John Paul was able to become friends with Soviet president Mikhail Gorbachev. Sulcz argued that in the summer of 1989 when the Soviets decided not to invade the countries of Eastern Europe that then appeared to be breaking away, the three-way friendship paid great dividends. In the midst of this unravelling of the Soviet Union, Gorbachev wrote to the pope at the end of August that same year, 'I know what you have written,' and asked for a visit with the pope. On 1 December 1989, John Paul welcomed Gorbachev and his wife Raissa to the Vatican. In 1992 Gorbachev acknowledged that 'everything that happened in Eastern Europe in these last few years would have been impossible without this pope' (Appleby 2000b, 12).

More specifically, Sulzc claimed that the three-way friendship among Jaruzelski, Gorbachev, and John Paul prevented the Soviet Union from invading Eastern Europe in the way that it invaded Hungary in 1956 and Czechoslovakia in 1968. Sulzc believed that the combination of broad popular support for change in Poland and the lack of any military threat were the main contributors to the peaceful revolution of 1989. It would seem that John Paul saw the situation in much the same way as Sulzc, when two years later, in his 1991 encyclical *Centesimus annus* (Daughters of St Paul), he suggested in paragraph 23 that the use of non-violent methods made the 'velvet revolution' possible, not only in Poland, but also in the rest of Eastern Europe. Again, Drew Christiansen draws attention to the following texts of John Paul II: 'It seemed that the European order resulting from the Second World War ... could only be overturned by another war. Instead it has been overcome by the nonviolent commitment of people who, while always refusing to yield to the force of power, succeeded time after time in bearing effective witness to truth. They disarmed the adversary, since violence always needs to justify itself through deceit, and to appear, however falsely, to be defending a right or responding to a threat posed by others' (1991, 49).

Two paragraphs later, John Paul rejected the so-called realist view of international affairs: 'The events of 1989 are an example of the success of willingness to negotiate and of the Gospel spirit in the face of an adversary determined not to be bound by moral principles. These events are a warning to those who, in the name of political realism, wish to banish law and morality from the political arena' (John Paul II 1991, 35).

Having rejected the political realist approach, he made clear in that same paragraph 25 his theological, and especially Christological, foundation for doing so: 'Undoubtedly, the struggle which led to the changes of 1989 called for clarity, moderation, suffering and sacrifice. In a certain sense, it was a struggle born of prayer, and it would have been unthinkable without immense trust in God, the Lord of history, who carries the human heart in his hand. It is by uniting his own sufferings for the sake of truth and freedom to the sufferings of Christ on the cross that man is able to accomplish the miracle of peace.'

In *Centesimus annus*, published on the hundredth anniversary of Leo XIII's *Rerum novarum*, John Paul presents his own Christ-centred spirituality as an alternative to the so-called realist approach that has typified his thinking about international affairs. Many realists would assume that such a Christ-centred spirituality would have little, if any, relevance to the brutal realities of military power and international conflict. But John Paul's spirituality forms the foundation for a whole host of practical decisions about the use of force. At the end of the passage just quoted, John Paul writes that the person who unites his own suffering to the suffering of Christ on the cross 'is in a position to discern the often narrow path between the cowardice which gives in to evil and the violence, which, under the illusion of fighting evil, only makes it worse' (para. 25).

This last quotation captures precisely the meaning of Christian courage in defending rights as opposed to the violence of the warrior. The Christian who is committed to non-violence opposes any violation of human rights and actively, but non-violently, opposes all such evil, but in doing so does not use coercion or force. The warrior, on the other hand, also opposes evil, but in using force and creating violence runs the risk of leaving things in an even worse state than before. In the United States, the statements about war and peace that appear in *Centesimus annus* have been largely ignored, in favour of debates led by liberals and neo-conservatives about the legitimacy of capitalism. To overlook what the pope wrote about war and peace is especially unfortunate

(Portier 1996) since this encyclical gives more attention to those issues than any since *Pacem in terris*, published in 1963.

The Middle East and Reconciliation

The last fifteen years of John Paul's papacy were especially important for the development of his views on war and non-violence. After 1989, he did not have to deal with tensions created by two superpowers with different economic and political systems squaring off against each other on the world stage. Instead, he confronted the tragedies of genocide, the rights of minorities, and the use of military power by the only remaining superpower, the United States. In facing these events the pope most directly developed new ways to interpret the traditional just war doctrine. As mentioned earlier, the pope already had stressed in 1981, as did the American bishops in their 1983 pastoral letter on war, 'The Challenge of Peace,' the importance of non-violence. He firmly opposed the 1991 Gulf War and the 2003 invasion of Iraq. It is obvious that during this period the pope supported and developed further what in 1983 the U.S. bishops had called the 'presumption against the use of force' in matters of war and peace.

That the pope found himself in opposition to U.S. foreign policy, especially, as we shall see later, under the presidency of George W. Bush, should be obvious. Nothing makes this opposition clearer than the effort of the Vatican to prevent an invasion of Iraq. (The civil war in progress, which resulted from the invasion and occupation and features sectarian violence in Iraq, is a story told more fully by chapter 8.) Weeks before the invasion, the pope sent Cardinal Pio Laghi to the White House for a conversation with the president that turned out to be a 'dialogue of the deaf.'

> Laghi, a friend and tennis partner of the elder President Bush, reported with dismay that the president did not even open the pope's personal letter of appeal. Later the White House denied Laghi the usual privilege of meeting reporters on the White House lawn. In the meantime, the assiduous U.S. ambassador to the Vatican, James Nicholson, a former Republican national chairman, invited Michael Novak to offer a defense of preventive war in the very shadow of the Vatican. It is very evident that most Americans, including American Catholics, know the White House hermeneutic and view the world through it. Fewer know the papal stand and fewer view the world through its prism. (Christiansen 2005)

Given the pope's emphasis on non-violence and the importance of learning how to build a lasting and just peace, a number of concerned Catholics, as stated earlier, worried, especially some conservative American Catholics, that the pope had become a pacifist. Between 2 August 1990 and 4 March 1991, John Paul II spoke publicly fifty-six times on the crisis in the Middle East. George H.W. Bush regularly used just war language to defend his administration's conduct of the Gulf War. Especially troubling to Catholic conservatives was a widely reported prayer that John Paul II uttered when he said, echoing Paul VI's dramatic call (Portier 1996) at the United Nations for the end of all war, 'Never again war, adventure without return, spiral of struggle and violence, never this war in the Persian Gulf ... threat to your creatures in the sky, on earth and in the sea ... No war ever again.' Had John Paul II become a pacifist? No, or not quite. On 17 February 1991 at a church in Rome he remarked to the congregation, mainly composed of youth, 'We are not pacifists; we do not want peace at any price' (Portier 1996, 53). It might have been more helpful had the pope recognized in his remark the fact that pacifists do not desire peace at any price, since they are willing to die, but not to kill, so that justice, the only lasting basis for peace, might prevail.

Nearly a decade before, in his 1 January 1982 World Day of Peace message, a tradition established by Paul VI of devoting the beginning of the New Year to reflections on world peace, John Paul II stated that 'peoples have a right and even a duty to protect their existence and freedom by proportionate means, against an unjust aggressor.' Such proportionate means could include the use of force. But John Paul continued immediately to qualify this statement in an important way: 'In the view of the difference between classical warfare and nuclear or bacteriological war, a difference so to speak of nature, and in view of the scandal of the arms race seen against the backdrop of the needs of the Third World, this right [of armed self-defence], which is very real in principle, only underlines the urgency' of finding alternatives to war. He stated (Sniegocki 2006, 231), finally, 'War is the most barbarous and least effective way of resolving conflicts.'[2]

The pope's emphasis on non-violence and peacemaking brought him to interpret in a much stricter fashion than ever before the criteria that must be met for a particular war to be considered just. After reading John Paul's 1991 encyclical, *Centesimus annus*, Bryan Hehir, the main advisor to the U.S. bishops in drawing up their 1983 peace pastoral letter, concluded, 'One surely comes away from the Gulf debate and this encyclical with a sense that the moral barriers against the use of force are now drawn more tightly by this pope' (1991, 231). In fact, John Paul rarely used the language of the traditional 'just war' doctrine. It would be no exaggeration to describe John Paul's position towards the end of his papacy as a theology of peace of which the theory of a just war is only a part. In addition, the pontiff's position is consistent with the non-violent efforts by states and FBOs, described in chapters 11–14, to deal with the underlying causes of civil and interstate war.

Taking all the above into consideration, it would still be incorrect to describe John Paul simply as a pacifist. He cautiously supported the toppling of the Taliban government in Afghanistan. After the 9/11 terrorist attacks, he stated, 'There exists therefore a right to defend oneself against terrorism, a right which, as always, must be exercised with respect for moral and legal limits in the choice of ends and means' (World Day of Peace Message 2002). He added that a response to terrorists required that those responsible be clearly identified, and that efforts be made to eliminate the contributing causes of terror. He also saw a role for the use of force for humanitarian purposes, that is, to protect 'whole populations' that might be at risk, as in the case of genocide. He was among the first international figures to advocate humanitarian intervention in the former Yugoslavia. His calls for similar interventions in the cases of Rwanda and the Congo were ignored. John Paul understood legitimate intervention in a broad way, a way that includes, for example, the use of international monitors. Actual military intervention, mounted preferably by international coalitions, remained in his thinking as only a last resort.

One of the clearest examples of John Paul's rethinking of the just war theory can be found in his 2002 World Day of Peace Message, entitled 'No Peace without Justice, No Justice without Forgiveness.' At the opening of this important statement, he located the events of 9/11 in the light of Christian hope: 'The enormous suffering of peoples and individuals, even among my own friends and acquaintances, caused by Nazi and communist totalitarianism, has never been far from my thoughts and prayers. I have often paused to reflect on the persistent questions: *how do we restore the moral and social order subjected to such horrific violence?* My reasoned conviction, confirmed in turn by biblical revelation, is that the shattered order cannot be fully restored except by a response that combines justice with forgiveness. *The pillars of true peace are justice and that form of love which is forgiveness.*'

Pope John Paul's preoccupation with justice and forgiveness was in sharp contrast with the so-called Bush Doctrine. War for the pontiff stood as an odious last resort, at best, and notions of preventive or pre-emptive war could not have been further from his thinking. But even before that, already in 1994, in an apostolic letter, 'Tertio adveniente millennio,' the pope called upon the whole church to prepare for the millennium by entering a period of self-examination and repentance. Against the advice of a number of the members of the Vatican curia, the pope called for the public expression of repentance for the failures and sins of the members of the church, present and past. Luigi Accatolli (see Komonchak 1997, 39) lists ninety-four texts in which John Paul II either acknowledged the historical faults of the church or, at least, of Christians, and asked pardon for them. The chapter headings under which Accatolli gathers these texts reveals the gamut of concerns: the Crusades, dictatorships, divisions among the churches, women, Jews, Galileo, war and peace, the wars of religion, burning of Jan Hus, the excommunication of Calvin and Zwingli, the enslavement of Indians, multiple injustices, the Inquisition, integralism, Islam, Luther, the Mafia, racism, Rwanda, the schism with the East, the history of the papacy, and the slave trade.

On the first Sunday of Lent, 2000, the pope had many church leaders confess such faults, including Cardinal Joseph Ratzinger, who then served as head of the Vatican congregation that monitors orthodoxy, and whom John Paul II directed publicly to ask forgiveness for the sins committed in the service of truth. Nor should it be forgotten that twice (1986 and 2002) the pope invited all the leaders of the world's religions to gather with him in Assisi to pray for peace; it was at those gatherings that the pope emphasized that religion should be a force for peace and justice, and never be a pretext for violence. He asked forgiveness for the many times in history when religion has been used to promote violence. Whatever reservations Cardinal Joseph Ratzinger had about syncretism as the Assisi meetings, he has, since being elected pope himself in 2005, strongly reinforced John Paul's teaching that religion and violence should have nothing to do with each other.

More could be said, for example, about Pope John Paul's commitment to improved relationships with the Jews and his dramatic visit to Israel in 2000, where he visited the Holocaust museum, Yad Vashem, and prayed and asked forgiveness at the sacred Western Wall. On the slip of paper he inserted into the space between the great stones of the wall he wrote, 'Lord of our fathers, you chose Abraham and his descendants to bring your name to the nations. We are deeply saddened by the behavior of those who in the course of history have caused these children of yours to suffer and, asking your forgiveness, we wish to commit ourselves to genuine brotherhood with the people of the Covenant.' Or about his tentative outreach to the Muslims, which his successor, Benedict XVI (2005–) initially aggravated through his September 2006 Regensberg address, but subsequently made good on with his visit two months later to Turkey, and most recently his extended discussion with representatives of an international group of Muslim religious leaders who in the fall of 2007 sent a lengthy statement, 'A Common Word,' inviting the West to consider the common ground that Christianity and Islam occupy. Or we could describe John Paul's largely unsuccessful outreach to the Orthodox Church, made difficult by the unravelling of the Soviet Union in 1989, and the subsequent aggressive proselytizing by mostly evangelical Christian missionaries of the largely religiously illiterate Russian people. We also could consider John Paul's many statements about capitalism. Martin Marty, the American Lutheran historian of Christianity, remarked that the pope 'said just enough to inspire free market ideologues to make him sound like St Adam Smith ... But no sooner would they quote such lines than their critics would counter with paragraphs in which the pope issued cautions, made criticisms, and prophesied: the market does not automatically produce activity congruent with human need' (2005, 32). Or we could develop further the Pope's important visit to India and his efforts to support inter-religious dialogue with not only Judaism and Islam, but also the religions of Asia where, especially in India, crushing forms of poverty perpetuate multiple forms of violence against the human spirit (Appleby 2000a, chap. 3; Phan 2004, chap. 12).

All of these other topics more or less affect John Paul II's reinterpretation of the just war theory – but they are best left to another study.

Conclusion

By way of conclusion, three remarks should be made. First, it may be asked whether the official teaching of the church developed under John Paul II in a way similar to the way it developed on the death penalty. The first English edition of the *Catechism of the Catholic Church* appeared in 1994. Its statements on the death penalty were not precise. Commentators who support the death penalty seized upon these ambiguities to continue to argue that that the death penalty is necessary. The next year, 1995, John Paul published his encyclical *Evangelium vitae* (Daughters of St Paul), in which he acknowledged a person's right to self-defence, but said that 'in the context of a system of penal justice ever more in line with human dignity and thus, in the end, with God's plan for man and society,' the death penalty should be strictly limited to cases of 'absolute necessity.' By that phrase the pope meant that without the death penalty 'it would not be possible otherwise to defend society.' He judged that such situations would be 'very rare, if not practically non-existent.' A few weeks later, Cardinal Joseph Ratzinger explained that the pope's reservations about the use of the death penalty were stronger than those mentioned in the *Catechism*, and that the *Catechism* would therefore need to be revised (see Portier 1996, 49–51). And it was. The American Sr Helen Prejean and other opponents of the death penalty had effectively underscored how some Catholics were interpreting the ambiguous phrases in the first edition of the *Catechism* to argue for its continued use.

The question then arises (Portier 1996) whether John Paul's thinking on the just war theory was moving in the same direction as his teaching on the death penalty – for all practical purposes, opposing it flatly. The answer has to be a qualified no. The pope's ever stricter restrictions have not completely excluded a very limited use for force under very carefully circumscribed conditions. However, Catholic restrictions on the death penalty are now nearly absolute.

Second, John Paul's views on war may be best understood as a recasting of the traditional just war doctrine within a more comprehensive theology of peace and reconciliation. Traditional just war theory distinguished *jus ad bellum* and *jus in bello*. The first describes the conditions that make entering a war morally defensible; the second describes how to fight a war justly. A growing number of theologians and ethicists now point to a third dimension that needs to be included as an essential part of the moral evaluation of a war. That dimension might be named the *jus post bellum*, or the consideration of the consequences of a war and the obligations all participants in a war have for rebuilding and for forgiveness. John Paul's commitment to non-violence was a principled one, but his acute awareness of the consequences of war, the primary one being the making of the evil worse, made him very reluctant to endorse the traditional just war theory without considerable revision. As mentioned earlier, John Paul wrote in paragraph 42 of *Centesimus annus* that wars leave 'a trail of resentment and hatred, thus making it even more difficult to find a just solution of the very problems which provoked the war.' Miles (2003) argues that the moral evaluation of a war must include not just a moral evaluation of *jus ad bellum* and *jus in bello*, but also of the *jus post bellum*, that is, the destruction of a society's social order, its medical facilities, and supply of clean water, and all the illnesses and diseases that take the lives of innocent civilians for months after the war has ended.

And third, it should by now be obvious how opposed John Paul was to the use of military force in the Bush/Cheney policy of pre-emptive war. In an article about *The Compendium of the Social Doctrine of the Church*, published by the Pontifical Council for Justice and Peace, one commentator argues that the Catholic Church's body of social doctrine, deeply influenced as is now evident by the writings of John Paul II, challenges some of the major directions of the then current American foreign policy, and especially what has been described as the Bush Doctrine, which typically ignored the United Nations and arrogated to the United States a right to initiate war unilaterally:

> On point after point – the document's deep respect for the United Nations and international law; its call for a universal public authority that will banish war; its conviction that poverty is the one contemporary issue that challenges the Christian conscience; its praise for unarmed prophets of conscience; the very strict restrictions it places on the just war doctrine; its call to end indiscriminate trading in arms; its conviction that preventive war cannot be waged without clear proof that an attack is imminent; its strong support for the International Criminal Court; and its call to fight the war on terrorism with respect for human rights and the principles of a state ruled by law – Catholic social thought is clearly at odds with the neoconservative philosophy that has been embraced by many in the Bush administration. (Fahey 2005, 19)

The American bishops have been consistently more vocal about abortion and same-sex marriage than they have been about the Iraq war. Unfortunately, many Catholics seem to be simply unaware of recent papal teaching on the morality of war.

When John Paul II was elected pope, his fellow Pole, Cardinal Stefan Wyszynski, told him, 'If the Lord has called you, you must lead the Church into the third millennium.'[3] And as he did, he significantly reshaped the just war doctrine, leaving behind a rich and challenging reflection on what needs to be done if the world is ever to establish a just international order. Appleby (2000b, 14) states that John Paul engaged 'world leaders with a more explicitly geopolitical analysis' and that he spoke 'more openly about power and how it should be directed and contained' than any of his predecessors. It is almost as though the position of the church on war has, since its beginnings, come full circle. More than any pope before him, John Paul II has erected important signposts for the creation of a more peaceful and just new millennium. Would that his teachings were more widely known and embraced.

NOTES

1 One of the last documents approved in 1965 by the Second Vatican Council was *Gaudium et spes* (The Church in the Modern World). It stated clearly the need for an international authority to ensure justice and respect for human rights: 'It is our clear duty to spare no effort to achieve the complete outlawing of war by international agreement. This goal, of course, requires the establishment of a universally acknowledged public authority vested with the effective power to ensure security for all, regard for justice, and respect for law' (Flannery 1996, 268–9).
2 John Paul II, 'Peace: A Gift of God Entrusted to Us' (Message for World Day of Peace 1982), 12. In another World Day of Peace message (1993), the pope stated, 'War worsens the sufferings of the poor; indeed, it creates new poor by destroying means of subsistence, homes and property, and by eating away at the very fabric of the social environment ... After so many unnecessary massacres, it is in the final analysis of fundamental importance to recognize, once and for all, that *war never helps the human community*, that violence destroys and never builds up, that the wounds it causes remain long unhealed, and that as a result of conflicts the already grim condition of the poor deteriorates still further, and new forms of poverty appear.' See Sniegocki (2006) for these and other key quotations of John Paul II.
3 John Paul II, in a sermon given in Poland in 1997, told the crowd that Cardinal Wyszynski told him this at the time of his election in 1978. See Gary (1998).

REFERENCES

Appleby, S. 2000a. *The ambivalence of the sacred: Religion, violence, and reconciliation*. Lanham, MD: Rowman & Littlefield.

- 2000b. Pope John Paul II. *Foreign Policy* 119 (Summer): 12–25.
Christiansen, D. 2005. John Paul II peacemaker: A nonviolent pope in a time of terror. Unpublished paper.
Fahey, J. 2005. On peace and war. *America* 193 (17 October): 16–19.
Flannery, A. 1996. *Vatican Council II: Constitutions, decrees and declarations*. New York: Costello.
Gary, Jay. 1998. John Paull II: At the threshold of the third millennium. http://jaygary.com/johnpaulii.shtml.
Gibbs, N. 2005. Editorial. *Time* 11 April.
Hehir, J.B. 1991. On Centesimus annus. *Commonweal* 118 (12): 394.
John Paul II, Pope. 1981. *Laborem exercens*. Boston: Daughters of St Paul.
- 1982. 'Peace: A Gift of God Entrusted to Us' (Message for World Day of Peace 1982).
- 1991. *Centesimus annus*. Boston: Daughters of St Paul.
Kelly, J.N.D. 1986. *The Oxford dictionary of the popes*. New York: Oxford University Press.
Komonchak. J. 1997. Preparing for the new millennium. *Logos* 1 (2): 34–55.
Lubac, H.D. 1993. *At the service of the church*. Connecticut: Ignatius.
Marty, M. 2005. Insights of a family friend. *America* 192 (18 April): 30–3.
McCormick, R. 2005. Deeds, not words. Commemorative issue. *Tablet* 259, no. 8583 (9 April): 30–1.
Metzger, Y. 2005. Yesterday, today and tomorrow. *America* 193:13–16.
Miles, J. 2003. 'The Iraqi Dead: Respect Must be Paid.' *Commonweal* 18 July. http://commonwealmagazine.org/iraqi-dead-0.
Phan, P. 2004. *Being religious interreligiously*. New York: Orbis Books.
Portier, W. 1996. Are we really serious when we ask God to deliver us from evil? The catechism and the challenge of Pope John Paul II. *Communio* 23:47–63.
Sniegocki, J. 2006. Catholic teaching on war and peace, and nonviolence since Vatican II. *Vatican II: Forty years later*, ed. William Madges. *College Theology Society Annual* 51:224–44. Markyknoll, NY: Orbis Books.
Time. Commemorative issue. 11 April 2005: 27.

11 Christian Mediation in International Conflicts

ROBERT B. LLOYD

> The wise and enlightened negotiator must of course be a good Christian, and he must let his character appear in all his speeches, in his way of living ... Justice and modesty should govern all his actions.
> – François de Callières, eighteenth-century French diplomat and theorist

Introduction

In recent years increasing scholarly attention has been devoted to the role of religious intolerance and religiously motivated violence in international conflict. Such research, as emphasized in chapter 3, naturally assumed greater prominence in the wake of deadly attacks by religiously motivated individuals and groups. Concurrently scholars, policymakers, and non-governmental organizations (NGOs) began focusing on the role of religion in *resolving* conflict. Johnston's seminal book *Religion: The Missing Dimension of Statecraft* (1994), was the first to systematically examine conflicts in which religious belief was an important factor in establishing just outcomes and promoting reconciliation. One well-known example in which a religious faith was introduced to promote reconciliation after a violent conflict was South Africa's Truth and Reconciliation Commission, established by Methodist and Anglican church leaders following the end of apartheid and the democratization of the country in the mid-1990s.

Both in *Religion* and in a subsequent book, *Faith-Based Diplomacy: Trumping Realpolitik* (2003), Johnston presented case studies from the world's five major religions in order to understand how religion can promote peacemaking within regions that include those particular religions. These case studies suggest that faith-based diplomacy is particularly useful if religion comprises a major element of the conflict, religious belief is vital to the contesting parties, and religion and society are closely but dynamically bonded. In cases where there is no religious component, faith-based diplomacy may still be useful through third-party mediation (Johnson 2003, 238–9). Understanding the nature and usefulness of such an approach is, in fact, the objective of this chapter.

NGOs have been prominent in increasing understanding of faith-based approaches to conflict resolution. The federally chartered United States Institute of Peace, for example, has published numerous books and held workshops on the role of faith-based mediation in the resolution of international conflicts. Of special interest to the institute have been Catholic and Mennonite contributions to conflict resolution. The Institute for Global Engagement, a Washington DC–based NGO that focuses on religious freedom, has sponsored numerous forums and publications on the topic of Christian mediation in international conflict. Some of its work is profiled in chapter 14.

In addition, debates on religion and conflict resolution increased among foreign policymakers. In *The Mighty & the Almighty*, former American secretary of state Madeleine Albright, writing from a policy perspective, affirms the importance of faith-based diplomacy as 'a useful tool of foreign policy' (2006, 78). She argues that 'American diplomats need ... to think more expansively about the role of religion in foreign policy and about their own need for expertise. They should develop the ability to recognize where and how religious beliefs contribute to conflicts and when religious principles might be invoked to ease strife. They should also reorient our foreign policy institutions to take fully into account the immense power of religion to influence how people think, feel, and act' (66–7).

Such growing academic research, NGO efforts, and policy recognition of the importance of religious belief in conflict resolution has done much to advance its appropriate inclusion into diplomacy. An example is provided by chapter 13, which focuses on religion and Canadian diplomacy. The current chapter examines the role of religion, identity, and global governance by examining third-party mediation in international conflict by Christians. This task is performed by asking a number of questions based on actual cases that exemplify the ways Christians have approached such international mediation. First, why have Christians been involved in third-party intervention in international conflicts? Second, within such a faith-based approach, how do various traditions influence their mediation effort? Are there any characteristics that distinguish Christian from non-Christian intercession? Third, what has been the response? And finally, how successful have Christian mediators been? Has Christian involvement made the conflict better or worse? This last question is important in that much of the literature suggesting that religion is a missing dimension of statecraft has produced approaches, stories, and analyses that illustrate the positive impact of religiously informed mediation on the resolution of conflict. Have there been cases, on the other hand, where such mediation has made matters worse or had no discernible impact? If so, was there some element in a faith-based approach that was deficient or even injurious?

Christianity is the focus of this chapter's examination of faith-based mediation for a number of reasons. First, Christianity is the world's largest religion, with some two billion people claiming to be followers of Christ. Second, the West has been strongly shaped by its Christian heritage and has had a major influence on international affairs for the past five centuries. Third, Christianity is becoming a religion whose locus is increasingly not in the West but the developing world, due to particularly rapid growth in Africa and Asia.

Christianity is by no means a monolithic faith but is composed of many different traditions that developed from historical circumstances, theological differences, the varying ethnic and linguistic backgrounds of religious adherents, and diverse geographical locations. Thus, both practitioners and scholars seeking to understand how Christians have mediated in international conflicts soon discover many historical and contemporary examples and a substantial body of research into the topic. This is particularly true for Christians who identify with the Roman Catholic or Mennonite traditions. This chapter examines what motivates self-identified Christians to mediate in international disputes, why varying traditions within Western Christianity differ from one another in their assumptions about and approaches to mediation, the impact of these assumptions on mediation, and the responses of parties in and outside the conflict. To understand better how Christians mediate this assessment draws solely on actual cases of non-official Track 2 mediation efforts. While there are examples of Track 1[1] mediation efforts by self-identified Christians working in an official capacity, limiting the level of analysis to Track 2 mediation by self-identified Christian NGOs and individuals makes clearer both the impact of tradition and how such faith-based mediation fits into the broader literature of third-party mediation in international conflicts.

Mediation Motivation

The world does not lack mediators willing to negotiate an end to a violent international conflict. Any number of reasons for such interest come to mind. These might include such self-evident positive principles as establishing justice, saving lives, ending destruction, and improving the overall future political and economic prospects for a country and its people. In some cases an unstated reason might be a simple desire to end an international irritant. Personal self-interest – even ego – plays a role in the professional and personal prestige that accrues to a successful mediator (Zartman 1986). It is not immediately apparent that any of these motivations differ substantively in a Christian and non-Christian mediator. Are there, then, any motivating factors differentiating Christian and non-Christian mediators?

Before proceeding further it is first necessary to define what is meant by the term *Christian mediator*. Roman Catholic scholar Appleby defines *religious actors* as 'people who have been formed by a religious community and who are acting with the intent to uphold, extend, or defend its values and precepts' (2000, 9). A Christian mediator is therefore a religious actor intentionally engaging as a third-party in an intra- or inter-state dispute to act as a catalyst in its resolution.

The Christian mediator's motivation is based on his or her relationship with God, reinforced by biblical precepts regarding consequential identity as a citizen and ambassador of the kingdom of God, a command to peacemaking, and recognition that all the earth is under God's sovereign purpose. This motivation may not be visible to others and indeed may be diluted or replaced by motivations shared with mediators not explicitly working from a Christian motivation. Furthermore, mediators from other religious traditions may share many of these faith-based motivations as well (Gopin 2000, 2002). Thus, a non-Christian (or a mediator from a different faith altogether) and a Christian Track 2 mediator – former American president Jimmy Carter, for example – may publicly pursue similar means and ends and indeed even share professional interests. Nevertheless, they may differ in underlying identity and motivation.

Christian Traditions and Mediation

One useful way to address how Christian mediation functions is to disaggregate Christianity into smaller divisions. This chapter argues that there are significant differences *within* a religious tradition that affect how individuals and groups within a belief system may approach conflict mediation. The philosopher MacIntyre demonstrated the importance of tradition, which he termed a 'historically extended, socially embedded argument,' in political and moral reasoning (1984, 224). In this sense Christianity itself is a tradition, but there are also well-known traditions within it that shape how their followers approach the task of international mediation. This chapter illustrates the impact of such traditions on international mediation focusing on the Western branch of Christendom – Roman Catholicism and the offspring of the Protestant Reformation. The very important Orthodox tradition is not included in this analysis because for the most part the Orthodox centre of gravity lies outside the West and the study focuses more specifically on the West.

The first task is to examine briefly the history and traditions within the Western branch of Christianity. Christianity has a two-thousand-year history that spans cultures, times, states, and continents. Differing understandings of the scripture, diverse historic experiences, and cultural dissimilarity have led to the emergence of identifiable traditions within Christianity. By understanding the religious tradition of the Christian mediator it is possible to make a number of observations about how individuals within each tradition will tend to approach international mediation.

Specific to the task at hand, many of these traditions are differentiated in part by their historical and theological responses to the precise relationship of church and state and the believer and unbeliever. In his classic book, *The City of God*, the African scholar St Augustine of Hippo grappled with this difficult question, writing in the context of the upheaval accompanying the gradual collapse of the Roman Empire early in the fifth century. St Augustine posited two kingdoms: the City of Man and the City of God. In his historical and theologically influential conceptualization, the Christian is a dual citizen, simultaneously possessing an identification and affinity with this world and with the kingdom of heaven. St Augustine's formulation proved robust for political conditions in the millennium that followed the disintegration of the Roman Empire in Western Europe.

Following the empire's collapse, the Catholic Church gradually extended its political influence in Western Europe. Medieval Europe became characterized by a complicated web of local realms and a supranational ecclesiastical organization. By the sixteenth century, however, growing movements to reform the Catholic Church – and the rise of national identities particularly in the Germanic regions of northern Europe – led to renewed attention to the relationship of St Augustine's two kingdoms.

There were two general approaches to the relationship of religious and secular authority within the movement that came to be called the Reformation. The *magisterial reformation* marked such groups as the Lutherans and Calvinists, and to a lesser degree the Anglicans. Protestant Reformers such as the German Martin Luther and the Frenchman John Calvin applied Augustinian concepts of the two kingdoms within a sixteenth-century political reality of Catholic political and church leaders opposed to their reforms. These reformers sought protection from their enemies through sympathetic Protestant political leaders. The physical protection and access to power, however, came at the price of close involvement in the affairs of magisterial churches by local political leaders.

A modern-day example of this magisterial reformation influence on Christian engagement within the political world was seen in Dag Hammarskjöld, a Swedish statesman and United Nations official, who served as secretary general of the United Nations between 1953 and 1961 when he was killed in a plane crash in Congo (Cordier 1967; Lash 1961). His successes as a mediator, seen in the release of American airmen in China and his intercession in the Suez crisis, won him praise as a statesman. He was posthumously awarded the Nobel Peace Prize in 1961.

Hammarskjöld's engagement with the political world was deeply influenced by his Christian faith. Hammarskjöld's journal of meditations, *Markings*, published after his death, shows the powerful impact his faith had on his thoughts and actions. His first Christian influences were his parents. His mother was an evangelical Lutheran Christian who came from a family of ministers. His father's side of the family included numerous government officials. As an adult, Hammarskjöld commented on his faith in a radio broadcast: 'I now recognize and endorse, unreservedly, those very beliefs which once were handed down to me. When I finally reached that point, the beliefs in which I was once brought up and which, in fact, had given my life direction even while my intellect still challenged their validity, were recognized by me as mine in their own right and by my free choice' (1961). Hammarskjöld was keenly aware of the two kingdoms, and his actions illustrate that he saw his mediation as UN secretary general as a way to advance biblical ethics and principles into the broader world.

Radical reformers, by contrast, rejected both what they viewed as the corruption of the Catholic Church and the compromises over scripture they believed magisterial reformist Christians were making with political leaders in such Reformed strongholds as Zurich, Switzerland. Often called Anabaptists, these Christians were composed of loosely organized groups of believers who rejected infant baptism, emphasized the importance of discipleship, stressed the need to love one's neighbour, and believed the goal was not merely to reform the church but to restore it to its original New Testament purity (Yoder and Kreider 1977, 399–403).

Two principles in particular affect Anabaptist views toward international mediation. First, the love ethics so permeated Anabaptist thinking that they soon became pacifists, refusing to go to war, defend themselves if attacked, or take part in coercion by the state. Second, and related, Anabaptists insisted on a strict separation of church and state because faith is a gift of God to the Christian sojourner in an alien land. Even had they wanted to engage in international mediation, Anabaptists did not enjoy the institutional resources used by the Roman Catholic or Reformed churches. The Mennonite churches are a modern representative of the Radical Reformation movement.

Compared with Reformation churches, the Roman Catholic Church is in many ways in a different class. The church has a central authority with a global jurisdiction, larger membership, and greater historical experiences – all of which give it a practical and theoretical reservoir on which to draw its mediation efforts. Of crucial distinction is the dual identity the Roman Catholic Church retains as both a sacred and temporal power. The special role of the pontiff in that regard comes out clearly in the account in chapter 10 of Pope John Paul II's record in the just war doctrine.

During the medieval era, in fact, the Roman Catholic Church existed essentially as a supranational organization in Western and Central Europe. Relatively high educational levels of church officials gave the mediator good training in handling complex international disputes. Even after the major changes in the international system following the Treaty of Westphalia in 1648, which established the primacy of state sovereignty and formalized recognition of a permanently religiously divided Europe, the Catholic mediator could at least expect to receive a hearing by political leaders.

One historical example illustrates this point. In the late fifteenth century, Spain and Portugal were great powers. Both had sought riches through new trade routes to the rich markets of Asia, bypassing the middlemen of the overland routes through Central Asia and the Middle East. Christopher Columbus's discovery of the Americas led to conflict over contested land in the New World.

To avert growing international conflict, Pope Alexander VII, a Spaniard, brought the two parties together, leading to a negotiated settlement in 1493. Issued as a papal bull (decree) entitled *Inter Caetera* in 1493, the agreement divided the globe in half along a meridian of 36°8'W, just west of present-day Portuguese Azores in the mid-Atlantic. Spain gained ownership of land west of the meridian and Portugal all territory to its east. The Treaty of Tordesillas in 1494 amended the north-south demarcation line, moving it farther west, allowing for Portuguese claims to Brazil.

The settlement thus awarded the Americas and Eastern Pacific (excluding at the time the Philippine Islands) to Spain. Portugal got the world east of a small sliver of South America through Africa, India, China, and to Formosa (Taiwan). The two treaties averted war, clarified ownership of (as yet unknown) disputed territories, and allowed the two states to tap into Asian markets through different routes. The signers of the treaty specifically requested papal approval of this agreement, which was granted in a decree by Pope Julius II in 1506.

Thus, mediation by individuals and institutions that have a Christian identity is not new, and furthermore has shaped profoundly the world we live in today. The long-term impact of that particular mediation effort is seen in the history, geography, and languages of such diverse places as India, China, Mozambique, the Philippines, Brazil, and Argentina.

Catholic interest in international affairs has continued into the modern era. In the latter part of the twentieth century, for example, the Vatican issued two encyclicals on the subject of international conflict and its management. The first, *Pacem in terris*, (Peace on Earth, 1963) by Pope John XXIII, presented human rights as a basis for the mediation efforts of the church. In 1991 Pope John Paul II, drawing upon his experience in Eastern Europe and emphasizing the importance of non-violence in international conflicts, issued *Centissimus annus* (The Hundredth Anniversary of Rerum Novarum).[2]

Table 11.1 shows the actors, conflict, and tradition of various third-party Christian mediators. Once again, the point made by chapter 2 about the neglect of religion, in spite of its clear and sustained presence in the international arena, is reinforced. Moreover, the table contains examples merely, not the full record of Christian mediation.

Table 11.1
Christian traditions and negotiation types

Christian tradition	Actor	Track 2 mediation
Roman Catholic	Holy See	Beagle Channel dispute
	Sant' Egídio	Mediation in Mozambique
Reformed	Anglican Church (Terry Waite)	Hostages in Lebanon,
	World Lutheran Federation (Paul Wee)	Guatemala
Baptist (Reformed/ Anabaptist)	Jimmy Carter	United States / North Korea
Anabaptist	Mennonite	Central America

For the Catholic Church, mediation is broadened analytically to include (semi-official) Track 1 negotiations conducted by the Holy See. Mediation by the Holy See is interesting because it is the only explicitly Christian organization that has official status with the United Nations. The Beagle Channel dispute was a border conflict in the 1970s and 1980s between Argentina and Chile over three small islands south of the Beagle Channel on the southern tip of South America. Following a series of failed negotiations, military tensions between the two countries nearly led to war. An offer by Pope John Paul II to mediate led to the de-escalation of military forces and the eventual signing of a treaty that resolved the conflict.[3]

A second example with the Roman Catholic Church is the successful mediation efforts of the Community of Sant' Egídio, a Rome-based Lay Public Association of the Roman Church. The Community played a pivotal role in mediating the end of the fifteen-year civil war in Mozambique (Almquist 1994). In the early 1990s, Jaime Gonçalves, the Roman Catholic archbishop of Beira, and a member of Sant' Egídio, began a dialogue with the rebel leader. Mozambique's government leader initially denounced these talks but eventually found them a useful means to pursue negotiations with rebel leaders. Sant' Egídio provided the forum for these negotiations, culminating in a peace accord in 1993.

Within the Reformed tradition are two examples. The Anglican churchman Terry Waite was an assistant for Anglican communion affairs to the archbishop of Canterbury. Experienced in diplomacy, Waite negotiated the release of several British hostages from revolutionary Iran in 1981. A few years later he negotiated with Libyan leader Moammar Gadhafi for the release of four British hostages. In 1987 he travelled to Lebanon to negotiate the release of four hostages with Islamic Jihad, a Syrian-based militant Islamic group that had begun kidnapping Westerners in Lebanon. Their goal was to gain the release of

Islamic Jihadists imprisoned after attempting to overthrow the Kuwaiti monarchy. But Waite's reputation as neutral was undermined when he used an American military helicopter to travel between Cyprus and Lebanon and appeared with Oliver North during the time of the Iran-Contra scandal. Promised safe conduct, Waite was nonetheless taken hostage by Islamic Jihad and held for five years until his release in 1991. Thus, this third-party mediation with Islamic Jihad ended in failure.

The second Reformed example occurred in the late 1980s and early 1990s, in which Catholic and Lutheran religious groups played a major role in mediating a Guatemalan conflict. The key actors were the Roman Catholic Church, the Lutheran World Federation, and a host of other groups like the U.S. National Council of Churches. Paul Wee, assistant secretary of the Lutheran World Federation, helped make possible a meeting between the Guatemalan government and rebels that helped break an impasse in negotiations.

In the case of the former American president Jimmy Carter, the mediation focuses on his Track 2 activities after his presidency. Jimmy Carter is an interesting case study because of his Southern Baptist background. This tradition has been influenced by elements of both the magisterial and radical reformation. Early Baptists in seventeenth-century Britain held to a radical polity yet served in high positions in government under Oliver Cromwell's Republican government. After ending his term as president, Carter became involved in international mediation. During the Clinton Administration he worked to negotiate between the United States and North Korea to avert armed hostilities. This effort was a factor that eventually led to the 1994 negotiated agreement between the two countries. Of particular interest is Carter's shift in mediation approach. During his presidency, Carter often created diplomatic strains with allies and enemies alike due to his insistence on human rights. Yet in his current capacity as a mediator with the Carter Center, he demonstrates a willingness to deal with morally disagreeable leaders in his attempt to seek peace.

The final approach is the mediation efforts by Anabaptist Moravians working in Nicaragua. Church members maintained close ties with the Miskito Indians living on Nicaragua's Atlantic Coast who had come into increasing conflict with the Marxist government in the 1980s.

Mediation Characteristics

The examples presented enable the Christian mediation approaches to be placed into conflict management literature, allowing greater under-

Table 11.2
The conflict resolution process and third-party mediation

Pre-settlement stage		Settlement stage		Post-settlement stage	
Non-violence phase Grievances	Violence phase	Negotiation phase Formula (agreement)	Implementation phase Formula institutionalized	Fragile phase	Durable phase
-Neglect -Discrimination	Unilateral solution (military)	*Justice* 1 Priority 2 Equality 3 Inequality -Equity -Compensation	-Ceasefire -Prisoner release -Demobilization -Elections	Grievances addressed satisfactorily	Stable regime
		Third-party Track 1 and Track 2 negotiations			
Preventive diplomacy	Pre-negotiations	Mediation 1 Communicator 2 Formulator 3 Manipulator	Post-agreement negotiations		

standing into the ways religious traits affect mediation. To aid this objective, table 11.2 presents a simplified model of the processes of international conflict resolution. A conflict is represented by three stages, marked by the way the grievances fuelling the conflict are addressed. The first, the pre-settlement stage, is marked by growing grievances, lumped under the general categories of neglect and discrimination. Failure to address such grievances to the satisfaction of one of the parties leads to a growing mobilization, which in the latter phases leads to violent confrontation. Responses of each party are unilateral, each side attempting to impose its own will on the other.

If such will cannot be imposed unilaterally, the conflict may progress to the settlement stage. The parties reach what Zartman (1986, 1999, 2001) terms 'a mutually hurting stalemate,' making the moment ripe for resolution. Negotiations focus on finding a common agreement or formula to overcome the differences. This formula is based on an agreed determination of what constitutes a just outcome. If such an agreement is reached, attention turns to critical implementation. In this phase many agreements have foundered, often seeing a return to violent conflict. In the final stage, the post-settlement, the formula that addressed the grievances is institutionalized, and a new, legitimate, and stable regime is established. Third-party intervention may occur at any point or phase in the conflict but is most commonly seen in the pre-settlement and settlement stages. The negotiation phase is obviously the main focus of such mediation efforts.

Christian mediators share with their non-Christian counterparts a strong interest in facilitating a peaceful end to a conflict. On the basis of these examples drawn from various traditions, can one find any notable aspects of actual Christian mediation? Attempting to answer this question is in line with 'thick religion,' the approach to research advocated by chapter 3. The present chapter will link theology, hierarchy, and knowledge – three key elements of thick religion – with Christian traditions to behaviour observed in mediation.

One characteristic of Christian mediation is an emphasis on *reconciliation*. This includes the restoration of strained or severed relationships or the building of new relationships where none existed.[4] One critical question facing any negotiator is how much of the conflict should be resolved to establish peace and justice. Should just enough conflict be resolved to end the fighting and establish relative peace? Or is ending the fighting necessary to end the conflict but not sufficient? Will failure to establish longer-term agreements and institutions lead to renewed fighting?

One approach, often called *conflict transformation*, argues that conflict management (ending the fighting) and conflict resolution (establishing the conditions for addressing deep-seated internal disputes through legitimate government institutions) do not really address the underlying causes of the conflict. The Mennonite John Paul Lederach, for example, contends a conflict will essentially disappear only when the interests and needs of the parties are legitimized and the relationships are restructured towards increased equality and justice (Lederach 1995, 14–19). Former American president Jimmy Carter, working from his Track 2 Carter Center, has likewise emphasized this approach in negotiations around the world.

A closely related concern is for a *just outcome*. Clearly, such a concern animates both those who identify themselves as Christian mediators and those who do not. The deep desire to reconcile relationships to establish justice is, however, a strong theme that runs throughout the length of scripture. Christian mediators who are animated by these commands thus attempt to implement this call directly into a political settlement. The question is, of course, how exactly one reconciles competing, and often conflicting, claims of justice into a settlement that transforms the relationships of the disputants. Underlying this approach, one not always expressed explicitly by Christian mediators, is a preference for justice based on equality.

To illustrate, in negotiation theory, a formula is a negotiated solution to end a dispute. It represents a shorthand for the trade-offs that lead both parties to feel sufficiently satisfied to sign an agreement and support its later implementation. Disputing parties end a conflict when there is agreement over substantive and procedural claims of justice. One aim of negotiations, therefore, is to satisfy competing claims for justice. The relationship of justice to the negotiation process is shown earlier in table 11.2. Justice by its very nature is an abstract and complex concept, but for the purposes of negotiation it can be broken down into three types: priority, inequality, and equality (Zartman 1999).

Priority (or partial) justice emphasizes a total allocation with no sharing. This approach designates a winner according to a general rule. A common example of this approach is the saying 'First come first served' or 'Winner takes all.' A second type of justice is equality (or impartial), which emphasizes fair treatment and equal outcomes. The motto is 'Split the difference.' Children dividing a cookie three ways take pains to ensure each portion is the same size. Where this exactitude is not possible, the mediator may use a variance of 'equivalence.' An example is each diner contributing an estimated amount for the tip at a restaurant when none at the table is exactly sure of the amount owed by each.

The third type of justice is inequality, of which there are two subtypes. The first, equity (or merit), is based on the principle of whoever contributes the most receives the most. An example is the distribution of power within the United Nations: the more powerful victors of the Second World War received a permanent seat on the Security Council. Compensation is the other subtype of inequality justice: whoever contributes the least receives the most. The international agreement to award former German territory to Poland, which was defeated in its war with Germany in 1939, might be considered one example of this type of justice.

This second distinctive element of Christian mediation is emphasis on using the equality definition of justice. Although the scriptures develop in various stories and parables the different types of justice, Christian mediators consistently equate justice with equality. Many Christian mediators are committed to equality justice on the assumption that relationships must be equal in order to be transformed.

A third characteristic relates to the *preferred role* of negotiation. Mediation in international conflicts involves the assumption of a role. Placing oneself in the midst of a conflict means introducing a new element into the conflict. This new variable, it is hoped, will change the dynamics of the conflict so as to end it. The mediator is dependent on leverage, which is a form of power, to achieve resolution. The leverage depends on a mixture of positive and negative inducements, ranging from the disputants' desire to maintain a good relationship with the mediator to the mediator deploying military forces. A mediator may play three roles during mediation. These roles are not mutually exclusive, but relate to the degree that the mediator is intervening in the dispute (Touval and Zartman 1985).

The first is the role of communicator. Here the mediator in essentially a human telephone, relaying messages between parties unwilling or unable to communicate. The second role is that of a formulator, which inserts the mediator more directly in the disputants' attempts to negotiate an end to the conflict. The mediator now actually presents possible solutions to the conflict, presented as possible 'formulas' to solve the conflict. Eventually, an acceptable formula may be found to resolve the grievances that led to the conflict. The final role is a manipulator, who pushes the parties by means of leverage in order to move them to a point of negotiations. The term *manipulator* is used as a warning. A man pulling two fighting dogs apart should not be surprised to be bitten. Likewise, a mediator manipulating disputants may suffer harm.

Christian mediators, like all mediators, must assume at least one of these roles in order to mediate a conflict. Do Christians prefer one role over the others? It is clear from many of the examples presented that Track 2 Christian mediators gravitate naturally toward the role of communicator. Christians often are able to develop relationships with parties precisely because they lack power of shared values and the parties' realization that the mediator has little leverage other than the relationship.

The mediation of the Sant' Egídio in Mozambique is a classic example of how Christian mediators developed lines of communication between disputants where none existed before. In another example, the Kenyan businessman Washington Okumu mediated in South Africa and helped to avert a last-minute breakdown in communication between the Inkatha Freedom Party and the African National Congress on the eve of the historic April 1994 elections that broadened South African democracy. This rupture threatened to increase violence and derail the elections (Cassidy 1995).

Christians also are involved in the formulator role. The Sant' Egídio mediators did turn to formulating solutions to the conflict once lines of communication had been established. The papal emissary sent to mediate the Beagle Channel dispute between Chile and Argentina also presented possible formulas for overcoming the conflict. Ex-president Jimmy Carter flew to North Korea to fend off a probable American attack by President Bill Clinton against nuclear facilities in the mid 1990s. Not only did the ex-president – a committed Christian – develop lines of communication, but he also developed a formula that proved mutually acceptable at the time to both sides.

The role of manipulator proves problematic for Christians for a number of reasons. First, manipulation does not give the appearance of a Christian virtue. The word conveys the sense of coercion, even in its positive inducements. The reluctance to use manipulation in negotiations relates to underlying views on the role of power and negotiations for theological and historical reasons. There are differences of opinion regarding questions of biblical interpretation of key passages regarding the legitimate use of violence and the relation of the individual Christian to the state. For many Christians the use of coercion – especially violent coercion – is seen as completely inconsistent with Jesus' own example, his command to love one another, and the God-given value of human life. The radical demands of the Gospel are seen as constraining the Christian's use of violence to achieve political ends. This is particularly relevant for Christians from a radical Reformation tradition. Opposition to a more realpolitik-oriented Bush Doctrine, therefore, would reflect such theological objections about the use of coercive and violent force to achieve political ends.

A final Christian characteristic of negotiation relates to the *timing of negotiation*. A classic case of a successful negotiated settlement to end a violent intra- or interstate conflict passes through a number of phases. In the pre-settlement stage the grievances of the parties, usually lumped into two bins of neglect and discrimination, are established and deepening. If demands to resolve the grievances are not satisfactorily met, then violence breaks out. Statistically, two-thirds of intra-state conflicts do not end in a negotiated agreement, but one side or the other is eliminated or surrenders (Pillar 1983; Stedman 1990). For those, however, that do in fact progress to the settlement stage there are certain preconditions – notably a mutually hurting stalemate – that push the parties to negotiation. Successful negotiations move the conflict to its final stage – the post-settlement stage. It is here that the agreements are implemented, and the parties navigate the treacherous shoals of making concrete the earlier agreements.

Christian mediators tend to focus on the earliest stages of negotiation. While a focus on the earliest stage is not unique to Christian mediators, it does seem to be a strong characteristic of their approach, for a number of reasons. First, an incipient conflict may be under the radar of a potential government. This relates in part to the dilemma related to preventive diplomacy in that negotiation occurs before there is an urgent demand for it (Zartman 2001). Second, in the earlier stages fewer resources are necessary to establish a communication or formula mode of negotiation. Third, in this stage of the conflict it is likely the parties are not even in contact with one another, so the demand for a neutral third party is greater. Fourth, intervention in the pre-settlement stage, at which point no coercion is necessary, avoids facing an unwillingness or inability to force an agreement or its compliance. The Sant' Egídio negotiation in Mozambique's civil war, for example, was successful because of its neutrality, trust, and relative weakness to enforce compliance by any party (Hume 1994). Once the agreement was made, however, additional resources to enforce compliance were necessary. The United Nations subsequently approved a peacekeeping force to oversee the transition from war and democratic elections.

Thus, for Christians who do become involved in international negotiation there is a marked difference in approach, depending on their theological tradition. The Reformation and Catholic experiences affect both the mediation *goals* and mediation *levels* of Christians within these traditions. Table 11.3 illustrates these differing approaches.

Roman Catholics argue that mediation goals include an emphasis on human rights, development, solidarity, and world order. Catholic theorists tend to emphasize the common good and believe that peace should be founded on principles of justice and human rights. Roman Catholic negotiators often prefer to mediate with the elite of a state and there is a strong presumption that leaders will give them an audience. The examples of the Holy See mediation with the elite of Argentine and Chilean society to avert a war and promote good relationships between the two Catholic countries illustrate this approach.

One crucial feature of the Reformed tradition is its emphasis on liberty. The Reformed writers emphasized the role of liberty in religious belief. Although there was a tension with the desire to implement Reformed beliefs throughout the polity, which involves coercion, the concept of freedom nevertheless holds great importance to Reformed

Table 11.3
Christian traditions and negotiating goals and levels

Tradition	Mediation goals	Mediation level
Anabaptist	Peace	Grassroots
Reformed	Liberty	Elite
Roman Catholic	Common good	Elite and grassroots

mediators. The work of Chris Seiple of the Institute for Global Engagement on religious liberty, conveyed in chapter 14 of this volume, is one example of this emphasis. It could also be argued that former president Bush's foreign policy that emphasized freedom reflected, in part, this Reformed tradition of liberty.

Individuals from the magisterial reformation often prefer to negotiate through the state and intergovernmental organizations, focusing their efforts on higher levels of government, partly because the Reformed tradition became the dominant political tradition in Germany, Britain, and the United States. Thus, Christian mediators are generally drawn from the ruling elite of these societies. The tension between the two kingdoms – the heavenly kingdom and the human or earthly kingdom – is experienced perhaps more acutely among Reformed mediators. Lacking a strong institutional affiliation with the church and identifying more strongly with the state, the Reformed mediator is forced to switch roles more often.

Christians from the radical reformation, such as the Anabaptists, have markedly different attitudes toward mediation. Anabaptist mediators prefer to use concepts such as peacemaking and peace-building rather than conflict management to describe the aims of their work. At the heart of this approach is a profound scepticism regarding the use of power, a commitment to pacifism, faithfulness to the biblical injunction to be peacemakers, and a readiness to make personal sacrifices in order to bring peace. Anabaptist beliefs lead to quite different approaches to mediation for those who subscribe to them. Modern-day Anabaptists such as the Mennonites tend to work at a grassroots level, show great sensitivity to local culture, and aim toward the transformation of a conflict rather than its management (Sampson and Lederach 2001).

Two examples illustrate the characteristics of Anabaptist mediation. First, the American Mennonite John Paul Lederach, a scholar on the international peacemaking activities of Mennonite churches, has written extensively on the need for deep-rooted conflicts to be transformed into positive relationships rather than negotiating a simple cessation of hostilities (1995). Second, in actual practice, during the 1980s civil war in Nicaragua the Moravian Church attempted peacemaking between the Marxist Sandinista government and Miskito Indian rebels on the country's Atlantic Coast.

As pointed out above, the role of manipulator is most problematic for Christians of all traditions because manipulation conveys the sense of coercion. For Christians of the Reformed tradition, this means a restriction of liberty. For Anabaptists it conveys a lack of love and possible use of violence. It is notable that former president Carter was accused of acting too independently of the White House in his mediation efforts with North Korea over its nuclear development program (Creekmore 2006). One could make the case that this was consistent with Carter's tradition because President Clinton was contemplating a military strike against North Korean nuclear facilities. For Roman Catholics, manipulation may go against the principle of non-violence and must be assessed within the context of Roman Catholic 'just war' teachings, which are a set of moral principles that determine the justice of entering into and engaging in a war. As described in chapter 10, Pope John Paul II, for example, spoke out against the impending war in Iraq, stating an American pre-emptive attack could not be justified on just war principles.

Christians from a Roman Catholic or Reformed background, however, may demonstrate a greater willingness than those within the Anabaptist tradition to use manipulation to move parties to negotiation. Both approaches see government as a powerful tool to reduce evil. In the case of failing or collapsed states, the reconstitution of civil authority is a critical first step in achieving this aim. In the case of post-independence Congo in the early 1960s, for example, active intervention to stop a bloody and destructive civil war was not inconsistent with either the Reformed or Roman Catholic just war traditions. Even so, Dag Hammarskjöld, the United Nations secretary general, was reluctant to use coercion to bring the warring parties to a negotiated settlement in his mediation role. Clearly there were also institutional and political constraints facing him and the United Nations at that time.

Responses to Christian Mediation and Mediation Outcomes

What has been the response of *disputing parties* and the *international community* to Christian mediation? The response of disputing parties to Christian mediation has varied from positive to negative, depending on how the mediation affected their own objectives. The response of the international community to Christian mediation has been quite positive where such mediation is seen as achieving goals otherwise unattainable. The mediation of the Sant' Egídio Community in Mozambique's conflict, while initially met with scepticism by professional diplomats, was eventually welcomed. In the Mozambique case there was strong international diplomatic support to resolve the long-standing conflict, and any assistance was welcomed.

There are, nonetheless, negative assessments of Christian intervention in international conflicts. First, mediation by Track 2 Christian organizations may be viewed as intervention by naive and inexperienced amateurs. A Christian mediator may be more easily manipulated by parties in the dispute. In the case of Terry Waite, for example, the mediator was simply seized as a valuable hostage.

Second, diplomats may view international negotiations as the natural domain of the state. Christian mediation may be perceived especially negatively if it interferes with state objectives. Jimmy Carter's mediation in North Korea was criticized by some because it was seen as freelancing by a former president and deliberately forcing or manipulating President Clinton's foreign policies. The case of the Palestinian-Israeli conflict shows the importance of trust and impartiality for a mediator, including one who also affirms the importance of his Christian faith in his beliefs and actions. During his time in office, President Carter had helped negotiate peace between Egypt and Israel. Afterward he maintained a strong interest in Middle East peace. Subsequent comments and writings that placed the primary sources of the Israeli-Palestinian conflict with Israeli policies and leaders and also comparing Israel to apartheid South Africa, however, undermined Israeli trust in Carter as a potential mediator. The Middle East example also demonstrates the potency of religious identity, competing claims to land and legitimacy, and insecurity, in negotiating compromises over core beliefs.

The Christian third-party mediation cases presented, with the exception of Terry Waite's involvement in Lebanon, are examples of success. In assessing what specific traits or approaches that Christians use in mediation that improve or worsen the management of a conflict, they are clearly biased in favour of improvement. Nevertheless, the cases permit an assessment of how such mediation might make things worse. While criticisms of such faith-based mediation were noted earlier, it is possible to evaluate these cases to make some initial propositions on Christian mediation and conflict management.

Christian mediation may worsen a negotiated outcome in two ways. First, the mediator may set very high, and unrealistic, thresholds for resolution of conflict. In the case of Track 2 Christian mediation this may mean an unrealistic desire to deeply resolve or transform the conflict. Achieving anything less would be seen as failure. Yet substantial progress may be possible even if relationships are not transformed. The strong normative commands of scripture can cause the mediator to be unwilling to compromise. If a conflict is 'spiritualized,' then any compromise is essentially a compromise with 'evil.' Thus, a non-Christian mediator may be more open to a settlement that pragmatically resolves a violent conflict but at the expense of justice for some individuals or groups involved in the conflict. In its extreme, an unwillingness to tolerate such inequality in outcome can cause negotiations to fail.

Second, dislike of force and power means that a very important tool in coercing parties to a settlement is not available, which may actually lessen the likelihood of settlement. This is particularly true for those who are mediating from an Anabaptist position. It also creates a moral equivalence between the parties that may, in fact, not exist. An example may be seen in the conflicts waged in Central America during the 1980s. The causes of the conflict were complex and related both to Communist expansion and centuries of oppression of ordinary citizens by the ruling elite. Anabaptist Christian Track 2 mediators seemed less concerned with the larger geo-strategic aspects of the conflict, preferring to keep the focus on the very real oppression and suffering of the largely Indian majorities caught up in the fighting.

Conclusion

This chapter has examined faith-based, third-party mediation in international conflicts. Christian mediation has strong intellectual roots and a long history of experiences in mediation, and has assumed increasing relevance in more recent times. The chapter explained the activities of Track 2 unofficial mediation by differentiating it from its secular counterparts, assessing mediators' motivations, goals, approaches, and effectiveness, examining the influence of varying traditions within Western Christianity, and evaluating the responses of those affected by the mediation. While tradition does not provide an overarching explanation of the entire range of Christian mediation in international conflict, it nonetheless provides one framework for understanding the phenomena.

The examples presented demonstrate that self-identified Christians are involved as third parties in international disputes. Furthermore, within each tradition, Christian third-party mediation clearly had a positive impact in resolving an international conflict. Like their secular counterparts, however, Christian mediators did not always succeed, as seen in the case of Terry Waite and his being taken hostage in Lebanon. Relating such mediation to the conflict resolution literature demonstrates that such Christian mediators demonstrated some success, particularly in the pre-negotiations and early negotiations stages of a conflict. One reason seen for this success is, first, that Christian mediators are seen as honest brokers. Second, at this point in the conflict relationships of the parties in dispute are so strained that it is difficult to initiate negotiations directly without the parties losing face. Third, the mediators had staying power, having sufficient resources and being committed to negotiations in the long haul. This is seen in the cases of Catholic mediation in Mozambique and Argentina/Chile. In the case of Track 2 negotiations, however, the inability of Christian Track 2 mediators to bring resources to bear usually precluded involvement in the more expensive stages related to implementation. Thus Track 2 groups, as seen in the Carter Center, are still useful in specific aspects of the implementation stage such as elections and human rights monitoring.

Some differences have been noted between mediators in their preferred level of mediation. Those from a Roman Catholic tradition often focused on working at an elite level, although the Sant' Egídio lay group did have a more grassroots approach. Even in the Mozambique case, however, Sant' Egídio mediators related primarily to government and rebel leaders. Christians from the radical reformer background tended to work without relation to the state, preferring mediation at the grassroots. Christians from a magisterial background tended to work with elites. One aspect of Christian mediation that may affect outcomes is that the bar for success – conflict transformation – was quite high for some Christian mediators, especially those from an Anabaptist background.

Responses of parties in and outside of disputes vary. Interested parties generally have reacted positively but tended to evaluate mediation in terms of their own interests. The religious identity of the mediators did not seem to be considered a negative trait in the cases covered, although this may not hold true in a broader and more comprehensive analysis.

This chapter reveals that a strong religious identity is not just a source of conflict but is also a means of peace and reconciliation. Such mediators act in a very complex international environment and are not always successful. They also act in ways that reflect their own understanding of their role as Christians working in an international system organized on the basis of states. As seen in varying responses to the war in Iraq, Christians' difference on the use of coercive force to resolve conflict is based in part on their theological perspectives. While this chapter has examined the work of self-identified Christians from the Western branch of Christendom mediating outside official diplomatic channels, such efforts of peacemaking are not unique to this religion. Nevertheless, this study does demonstrate that one aspect of understanding how believers from religions such as Islam, Hinduism, and Buddhism also contribute to the resolution of conflict is in understanding that even within Christianity there is a great variation in perspective and practice in international mediation. This provides at least one point of comparison with individuals and groups from other faiths engaged in similar efforts.

NOTES

1 Track I diplomacy is traditional negotiations practised by 'official' government representatives. Track II diplomacy is unofficial diplomacy practised by representatives of nongovernmental organizations to resolve an international conflict.
2 An excellent overview of Roman Catholic approaches to international mediation resulted from a workshop in April 2001 sponsored by the Washington DC–based United States Institute of Peace. The Special Report, entitled 'Catholic Contributions to International Peace,' is available from their website at http://www.usip.org/ resources/catholic-contributions-international-peace.
3 A brief review of these negotiations is found in Amstutz (1999).
4 Appleby (2000) makes the case that religious peacemaking is the primary goal of Christian negotiation.

REFERENCES

Albright, M. 2006. *The mighty & the Almighty: Reflections on America, God, and world affairs*. New York: HarperCollins.

Almquist, K. 1994. The role of nongovernmental organizations in international mediation: The Case of Sant' Egídio. Unpublished manuscript. Washington, DC.

Amstutz, M.R. 1999. *International conflict and cooperation: An introduction to world politics*. Boston: McGraw-Hill.

Appleby, R.S. 2000. *The ambivalence of the Sacred: Religion, violence, and reconciliation*. Lanham, MD: Rowman & Littlefield.

Augustine. 1993. *The city of God*. Trans. Marcus Dods. New York: Random House.

de Callières, F. 2000. *On the manner of negotiating with princes: Classic principles of diplomacy and the art of negotiation*. Boston: Houghton Mifflin.

Cassidy, M. 1995. *A witness forever: The dawning of democracy in South Africa, stories behind the story*. London: Hodder and Stoughton.

Cordier, A.W. 1967. Motivations and methods of Dag Hammarskjöld. In Cordier and Maxwell, 1–21.

Cordier, A.W., and K.L. Maxwell, eds. 1967. *Paths to world order*. New York: Columbia University Press.

Creekmore, M.V. 2006. *A moment of crisis: Jimmy Carter, the power of a peacemaker, and North Korea's nuclear ambitions*. New York: Public Affairs.

Gopin, M. 2000. *Between Eden and Armageddon: The future of world religions, violence, and peacemaking*. Oxford: Oxford University Press.

– 2002. *Holy war, holy peace*. Oxford: Oxford University Press.

Hammarskjöld, D. 1961. *This I believe*, radio program moderated by Edward R. Murrow. In Lash, 24.

– 1964. *Markings*. Trans. L. Sjöberg and W.H. Auden. New York: Ballantine Books/Random House.

Hume, C.R. 1994. *Ending Mozambique's war: The role of mediation and good offices*. Washington, DC: United States Institute of Peace.

Johnston, D. 1994. *Religion: The missing dimension of statecraft*. New York: Oxford University Press.

– 2003. *Faith-based diplomacy: Trumping realpolitik*. New York: Oxford University Press.

Lash, J.P. 1961. *Dag Hammarskjöld: Custodian of the brushfire peace*. New York: Doubleday.

Lederach, J.P. 1995. *Preparing for peace: Conflict transformation across cultures*. Syracuse: Syracuse University Press.

MacIntyre, A. 1984. *After virtue: A study in moral theory*. 2nd ed. Notre Dame, IN: University of Notre Dame Press.

Pillar, P.R. 1983. *Negotiating peace: War termination as a bargaining process*. Princeton, NJ: Princeton University Press.

Sampson, C., and J.P. Lederach, eds. 2001. *From the ground up: Mennonite contributions to international peacebuilding*. Washington, DC: United States Institute of Peace.
Stedman, S.J. 1990. *Peacemaking in civil war: International mediation in Zimbabwe, 1974–1980*. Boulder, CO: Rienner.
Touval, S., and I.W. Zartman. 1985. *International mediation in theory and practice*. Boulder, CO: Westview.
– 1996. International mediation in the post–Cold War era. In *Turbulent peace: The challenges of managing international conflict*, ed. C.A. Crocker, F.O. Hampson, and P. Aall. Washington, DC: United States Institute of Peace Press.
Van Dusen, H.P. 1967. Dag Hammarskjöld: The inner person. In Cordier and Maxwell, 22–44.
Yoder, J.H., and A. Kreider. 1977. The Anabaptists. In *Handbook to the history of Christianity*, ed. T. Dowley. 399–403. Grand Rapids, MI: Eerdmans.
Zartman, I.W. 1986. Ripening conflict, ripe moment, formula, and mediation. In *Perspectives on negotiation: Four case studies and interpretations*. Washington, DC: Foreign Service Institute, United States Department of State.
– 1999. Justice in negotiation. In *International negotiation: Actors, structure/process, values*, ed. P. Berton, H. Kimura, and I. Zartman. New York: St Martin's.
– ed. 2001. *Preventive negotiation: Avoiding conflict escalation*. Lanham, MD: Rowman & Littlefield.

12 The Role of Religious NGOs in Shaping Foreign Policy: Western Middle Powers and Reform Internationalism

STEVEN L. LAMY

Introduction: Pursuing the Common Good

This chapter focuses on the foreign policies of Western middle powers or what have recently been called *Good Samaritan states*. These reform internationalist states make up what Pratt (1990) and Stokke (1989) called the 'like-minded states' or small or middle powers interested in promoting economic and social justice, defending human rights, and maintaining peace and stability by supporting multilateral institutions and the rule of law.

Lawler (2005, 441–2) defines the 'Good State' in philosophical and policy terms: 'The Good State is simply a state committed to moral purposes beyond itself, to a robust internationalism in its foreign policy. By internationalism is meant a philosophy of foreign policy constructed around an ethical obligation on the part of states actively to pursue authentically other-regarding values and interests.' Lawler goes on to suggest that in these 'good states,' the internationalism is not accidental or momentary. It is 'a transcendent rather than an immanent moral ideology' that suggests a commitment to more than just a national interest foreign policy (442).

These states are more likely to be part of global efforts to pursue the 'common good.' Leaders and citizens in these states strive to integrate ethical obligations with policy practices (Steenland et al. 2007, 3). The leaders of religions and secular organizations are pressuring governments to work with public and private actors to address global challenges that threaten populations across the world. Our 'shared humanity' provides all the incentive we need to act. This 'responsibility to act' is clearly articulated in the report of the International Commission on Intervention and State Sovereignty (ICISS 2001), commissioned by the Canadian government after the success of the International Campaign to Ban Landmines and the human security movement. (Canadian diplomacy and religion are covered in depth by chapter 13.) The Responsibility to Protect Doctrine (R2P) was first adopted as a norm by a UN High Level panel in 2004. Then the 2005 *Report of the UN Secretary General* was submitted and approved by all heads of state and government representatives attending the sixtieth session of the UN General Assembly. All agreed to the R2P document in principle. Further, the UN Security Council Resolution 1674, affirmed in April 2006, provided for protection of civilians in armed conflict but also supported again the R2P principle. The R2P doctrine clearly affirms that states have the responsibility to protect civilians from violence and deprivation and to prevent further violations of human security. When a state fails to protect its citizens, responsibility shifts to the international community.

A shared moral vision and pursuit of a global common good are not novel ideas. However, recently religious leaders and progressive religions and secular non-governmental organizations (NGOs) have been working across boundaries of faith and geography to pursue common solutions and to promote global governance that addresses issues like torture, human rights, global climate change, and war (Fuchs and Buckley 2007, 8). Furthermore, Christian faiths and various religious NGOs have advocated policies that promote the common good. These religious organizations provide relevant information for policymakers, educate their fellow worshippers, and, in many cases, actually participate in programs that provide for those left behind (9). Many of these Christian groups refer to St Thomas Aquinas as a foundational advocate for the common good: 'He that seeks the good of the many seeks in consequence his own good' (1981).

Fuchs and Buckley also discuss the importance of doing justice in both the Jewish and Islamic traditions. The Jewish tradition, *tikkun olam* (repairing the world), emphasizes acts that 'repair the world' and is a theme used by contemporary Jewish NGOs and activists to promote acts of social responsibility. This may mean promoting policies that protect the disadvantaged or supporting actions that address human rights and social justice.

The Qu'ran and Islamic traditions also emphasize giving to the poor (*zakat*) and the idea that wealth is held by individuals in trust. All material things belong to God and we purify all our possessions by alms giving. *Maslaha* is translated as 'public interest' or 'public welfare,' and *maslaha* and *istislah*[1] or seeking the best public interest are important concepts in traditional Islamic law. These concepts guide governments to pursue the common good and provide for public needs.

Eastern religious traditions such as Buddhism and Confucianism all suggest that we are human because we assist others in need. Fuchs and Buckley (2007, 11) quote the Dalai Lama: 'Ultimately, humanity is one and this small planet is our only home. If we are to protect this home of ours, each of us needs to experience a vivid sense of universal altruism.' The Good Samaritan states work in partnership with a number of secular and religious NGOs to pursue the common good. These states and their NGO allies have worked relentlessly since the end of the Cold War to address the particularistic and state-centric factors that continue to prevent the achievement of the global common good.

The human security, responsibility to protect, and duty to prevent movements focus on the conditions that Fuchs and Buckley (2007, 13–14) claim are obstacles to realization of a world that promotes cosmopolitan rights, social justice, non-violence, and environmentally sustainable development. These obstacles include:

- Weak and failed states that do not have the means to provide for their citizens and lack the interest or means to pursue the global common good
- A dominant belief system in most rule-making and rule-taking states that promotes national interests over human interests
- International institutions that serve the interests of powerful and wealthy states and not the interests of the poor and marginalized people of the world.
- The predatory aspects of globalization that often put profits over principles (for example, the search for the 'lowest common denominator' means that political and economic actors set aside laws that protect workers and fundamentally support human security)
- Racism, ignorance, and the acceptance of Huntington's theory of a threat of a clash of civilizations by many citizens around the world that has led to fundamentalism and extremist movements within all religious traditions
- Instrumental thinking (i.e., cost-benefit analysis) that dilutes the commitment to the ideas of a global community and privileges profits over people

In partnership with progressive secular and religious NGOs, Good

Samaritan states lead efforts to address these obstacles and achieve a global common good.

The first part of this chapter has explored the factors that make a Good Samaritan state. In the second section, I explore the foreign priorities of the Good Samaritan states. Specifically, I review their policy objectives and practices in two critical areas: the responsibility to protect and duty to prevent policy sector and the campaign to achieve the Millennium Development Goals (MDG). Also, I look at the role of religious NGOs who partner with social democratic Good Samaritan states in the aforementioned policy areas. I attempt to answer two critical questions. How do these religious NGOs influence the foreign policy process? Why are these religious NGOs influential in these states?

In the final section of the chapter I discuss the implications for future efforts to achieve the global common good in an international system that remains state-centric and where nationalism and ethno-nationalism seem to be on the rise.

The Foreign Policy Priorities of Good Samaritan States

Most of the Good Samaritan states referenced by Fossum (2006), Lawler (2005), and Lumsdaine (1993) are Western social democratic states or what we have come to call 'middle powers.' Norway, Sweden, Denmark, the Netherlands, and Canada see themselves as *guide states* and as promoters of global social democratic values and policies. As Lumsdaine (21) suggests, states can choose to be 'public spirited,' and national interests therefore may emerge from a 'social process of choice and self-definition.' Thus, those social democratic states that provide well for their own citizens seek to do the same for outsiders. Lumsdaine's study of the international foreign aid regime confirms this point (22–3). He confirms three hypotheses that emphasize the special role of Good Samaritan middle powers:

- Beliefs, values, and practices of moral discourse among citizens and domestic political life are transferred to foreign policy.
- A state's foreign policy is influenced by its previous experience and the role it plays in international society.
- International regimes (e.g., foreign aid) and practices have an inherent social meaning so that change in those practices tends to be ongoing norm-governed change.

Lumsdaine's research suggests that among the major aid donor states only about one-third of the aid serves commercial and security purposes. Thus, most of the aid given is for humanitarian purposes.

In describing the importance of a 'behavioural' measure of middle powers, Cooper, Higgot, and Nossal (1993) describe their attributes as follows:

- Catalysts: states that provide resources and expertise to lead in global initiatives
- Facilitators: states that set agendas in global policy discussions and build coalitions for collaborative responses
- Managers: middle powers that support institution-building at the international level and encourage support for existing international organizations and multinational activities

The same authors quote Gareth Evans, a former Australian minister of foreign affairs and trade, and head of the commission that developed the *Responsibility to Protect Report* (2001), in describing a concept called 'niche diplomacy.' This form of middle-power activism 'involves concentrating resources in specific areas best able to generate return worth having, rather than trying to cover the field' (Cooper, Higgot, and Nossal 1993, 25–6).

Middle powers, because of their normative position and past roles in international affairs, have very distinctive interests in the future world order. Middle powers are activists in international and regional forums and are confirmed multilateralists in most issue areas. These states actively support an equitable and pluralistic rule-based system. They are, for the most part, trading states and thus favour a relatively open and stable world market. Since stability is so important to them, most middle powers see themselves as global problem-solvers, mediators, and moderators in international disputes (Holbraad 1984; Woods 1988). Middle powers usually lead in regional organizations (e.g., European Union) and in functionally specific institutions such as the World Health Organization and the Development Assistance Committee of the Organization of Economic Cooperation and Development.

A third view of middle powers places emphasis on the *normative orientation* of this group of states. Although subject to much criticism, the image of middle powers as 'potentially more wise and virtuous' than other states is usually promoted by national leaders and progressive interest groups in order to gain domestic support for international activism and enhance the reputation of their states in the international community. This image of global moral leaders, which bridges the gap between rich and poor communities, fits well with the egalitarian social democratic values of most Western middle powers. Robert Cox (1989, 834–5) argues that the traditional normative aims of middle powers – greater social equity and a call for more diffusion of power in the system – might give them more leverage as principal problem-solvers in continuing economic and political challenges faced by all states. Other advantages enjoyed by Western middle powers with social democratic values include their commitment to using public interventions to create more equitable societies and their experience with corporatist structures of decision-making.

Cox and others observe that non-governmental forces will play a major role in future policymaking. In corporatist systems, these non-governmental actors, including religious NGOs, play a pivotal role in policymaking. Leaders of middle power states may be more capable of organizing regional and international policymaking programs because they have experience with accommodating diverse interests in corporatist bargaining. The traditional commitment of middle powers to rule-based systems, establishing and maintaining international and regional organizations to resolve common problems, and power-sharing and burden-sharing in international issue areas suggests these states may play a critical role as the catalysts of problem-solving initiatives or the managers of regimes initiated by greater powers with less interest in internationalism and little domestic support for egalitarian goals and values.

Both Sweden and the Netherlands see themselves as *mentor* or guide states. The Dutch version of *gidsland* is described by Fossum (2006, 783) as 'a nation that progressively guides other countries locked in pitiful nationalist struggles for power, dominance, and religious zeal to proper international behavior consisting of respect for international legal order, rights of men, and free trade as the best way of ensuring prosperity for all.'

A *guide state* takes on a cosmopolitan paradigm that includes rejecting the distinction between domestic and international politics. Cosmopolitan norms and values are promoted in both political arenas. Further, guide states lead in policy areas in which that state and its citizens have special interests and expertise. As global problem-solvers, most *guide states* assume global stewardship in security, poverty, human rights, trade and aid, the environment and global governance.

Good Samaritan states project their internal political culture and belief system externally. These social democratic values are embedded within both domestic and foreign policy institution and policy narratives. However, it is about more than being social democratic states with a commitment to social justice and a rule-based international system. Fossum (2006, 825–6) suggests that guide states are both *permeable* and *reflexive*. A permeable society is responsive to external norms and rules. It is also very attentive to public opinion at home and abroad. Further, these societies work extensively with both secular and religious NGOs promoting cosmopolitan rights and values. Global NGOs are described as 'push factors,' promoting values and goals and partnering with states in foreign policy.

Reflexivity describes the dynamic interaction that a state, meaning its leaders and citizens, have with the world. Are the citizens of a state open to change and are they engaged in constant critical self-reflection? Clearly, interest in foreign policy and global issues must be high and citizens must be fairly knowledgeable about international politics. NGOs play an important role in providing information and presenting options for citizen participation. Reflexivity and permeability combine to create a globally engaged citizenry and a government committed to promoting its domestic values and beliefs at home and abroad.

Religious NGOs and the Shaping of Foreign Policy

A number of major global policy campaigns are being led by Good Samaritan states and a significant number of secular and religious NGOs. The responsibility to protect (R2P) and duty to prevent campaign and the UN Millennium Development Goals are prominent examples. Each represents a significant attempt to address persistent global problems and reform global governance to better address transnational security challenges and the failure of many states to meet the needs of their citizens. Before I cover these issues in more detail it may be important to discuss the nature of power and influence that religious or secular NGOs can have in policy formulation and implementation. The goal of most NGOs is to persuade the public and political elites to act on their issues, to pressure policymakers, and to educate the general public. In their ground breaking study, *Activists beyond Borders* (1998), Keck and Sikkink discuss four sources of power and influence for NGOs: information politics, symbolic politics, leverage politics, and accountability politics. I will add a fifth form of influence, and that is the global campaign. Each is discussed in the next few pages.

Information Politics

Few political leaders are experts in the policy areas they are asked to address. NGOs, both secular and religious, provide *valuable information* to those who make policy and to the citizens who vote. It might be an 'emergency alert' from Lutheran World Relief on the crisis in Darfur or a Project Ploughshares research report on arms trade and child soldiers. These NGOs use e-mail, fax machines, newsletters, Web pages, and reports to keep their followers informed and to mobilize citizens to pressure decision-makers to act.

These same NGOs use their expertise and their access to critical voices in crises to provide important technical and strategic information. NGO fieldworkers and researchers are on the front lines and are often the first to know about conflicts and crises. Again, these organizations are essential in both the 'initiation or articulation' of policy and the eventual 'formulation and implementation' of that policy. They also cross the domestic and international divide, linking their home base with distant communities. In this sense, many of these religious communities act as truly transnational actors: Kantian universalists in their perspectives and goals and local and global (i.e., glocal) in their policy strategies.

Symbolic Politics

Religious and secular NGOs use their position in society to increase awareness and expand support for their cause. When a NGO like the International Campaign to Ban Landmines is awarded the Nobel Peace Prize, it calls attention to its cause and gives the NGO more legitimacy around the world. For example, Caritas Internationalis works in over two hundred countries and territories to assist the poor and to fight intolerance and discrimination. When they promote specific causes and advocate for the poor using the words and symbolism of Pope John Paul II (covered extensively in chapter 10), they are attempting to influence both policymakers and citizens alike.

Leverage Politics

Many religious NGOs often use material (e.g., donations or the promise of political support) or moral leverage to persuade governments to act in certain ways or to encourage other religious or secular NGOs to support their position on an issue. Often these religious NGOs will shame governments into acting in a certain way. These groups, especially those with significant resources, are adept at using the media and the Internet to expose certain behaviours and to make the public aware of practices of government, transnational corporations, or other actors with authority in a given policy area. With greater access to media and new information technology, both religious and secular NGOs have greater access to larger audiences. Religious NGOs often use religious values and principles to demand greater accountability from public officials. The World Council of Churches (WCC), along with other religious groups, has created 'an alternative to corporate globalization,' the Ecumenical Earth Program. This program focuses on issues like climate change, biological and cultural diversity, and biotechnology (Forum on Religion and Ecology 2004). The WCC project is co-sponsored by other Christian development agencies from several middle powers or 'guide states,' including Norwegian Church Aid and Church of Sweden Aid. These are influential domestic and international actors that can deliver votes and support critical policy programs when called upon. Votes and policy support along with money and goods are *material leverage* strategies.

Another effective strategy involves religious NGOs in *moral leveraging*. Sometimes called the 'mobilization of shame,' NGOs use their communication resources and their members to mobilize public opinion and make the world aware of certain polices. The longstanding campaigns to free Tibet and to overthrow the military junta in Burma are two examples. In both cases, Buddhist monks and religious leaders have led the campaigns. Shaming campaigns were clearly effective against South Africa's apartheid system, but shaming campaigns aimed at leaders in China, Sudan, and Burma have not resulted in a change in policies in the target state.

A frequent target of many NGOs is China and its domestic human rights policies and its indifference to problems in states with which it trades and invests. Lately, these progressive actors are hoping to change Chinese policies at home and in Darfur and Tibet. Their attempt to create a global boycott of the 2008 Olympics failed. Clearly economic concerns are trumping moral concerns. China is a big market and is an important provider of essential goods and services, and in this case, states do not believe they can afford to take the moral high ground.

Accountability Politics

Often religious and secular NGOs are able to convince governments or individual politicians to support a particular position or program. Then these same NGOs keep track of what the government actually does. These groups hold the government or political leader accountable by making certain everyone is made aware of gaps between promises and performance.

Many religious NGOs concerned about global poverty have focused their attention on making certain the G-8 countries keep their promises. Caritas Internationalis and a delegation of Roman Catholic religious leaders from Africa, Asia, Latin America, and Europe met with political leaders on the eve of the 2007 G-8 Conference in Germany to urge them to keep their promises made at previous summit meetings. In previous conferences, G-8 members had promised to increase resources to fight global poverty, especially in Africa. As the *Caritas Report* (2007) suggests, progress has been uneven at best and few states are meeting their obligations. This was also the purpose of the global One Campaign led by U-2, Radiohead, and other celebrities. With an increasing awareness of the transnational nature of these global crises, campaigns like the One Campaign provide information about global poverty, suggest ways all citizens can contribute to a solution, and put pressure on political and business leaders to act. They can deliver votes and they certainly make strong moral arguments. The alliance of rock stars and Christian conservative political leaders in the United States led to Congressional support for the Jubilee Movement's campaign to forgive the debts of many African countries.

Global Campaigns

A relatively new tool for NGOs and other civil society actors is a global campaign that uses the media, local activist networks, and the Internet. More recent examples include the International Campaign to Ban Landmines, the One Campaign aimed at ending global poverty, and the Save Darfur Campaign. With celebrity spokespersons, concerts, and teach-ins, these campaigns aim to educate people about the issues and to mobilize citizens to pressure political leaders to act. Religious NGOs often play a major role in educating and mobilizing people of faith.

The religious NGOs that we highlight in this chapter are the progeny of the late-nineteenth-century *Social Gospel* movement. This progressive religious tradition rejected a more conservative individualistic social ethic and sought to establish a 'Kingdom of God' with social justice, peace, and collective action for the common good as its goals (Hutchinson 1975). This tradition of social action informs some of the most powerful religious movements in the United States today. Globally, religious NGOs have focused their energies on some of the greatest challenges facing humanity, including poverty, environmental degradation, disease and HIV/AIDS, and the failure of some states to provide basic human security for their citizens.

Background on the Social Gospel Movement

The Social Gospel movement was a response to rapid urbanization, industrialization, and the treatment of workers in America in the late nineteenth century, though its impact extended to Canada and the United Kingdom. Its goal was to organize humanity according to the will of God. Followers believed that Christians could make society more like the society Christ sought to create. Jesus was seen as moral exemplar who worked to liberate the poor and transform society by focusing on social justice. This movement clearly inspired present-day activists in the Roman Catholic *liberation theology* community and in many of the contemporary Islamic, Jewish, and Protestant religious communities.

The Social Gospel movement was not a radical attack on capitalism but a call for reform of the capitalist system. The movement's goals were similar to the current emphasis by secular and religious NGOs on addressing the predatory aspects of globalization. Current progressive NGOs argue that if profit is the only motivation for global corporations, then these corporations will make their investments in countries without unions, minimum wage laws, or safety and environmental regulations. Today, many religious and secular NGOs are working to protect workers and to provide for those at the bottom of societies. Many of these NGOs talk about creating a capitalist system with a human face.

The Social Gospel movement tied salvation to good works, arguing that all Christians should do their best to emulate the life of Jesus Christ. The wealthy, they believed, had a responsibility to share their wealth with those in need. One major spokesman for the movement was Walter Rauschenbusch (1861–1918), a minister and a professor of divinity. A pacifist, Rauschenbusch argued that we should pay attention to *social sins*, not merely personal sins. He believed that war, brought on by greed and deceit, was the worst of any social sin (Dyck 1989). Rauschenbusch described the social gospel in his book *Christianity and the Social Crisis* (1944, 286). 'Will the twentieth century mark for the future historian the real adolescence of humanity, the great emancipation from barbarism and from the paralysis of injustice, and the beginning of a progress in the intellectual, social, and moral life of mankind to which all past history has no parallel? It will depend almost wholly on the moral forces which the Christian nations can bring to the fighting line against wrong, and the fighting energy of those moral forces will again depend on the degree to which they are inspired by religious faith and enthusiasm.'

Today, the ideas promoted by the Social Gospel followers are important to a number of religious groups in the United States, including the Evangelical Lutheran Church, the Presbyterian Church, the United Church of Christ, and the United Methodist Church. Many of these religious denominations have supported the One Campaign and the UN Millennium Development Goals. In the next few pages, we explore how religious organizations representing Christian, Jewish, and Islamic traditions have continued the Social Gospel values and promoted a more humanitarian emphasis in international relations.

Responsibility to Protect and the Support of Religious NGOs

At the UN Millennium Assembly in 2000, Canada's Prime Minster Jean Chrétien announced that Canada would sponsor an International Commission on Intervention and State Sovereignty (ICISS). The government invited Gareth Evans, head of the International Crisis Group, and Mohamed Sahnoun, a former Algerian diplomat and an experienced UN advisor, to serve as co-chairs.

In September 2000, the Commission was charged by Canada's Foreign Minister Lloyd Axworthy to find 'new ways of reconciling seemingly irreconcilable notions of intervention and state sovereignty' (ICISS 2001, 81). This was a very careful review of the right of humanitarian intervention. The key question the Commission explored is whether it is appropriate for states to take coercive military action in another state to protect citizens at risk in that other state.

The *basic principles* (ICISS 2001, xi) of the report fit nicely with many of the universal goals of religious NGOS.

Basic Principles:

1. State sovereignty implies responsibility, and the primary responsibility for the protection of its people lies within the state itself.
2. Where a population is suffering serious harm, as a result of internal war, insurgency, repression, or state failure, and the state in ques-

tion is unwilling or unable to halt or avert it, the principle of non-intervention yields to the international responsibility to protect. The elements or three specific responsibilities are:

1. *The responsibility to prevent* entails addressing the causes of conflict and other crises that put populations at risk.
2. *The responsibility to react* is the necessity to respond to situations that put individuals at risk with appropriate measures, which might include intervention.
3. *The responsibility to rebuild* after a natural disaster or military intervention means the international community must provide assistance for recovery and reconstruction. In addition, the international community should assist, with reconciliation efforts aimed at addressing the causes of conflict and violence.

The Responsibility to Protect (R2P) documents and resulting strategies all emphasize the importance of prevention. Clearly stated, that means addressing fundamental *human security* issues: freedom from fear, freedom from want, and the need for the rule of law to provide for a just and peaceful society. A significant number of religious NGOs devote their energies and resources to these issues. The five examples discussed here are the American Jewish World Service, My Sister's Keepers, Project Ploughshares, Caritas Internationalis, and the Religious Society of Friends.

American Jewish World Service

The American Jewish World Service (AJWS, http://ajws.org) is a partner in the R2P Coalition (http://r2pcoalition.org), and they have recently focused their attention on the genocidal campaign waged by the government of Sudan in Darfur since 2003. In his advocacy and education materials, Dorfman (2007) asks a fundamental question: What is the nature of our responsibility to prevent unjustified killing? In its programs and activities to educate students about genocide, the organization suggests that, as Jews, the community has a responsibility to respond to the Darfur conflict. The material begins with a clear message: 'The values of *tikkun olam* (repairing the world) and *pikuach nefesh* (saving human life) obligate us to take action to protect the people of Darfur.' The term *tikkun olam* was first used by activists taking social action in the 1950s and it is now used to refer to both charitable giving and general acts of kindness. As with the Social Gospel movement, the emphasis is on repairing the world – fixing it – and not radically transforming it.

Referring to religious texts, the AJWS makes a clear and powerful case for intervention and recognition of their community's 'responsibility to protect' innocent people:

Vayika/Leviticua 19:16: 'You shall not stand idly by the blood of your neighbour; I am God.'

Deuteronomy 21: 1–9, 'And they shall make the declaration: our hands did not shed this blood, nor did our eyes see it done.'

Rambam Laws of the Courts and the Penalties Placed under Their Jurisdiction 12:3, 'For this reason, one human being was created alone in the world. This teaches us that a person who eliminates one human life from the world is considered as if he eliminated an entire world. Conversely, a person who saves one human life is considered as if he saved an entire world' (Dorfman 2007).

These religious texts and moral prescriptions suggest a commitment to empathy and compassion for all humankind. The *not on our watch* view shapes the AJWS view on Darfur that is shaped by the history of persecution and genocide against the Jewish community. The AJWS position supports the elements of the responsibility-to-protect document as a fundamental duty to contribute to the welfare of humankind.

AJWS is using informational, symbolic, and leverage strategies to get its point across. AJWS has focused its resources on developing educational materials for Jewish schools, summer camps, and more informal educational programs (AJWS 2007). As a partner in the R2P coalition, they are also participants in the global campaign to address the crisis in Darfur.

Project Ploughshares

Founded in 1976, Project Ploughshares is an agency or organization of the Canadian Council of Churches. The Project works with public, private, and global civil society actors to 'build peace, prevent war and promote peaceful resolution of conflict' around the world (Project Ploushares n.d.). Ploughshares has programs dedicated to four related goals:

- Promoting research and information about and advocating for the elimination of weapons of mass destruction

- Advocating for non-force responses to conflicts and thus reducing the resort to military force
- Promoting controls of small arms and light weapons and working to eliminate the use of child soldiers
- Supporting global civil society programs to provide human security including the elements of responsibility to protect as supported by the members of the UN.

Ploughshares works alone and in partnerships to encourage governments to transfer resources they now use for war and the preparation for war to human security programs. In partnership with the Africa Peace Forum in Kenya, Ploughshares launched a program to implement the January 2005 peace agreement in Southern Sudan. A 2006 workshop focused on power-sharing, disarmament, demobilization, and reintegration of soldiers from the conflict and development programs essential for building sustainable peace in the region (Schroeder 2007). This dialogue and research project has been extended and broadened to include security in the Horn of Africa.

Ploughshares is a member of the International Action Network on Small Arms (IANSA), which is funded by governments including the United Kingdom, Belgium, Sweden, and Norway, and religious NGOs like Christian Aid, Pax Christi, World Vision, and Franciscans International. This is a global movement made up of over 800 civil society organizations that work in over 120 countries to stop the proliferation of small arms and light weapons and to prevent armed violence. In 2006, IANSA was instrumental in the formulation and acceptance of a global arms trade treaty by 153 governments in the UN General Assembly. The United States voted to oppose the treaty and twenty-four governments, mainly arms developers, abstained. The resolution captured the spirit of the R2P Movement: 'The absence of common international standards on the import, export and transfer of conventional arms is a contributory factor to conflict, the displacement of people, crime and terrorism, thereby, undermining peace, reconciliation, safety, security, stability and sustainable development' (Epps 2007, 21).

IANSA tools to control small arms and prevent gun violence fit well with the Keck and Sikkink framework (http://www.iansa.org):

- Advocate policy at the local, national, and international level aimed at arms control and preventing gun violence

- Provide information about small and light arms and sponsor public education campaigns
- Maintain and strengthen the global network committed to controlling if not ending small arms proliferation (including extending the reach of the network and linking it with other global campaigns)

An important element of IANSA's global strategy is promotion of the voices of survivors and victims of gun violence. The worldwide control arms campaign used the resources of hundreds of NGOs and the symbolic power of a million people who lent their portraits to the 'Million Faces Petition' to raise awareness, shape public opinion, and pressure political leaders to support the arms trade treaty.

My Sister's Keeper

This is a faith-inspired, multi-racial collective of women working in human security. Two women, Gloria White-Hammond (a minister and physician) and Liz Walker (a minister and journalist) started this organization after being invited to participate in a slave redemption program in southern Sudan by Christian Solidarity International, a Swiss human rights organization. The essence of My Sister's Keeper is support for 'the hopes of women who dare dream in the face of dire economic conditions.' The organization promotes the idea that 'knowledge is power' and dares to imagine a world 'where women can create and sustain vibrant and joyous communities' (My Sister's Keeper 2010a).

My Sister's Keeper (http://www.mskeeper.org) is a partner in the Responsibility to Protect coalition and its program priorities fit directly with efforts to provide human security in areas of conflict. Although focused on Sudan, the organization provides valuable information for those who want to understand the plight of women throughout the world and for those who want information about humanitarian programs that might benefit women. Although originally focused on finding ways to free women from slavery, the organization's projects now include education for girls, health care, and HIV/AIDS programs. The leaders of this organization clearly understand the connection between economic development and societal violence. Thus, My Sister's Keeper purchased a grinding mill to help prepare meals, and soap-making equipment, supplies, and sewing machines to provide jobs and create opportunities for women to be become self-reliant in the villages of

Sudan. The organization's members are committed to the goals of R2P and are major advocates for global action in Darfur.

The uniqueness of this project stems from its identity as a women-led humanitarian action program that emerged from conversations between Christian women from the affluent North and women barely surviving in violent and poor communities in Sudan. The members of this organization are inspired by a simple but powerful statement: 'I understand that each day as I wake up on this side of freedom, I have a gift that comes with a responsibility' (My Sister's Keeper 2010b).

Caritas Internationalis

Caritas Internationalis is a confederation of 162 Roman Catholic relief, development, and social service NGOs working in over two hundred countries and territories (http://www.caritas.org). Caritas works to provide human security – freedom from fear and freedom from want – for the poor and oppressed. Caritas programs also emphasize social justice, peace, and an appreciation of the environment. The religious approach of Caritas is based on the social teachings of the Roman Catholic Church that focus on human dignity, non-violence, stewardship, and respect for human rights. Caritas is primarily an *advocacy* organization that is defined as seeking a voice in all public policy debates in an effort to influence policy formulation and implementation. Caritas seeks to influence global policy by mobilizing citizens locally, nationally, and globally. In addition, Caritas has programs that assist 24 million people in two hundred countries and territories with a budget of $5.5 billion. One area that Caritas is working in is peace and development. Pope Paul VI's words inspire the organization's work in Iraq and other conflict regions: 'The new name of peace is development.'

An example of an on-site program is the peace-building course Caritas offers in primary schools in Baghdad promoting coexistence between Muslim and Christian children and it explores causes of conflict, healing, and reconciliation (Caritas 2008a). Caritas has developed a peace-building toolkit for local trainers who are engaged in grassroots efforts to build stable communities in developing countries. The essence of these programs is captured by Father Cibamo, a priest and community activist in the Congo: 'Peace isn't just an absence of war. Peace is about how we live with ourselves in our families and in our communities. It's about how resources are managed, about social conditions and the political situation' (Caritas 2008b).

Catholic Relief Services (CRS) in the United States is part of the Caritas family of organizations. CRS runs programs in nine different sectors including agriculture, education, peace building, and health care in thirty-six countries in every region of the world. The CRS program budget is near $600 million. Another Caritas partner is the Canadian Catholic Organization for Development and Peace, an educational advocate and sponsor of development projects. In 2007, it spent approximately $11.2 million on 234 development projects and about $5 million on emergency relief projects.

Most recently, Caritas has begun a campaign for an equitable and binding Copenhagen Climate Change agreement and mobilized a coalition of some 170 Catholic organizations called Grow Climate Justice. These organizations are emphasizing the human rights issues associated with environmental degradation and the responsibility to protect those people who will be victims of the consequences of climate change (Caritas 2008c).

The Religious Society of Friends (Quakers)

The Religious Society of Friends or Quakers sponsors several organizations that are involved in peace, social justice, and poverty alleviation. The Friends Committee on National Legislation is the oldest ecumenical lobby in Washington, DC, founded in 1943. The Friends Committee mission statement captures the idea of Christian responsibility and service (Friends Committee on National Legislation 2007): 'We seek a world free of war and the threat of war. We seek a society with equity and justice for all. We seek a community where every person's potential may be fulfilled. We seek an earth restored.' Quaker testimonies and shared beliefs and Quaker practices shape the agenda for the Friends Committee. Recently, this policy advocacy list has included R2P issues like civil liberties, Darfur and genocide, control of arms, torture, peacekeeping, and global poverty.

A second Quaker organization that has had a significant impact on global policy debates is the Quaker United Nations Office (http://www.quno.org), which works with all UN agencies and in partnership with other NGOs and faith-based organizations to promote a progressive Social Gospel agenda. They have pushed for UN action on disarmament, human rights, global poverty, and fair trade and development. In general, the Quaker UN Office has been the guardian of the moral dimension in all issues related to global governance. The Quaker UN

Office has strongly supported the goals of the Responsibility to Protect agreement and the policies aimed at achieving the Millennium Development Goals (MDG).

A third Quaker organization is the very successful and seemingly omnipresent actor when issues related to peace, non-violence, and social justice are on the agenda – the American Friends Service Committee (AFSC). The AFSC sponsors educational and advocacy campaigns in areas such as the war in Iraq, the impact of debt on African countries, the Palestinian-Israeli conflict, militarism and child soldiers, and the rights of immigrants around the world.

Which Quaker values guide the AFSC? The AFSC is an inclusive spiritual organization that welcomes people from all faiths. The AFSC values suggest that 'ultimately goodness can prevail over all evil':

- We believe that there is God in each person and we respect the worth and dignity of all people.
- We regard no person as our enemy. We seek to address the goodness and truth in each individual.
- We assert the transforming power of love and non-violence in a dangerous world.
- We search for and put our trust in the power of the Spirit to guide the search for truth and action.
- We accept the fact that our view of the world and understandings of the truth may be incomplete. New perceptions of truth will continue to be revealed and influence our world view. (AFSC 1994)

Again, members of the AFSC are committed to a life of political activism or what is called 'a spirit-led journey' to address the root causes of poverty, injustice, and war. AFSC activists work with the rich and poor, powerful and weak in the pursuit of global justice.

Since the end of the Cold War there has been a dramatic increase in global activism by both secular and religious NGOs. Most of these NGOs have focused their efforts on providing services related to global poverty. Providing for the poor is a priority in all religious traditions. Indeed, most of those NGOs working to support R2P are concerned about failure of governments to provide for basic human needs. In addition, support for R2P prescriptions indicates support for humanitarian intervention to address gross injustices like genocide or ethnic cleansing in Darfur. The Christian 'just war tradition' serves as a guideline for any form of intervention. These NGOs join the majority of

UN members who supported R2P to challenge the traditional view of national sovereignty.

All of these religious NGOs use all of the tactics and strategies discussed by Keck and Sikkink. They provide valuable information for policymakers and citizens alike. They also advocate for peace, reconciliation, human rights, sustainable development, and the environment. They use their members to put pressure on policymakers and they all sponsor in country programs.

Millennium Development Goals

In September 2001, the 189 member countries of the United Nations signed the Millennium Declaration, which committed the global community to work towards achieving eight Millennium Development Goals (MDGs). These goals were developed over the years by a variety of international, regional and national actors. The MDG process began in 1995 when the Development Assistance Committee (DAC) of the Organization of Economic Development (OECD) began a review of past development policies with the goal of making recommendations for development priorities in the twenty-first century. This report, *Shaping the 21st Century* (1996), became the centrepiece of discussions among experts in development from the OECD, World Bank, UN, national governments, and global civil society. These experts recognized conditions that contributed to the growing gap between rich and poor countries. Their final report presented eight goals to be achieved by 2015, with 1990 as the base year:

1. Eradicate extreme poverty and hunger
   - Reduce by half the proportion of people living on less than a dollar a day
   - Reduce by half the proportion of people who suffer from hunger
2. Achieve universal primary education
   - Ensure that all boys and girls complete a full course of primary schooling
3. Promote gender equality and empower women
   - Eliminate gender disparity in primary and secondary education preferably by 2005, and at all levels by 2015
4. Reduce child mortality
   - Reduce by two-thirds the mortality rate among children under five

5. Improve maternal health
   - Reduce by three-quarters the maternal mortality rate ratio
6. Combat HIV/AIDS, malaria, and other diseases
   - Halt and begin to reverse the spread of HIV/AIDS
   - Halt and begin to reverse the incidence of malaria and other major diseases
7. Ensure environmental sustainability
   - Integrate the principles of sustainable development into country policies and programs; reverse loss of environmental resources
   - Reduce by half the proportion of people without sustainable access to safe drinking water
   - Achieve significant improvement in lives of at least 100 million slum dwellers by 2020
8. Develop a global partnership for development
   - Develop further an open trading and financial system that is rule-based, predictable, and non-discriminatory. Includes a commitment to good governance, development, and poverty reduction – nationally and internationally
   - Address the least-developed countries' special needs. This includes tariff- and quota-free access for their exports; enhanced debt relief for heavily indebted poor countries; cancellation of official bilateral debt; and more generous official development assistance for countries committed to poverty reduction
   - Address the special needs of landlocked and small island developing states
   - Deal comprehensively with developing countries' debt problems through national and international measures to make debt sustainable in the long term
   - In cooperation with the developing countries, develop decent and productive work for youth
   - In cooperation with industrial pharmaceutical companies, provide access to affordable essential drugs in developing countries
   - In cooperation with the private sector, make available the benefits of new technologies – especially information and communications technologies (http://www.un.org/millenniumgoals, http://www.undg.org/login.cfm, http://www.undp.org/mdg)

A significant number of religious and secular NGOs are working to help the world achieve these goals. Not surprisingly, the European social democratic *middle powers* or *guide states* lead the world in meeting these goals. To illustrate, only Norway, Sweden, Denmark, Luxembourg, and the Netherlands have reached the 0.7 per cent target for development assistance. Many religious NGOs within these states work in partnership with more global religious NGOs like World Vision and Church World Services to reach the MDG goals.

The Church of Sweden and Church of Sweden Aid coordinate the international activities of Church of Sweden parishes. The Church of Sweden recognizes that the societies of the wealthy North are a part of the problem in the struggle for a just and sustainable global community. Thus, church members in partnership with religious communities in the South seek to inform, educate, and advocate in favour of those who are the most vulnerable and marginalized. The church promotes informed lobbying at local, national, and international centres of power. The challenges are significant but not insurmountable: 'Unjust global conditions are often felt to be difficult to understand and change. That creates powerlessness. It is therefore important that people are given the opportunity to meet, in order imaginatively and creatively to find instruments that may in various ways counteract and affect these injustices' (Church of Sweden 2001).

Another Nordic religious NGO that works in partnership with other NGOs around the world to improve people's living standards and to challenge the political authorities to address poverty and violence is Norwegian Church Aid. The challenge from their perspective is clearly stated in scriptures: 'The Kings of old Israel were crowned during a liturgy in which the entire population participated, and thereby received their ruling mandate from God' (2005, 3). But the core of the mandate of the kings was as follows: 'May the King judge the poor fairly; may he help the needy and defeat their oppressors.' (Psalms 72:4). Norwegian Church Aid bases its work upon five core values of compassion, justice, participation, integrity of creation, and peace. To them, poverty is a violation of human dignity and cannot be properly addressed unless changes are made to the policies of wealthy states. Meeting the MDG goals by 2015 is certainly a priority. They are pushing Norway to increase its ODA contribution to 2 per cent of GDP by 2015.

The ten-point political platform of Norwegian Church Aid represents a Kantian focus on universal cosmopolitan rights and realization of human security goals:

1. Place human dignity first.
2. Demand quality and results.

3. Strengthen democracy and civil society.
4. Combat terror and violence.
5. Secure women's rights.
6. Provide access to clean water and safe sanitation.
7. Combat HIV and AIDS.
8. Cancel all illegitimate and unpayable debt.
9. Develop a fair trade system.
10. Strengthen the UN and other institutions of global governance (Norwegian Church Aid 2005, 5–17).

Most of these ten elements of their political platform fit well with the MDG goals. However, Norwegian Church Aid supports these as intermediate objectives in the fight against global poverty. The leaders of this NGO believe that the only way to truly address global poverty and structural violence is to dramatically reform the global institutions that manage trade, debt, financial activities, and political and military policy.

Any discussion of religious NGOs working to address global poverty must include reference to World Vision International (http://www.wvi.org). World Vision works to 'empower communities to know and speak up for their rights' in programs in six continents with a budget of $2.6 billion (World Vision 2008). World Vision sponsors campaigns on six continents to bring the concerns of the poor and disenfranchised to the powerful. It is an international partnership of Christians whose mission is to follow Jesus Christ in working with the poor to promote human transformation, seek justice, and bear witness to the good news of the Kingdom of God (World Vision n.d.).

One example is a current campaign to hold the leaders of the G-8 countries accountable for child health care. This World Vision campaign aimed to pressure leaders to address these issues at their summit in Japan in 2008. World Vision states that 26,000 children below the age of five die each year as a result of preventable diseases. If G-8 countries meet the MDG goals they will boost the funds for programs for child health care and serve as a model for other donor countries. Unfortunately, as table 12.1 suggests, meeting these goals for 2015 may not be possible. World Vision, like all religious NGOs, believes that the only solution to ending global poverty is to demand an end to injustice and inequality. Thus meeting the MDG obligations is only part of the solution.

Every major religion has inspired NGOs that work to alleviate pov-

Table 12.1
Progress in meeting MDG goals in developing countries, 1990–2002

Indicator	1990	2002
Extreme poverty (%)	28	21
Undernourishment (%)	20	17
Under five mortality rate (deaths per 1,000 live births)	103	88
Life expectancy at birth (years)	63	65
Access to improved drinking water (%)	71	79
Access to improved sanitation facilities (%)	34	49

Source: Millennium Project, UNDP, New York (2007, 14)

erty and provide human security. Islamic Relief Worldwide and Islamic Relief USA follow the words of the Qu'ran (5:32): 'Whoever saved a life, it would be as if he saved the life of mankind.' Both organizations founded in 1984 operate programs worldwide and support the MDG goals. Islamic Relief Worldwide states that the alleviation of poverty and suffering lies at the heart of Islam (Islamic Relief Worldwide 2010).

Concluding Remarks

We are living at a time when religion is seen as a negative force dividing societies and promoting limited and exclusive fundamental positions. The more exclusive and fundamentalist religious groups promote a Manichean view of the world – believers versus non-believers, us versus them, and certainly not promoting cooperation among religious communities. This chapter suggest that religious NGOs do play a very active role in building community and responding to major human security challenges. The evidence suggests that many of these religious NGOs are continuing to promote the values and goals of the Social Gospel movement. They seek to create God's Kingdom on Earth and they closely follow religious scriptures that emphasize compassion, caring, and non-violence.

As stated earlier in the chapter, these progressive religious NGOs always have focused on taking care of the needy and victims of violence, war, and natural disasters. But what is clearly different here is that the progressive religious NGOs in this study are not just focused upon charity and assisting those in need. Instead, these groups are promoting strategies for reform of the international system. These NGOs are interested in *repairing the world* and dealing with structural violence or the deaths caused by poverty, failed states, and the failure to provide basic human needs in a number of regions.

Both secular and religious NGOs with these progressive policy priorities have found real partners in the middle powers and guide states. Cosmopolitan values like peace, social justice, economic well-being, and respect for the environment are embedded in the domestic political cultures and political narratives of these social democratic states. These states are comfortable working with global civil society actors, especially those NGOs that are defined by more Kantian universal values. It is therefore not surprising that these NGOs and middle powers have gone forward with global governance projects like the Responsibility to Protect, Millennium Development Goals (MDG), and campaigns within the human security movement. These new moral coalitions will continue to challenge the dominant great power politics narratives and the resulting national interest policy agenda. They are likely to become more influential as global problems persist and the demands from citizens for effective policy responses increase.

NOTES

1 *Maslaha* (concept in traditional Islamic law) means to prohibit or permit something on the basis of whether or not it serves public benefit and welfare. *Istislah* is a method employed by Muslim jurists who find no clear answer to a problem in the sacred texts. *Istislah* is the method in which *maslaha* is practised.

REFERENCES

American Friends Service Committee (AFSC). 1994. AFSC mission and values. http://afsc.org/mission-and-values.

American Jewish World Service (AJWS). 2007. Not on our watch: A Jewish informal education resource on the genocide in Darfur. American Jewish World Service and the Foundation for Jewish Campaign. http://www.ajws.org/what_we_do/education/resources/not-on-our-watch-booklet.pdf.

Aquinas, T. 1981. *Summa theologica.* Grand Rapids, MI: Principal Christian Classics.

Caritas. 2007. *CI Advocacy Bulletin* 3 (April). http://www.caritas.org/templates/printnews.

- 2008a. http://www.caritas.org/activities/peace_reconciliation/building societiesbasedonpeaceinIraq.html.
- 2008b. http://www.caritas.org/peace_reconciliation/peacebackground.html.
- 2008c. http://www.caritas.org/activities/climate_change/caritas advocacy.html.

Church of Sweden. 2001. The international mission of the Church of Sweden: Commitment to international community and solidarity. http://www.svenskakyrkan.se/svk/lhskm/international_mission6.htm.

Cooper, A., R.A. Higgot, and K. Nossal. 1993. *Relocating middle powers: Australia and Canada in a changing world order*. Vancouver: University of British Columbia Press.

Cox, R. 1989. Middlepowermanship, Japan, and future world order. *International Journal* 44:834–5.

Development Assistance Committee (DAC), Organization of Economic Development (OECD). 1996. Shaping the 21st century: The Contribution of Development Co-operation. http://www.oecd.org/departmentdataoecd/23/35/2508761.pdf.

Dorfman, Aaron. 2007. Jewish responses to genocide. http://www.ajws.org/what_we_do/education/resources/jewish-responses-to-genocide-2007.pdf.

Dyck, Cornelius J. 1989. Social gospel. Global Anabaptist Mennonite Encyclopedia Online. http://www.gameo.org/encyclopedia/contents/S65ME.html.

Epps, Ken. 2007. Landmark step toward an international arms trade treaty. *Ploughshares Monitor* 28 (2). http://www.ploughshares.ca/libraries/monitor/monm07h.pdf.

Forum on Religion and Ecology. 2004. Christian Engaged Projects. http://fore.research.yale.edu/religion/christianity/projects/envt_partner.html.

Fossum, J.E. 2006. Gidsland and human security: Cosmopolitan vehicles? *International Journal* 61 (4): 783–91.

Friends Committee on National Legislation. 2007. FCNL policy statement. http://www.fcnl.org/priorities/freewar.htm.

Fuchs, M.H., and D. Buckley. 2007. Pursuing the global common good. In Steenland et al., 5–15.

Holbraad, C. 1984. *Middle powers in international politics*. New York: St Martin's.

Hutchinson, W.J. 1975. The Americanness of social gospel: An inquiry in comparative history. *Church History* 44:376–81.

International Commission on Intervention and State Sovereignty. 2001. Report of the International Commission on Intervention and State Sovereignty. http://www.iciss.ca/report2-en.asp.

Islamic Relief Worldwide. 2010. Who we are / About us. http://www.islamic-relief.com/WhoWeAre/Default.aspx?depID=2.

Keck, M., and K. Sikkink. 1998. *Activists beyond borders: Transnational advocacy networks in international politics.* Ithaca, NY: Cornell University Press.

Lawler, P. 2005. The good state: In praise of 'classical' internationalism. *Review of International Studies* 31:427–49.

Lumsdaine, D.H. 1993. *Moral vision in international politics: The foreign aid regime 1949–1989.* Princeton, NJ: Princeton University Press.

My Sister's Keeper. 2010a. About us. http://www.mskeeper.org/site/index.php?option=com_content&task=view&id=41&Itemid=82.

– 2010b. Our projects. http://mskeeper.org/site/index.php?option=com_content&task=view&id=27&itemid=50.

Norwegian Church Aid. 2005. Norwegian Church Aid's 10-point political platform 2009–2013. http://www.kirkensnodhjelp.no/Documents/Kirkens%20N%C3%B8dhjelp/arbeidet_vart/Political%20platform%202009-2013_English.pdf.

Pratt, C. 1990. *Middle power internationalism: The north-south dimension.* Montreal and Kingston: McGill-Queen's University Press.

Project Ploughshares. n.d. Who we are. http://www.ploughshares.ca/who/index.html.

Rauschenbusch, W. 1944. *Christianity and the social crisis.* New York: Harper and Row.

Schroeder, E. 2007. Exploring security challenges to peace in Sudan. *The Ploughshares Monitor* 28 (3). Waterloo, Ontario, Project Ploughshares.

Steenland, S., P. Rundlet, M. Fuchs, and D. Buckley. 2007. *Pursuing the global common good: Principle and practice in U.S. foreign policy.* Washington, DC: Center for American Progress.

Stokke, O., ed. 1989. *Western middle powers and global poverty: The determinants of the aid policies of Canada, Denmark, the Netherlands, Norway, and Sweden.* Uppsala: Scandinavian Institute of African Studies.

Woods, B. 1988. *Middle powers in the international system.* Ottawa: North-South Institute.

World Vision. 2008. Seeking global change. http://www.wvi.org/wvi/wvi-web.nsf/section/768CC337EFC5C83D8825737F007DB7A2?opendocument.

– n.d. Our mission. http://www.worldvision.org/content.nsf/about/our-mission.

13 Religion and Canadian Diplomacy: Promoting Pluralism on the Global Stage

EVAN H. POTTER

> Canada – Canada. I have dealt with Canada since Vietnam. The word that comes to mind when I think of Canada is 'self-righteous.' Yes, self-righteous. In Canada you get to do what is desirable. In America we must do what is necessary.
>
> – Henry Kissinger[1]

Introduction

The politicization of religion in global politics – a product of globalization, the end of the Cold War, the ubiquitous global mass media, the failure of certain secular regimes to deliver necessary economic and social benefits, and the emergence of more faith-based political parties as a result of increased democratization – is unlikely to abate in the decades ahead. Religion, as chapters 2 and 3 establish for better or worse, is back on the agenda of international relations.

Islam and Christianity (in particular Evangelical Protestantism), the world's fastest-growing religions, are encountering each other in both developed and developing countries, creating a social and political environment that has not existed since the Middle Ages. This religiousization of international affairs is also having direct effects on domestic public policy debates about 'reasonable accommodation'[2] in countries with significant and growing minority populations such as Canada, Australia, the United States, the Netherlands, France, Germany, and the United Kingdom.

Historically, though religious questions have been a thorny issue in Canadian domestic politics, revolving around tensions between Protestants and Catholics, religion itself has not been a determining factor in the conduct of Canada's foreign policy, though, as this chapter will show, Canadian governments have worked with faith-based organizations to achieve mutual goals to promote global peace and development.[3] Foreign policy practitioners view religion as one element of identity that includes ethnicity, language, social/professional class, and ideological affiliation, and are careful not to privilege one aspect of identity more than others; identity, for its part, is only one factor in the equation of a foreign policy decision. Although foreign policymaking has no doubt been affected by organized religion in Canada, there is no evidence that Canadian governments have ever launched a faith-based foreign policy initiative.

This chapter will argue that religion intersects with the conduct of Canada's foreign policy in two fundamental ways: the promotion of the principle of pluralism in Canada's foreign policy, which has its roots in a generation-long experiment with multiculturalism on the domestic front, and the federal government's interaction with faith-based communities as interest groups, who certainly have to be listened to, but who are also competing with labour and business lobbies in the 'pulling and hauling' of the bureaucratic foreign policy process.

The first part of this chapter will describe how the discourse on a Canadian model of pluralism underpinned by the philosophy of multiculturalism serves to forge the 'Canadian values' narrative that is so often invoked by Canadian politicians, diplomats, aid officers, and soldiers when promoting Canada's international role. To be sure, many of the values such as respect for human rights, peace, and sustainable development are not unique to Canada's foreign policy, but some, like the value of diversity and pluralism, are viewed as more distinctly Canadian and are promoted by the federal government as a defining characteristic of Canadian society and identity (Ignatieff 2004). Canada's ability to acknowledge tensions among some of its ethnic, religious, and linguistic groups, along with its ability to manage this diversity in a non-violent and cooperative way, are said to offer valuable lessons to other countries. The public policies underpinning pluralism have thus become an important component of Canada's global soft power.

The second part of the chapter provides specific examples of how the Canadian government promotes the discourse of pluralism in its international policy through development assistance and diplomacy. Most examples will focus on relations with the Islamic world, but this is only one component of the government's broad approach to promoting

Canadian pluralism as a defining feature of Canadian foreign policy. Diplomatic efforts are not confined to explaining the Canadian model to foreign audiences. Given that the Canadian media and international media (notably American networks that are available to most Canadian households through their local cable systems) have largely framed the public's conception of Islam in security terms, there is an added responsibility for the government's international departments to reach out to domestic Muslim communities in Canada, to assuage their concerns about being targets and to explore ways in which these communities can act as 'bridges of understanding' back to their countries of birth.

The Roots of Canada's Approach to Pluralism in Its Statecraft

The tradition of Pearsonian internationalism in the service of global peace – encompassing elements of multilateralism, good international citizenship, and voluntarism – continues to exert a powerful hold on Canada's foreign policy (Munton and Keating 2001, 527–31).[4] The strong ethical strain to this tradition in Canada's international relations has created the tendency to promote the idea of a values-based foreign policy that eschews references to the 'national interest.' Respect for differences – political, religious, cultural – is thus implicit in Canada's statecraft. One of the distinguishing features of the Canadian approach to religion in its statecraft is that, for the most part, it does not actually focus on the world's religions. Indeed, it is difficult to even find references to the word *religion* in public statements on Canada's foreign policy. Ottawa prefers to focus on communities rather than on their religions, the overarching philosophy being to see the world as a 'community of communities' in addition to a collection of nation-states. Canada, as chapter 12 has established already, is one of several middle powers with a track record of collaborating with religious NGOs to promote international peace and development.

Canada's engagement is, therefore, with Muslim *communities*, not with Islam (or any other religion) directly. This is more than a matter of semantics. It is intended to demonstrate that Canadian policy is addressing people, not a religion, in order to challenge the thesis that it is fundamentally the values embodied in religions such as Islam that are the primary source of conflict or misunderstanding between communities. (It is, of course, true that religious communities are underpinned by shared values and it is at times not easy to disassociate the communities from the values to which they adhere.)

The desire to engage with Muslims as citizens and not just as Muslims stems from a growing body of evidence that suggests that communities who are targeted or marginalized on the basis of their religion can respond with a stronger and at times more radicalized religious expression (Haynes 1995). Thus issues such as the eligibility of sharia law for use in arbitration, covered in the context of the Canadian province of Ontario in chapter 9, are significant precisely for such reasons.

The Canadian government underscores the need to distinguish between political and religious agendas since the two are often conflated, with religion used for political ends or to justify cultural practices that have no religious basis. Religion does not cause things to happen but informs the manner in which they occur. For this reason, the Canadian response to the rise of religion in a post–11 September 2001 global context is not premised exclusively on a counterterrorism paradigm, though Canada has invested significantly in counterterrorism efforts at home and abroad, but on a paradigm based on the promotion of the values of pluralism and democratic governance as essential to countering violent extremism. How has an emphasis on pluralism emerged as the central value underpinning Canada's approach to responding to the increasing politicization of religion?

Canada has been conducting an innovative but fragile experiment over the past half-century. It has developed policies and instruments to give expression to pluralism as one of Canada's foundational values, recognizing that diversity rather than assimilation is a source of strength and that every individual and community has an equal voice and can and should use that voice to participate as a full member of society. An evolving multicultural and social policy framework supports inclusion and integration. Canada was the first country to institute an official policy of multiculturalism (Multiculturalism Act 1970) and is the only one to have a law recognizing the cultural diversity of its population. The Canadian Charter of Rights and Freedoms (1982) along with provincial charters of rights of freedoms prohibit discrimination based on race, national or ethnic origin, colour, religion, sex, or mental/physical disability. Canadian multiculturalism is rooted in the long-standing policy of biculturalism, which Paulston (1978) describes as an eclectic process through which an individual acquires a secondary cultural identity. In the Canadian context this has meant the promotion of the English and French 'founding nations' in government policy and thus society at large. Canadian scholar Kymlicka (2004, 840–1) argues that the alienation of so-called white ethnics (e.g., Ukrainians,

Poles, Finns, Germans, Dutch and Jews) by this policy of biculturalism eventually paved the way for the recognition of the contribution made by non-white immigrants to Canada's development and pluralistic character. Kymlicka (2004, 836) pithily encapsulates Canada's model of diversity as 'multicultural citizenship to accommodate ethnic communities formed by immigration; bilingual federalism to accommodate the major substate national(ist) group in Quebec; self-government rights and treaty relationships to accommodate indigenous peoples.'

The 'paeans to "unity in diversity"' in Canada's public diplomacy abroad through, for example, financial and logistical support for academic research, conferences, and cultural exhibits that expose foreign audiences to a Canadian model of achieving social cohesion, have helped to reinforce a very positive and peaceful international image of the country (Kymlicka 2004, 830). This, in turn, has paid handsome economic and social dividends for Canada in the form of economic growth (e.g., foreign investment and skilled immigrants) and a reputation for tolerance (a 'force multiplier' for the Canadian diplomatic 'brand').[5] At the same time, according to Kymlicka (832), the marketing of Canadian pluralism abroad also legitimizes the federal government and its policies in the eyes of its critics at home.

The confidence of these minority communities in their legal rights as citizens has given rise to a spirited – but, it should be added, non-violent – national debate on how Canadian society should accommodate citizens from other cultures. The issues ranged from whether members of the Royal Canadian Mounted Police should be allowed to wear turbans (they can) to whether a kirpan, a ceremonial dagger worn by Orthodox Sikhs, could be worn by a Sikh student in Quebec's public school system (Blackwell 2006).[6] The fissures in what has sometimes been referred to as the 'ideology of Canadian multiculturalism' became readily apparent in the debate over 'reasonable accommodation' in Quebec. In February 2007, under public pressure about where Quebecers should draw the line on religious freedom following a number of highly publicized incidents of apparent religious intolerance, Quebec's Premier Jean Charest launched a commission to discern from Quebecers what they thought constituted fair treatment of the province's religious and cultural minorities.[7]

Fearing the prospect of ghettoization and ethnic tensions, not all Canadians have viewed Canada's official multiculturalism as necessarily in the best interest of the minority communities or the country as a whole. There have been broadsides against the policy itself (Bissoondath 1994) and suggestions that Canada's promotion of its model to the world is more rhetoric than reality (e.g., given the history of its treatment of its Aboriginal people). Snide references to so-called hyphenated Canadians and to 'hotel Canada' belie official speeches extolling the Canadian model (Cohen 2007; Ghoreishi and Ford 2006).[8]

That being said, Canada's particular model of multiculturalism and accommodation, which has aided the integration of immigrants into national life, has made the country a magnet for the world. In 2006, Canada, with one in five of its citizens foreign-born, accepted 250,000 new permanent residents, with the top four source countries being China, India, the Philippines, and Pakistan, giving it the highest intake of immigrants of any industrialized country.[9] Some 800,000 Canadian Muslims, most of whom are the successors to large migrations of Christian Europeans to Canada early in the twentieth century and again after the Second World War, are an integral part of this expanding cultural mosaic. In fact, Muslim Canadians – 600,000 of whom are Arab Canadians – represent one of the fastest growing demographics of Canada, doubling in size in the 1990s. This Canadian Muslim umma, to take just one example of a minority community in Canada, has succeeded in every facet of Canadian life – business, media, academia, journalism, and government. Research has shown that at the university level, 'the percentage of Muslims is twice as high as that of other immigrants and close to three times as high as the total Canadian population' (Karim 2002, 264).

However, the actions of a small minority of Muslims have cast a negative light on how Muslims are perceived in Canada and worldwide.[10] (Chapters 4 and 6, on human rights and religious humanitarianism, respectively, bring out that point in different and mutually reinforcing ways.) Islam and its followers have become objects of misunderstanding and, in some cases, intolerance (Gerges 2003). Few moderate Muslim have condemned the use of radical violence in the name of their religion. If more recently an increasing number of prominent Muslims around the world – religious leaders, politicians, scholars – have spoken out strongly against acts of violence wrongly perpetrated in the name of Islam, the renewed discussion of the 'clash of civilizations' perpetuated by twenty-four-hour cable news networks has contributed to a perception of incompatibility of Islam and western societies. As noted in *Strong Religion*, an authoritative study, the strains of violent fundamentalism have been associated throughout history with all of the world's major religions (Almond, Appleby, and Sivan 2003).

The Canadian government has long held the view that religion is not the cause of extremism but that people who are extremists distort religion and exploit vulnerabilities in societies and individuals in order to further a political cause. The terrorist attacks in London and Madrid, the controversy over the Danish cartoons depicting Prophet Mohammed, and ongoing violence in Afghanistan, Sudan, and Iraq all serve to highlight the need for greater mutual understanding between the West and the Muslim world.

While Canada has not, in its modern history, directly experienced the combustible consequences of the intersection of religion and international politics on its soil, in 2007 a commission of inquiry was established into the 1984 bombing of an Air India plane (en route from Vancouver) off the coast of Ireland by extremists based in Canada who were calling for the creation of a Sikh homeland in India (Galloway 2007, 4). Over three hundred people were killed, making it the single largest mass murder of Canadian citizens though, as a telling reflection on the relative depth of Canadian multiculturalism, the Canadian citizenship of the passengers (the majority of whom were of Indian descent) was publicly asserted only years later by Canadian politicians.

It is against this domestic backdrop of an often imperfect experiment in creating what some have called the world's 'first post-modern state' that I would like to turn now to the question of how this value of pluralism has been operationalized through Canadian diplomacy to achieve Canada's national interests in the international arena (Giddens 1993).[11]

Promoting Pluralism in Canada's Diplomacy

I will begin by stating the obvious: Western diplomacy is at the crossroads in trying to respond to a global effort to contain extremist groups within Muslim communities, while managing the Israeli-Arab and Israeli-Palestinian conflicts, and all the while keeping a wary eye out for how these and other conflicts with ethno-religious dimensions spill over into the growing minority communities within the Western countries themselves. These communities live in a true global infosphere, one that could hardly have been imagined by Marshall McLuhan (who coined the term *global village*), and are attuned in their homes and places of work in their adopted countries to the nuances of international politics facing their homelands. For this very reason, the successful new diplomacy of the twenty-first century will have to be Janus-faced – facing inwards to domestic minority communities and at the same time outwards to their homelands.

Diplomacy, in both theory and practice, has tended to foist peace and coexistence upon whole populations, expecting that the promises in abstract treaty documents will be enough to quell the rage and injury of centuries. There is little attention to how whole communities actually move from unbridled hatred to tolerance and eventually to reconciliation. Diplomacy has thus far demonstrated little understanding of how to actually inculcate the values of coexistence and human rights in the context of many unresolved grievances that run very deep. There is a good understanding of the importance of economic development as a major factor in relieving stresses that contribute to extremist violence. But this ignores the full panoply of human tendencies that contribute to war or peace. Gopin (2002)

One of the conceits of traditional diplomacy is not only the belief that average citizens will appreciate all the work that has gone into a negotiated statement, but also the belief that today's leaders truly lead and that official-to-official negotiations will suffice to reach deals. This of course ignores the reality that the mood of the 'street,' often with memories of occupation, in the case of Palestinians, soaked in humiliation and suffused with images and information from competing national and international broadcasters ranging from CNN International, Deutsche Welle, BBC World, Al-Jazeera, Al-Arabiya, and Voice of America, to name just a few of the more prominent broadcasters, can determine whether leaders – even authoritarian ones – undertake workable compromises. As Johnson (2004) has written, 'almost anywhere one turns one finds a religious dimension to conflict, and the West woefully ill-equipped to deal with it.' With the effectiveness of traditional diplomacy waning in the face of ethnic conflict and other problems of communal identity, religious actors and greater cultural engagement have the potential to help governments to deal with identity-based conflicts. That being said, foreign ministries have been providing their staffs with more specialized training on religion. For example, the U.S. State Department's Foreign Service Institute has courses on religions for officers assigned to countries where faith plays an important role. The Quai d'Orsay has a unit dealing with religions, which reports to senior officials and the minister's office.

How then has Canada's diplomacy adapted to these realities? Certainly, religion has always been a variable for Canada's national security and foreign policy practitioners. It has been approached multilaterally in a human rights context, primarily within the United Nations, whether through Canada's participation in UN bodies such as the UN Human Rights Council or UNESCO or as a signatory to a wide array of UN treaties addressing the importance of respecting religious freedoms. This is not different from most countries' declaratory policies of promoting the principle of religious freedom and tolerance in international forums. The real question concerns the detectable influence of Canadian ecumenical organizations on the formulation and articulation of Canadian foreign policy.

Reflecting on the history of church involvement in Canada's foreign policy, one is struck by how the influence of ecumenical organizations appears to correlate with the prominence of Canada's role on the international stage. As Matthews (1990, 162) notes, peace and disarmament tended to dominate church concerns in the 1950s; development and human rights were added in the 1960s.[12] The Vietnam war and the apartheid systems in Zimbabwe and South Africa mobilized church action on behalf of concerned congregations, pressuring the federal government to, for example, provide sanctuary to American war resisters (labelled 'draft dodgers' by the media) and to lead an international coalition against the two African regimes. In the 1980s, there was a more visible social and political activism by ecumenical organizations and the Christian churches in the Central American Peace Process, in Canada's leadership in organizing a Commonwealth-wide campaign against apartheid in South Africa, and in the campaign for nuclear disarmament (Bromke and Nossal 1983–4, 341–2; Matthews 1990).[13] There appears to have been an ideational connection between religious activists in Canada and a wave of liberation theology in Latin America.

In the post–Cold War 1990s, events coalesced again to attract support for Canada's human security agenda, an agenda that is closely identified with Canada's Foreign Minister Lloyd Axworthy (1996–2000).[14] Here was a natural convergence between the underlying principles of human security (freedom from want and freedom from fear) with the tenets of Christianity – social and economic development.[15] Robert Matthews (1990, 161) perhaps best summarizes the relationship between church and state in Canadian foreign policy at the end of the Cold War: 'With increasing vigour over the last two decades the mainstream Christian churches have campaigned publicly and have lobbied the federal government to ensure that Canada's foreign policy and programs better reflect a concern for human rights and social justice. Although they have been increasingly sophisticated and systematic in approaching this task, the churches have not had much *direct* impact on public policy' (161; my emphasis).[16] The major Canadian public foreign policy reviews of the last fifteen years – the joint House of Commons and Senate parliamentary review in 1994, and *A Dialogue on Foreign Policy* (Canada. Department of Foreign Affairs and International Trade 2002) led by Canada's foreign ministry – offered ecumenical organizations ample opportunity to publicize their views on Canada's global role. However, it should be observed that these reviews elicited little comprehensive media coverage and thus did not offer any meaningful agenda-setting power for these organizations. With a few notable exceptions (e.g., nuclear disarmament, the campaign against apartheid), in the period between 1960 and 1995 the organized church in Canada sat largely on the periphery of the foreign policy process, though its *indirect* impact, as difficult as it is to confirm and quantify through public opinion surveys, may well have been greater. In light of this brief history, have ecumenical organizations continued to play a relatively peripheral role or have they inserted themselves more forcefully into the foreign policy process?

A striking change in Canada's aid program in the new century was the shift to supporting democratic governance. In 2006, the Office for Democratic Governance was created within the Canadian International Development Agency (CIDA) with a specialized mandate to promote freedom and democracy and human rights, including programs to build 'inclusive' societies. And CIDA, through its partnership programs, has for years supported the international development work of both large and small Canadian non-governmental organizations, some of which happen to be faith-based. For example, half of the Mennonite Central Committee's total worldwide income of $114 million in 2005–6 came from its Canadian chapter, MCC Canada, with CIDA contributing $6 million of public money for the MCC's work in such areas as food security programs, income generation, health, education, peacebuilding, and the regions affected by the tsunami in December 2004. MCC Canada is also a member of Mines Action Canada, an advocacy NGO, which represents a coalition of civil-society-based organizations in Canada that supports the Ottawa Convention, the international treaty that bans landmines. It is interesting that one-third of the thirty-three major Mines Action Canada coalition members listed on its website are explicitly faith-based Canadian civil society organizations running the gamut from the Christian Aid to Under-Assisted Societies Everywhere to Presbyterian World Service International. Half the budget of Mines Action Canada came from Foreign Affairs and International Trade Canada (direct funding ceased in 2008).

But cooperation with faith-based organizations is not faith-based diplomacy; rather, it occurs when the government's and NGO interests converge, such as on matters of human security.[17] A pamphlet available on the MCC Canada's website entitled *O Canada: Armed and Ready* decries the militarization of Canada's foreign policy and calls on concerned citizens to act by, among other things, sending letters to their members of Parliament and the prime minister to advance security through non-military means and to withhold the 'military portion' of their taxes and put it in a peace trust fund. The pamphlet, while acknowledging that some armed force may be necessary in the short term for security (for example, to protect civilians in refugee camps in Darfur), nonetheless in a section on 'faith reflection' exhorts Canadian Christians to embrace the idea that 'nations loving enemies is the vision toward which God is moving history' (Mennonite Central Committee n.d., 3). It is difficult to imagine the Canadian military in Afghanistan, which has been engaged in its biggest combat mission since the Korean War, unilaterally laying down its arms in Kandahar province. That being said, the existence of a Canadian-led Provincial Reconstruction Team in the province, whose success depends on developing the trust of tribal leaders, points to the importance of understanding the *role* of culture and religion in managing this complex intervention.

However, what really begins to distinguish Canada's approach to addressing the intersection of religions and foreign policy from that of other like-minded countries is its more indirect and 'quieter' approach to engaging faith communities around the world or navigating the often tense sectarian strife within other societies. For example, in the immediate aftermath of the 2004 tsunami, Canadian diplomats established an aid presence in the devastated Indonesian province of Aceh, a province with a large non-Muslim population that was at loggerheads with the central government. Canada, it was said, was able to gain the confidence of all parties, given its reputation for even-handedness even though there was an active guerrilla movement on the island.

Canada promotes its pluralist model most explicitly through its modest international cultural relations and international education programs, which are managed by the Canadian foreign ministry. Unlike Germany, with a Commission for Dialogue with the Islamic World, or the State Department, which has had its employees participating in religious chat rooms, Canada prefers to use non-religious instruments such as its Canadian Studies program around the world to engage in dialogue. There is a realization that longer-term forms of public diplomacy, often based within non-confrontational forums such as those provided by cultural and educational exchanges, can help to rebuild relationships and make the necessary concessionary adjustments wherever possible.

Perhaps the most highly visible example of Canada's commitment to promoting pluralism on the international agenda as a means of reaching out to faith communities is the establishment of the Global Centre for Pluralism, a major new forum for education, research, and exchange. Jointly inaugurated in 2006 by the Aga Khan, the spiritual head of the world's Ismaili Muslims, and the government of Canada, the Centre is located in Ottawa in Canada's former War Museum and in close proximity to the Lester B. Pearson building, the headquarters of the Canadian foreign ministry (Ross 2007).[18] The press release announcing the new Centre said that it draws inspiration from the Canadian experience and 'will work with countries to nurture successful civil societies in which every citizen, irrespective of cultural, religious or ethnic differences, is able to realize his or her full potential' (Global Centre for Pluralism 2006). The decision to locate this global centre in Ottawa was apparently a natural one because of what the Aga Khan calls 'Canada's gift to the world' – what he sees as the Canadian practice of seeking unity in diversity. The mission of this C$60 million Centre supports several key Canadian international policies, among them the promotion of democracy and good governance, a more equitable sharing of the world's resources between developed and developing countries, and the projection of Canadian values, such as the rule of law, human rights, and respect for diversity. Given its commitment to long-term, generational change by developing human capacity through its outreach to a cross-section of opinion-formers from around the world, the Centre will become an important instrument of Canada's soft power. In keeping with a new diplomacy that must be both inward- and outward-looking at the same time, the Canadian government is following in the footsteps of other Western countries with sizable minority communities, notably, Australia, Germany, and the United Kingdom, in developing inter-cultural, inter-religious and inter-ethnic partnerships to foster greater cross-cultural understanding.

The official instrument within Canada's foreign ministry to give expression to this renewed effort to build inter-cultural understanding in a post–11 September environment, the Muslim Communities Working Group (MCWG), was established in 2005 to ensure a well-informed approach to Canada's relations with Muslim communities abroad. It provided policy input to work involving Muslim communities, which in turn is supposed to help address common challenges of democratization, good governance, human rights, and integration. The mandate of the MCWG was rooted in the tradition of Canada's internationalism and its promotion of the benefits of pluralism; more practically, the working group ensured communication is a two-way street and that Canada's foreign policy is properly understood in the Muslim world.

In Canada, the response to the Danish cartoon controversy in 2005, for example, underscores the importance that Canada accords to both rights to freedom of expression and the respect for cultural, ethnic, and religious differences on which Canada is founded. Canadian editors, while upholding the principle of free speech, exercised their judgment in light of the potential for violence in Canada resulting from the publication and the cartoons. Consequently, the cartoons were not reprinted in any major Canadian media outlets.[19] As a measure of the recognition that a link had to be established between inter-cultural dialogue and security, in 2005, Canada also established a Cross-Cultural Roundtable on Security to engage Canadians from diverse communities and to get their advice on matters of national security.

It is to be noted, however, that Canada faces a major handicap in getting its messages out to the world on its inter-cultural dialogues because it is one of the few G8 countries that does not have an English-language global television presence. Whereas Canada must rely on the French-dominated TV-5 global television network or on Radio Canada International, other G8 members are spending hundreds of millions of dollars on a sophisticated multi-platform international information presence. And with respect to money for inter-cultural dialogues, the €6 million at the disposal of Germany's Goethe Institute, the German Academic Exchange Service, and the Institute for Foreign Relations for outreach to the Muslim world have dwarfed Canada's financial commitments for similar dialogues. The Canadian government's investment in the Global Centre for Pluralism, as a focal point for intercultural dialogue, therefore offers Canada the opportunity to make up lost ground by combining the rich internationalist tradition in its foreign policy with its more recent experience as a multicultural society to create a powerful voice for reconciliation and moderation on a world stage in which the forces of intolerance are holding increasing sway.

Conclusion: Is There a Model of Accommodation for the Future?

This chapter has shown that the growing politicization of religion in global politics has forced Canada to respond to the intersection of politics and religion in its own foreign policy. Drawing on a history of accommodating multiple identities, starting with the founding peoples (Aboriginal, English, and French) and now with an increasingly diverse society representing the world, Canada's response has been to promote the principle of pluralism through its international policy. The secular nature of Canada's political culture has not allowed it to pursue a faith-based diplomacy. Rather, the Canadian state has worked with faith-based communities and ecumenical organizations in promoting common interests of social justice and development. Within its diplomacy, the Canadian government addresses religion primarily through multilateral organizations such as the UN to which it has accorded high status in its diplomacy, through emphasis on democratic governance in its aid program, bilaterally through long-term public diplomacy using cultural and educational programs, and increasingly domestically, given the interest in the issue of reasonable accommodation for minorities, through direct outreach by the foreign ministry to the Canadian Muslim umma.

Canada's approach to dealing with religion in world politics has been incremental, firmly anchored in its broader approach to support democratic governance and, unlike, British or American engagement, is not explicitly linked to a domestic and global counter-terrorism mandate. Canada sees the global Muslim umma as a political and cultural polity and supports the values of pluralism and diversity within this umma, just as it supports this umma within Canada, and, just as it supports pluralism and respect for diversity in communities around the world, whether encouraging rapprochement between Muslims and Hindus in India or promoting human rights (including religious tolerance) in its foreign policy with China. In this way, Canada's domestic model for social cohesion is used to promote Canadian interests at the international level to address the growing politicization of religion in global affairs.

Given the United States' quasi-hegemonic status as a world power, as noted in chapter 1, it is not surprising that a middle power such as Canada – whose economy and security are so intimately intertwined with those of its southern neighbour – would accord significant importance to understanding American motivations and perspectives in responding to international challenges, including the almost simultaneous launches of a global 'war on terror' and the most far-reaching attempt to engage civil society since the Cold War – the Bush Administration's public diplomacy campaign to win 'hearts and minds' in the Muslim world (particularly in the Middle East). However, the act of seeking to understand another nation's intentions and behaviour, the sine qua non of diplomacy, is not the same as agreeing with or following them. As noted in a cross-section of global public opinion surveys taken between 2001 and 2008,[20] the legacy of the Bush Doctrine – its self-conscious return to realpolitik through a doctrine of pre-emption (as evidenced by its invasion of Iraq) and its establishment of prisons to house predominantly Muslim suspects in Guantanamo and at CIA-operated 'black sites' in other countries – is that the Obama Administration must contend with a world in which there is widespread opposition to U.S. policy and where the image of America has fallen into precipitous decline. It can be inferred from the survey findings that the Bush Administration's attempts to promote inter-faith dialogue as part of its reinvigorated global public diplomacy could not overcome the global antipathy generated by its foreign policy.[21]

Understanding the collective feeling of existential threat within the Bush Administration following the 9/11 attacks (i.e., that weapons of mass destruction could be employed by Islamists), the Canadian government enhanced continental security (thereby also protecting its economic interests) by investing over $7 billion in public safety and then deployed a substantial Canadian military force to Afghanistan where, for six years (2003–9), the Canadian Forces were responsible for keeping the peace in the Taliban's heartland of Kandahar province as part of a NATO mission under a UN mandate. A legacy of the Bush Administration is that Ottawa has been able to demonstrate an ability to pursue its own national interest in a very volatile period of global politics by acting in 'common cause' with the United States. It has been a delicate domestic and international balancing act. Canada chose not to join the 'coalition of the willing' in Iraq, but it did reorient its international policy – defence, diplomacy, and development – to stabilize Afghanistan and ramped up its global efforts to prevent the proliferation of weapons of mass destruction (including participating in the U.S.-led Proliferation Security Initiative). Domestically, the federal government in its declaratory policy was careful to spell out that Canada was not engaged in a war against Islam, a position that, as noted in this chapter, was accepted by the Muslim communities in Canada and abroad in large part because of the Canadian government's decades-long effort to encourage the creation of a multi-ethnic polity at home. With the notable exception of the commission of inquiry in Quebec, there has been no national soul-searching (as there has been in the United Kingdom, the Netherlands, and Germany) about how to manage differences between dominant and minority cultures in Canada as a result of 9/11. While the Bush Administration's policies contributed to a resurgence of anti-American nationalism around the world, often with direct or indirect religious overtones, it can be concluded from this chapter that the Obama Administration would likely benefit from Canada acting in 'common cause' with the United States again by promoting a Canadian 'brand' of democratic development around the world that is anchored by the value that Canadian society accords to pluralism at home. That is to say, the Canadian government subscribes to the idea that stability and peace can be achieved when there is a healthy civil society and that such a society is premised on pluralism, which 'fosters the equal participation of all people in political, economic, educational and sociocultural life and allows individuals to retain their cultural, linguistic and religious heritage within a framework of shared citizenship.'[22] Eck suggests that increasing inter-faith understanding will require more than a global environment that values tolerance: 'Tolerance is a necessary virtue ... it does not require Christians and Muslims, Hindus, Jews, and ardent secularists to know anything about one another. Tolerance is too thin a foundation for a world of religious difference and proximity.'[23] What is needed, according to Eck, is dialogue and 'energetic engagement with diversity.'[24]

While Canada has eschewed faith-based diplomatic initiatives, it appears that pluralism as a value will embody an activist Canadian international agenda that promotes encounter and debate among communities, which may include inter-faith dialogues. We can foresee that a major component of Canada's foreign policy in the years ahead will focus on the promotion of democratic development, a central tenet of which is pluralism (cultural, religious, ethnic, political). It could be said that the ongoing development of a democratic development framework premised on the core value of pluralism, as reflected in Canada's bilateral and multilateral relations (particularly through its development assistance), will be an important dimension of Canada's future 'smart power.' This is the 'Canadian' response to the rise of religion in world politics.

In the end, can religion and diplomacy reinforce each other to mutual advantage rather than acting in isolation? The simple answer is that it depends. Certainly, if both parties see advantage in doing so, they will. It is now commonly acknowledged that the Vatican under Pope John

Paul II, in collaboration with members of the Western alliance, played an important role in helping to sow the seeds of the Soviet empire's eventual and largely peaceful dissolution. This accomplishment, along with others of the late pontiff vis-à-vis the peaceful pursuit of freedom and social justice by non-violent means, is detailed already in chapter 10. Today, conflicts with countries such as Iran and Burma are on smaller – perhaps even more manageable – scales and may lend themselves to 'Track-2' style efforts that would incorporate members of faith communities. In the end, power politics, an old and enduring concept, will likely be forced to recognize the contributions of faith-based non-governmental organizations.

NOTES

1 Henry Kissinger to Colin Robertson, a Canadian diplomat, at 2004 GOP Convention, New York. It is a variation of Dean Acheson's description of Canada as 'the stern daughter of the voice of God.' Personal communication with Colin Robertson, 25 July 2008.
2 In Canada, the term, which entered public debate in 2007 to describe Quebec society's relationship with newcomers from other cultures, soon came to symbolize a national debate, given the increasing number of immigrants from Asia.
3 For example, since 1969, Canada has had direct bilateral diplomatic relations with the Vatican. According to the fact sheet 'Canada and the Holy See' (Canada 2009), 'Canada benefits from the perspective of an important international player, both at the regional level and on global issues. The Holy See has, for example, been at the forefront of intercultural and interreligious dialogue at a time when religions have re-emerged as an important dimension in relations between states ... Canada and the Holy See have a long tradition of promoting human rights and fundamental freedoms.'
4 Internationalism has long been central to Canadian foreign policy and is associated, in particular, with the decade after the Second World War during which Canada, arguably, punched well above its weight in international affairs. This internationalism was embodied by the career of Lester B. Pearson, foreign policy mandarin, secretary of state for external affairs, and Canadian prime minister, who received the Nobel Peace Prize in 1957 for his efforts to mediate the Suez crisis, leading to the establishment of a

United Nations peacekeeping force in the Middle East. This internationalism has been closely associated with the notion during the Cold War of Canada as a middle power and an international mediator, something that continues to resonate in Canadian society. Munton and Keating (2001) provide a comprehensive account of the evolution of Canada's internationalism.

5 Canada uses its international reputation for tolerance – religious, linguistic, same-sex unions – as a means of enhancing its international prestige as a diplomatic actor. The appointment of prominent Canadians as international mediators, such as former Canadian chief of defence staff John de Chastelain in his role as chairman of the Independent International Commission on Decommissioning (which culminated in the creation of a Northern Ireland Assembly in 2007), is an example of such an extension of the Canadian diplomatic brand.

6 In March 2004, the Quebec Court of Appeal ruled that a school board was justified under Section 1 of the Canadian Charter of Rights and Freedoms in prohibiting a twelve-year-old Sikh boy from wearing his kirpan in its school. The kirpan is a ceremonial curved dagger that all baptised orthodox Sikh men and women are obliged to wear at all times. In 2006, the Supreme Court of Canada overturned the Quebec court's ruling in a unanimous decision that was said to have upheld the value of religious tolerance in Canadian society.

7 The media breathlessly catalogued the incidents, including Muslim women refusing to be seen by male doctors in the province's public health system and a young girl being denied the right to play on her soccer team because she wore a hijab. A national controversy erupted when a municipal council in the small Quebec town of Hérouxville issued a 'code of conduct,' which stated that stoning women or burning them alive was prohibited. The official title of the two-person commission, which held public consultations throughout the province, was the Consultation Commission on Accommodation Practices Related to Cultural Differences. The Commission's report was published in 2008.

8 The *Toronto Star* in its editorial on 15 October 2007, reported on an opinion poll in Quebec showing that the province's citizens had in fact become less tolerant: Quebecers, by a wide margin, opposed virtually all cultural or religious accommodation with new immigrants and other minority groups, and 70 per cent opposed females wearing a hijab on a soccer field.

9 On the number of foreign-born Canadians, see Statistics Canada (2007).

10 Indeed, many Muslims deny that the Islamists actually practise their religion at all.

11 Canada as a postmodern state refers to a national identity that is increasingly socially constructed rather than territorially determined as Canadian society assumes greater openness to new identities. The idea of Canada is thus constantly contested and revised.
12 Matthews limns the history of how Christian churches in Canada responded to major episodes in postwar Canadian foreign policy (1990, 161–3).
13 Although Canada's ecumenical communities should never be seen as a monolith, it would be accurate to conclude that there was a broad coalition of religious leaders from different faiths who supported the government's efforts to promote peace through negotiation in Central America and who supported sanctions against South Africa. However, on the issue of disarmament, it is clear that there continued to be a considerable gap between official Canadian policy and the aspirations of Canada's church leadership. As Bromke and Nossal note, church leaders were troubled by the Trudeau government's agreement to allow cruise-missile testing on Canadian soil.
14 For example, Canadian ecumenical organizations played a prominent role in the lead up to the Ottawa Convention on Landmines.
15 I am indebted to Daryl Copeland, a senior Canadian diplomat and analyst, for this observation.
16 Matthews offers the most cogent analysis of the involvement of Canadian Christian churches in the foreign-policymaking process.
17 Faith-based diplomacy refers to diplomacy undertaken by the nation-state, either directly or indirectly, that is driven by religious imperative.
18 The Shia Imami Ismaili Muslims, generally known as the Ismailis, belong to the Shia branch of Islam and comprise ethnically and culturally diverse peoples living in over twenty-five countries.
19 The now-defunct *Western Standard*, a regional newsmagazine associated with the Conservative movement in Western Canada, did reprint eight of the offending cartoons in 2006. Predictably, other Canadian media accused the magazine's publisher and co-founder, Ezra Levant, of acting irresponsibly.
20 See, for example, the Pew Global Attitudes Project, which has tracked the decline of the United States' favourability in the eyes of the world since 2000. See also the catalogue of Pew global surveys at http://pewglobal.org. See also the regular surveys on how the United States is viewed internationally as reported by http://www.worldpublicopinion.org.
21 A poll by the Environics Research Group for a consortium of media groups and foundations in 2008 reported that when asked to name the country that stood out as a negative force in the world, the United States was cited most often (52 per cent). Iran was next at 21 per cent. http://erg.environics.net/media_room/default.asp?aID=665 [accessed in March 2009].

22 Prime Minister of Canada, 'Canada's New Government joins with the Aga Khan to create the Global Centre for Pluralism,' *Speech*, 25 October 2006, http://pm.gc.ca/eng/media.asp?category=2&pageid=46&id=1381.
23 See Diana L. Eck's full definition of pluralism at http://www.pluralism.org/pluralism/what_is_pluralism.php.
24 Ibid.

REFERENCES

Almond, G., R. Appleby, and E. Sivan. 2003. *Strong religion: The rise of fundamentalisms around the world*. Chicago: University of Chicago Press.
Bissoondath, N. 1994. *Selling illusions: The cult of multiculturalism in Canada*. Toronto: Penguin.
Blackwell, R. 2006. Kirpan ban overturned: Ceremonial dagger can be worn by Sikhs at school, Supreme Court justices rule. *Globe & Mail*, 3 March.
Bromke, A. and K. R. Nossal. 1983-84. Tensions in Canada's Foreign Policy. *Foreign Affairs* 62:335-53.
Canada. Department of Foreign Affairs and International Trade. 2002. A dialogue on foreign policy. http://www.dataparc.com/projects/www.foreignpolicy-dialogue.ca/pdf/DialogueEng.pdf.
Canada. 2009. Canada and the Holy See. http://www.canadainternational.gc.ca/holy_see-saint_siege/bilateral_relations_bilaterales/index.aspx?lang=eng&menu_id=9&menu=L.
Cohen, A. 2007. *The unfinished Canadian*. Toronto: McClelland and Stewart.
Eck, Diana L. n.d. What is pluralism? http://www.pluralism.org/pluralism/what_is_pluralism.php.
Environics. 2008. The Canada's world poll. http://erg.environics.net/media_room/default.asp?aID=665.
Galloway, G. 2007. A murky ending to the Air India whodunit. *Globe & Mail*, 15 December.
Gerges, F. 2003. Islam and Muslims in the mind of America. *Annals of the American Academy of Political and Social Science* 588:73–89.
Ghoreishi, O., and C. Ford. 2006. Hotel Canada. *Epoch Times* 3 August. http://en.epochtimes.com/news/6-8-3/44549.html.
Giddens, A. 1993. Canada: The first postmodern state? Keynote address, Conference of the British Association of Canadian Studies, University of Cambridge.
Global Centre for Pluralism. 2006. Government of Canada and Aga Khan sign funding agreement for global centre for pluralism. News release. http://www.pluralism.ca/press_releases/press_release_oct25-2006.shtml.

Gopin, M. 2002. The practice of cultural diplomacy. Center for World Religions and Diplomacy Conflict Resolution. http://www.gmu.edu/departments/crdc/docs/culturaldiplomacy.html.

Haynes, J. 1995. *Religion, fundamentalism and ethnicity: A global perspective.* United Nations Research Institute For Social Development. http://www.unrisd.org/80256B3C005BCCF9/(httpAuxPages)/265FAA83B0EA35EB80256B67005B67F6/$file/dp65.pdf.

Ignatieff, M. 2004. Peace, order and good government: A foreign policy agenda for Canada. OD Skelton Lecture, Department of Foreign Affairs and International Trade, Ottawa, 12 March.

Johnson, D.M. 2004. Conflict prevention and peacebuilding: The religious letter. International Center for Religion and Diplomacy. http://www.icrd.org/index.php?option=com_content&task=view&id=200.

Karim, K. 2002. Crescent dawn in the Great White North: Muslim participation in the Canadian public sphere. In *Muslims in the West: From sojourners to citizens,* ed. Yvonne Yazbeck Haddad, 262–78. New York: Oxford University Press.

Kymlicka, W. 2004. Marketing Canadian pluralism in the international arena. *International Journal* 59 (4): 829–52.

Matthews, Robert O. 1990. The Canadian churches and foreign policy: An assessment. In *Canadian Churches and Foreign Policy,* ed. Bonnie Green, 161–79. Toronto: Lorimer. http://books.google.com/books?id=Ag6n2cBXeTsC&pg=PA161&lpg=PA161&dq=%22Robert+Matthews%22+and+%22Canadian+Churches+and+Foreign+Policy%22&source=web&ots=iyN5y03hNU&sig=x0016cnVksZJjgk6ZWq33f1XDlQ&hl=en.

Mennonite Central Committee. n.d. *O Canada: Armed and ready.* http://canada.mcc.org/peace/projects/canadaarmed.

Munton, D., and T. Keating. 2001. Internationalism and the Canadian public. *Canadian Journal of Political Science* 34 (3): 517–49.

Paulston, C. 1978. Biculturalism: Some reflections and speculations.' *TESOL Quarterly* 12 (4): 369–80.

Ross, V. 2007. Tories fast-track Aga Khan centre. *Globe & Mail,* 1 February.

Statistics Canada. 2007. 2006 Census: Immigration, citizenship, language, mobility and migration. http://www.statcan.ca/Daily/English/071204/d071204a.htm.

14 From Ideology to Identity: Building a Foundation for Communities of the Willing

CHRIS SEIPLE

International Relations: From Theory to Reality

I begin with three absolute 'truths':

- Religion pre-dates the field of international relations (a point made emphatically in chapter 2).
- Religion has been and will always be integral to human identity.
- Religion has been and will always be a part of the problem, and a part of the solution.

We in the international relations field have not always recognized these 'truths' – even now. So why should we think about religion? How does using religion help us understand critical international relations issues?

I am going to wrestle with these questions as I examine the one thing that I might have some expertise on: myself. I want to walk you through my own case study as someone who takes quite seriously – and has practical experience with – international affairs, belief, human rights, and American engagement of the world. I will not be as deep or penetrating as I would like to be in each arena, but that is the price of considering them together according to the dual presupposition that each has its own ideology to be shed, if they are to be related as they should.

My argument is a simple one: if we want to practise that first part of wisdom – naming something properly – we must move past the ideologies of our tools of analysis and, yes, our alleged identities, both personal and professional, if we, as potential communities of the willing, are to be relevant to the complex solution sets this world requires. Accordingly, the chapter discusses how international relations is moving from theory to reality; belief is moving from religion to faith; human rights is moving from tolerance to respect; and American policy is moving from defence to security. As such, this chapter hopefully positions us to explore what 'communities of the willing' might look like. It does so in a way that is consistent with the call in chapter 3 for 'thick religion.' Theology and religious knowledge play a direct part in the following analysis. The chapter concludes with a brief discussion of two practical examples – ripped from reality but not, unfortunately, from the headlines – that might suggest potential areas of research and even hope.

> Americans are baffled by Iraq because we have spent three and a half centuries in a post-Westphalian world where state trumps faith and tribe ... Before we can understand our enemies, or our allies, in the Middle East, we have 350 years of assumptions to unlearn.
> – Freedberg Jr (2003)

The real conversation for American society today might just be about unlearning more than 350 years of Westphalian assumptions.[1] As someone who took all of his international relations courses during the mid- to late 1980s and mid- to late 1990s – that is, before 9/11 – it is rather easy to prove that religion came up seldom in class. In fact, in all of my undergraduate and thirty-six graduate courses, I can think of but one class where religion was regularly discussed. There simply was little room for religion in the parsimonious paradigms that the discipline of political science imposed on studying the international world.

In September 2007 I interviewed Madeleine Albright at our annual Global Leadership Forum (which focuses on Christians and international affairs). She reflected that in her own academic training and practice during the Cold War, God did not come up. If it did, it was only in the context of 'godless communism,' and that was about it (Global Leadership Forum 2007).[2] If international relations theory was allegedly so good for so long (at least before 9/11), why did it fail so dramatically – and why are we playing so much catchup, still, seven years after 9/11? Consider this answer: 'The sweet dream of American political thought – reborn in each generation, it seems – is that cultural factors like religion will shrink into insignificance as blessed pragmatism finally comes into its own' (Miles 2005, 25). This disposition parallels the long-term dominance of secularization theory in academe as observed in chapters 2 and 3. Taught not to speak of religion and politics in polite company, American foreign policy elites – products of academic institutions that generally dismiss religion – are now forced to understand a world where religion *is* politics in many regions. This process has not been easy or fun. And it certainly has not been successful.

To take one brief example, consider Uzbekistan, where 'to be Uzbek is to be Muslim.' Islam, since its eighth century AD arrival in Central Asia, permeates the culture of Uzbekistan and has reinforced the strong traditions of hospitality, respect, and intellectual thinking. For example, Uzbeks are very proud of Samarkand, where a madrassa was established in fifteenth century to study theology and science. Uzbeks are so proud that they will gladly take you there for the day.

Common sense demands that American engagement begin with an awareness of the relationship between Islam and culture. In general, however, U.S. policymakers – formed and informed by international relations theory – consistently have ignored religion as a factor in understanding Uzbekistan's civil society, let alone foreign policy (Seiple 2006b).[3] Why is that so? Since the Enlightenment the West has separated church and state, and the results have generally been good for religious and political liberty. The casualty, however, has been the West's theories of global politics, which have not provided a role for religion in their analysis: 'To the extent that religion is included as a factor of analysis, it is often framed as a simplistic ideology ... and catalyst to conflict, rather than a complex worldview that forms and informs culture and action, and therefore deserves more subtle discussion' (Seiple and White 2004, 45).

Indeed, traditional international relations theory generally fails to provide for the 'irrational choice' and/or influence of a moral imperative. Carr's (1964) critique of realism serves equally well for conventional international relations theory: *'Realism breaks down because it fails to provide any ground for purposive or meaningful action ... realism can offer nothing but a naked struggle for power which makes any kind of international society impossible'* (92–3; emphasis added). In other words, the theory of international relations, at least in my educational experience, has made little allowance for a greater good or higher meaning as a reality that affects international relations. That this religious reality might also be catalytic, even an explanatory variable, has traditionally been too much for the academician studying international relations in the post-Enlightenment-empiricist world of scientific secularism. Indeed, what place could there be for an Absolute in a field where absolutely nothing was for sure, except the great power of the period (which, ironically enough, has always fallen)?

Belief: From Religion to Faith

In an era of globalization – where ideas, images, and information lay siege to our identity through technology, trade, and travel – religion is a reliable redoubt on two fronts.[4] First, it provides a meta-narrative, an explanatory framework that, anchored in an Absolute, provides understanding of the complex dynamics in our world today. Compared to the non-narrative of secularism – where truth is relative – the Absolute of religion is comforting indeed. Second, especially for those children of Abraham, religion was global before globalization. To believe in a deity who created the globe in the first place is to believe in a God who is sovereign over globalization. Christ, for example, created the first international NGO when he established his church through Peter. Christ and Muhammad both asked their followers to spread their faith to the ends of the earth. In other words, Christianity and Islam invented globalization long before Thomas Friedman's insight-in-India that the world was flat.[5]

The 'down side' to belief, of course, is the notion that one's fervour might result in the erroneous conclusion that it is possible to know the Absolute absolutely. Once one feels confident enough to speak for the Absolute, it is not long before ideology sets in; that is, a checklist for living life, where everything is reduced to simple black-and-white issues that the religious adherent is either for or against. Often concomitant with this perspective is a hubris disdainful of non-religious people and secular accomplishments. Worse, with such an ideology as a foundation, it is not hard to construct a house of extremism, even terrorism. All religions have been guilty of this process, and product.

In my own case, I grew up in a strong faith community. These were and are good people with whom I went to church. Nonetheless, my faith communities growing up were essentially all white, and it was assumed that you were Republican and supportive of Republican issues. We were also fairly certain, or so it seemed, about the meaning of scripture and who was going to Heaven and who was not. Religion was my world. I did not think much about religion's role in international affairs but it was inconceivable that faith and flag could be two separate things.

In 1986 I went to college amidst a spate of televangelist scandals. (If you remember, for example, this was the time when Jimmy Swaggart was caught up in a sex scandal and Jim and Tammy Faye Bakker were involved in a financial scandal.) With a fairly good impression of myself after living in my suburban cocoon, I was unprepared for my encounter with other world views. I was certainly not prepared to have others condemn my evangelical world view with pejorative pleasure. And so I was forced to begin thinking through what about my religion was real.

As I experienced all the issues of my fellow dorm mates my freshman year – I had been placed in the African-American house – I realized that I could not recall one church conversation about, for example, diversity, the urban poor (despite being relatively close by), caring for the environment, or working for human rights. While we cared deeply for those suffering overseas through development and missionary work, we simply did not think about those other issues when I was growing up. After graduation, I continued to think about these and related issues in the Marine Corps (where I spent nine years). It was not until my time at the Institute for Global Engagement (IGE), however, that I began to truly understand my faith as a way of life ... and as a practical engagement strategy requiring me to understand how to love my neighbour in a language and logic that she or he understands.

Today I understand every major issue we face to be in part a faith issue, one over which a global God has sovereignty, and about which a loving Jesus seeks to have compassion ... sometimes through me as his disciple. I read Matthew 23 – where Jesus condemns the religious ideologues for forgetting the larger picture of 'faith, mercy, and justice' – and I begin to grasp the perverse and ironic danger of an ideological checklist. While I am absolutely certain of an Absolute, I also recognize that I cannot know the Absolute absolutely. Therefore there is all the more reason to proceed with humble and prayerful caution regarding the majesty and mystery that is God.

Human Rights: From Tolerance to Respect

Tolerance is the legal term of international covenants that expects people and states worldwide to live with one another. Unfortunately, it took 9/11 to make clear what the identity wars of the 1990s should have already taught us: tolerance is not enough.

What we need is *respect*. Respect is the moral obligation to take the time to understand our neighbour's identity, acknowledge deep differences, and, as a result, build a common space of mutually accommodated identity – identity that is, by definition, rooted in the other. You cannot legislate respect, but you can live it in your personal life and you can work in practical ways through governmental and civil society channels to promote it.

My organization, IGE, works for sustainable religious freedom around the world. A few years back, I was forced to meet an experienced Asian diplomat from an authoritarian country. (He had been assigned to me, by his government, as my handler.) After spending some time with us and talking about some of these issues, he simply said about the IGE, 'I appreciate very much that you first seek to understand, then engage. You are the first Americans not to give me a list and tell me what to do.' I apologized. I made clear that, while there was no excuse for the way his government had violated human rights, those violations were no excuse for the way he had been treated as a person.

In October 2007 I spoke to fifty 'staffers' on Capitol Hill concerned about issues of faith and law. One senior staffer came up to me afterwards and reacted specifically to the idea that Americans give lists and tell people what to do. She said, 'That's all we ever do.' It was a quiet confession. Like many elites of the foreign affairs establishment, she had the best of intentions to be intolerant of intolerance, but by operating exclusively out of an ideology of tolerance she had neglected a broader and deeper imperative: *respect*.

Showing respect is difficult for Americans sometimes, particularly in the Muslim world. This is not surprising, given the generally negative and distorted image of Islam in relation to human rights as reported in chapter 4. For example, the overwhelming majority of U.S. policymakers cannot distinguish between Sunni and Shia (Stein 2006). In fact, it is almost impossible for Americans to respect Islam when a recent Gallup poll of Americans revealed that five years after 9/11, 57 per cent of Americans essentially know 'not much' or 'nothing' about the 'beliefs and view of Muslims' (the same percentage as just after 9/11). This same poll asked what Americans admired most about Muslim societies. Fifty-seven per cent of Americans said 'nothing' or 'I don't know.' This poll concluded that Americans 'see conflict with the Muslim world' as a function of 'public relations' while Muslims 'see conflict with the U.S.' as a function of 'policy and respect' (Esposito and Mogahed 2008).

Encouraging examples are out there, however, even from the most unlikely places. Consider the recent initiative at the United Nations called the Alliance of Civilizations (AoC) project. That the UN could be a major new catalyst for respect rather than mere tolerance is ironic, of course, as traditionally the UN has been so tolerant of other perspectives that perpetual human rights violators sit on the Human Rights Council. And while religious freedom is enshrined in Article 18 of the UN Universal Declaration of Human Rights, in UN circles there has long been a disregard for religion as a factor in international affairs.

Fortunately, there is potential for these patterns to change with the establishment of the AoC.

Emerging from Iranian President Khatami's 1999 call for a Dialogue among Civilizations (which was adopted by the UN as the theme for 2001), the AoC began to take form in 2005 when Spain and Turkey co-sponsored the idea. Secretary General Kofi Annan formed a High Level Group (HLG) to explore the goals and framework of the AoC, reporting its findings on 13 November 2006. The HLG's report stated that the AoC should contribute by 're-affirming a paradigm of *mutual respect* among peoples of different cultural and religious traditions and by helping to mobilize concerted action toward this end' (Alliance of Civilizations 2006b, 4). Seemingly, the UN was signalling that, in fact, tolerance was not enough.

Yet the HLG 'highlights' report, or executive summary, did contain an odd comment. In reference to the relationship between Muslim and Western societies, the report noted that 'because the causes of current tensions are political – and not religious or cultural – they are also solvable' (Alliance of Civilizations 2006a).[6] In other words, religion is not a part of the problem; and if it was, then the problem would be insoluble. At the very least, this type of language betrays the difficulties of a paradigm shift. In this case, the quote simultaneously reveals an implicit ideology rooted in international relations theory that had littler tolerance for religion's role in international affairs, except as the negative ingredient that makes solutions impossible.

On 26 April 2007, Secretary-General Ban Ki-moon appointed the former president of Portugal, Jorge Sampaio, as the first-ever UN high representative for the Alliance of Civilizations. Since that time, Sampaio has been setting up a small AoC Secretariat and developing the AoC's two-year implementation plan.

In October 2007, it was my privilege to moderate a discussion with President Sampaio at the Council for Foreign Relations. In preparation for that discussion, we talked by phone and I asked him about the quote from the HLG's 'highlights' report. Although he did not participate in the meetings that produced it, he assured me that religion was 'very much connected' to the solutions that our world requires.[7] All of his statements since assuming the post of high representative, in fact, confirm this understanding – and therefore the possibility of a paradigm shift at the United Nations.

On 19 September 2007, Sampaio told his UN colleagues that a comprehensive approach was needed, one that focused on 'glocal deliverables ... [that is] deliverables that must be underpinned by a global approach and implemented at a local level' (Sampaio 2007a). Within this philosophy of engagement, Sampaio shared his goals for the AoC with the UN's General Assembly on 4 October 2007. He described 'confessional organizations' as 'active and influential ... key partners.' In the same speech, he called upon member states to 'create or strengthen national strategies for cross-cultural dialogue,' while further requesting that international organizations create a 'chart for partnering with the Alliance' (2007c).

Within this broad framework, Sampaio is beginning to tackle the toughest issue of our day: relations between Western and Muslim cultures. For example, he recently warned the Organization for Security and Cooperation in Europe about using 'inaccurate concepts' to understand Islam and the need to 'move beyond facile stereotypes, simplistic dichotomies, and ready-made images.' He also acknowledged that 'intolerance and discrimination attitudes exist within Muslim societies, let alone between different Islamic communities' (2007b).

Despite the UN's ideology, the Alliance of Civilizations' concept of identity is seemingly off to the right start –rooted in respect and dialogue, as well as an honest understanding that religion is a part of the problem and therefore must be a part of the solution.

American Engagement: From Defence to Security

I served in the Marine Corps throughout the 1990s. My last tour was at the Pentagon where I worked directly for the commandant of the Marine Corps in the Strategic Initiatives Group – a special think tank whose job was to consider the origin of our present national security system and how global trends might force change. I still follow these trends and their impact closely, especially as my own travels have taken me to places like the Afghanistan-Pakistan border (three times in the last two years). As a result, I speak often with NGOs, as well as national security officials and our military. This ongoing perspective enables the following observations.

Nine years after 9/11, America is just now beginning to return to the comprehensive understanding of security that was intended in 1945. On 1 December 1947, Ferdinand Eberstadt – whose 1945 report served as the basis for the 1947 National Security Act – wrote to Senator Taft, laying out his vision of security: 'National Security policy is like a mosaic made up of a multitude of actions and relationships, but, like a mosaic, there must be a guiding and dominating theme, and in our case that theme should be the maintenance of peace by all means and forces at our disposal' (qtd in Dowart 1991, 8–9). George F. Kennan also supported such an approach. In his own analysis of the Soviet Union, Kennan felt it critical that U.S. policy must focus on the political and economic intentions of the Soviet Union, not just its military capabilities.[8]

Unfortunately, Eberstadt's best friend, the first secretary of defense, James Forrestal, did not agree and soon began to organize the Defense Department singularly around Soviet military capabilities (Dowart 1991, 135). This set the stage and pattern for the rest of the nascent national security establishment. Forrestal was 'proved' right when North Korea invaded South Korea (an event that was perceived as part of 'global communism' on the march). Given the recent promulgation of NSC-68 – a secret memo designed to beef up the American military, among other things – it was not long before the Department of Defense was receiving the lion's share of the national security budget.[9] U.S. 'national security' was soon reduced to American military response capabilities, something that was easy to count as policymakers and political scientists quantified international relations and national security while ignoring religion, ethnicity, and identity.

By the 1990s, the United States suffered from a militarized national security. This logic – as much a response to the 1990s military interventions (from Somalia to Kosovo) as it was the longing for a clearly defined enemy who fought conventionally – reflected a 'Cold War hangover.' The hangover stumbled after a simple logic: national security = the military = overseas warfighting only. Having forgotten that defence is a lesser included set of security, it came as no surprise that Governor George W. Bush ran for president in 2000, promising not to do 'nation-building.' He would save the military to fight and win the nation's wars.

Adding insult to injury, however, was the non-evolution of the rest of U.S. national security structure according to the primary lesson of the 1990s interventions: there were no more 'pure' battlefields; Washington's 'interagency' would have to find ways to be effective in the field (Seiple 1999, 2000). The only thing worse than a military reluctantly engaged in the operational reality of 'nation-building' missions – and refusing to have its identity significantly affected by it – was an 'interagency' that completely ignored that reality. The 9/11 commission report details these facts in painful detail (National Commission on Terrorist Attacks 2004, 399).

It was not until Iraq, however, that these fault lines were decidedly revealed as psychological and bureaucratic chasms that demanded a comprehensive approach. Foremost among them was the American inability to address religion. For example, on 28 June 2003, Grand Ayatollah Sistani, the senior Shia cleric in Iraq, issued a fatwa against the U.S. democratization plan for Iraq, calling it undemocratic. It was not until mid-November that U.S. policymakers realized how important Sistani was to a peaceful transition. They then called Administrator Paul Bremer home for 'emergency consultations': 'Said one [Iraqi] council member, speaking on condition of anonymity: "We waited four months, thanks to Bremer." "We could have organized [this transition] by now had we started when Sistani issued his fatwa. But the Americans were in denial"' (Chandrasekaran 2003).[10] By most accounts, it was during this time – from June to November 2003 – that the insurgencies organized and began fighting American troops. The United States has still not recovered from this inability to understand the role religion plays in realpolitik.

To be fair, especially since 9/11, the U.S. government has naturally focused its domestic and international attention on physical security, promising gates, guards, and guns against the terrorist threat. It was the right course of action; it was also the course that, given the U.S. Cold War hangover, America could quickly and easily implement. Nonetheless, it was a still a tactical reaction to symptoms, not a strategic move against the root causes. If America, and the world, wants to avoid merely hacking at the leaves of evil, to paraphrase Thoreau, then it must begin to strike at the root – an identity that is simultaneously ideological and theological.

In some ways, militant Islam is an ideology, with characteristics that are conceptually no different from other radical ideologies like communism or fascism. It provides a simple and ordered explanation of the world and identifies the enemy. It acts as a catalyst, motivating its followers against the enemy, while painting a portrait of a better world absent the enemy. Understanding militant Islam as an ideology is useful because it helps us name the dynamics at play and to recognize and predict the associated patterns. Yet militant Islam is also rooted in very bad theology. And only good theology beats bad theology. Working with Muslims to better understand, promote, and institutionalize the best of the Islamic faith is the only means to defeat this terrorist threat. It is incumbent upon Muslims and U.S. policymakers alike to know Islam's identity at its theological best, not its ideological worst. The same goes for all religions (Seiple 2004a, 2006a).[11]

Nevertheless, it is still a 'new' thing to incorporate religion in realpolitik analysis. In 2004, for example, the *Atlantic Monthly* published an article on 'forensic theology,' revealing the work of a few analysts – 'pioneers,' the article called them – who have been working since the 1990s to better understand the theology behind the religious edicts, or fatwas, of militant Islamic clerics (Grey 2004). As encouraging and much needed as this news was, it did present a question. If the United States has been at war with variants of militant Islam, Shia and Sunni, since the capture of its embassy in Tehran in 1979, why has it taken so long to finally examine the theology of militant Islam in some kind of systematic manner?

To be sure, there are pockets of good people beginning to wrestle with the key issues – especially in the military. The Army and the Marine Corps have developed a new counterinsurgency manual that calls for a 'flexible, adaptive force' led by 'agile, well-informed, culturally astute leaders' (Seiple 2003a)[12] (although the manual, strangely, does not address religion itself). The very need for such a document – five years after 9/11 and three years after the insurgency had begun in Iraq – indicates how unprepared the United States is, and remains (Petraeus and Amos 2006).

As usual, it is worse with the interagency. Secretary of State Rice told Congress in 2007 that 40 per cent (129 people) of the 300 State Department slots for Iraq would have to be filled by military personnel. Because the civilian elements of U.S. national power have not been prepared, American military personnel would take on such responsibilities as 'business development' and 'city management' (DeYoung 2007).

In short, operational reality has finally forced the U.S. military to shed the ideology of its Cold War hangover, while this reality has had much less impact on the rest of the interagency. Sadly, U.S. governmental agencies, as most policymakers will say off the record, are not outfitted – organizationally and, more importantly, conceptually – to fight a multi-generational war that is both ideological and theological (Danan 2007; Seiple 2002). If the American government accepts this reality, the foremost recommendation is to revamp the education of our national security officials – from the military to the chaplains to the State Department to our intelligence community – such that they are equipped to think about religion in their strategic assessments, planning, and operations.[13]

If this is the operational context for how well our agencies are educated and trained to implement foreign policy – irrespective of whether one agrees with that policy or not – it is worth reflecting, briefly, on the strategic and historic context of the 'Bush Doctrine,' whose application has revealed the tremendous shortcomings of our governmental agencies to work together with a common world view pursuant to common cause.[14]

The Bush Doctrine was not a simply defined term. It is a U.S. military strategy of pre-emption, with precedent. (See, for example, Gaddis 2004.) It is a second inaugural address that echoed John F. Kennedy's call to 'bear any burden' for the 'survival and success of liberty.' It is, as discussed above, the outgrowth of a national security that has become militarized over two generations – a national security where the military has been the 'piggy-back' for the rest of U.S. agencies, and the 'piggy-bank,' because the U.S. government is not organized or funded to wage peace. It is short-hand for an un-nuanced engagement of the world.

Simply, the Bush Doctrine is merely the latest form of American exceptionalism: something a cursory review of the book by McDougall (1997) – would reveal. Meanwhile, McDougall's very title, which includes the words *promised land*, confirms how much religious rhetoric is part and parcel of the presidential pulpit. President Bush certainly couched his multi-faceted doctrine in religious terms, but such diction is unexceptional in America's export of its exceptionalism.

Practical Application

Shedding ideological skins at several levels in order to recover identity is not easy. It takes honesty, time, patience, and respect. As Sampaio (2007c) has reflected, 'This way of formulating the question of what an identity consists of is probably very personal and indeed quite provocative. But it helps to make the case for building open and pluralistic identities, free from the burden of possessions, memorabilia and reminiscences from the past which fuels national conflicts and identities as well as xenophobia.'

It is difficult, but an identity that is authentic – defined by what it is for, instead of what it is against – is an identity that can accommodate other identities. Mutually accommodated identities that acknowledge and celebrate deep differences also position people to develop and deepen what they have in common, beginning with the value of respect. Again, it is a difficult process, requiring all to 'walk their talk.' But there simply is no other approach, let alone solution.

As previously noted, my organization, the IGE, promotes sustainable environments for religious freedom worldwide. We do so through a strategy we call 'relational diplomacy,' working simultaneously from the top down and the bottom up.[15] IGE's work is an example of collaboration between government and religious NGOs toward the ends of peace and stability as reported in chapter 12.

I have three degrees in international relations. None of them taught me about the role of religion in international affairs. To be fair, I never even thought to ask until the third degree. But one day in 1999, the following thought occurred to me: 'I take my faith seriously and I know that religion has a positive role to play in the world; yet religion is never addressed in the academic disciplines of international affairs ... except as a catalyst to conflict.'

In the months following 9/11, the Institute for Global Engagement twice convened a small group of Christians to discuss how Christians contributed to the problems and solutions of international affairs, and whether or not there was some vehicle through which we could provide practical thought leadership for this new era where religion was necessarily a key factor. The Center on Faith & International Affairs emerged from these discussions, as did its flagship publication, the *Review of Faith & International Affairs* (the field's journal of record). Although originally designed as an intra-Christian discussion across denominations and traditions, we soon realized that there was a tremendous void in the national and global discourse – there was no organization, let alone journal, that encouraged all faiths and world views to actively and practically discuss the role of religion in global events. There had to be a place where deeply held differences could be discussed respectfully and authentically. As a result, CFIA and the *Review* have been multi-faith since 2005.

This journey has been a wonderful one, especially as we have had the conversations of identity necessary to establishing our multi-faith board of advisors and contributors. While we are definitely multi-faith, we have found that many of our conferences and published articles focus on Christianity and/or Islam. Three reasons drive this focus. First, CFIA – indeed, books like this one – would not take place if it were not for the catalytic events of 11 September. Second, American and global security depends on a super-region where Islam is the majority religion – along the 'I-Axis' from Israel to India.[16] Third, Islam and Christianity are global religions with global goals; no matter the issue or region, it is more than likely that believers from both faith traditions will be involved, and relevant.

There is much work to be done at CFIA and the *Review*. Still, both are now a known and safe space to discuss identity while building and contributing to a new body of knowledge that also informs policymakers and practitioners.

Ideas without implementation, however, remain worthless. Our work in Pakistan's Northwest Frontier Province (NWFP) demonstrates the practical process of creating a space in which one can talk about deep differences and common values ... shedding mutual stereotypes as a result. In the fall of 2003, we were approached by a Pakistani American who told us, 'I don't know what you do, but I think you're bridge-builders. Would you like to work with the NWFP's Islamist chief minister who was freely elected last year on a pro-Sharia and anti-American platform?' IGE agreed to do so.

After many months of mutual vetting – via fax and telephone conversations – our mutual ideologies softened enough. In July 2005, at IGE's invitation, the Chief Minister Akram Khan Durrani, his two senior aides, and his three sons arrived in America. During our first meeting, I asked the Minister Durrani why he was in politics. He told me that one day he would stand before God and would be held accountable for his actions. I told him that while we disagreed on the divinity of Christ, I shared the same conviction, and that was all the common ground we needed to begin a relationship.

Over the next ten days our team and his delegation got to know each other quite well, discussing everything from politics to God. Minister Durrani invited us to his country. From that October 2005 visit emerged a memorandum of understanding (MOU) to work together in promoting religious freedom – an MOU that Minister Durrani insisted on writing and signing the day after that terrible earthquake struck NWFP.

We soon visited again in May 2006, bringing with us a delegation of American leaders who also happened to be devout Christians and Muslims. From this experience emerged another MOU to provide a cohort of students an alternative to extremism along the Waziristan border by funding their education. We are now funding our second cohort at the University of Science and Technology in Bannu. The fruit of this visit came to bear in May 2007 when we co-sponsored the NWFP's first-ever conference on 'Peace & Religion.' It was the first time that imams and student leaders from throughout the entire province had the opportunity to listen to the perspective of the minority faiths in their province (including Shia, Sikh, Hindu, and Christian).

Incredibly, this entire process of moving past mutual and monolithic stereotypes would not have happened except for a secular donor who believes in religious freedom. It took a secular individual to fund a Christian religious freedom organization to talk to Islamists with whom no one else would engage.

The subject of another study, my sole desire in sharing these two stories with you is this: communities of the willing do not happen out of ideological lip service. They are possible only through the persistent work of a relational diplomacy that enables authentic differences of identity to be acknowledged and respected, such that additional identities of common values and purpose can develop, deepen, and even transcend. This kind of work is exhausting, and there are too few donors who want to support it. But whenever I get pessimistic, I think of my 'brother in humanity,' as he calls me, Qibla Ayaz. He is the dean of Islamic theology at Peshawar University. Whenever I feel pessimistic, he indefatigably reminds me that it is not ours to complete the task, but neither is it ours to withdraw from it.

Conclusion

I conclude with the reminder that this chapter is but a mid-stream snapshot of my own journey of faith as an American who loves this world. I trust that it reveals a journey where deep differences are acknowledged and celebrated as we learn to cooperate across them, pursuant to potential and positive effect. For example, conservative Muslims and conservative Christians working together – based on common values – just might be a missing ingredient that our world desperately needs.

Perhaps the greatest divide, however, remains in the West: between secular-based understandings and approaches and faith-integrated understandings and approaches. This fundamental difference is reflected in how we think about global affairs. For the secular international relations student and theorist, religion is something to be (re-) discovered. In this world view, 'international relations' is the umbrella, and things like culture and its sub-components – e.g., religion – are lesser included sets. For the person of faith, especially from the Abrahamic tradition, a much different view of the world ensues. If God is a global God – something held to be true by those who believe he created the universe – then culture, international relations, etc. are lesser included sets of his divine intent. And they are things in which he is already at work.

Time will tell the impact of this divide. For now, naming it is sufficient as we better understand our own identities even as we develop identities that are rooted in deep respect for the other.

NOTES

1 The 1648 Treaty of Westphalia ended Europe's religious wars and ushered in the international system of sovereign states that we know today.
2 Video highlights from the conference are accessible from http://www.globalechristian.org/. These highlights also include presentations by Muslim-American leaders and a reflection on why Christians should listen to Muslims.
3 For additional detail, see Seiple (2006b), particularly chapter 3, which examines the development of civil society in Uzbekistan, and especially the role of Islam therein.
4 The reference here is specifically the Abrahamic traditions of Judaism, Christianity, and Islam.
5 This awareness makes cause for a good conversation: instead of trying to fit religion into international relations, maybe we ought to be trying to fit international relations into religion. But that discussion can be saved for another book, although I will return to this point at the end of the chapter.
6 The report itself later notes that 'religion is an increasingly important dimension of many societies and a significant source of values for individuals. It can play a critical role in promoting an appreciation of other cultures, religions, and ways of life to help build harmony among them' (6). Five years after 9/11, this statement is underwhelming and further demonstrates an uncomfortable and incomplete understanding of the role that religion plays in the world as a profound spiritual force that anchors identity.
7 Telephone conversation, 12 October 2007.
8 For example, see *American Diplomacy* by Kennan (1985, 172–4).
9 Ironically enough, perhaps, this militarized national security became a clear pattern with the transition from the Eisenhower Administration to the Kennedy Administration. Ike closed out his eight-year term by warning against the 'military-industrial complex,' while Kennedy initiated a 'liberty agenda' in his inaugural. Who can forget these words: 'Let every nation know, whether it wishes us well or ill, that we shall pay any price, bear any burden, meet any hardship, support any friend, oppose any foe, to assure the survival and the success of liberty. This much we pledge – and more.' And so a retrospective Republican president with nothing to

lose warned against a militarized national security while an energetic and young Democratic president eager to prove that he was not 'soft' on communism essentially committed the United States to the defence of liberty everywhere, at any cost.

10 See also Weisman (2003): 'The [Bush Administration] official said that fears of an Iranian-style – and Iranian-influenced – theocracy in Baghdad have faded because it has become clear that Iraq's Shiite population is not a monolithic bloc and not necessarily dominated by Tehran ... [Said an administration official:] "Our basic position is that as we get to know more of Iraqi society, we're more comfortable with a democratic process, and if that emerges with a predominant Shiite role, so be it ... There's been a steady education process here."'

11 It is important to note that I do not possess theological expertise on any faith, least of all my own. But I do believe it is fair to state that any 'religion' that condones and encourages the killing of innocent people is not, in fact, religion, but terrorism. For more on this discussion, see Seiple (2004b, 38–9); also see Seiple (2006a).

12 I first wrote about this in Seiple (2003a).

13 For example, see Douglas M. Johnston's recommendation for a 'religious attaché' at U.S. embassies worldwide (2006); also see Seiple (2004b).

14 For more on this topic, see Seiple (2003b).

15 For a detailed example of our work, see Galli (2007).

16 See, for example, Freedberg Jr. (2008).

REFERENCES

Alliance of Civilizations. 2006a. *Highlights of the High Level Group Report, 13 November 2006*. New York: United Nations Publications.

– 2006b. *Report of the High Level Group, 13 November 2006*. New York: United Nations Publications.

Carr, E.H. 1964. *The twenty years' crisis, 1919–1939*. New York: Harper & Row.

Chandrasekaran, R. 2003. How cleric trumped U.S. plan for Iraq. *Washington Post*, 26 November.

Danan, L. 2007. *Mixed blessings: U.S. government engagement with religion in conflict-prone settings*. Center for Strategic and International Studies Report, August 2007. Washington, DC: Center for Strategic and International Studies.

DeYoung, K. 2007. Military must fill Iraq civilian jobs. *Washington Post*, 8 February.

Dorwart, J.M. 1991. *Eberstadt and Forrestal*. College Station, TX: Texas A&M University Press.
Esposito, J.L., and D. Mogahed. 2008. *Who speaks for Islam? What a billion Muslims really think*. Washington, DC: Gallup.
Freedberg Jr., S.J. 2003. Forget Vietnam. *National Journal* 35 (47/48): 3572–5.
– 2008. The I-axis. *National Journal*, 20 December.
Gaddis, John Lewis. 2004. *Surprise, security, and the American experience*. Cambridge: Cambridge University Press.
Galli, M. 2007. A new day in Vietnam. *Christianity Today*. http://www.christianitytoday.com/ct/2007/may/24.26.html.
Global Leadership Forum. 2007. Category videos (Global Leadership Forum 2007). http://www.globalengage.org/forumabout/media/videos.html?task=viewcategory&cat_id=14.
Grey, S. 2004. Follow the mullahs. *Atlantic Monthly* 294 (4): 44–5.
Johnston, D.M. 2006. Faith-based diplomacy: Bridging the religious divide. Unpublished presentation, Washington DC, 8 December. http://www.icrd.org/storage/icrd/documents/bridging.pdf.
Kennan, G. 1985. *American diplomacy*. Chicago: University of Chicago Press.
McDougall, Walter A. 1997. *Promised land, crusader state: America's encounter with the world since 1776*. New York: Houghton Mifflin.
Miles, J. 2005. Religion and American foreign policy. *Survival* 46 (1): 23–37.
National Commission on Terrorist Attacks. 2004. How to do it? A different way of organizing government. In *The 9/11 Commission Report*, 399–428. New York: Norton.
Petraeus, D.H., and J.F. Amos. 2006. *Counterinsurgency* FM 3-24 MCWP 3-33.5. http://usacac.army.mil/cac2/coin/repository/FM_3-24.pdf.
Sampaio, J. 2007a. Memo to participants in the AoC Group of Friends Ministerial Meeting. 26 September.
– 2007b. Presentation to 'OSCE chairmanship conference on intolerance and discrimination against Muslims.' 9 October. Cordoba, Spain.
– 2007c. Presentation to the U.N. General Assembly on 'high-level dialogue on interreligious and intercultural understanding and cooperation for peace.' 4 October. New York.
Seiple, C. 1999. Window into an age of windows: The U.S. military and the NGOs. *Marine*
– 2000. The 'lessons' of Kosovo. *Marine Corps Gazette* June, 39–41.
– 2002. Homeland Security concepts and strategy. *Orbis* 46 (2): 259–73.
– 2003a. *Religion and the new global counterinsurgency*. Institute for Global Engagement. http://www.globalengage.org/issues/articles/security/582-religion-and-the-new-global-counterinsurgency.html.

- 2003b. Waging peace. Government Executive. http://www.govexec.com/dailyfed/0503/052003db.htm.
- 2004a. Interrogating Islam ... and ourselves. *Review of Faith & International Affairs* Fall:38–9.
- 2004b. From the president: Religion & realpolitik: Recommendations for the next president. Institute for Global Engagement. http://www.globalengage.org/pressroom/ftp/443-from-the-president-religion-realpolitik-recommendations-for-the-president.html.
- 2006a. From the president: Ramadan and reason. http://www.globalengage.org/pressroom/ftp/478-from-the-president-ramadan-reason.html.
- 2006b. Re-visiting the geo-political thinking of Sir Halford John Mackinder: U.S.–Uzbekistan relations, 1991–2005. http://www.globalengage.org/attachments/771_seiple_dissertation.pdf.

Seiple, C., and J. White. 2004. Uzbekistan and the Central Asian crucible of religion and security. In *Religion and security: The new nexus in international affairs*, ed. D. Hoover and R. Seiple, 37–57. New York: Rowman & Littlefield.

Stein, J. 2006. Can you tell a Sunni from a Shiite? *International Herald Tribune*. 17 October. http://www.nytimes.com/2006/10/17/opinion/17stein.html.

Weisman, S.R. 2003. Sensing Shiites will rule Iraq, U.S. starts to see friends, not foes. *New York Times*, 20 November.

PART FIVE

Conclusion

15 Religion, Identity, and Global Governance: What Have We Learned?

PATRICK JAMES

Looking Back, Looking Forward

This study began in chapter 1 with a series of questions about religion, identity, and global governance. It moved toward answers by focusing on ideas, evidence, and practice. Each of the questions from chapter 1 will be answered in a tentative and summary way. This includes references to a few other studies. The discussion that follows regarding each set of questions is based on insights derived from the intervening chapters. The chapter concludes with a few thoughts about the way forward.

Religious Identity

How is it established that religious identity is a relevant factor in explaining or understanding politics? How can it be known whether religion is 'real' versus a cover for some other factor such as ethnicity or group power?

These questions, in an overall sense, already are important ones in the study of religion and politics. The answers offered in this study parallel some of what is established now about the role of religion in politics and society. Religion very frequently plays a genuine role in politics. Witness what Appleby (2000) labels as 'militance.' Many instances of self-sacrifice in the name of religion are observed; attempts to label this behaviour as purely instrumental across the board are not convincing. Moreover, religion overlaps with significant transnational issues like fundamentalism, human rights, and political Islam (Fox and Sandler 2004). As for the related question about whether religion is just a front for something else, other studies have challenged this way of thinking quite effectively in both theory and evidence (Appleby 2000; Fox and Sandler 2004). The tendency to pose the question so persistently, in fact, is a telltale sign of bias against religion as an established part of human life.

This volume offers a number of illustrations that establish the value of religious identity in understanding and explaining political processes. The chapters on evidence and practice are most helpful here. Consider analysis of the Iraqi civil war in chapter 8. The evolution of that conflict shows how religion is used by factions to interpret the world. Militias with a religious designation, such as the Mahdi Army under the radical Shia cleric Muqtada al-Sadr, are formidable threats to peace and security. This chapter, in fact, shows that a security dilemma with a *religious* foundation is at work in sustaining civil strife in Iraq. Saddam Hussein's brutal dictatorship, which turned to Islam for legitimacy as it became increasingly threatened from within, clearly made religious identity more salient. After the regime's fall, that tactic produced unintended consequences. Sectarian violence between Sunni and Shia ensued once the U.S. invasion and occupation removed Saddam's iron grip on Iraq.

Very different in how it played out, but also convincing about the impact of religious identity, is the account in chapter 9 of the debate over sharia law in Canada's province of Ontario. It is interesting to note that the debate included citations of Islamic beliefs by both advocates and opponents of sharia as an alternative to the court system vis-à-vis family law. The arguments back and forth are grounded in different visions of society on the role of religion. The main points of division, at a basic level, concern religion as a private versus public part of identity and the degree to which some forms of the latter, most notably regarding Islam, are consistent with a free society.

Religious beliefs also affect substantive matters of negotiation as practised by NGOs. This is well-established by the account in chapter 11 of Christian mediation. For example, Christian mediators in general prefer the role of communicator over manipulator in attempting to move those in conflict closer to agreement. Stylistic nuances also are revealed and follow from doctrinal differences among Christian traditions. For example, the Reformed and Anabaptist traditions prefer elite and grassroots mediation levels, respectively.

Chapter 12 tells a convincing story about the political efficacy of religious NGOs. (Chapter 13, which focuses on Canadian foreign policy, reinforces this main point in a more specific context.) Put simply, these NGOs indeed are religious in that their priorities about policy match well with self-proclaimed belief systems. For example, chapter 12 shows how religious NGOs such as Project Ploughshares work with Western middle powers toward the goal of enhanced human security. This is understood in the sense of peace and social justice in tandem – goals that eschew power politics and can be traced to the altruistic and pacific doctrines of the Abrahamic religions. The same could be said of the objectives pursued successfully by the IGE, which are covered in chapter 14. Moreover, the altruistic and pacific doctrines espoused are common to all the world's major religions, in spite of how these belief systems are distorted in some instances to justify mayhem.

What comes out of this evidence, collectively speaking, is that religion generally is more important vis-à-vis understanding and explaining the actions of NGOs rather than states – at least when it comes to positive behaviour. In that sense, as the volume's title anticipates, religion fits in substantively with global governance. It clearly is part of the problem, but also part of the solution, in achieving human security worldwide.

With regard to the related question about the reality of religious identity, the answer begins with the observation in chapter 2 that faith antedates the international relations theories that have ignored it for so long. As the chapter points out, religion creates a community of believers. Thus the potential for mobilization is omnipresent and goes beyond instrumental rationality into *affective motivation*. As chapter 3 goes on to argue, such motivation inherently blurs the boundary between what is regarded as public versus private. It always is possible to challenge whether self-stated religious motivations are real, of course, but sustained, extreme actions in the name of religion make it increasingly difficult to imagine that religion is just a cover for what is observed. Examples include homicide bombing and implicitly suicidal acts of insurgency against more numerous, better-equipped, and highly trained adversaries. Chapter 5 uses cross-national, aggregate data to show that religious exclusivity on the part of a government is associated with its involvement in international crises. More in-depth, case-based research would be needed to establish a causal process there, but the evidence on the surface points in the direction of religious beliefs influencing at least some aspects of foreign policy.

One example of just that type of research appears in chapter 7. Muslims in India, while experiencing violence, are observed to be very restrained in their responses. The chapter traces this to the evolution of Islamic theology in that part of the world to favour pacific relations with others, even in the face of violence.

Religious identity can be malleable. This comes out clearly in chapter 10 as a feature among even of those in positions of high leadership. The chapter's recounting of Catholic doctrine on just war shows how pontiffs evolved from pacifists into warriors and then back into a belief that violence should be used only in the most extreme circumstances. Chapter 14, which is autobiographical, tells the story of one person's evolution in religious identity. The author moves toward social consciousness as a result of reflection on his Christian beliefs and takes action through the Institute for Global Engagement, which promotes dialogue and religious freedom around the world.

Religious identity interacts, as chapter 6 points out, with other aspects of identity, such as ethnicity, class, and language. This chapter uses the example of the 'War on Terror' to show how religious identity can be shaped by historical context. Muslims in general and Islamic humanitarian organizations in particular are put on the defensive by the War on Terror's dichotomy of good versus bad in the context of their religion.

While the weight of evidence in this volume favours the position that religion is real rather than a cover for other motivations, it also is important to point out limitations. Happily, not all violent behaviour that superficially might be attributed to religion is in fact traced to differences over faith. The investigation in chapter 7 of the Sri Lankan conflict establishes that material differences between ethnic groups, not religious belief, explain the horrific violence between Tamils and Sinhalese. And sometimes good things happen – consistent with the best aspects of religious faith – but not because of religious adherence. An example of that is Canadian coordination with religious NGOs in pursuit of human security, as described by chapter 13. This is *not* faith-based diplomacy. Instead, the Canadian government sees religious NGOs as targets of opportunity to more effectively carry out its foreign policy goals.

Religion, in sum, is real. So are the effects of religious identity on politics.

Religion and Global Governance

When and how can religion be applied to advance positive, peace-oriented agendas? What is the balance between religion as a cause of violence versus a possible source for achievement of a more peaceful world? In an overall sense, how do religion and global governance relate to each other?

Religion indeed can be applied in a positive way. It gives legitimacy to constructive as well as destructive acts committed by those who claim to act out of faith (Appleby 2000; Fox and Sandler 2004). As will become apparent, the glass is either half empty or half full, depending on the point of view, regarding the overall role played by religion. Relevant here is the established finding that a significant number of religious groups find secularization threatening (Almond, Appleby, and Sivan 2003). This is at the root of many problems encountered in the world vis-à-vis religion.

With regard to the context for a positive role for religion, three ingredients emerge as important in this volume: theology, NGOs, and a minimal level of state non-interference, if not support, for their actions.

Theology matters. While only alluded to at various points in this volume, the coercive and even violent message of Al Qaeda and its fellow travellers is well known. Less familiar is the important story told in chapter 7 about Islamic theology in South Asia. Among Indian Muslims, beliefs evolved in a manner that promoted peaceful responses even to violent provocations. (Only Kashmir is an exception.) Examples of this occur elsewhere, although, as chapter 3 points out, there is a bias against seeing religious pacifism as sincere. Consider also the importance of religious doctrine in the story told by chapter 10 about the evolving role of the pontiff in world politics. Changing interpretation of the Bible produced pacifism, subsequent direct involvement in power politics and even violence, and ultimately a sense of responsibility to promote peace and avert war in all but the most extreme circumstances.

Religious NGOs are important builders of a more peaceful world. This is a more specific observation that follows from the prescient designation of an essential role for NGOs per se in global governance (Murphy 2000, 795). Consider the account in chapter 11 of Christian mediation. The international community generally reacts well to such efforts. Success stories such as Sant' Egídio's role in quelling the Mozambique civil war demonstrate that religious intermediaries can succeed. The chapter also points out limits: NGOs can succeed when they set realistic goals, especially given their inherent inability to use coercion to move negotiations forward. When religious NGOs operate with awareness of those realities, they can achieve great success. Other positive examples are provided in chapter 12 vis-à-vis partnership with Good Samaritan states to promote the UN's Millennium Development Goals, chapter 13 with respect to coordinated efforts with the government of Canada in delivering its message in favour of religious pluralism, and chapter 14 in regard to the activities of the IGE in Pakistan and elsewhere to achieve higher levels of dialogue and religious freedom.

While NGOs matter, states still hold the overwhelming amount of power in this world and need, at the very least, to get out of the way for NGOs to do their work. More than that would be desirable, but a permissive environment is essential for NGOs to effect change. Western middle powers are cited in chapter 12 as working in tandem with NGOs to remove the underlying causes of strife within and between states. An especially notable government action is Canada's establishment of a Global Centre for Pluralism. It might be added that NGOs in such collaboration may be able to address the 'moral insufficiency' of global governance as Murphy (2000, 791) described the situation a decade ago – a description that regrettably still seems on the mark today.

Chapter 4 shows interesting possibilities for states to behave in different ways within and beyond their borders with regard to religion. While supporting human rights at the UN, various Islamic states continued to oppress their own people. Ironically, as chapter 6 points out, Western states fiercely protect the rights of their citizens but do unintended harm with the discourse coming out of the War on Terror. This divisive language, which categorizes Muslims simplistically as good or bad, inhibits efforts by Islamic humanitarian organizations. It creates a climate of fear and may even produce the very reaction it is intending to head off – hostility to Western institutions and values.

What about the balance between positive and negative aspects of religion? The best answer to this question is perhaps one provided by chapter 14: religion has been and will always be a part of the problem, and a part of the solution. Chapters 2 and 3, however, provide ample warning that the world after 9/11 is likely to answer the question in a biased way that overlooks the positive side of the ledger. Bias is twofold: against religion in general and against Islam in particular. The chapters in Part Four of this volume already make it clear that the story of religion is not just one of fanaticism and violence. Religious NGOs obviously are making efforts, sometimes individually and others in alliance with governments, toward a better world.

Unfortunately, religious fanaticism – within Islam but also other religions – continues to wreak havoc around the globe. Iraq's civil war, retold in chapter 8, is just the latest glaring example. Chapter 5, which takes a cross-national approach, reveals the importance of state religious exclusivity in not only creating resentment at home but also stimulating conflict abroad. States with an official religion or religious legislation tend to be more involved in international crises, especially within a protracted conflict. This generalization points toward the importance of working on behalf religious freedom in order to reduce or even eliminate the forces that can set in motion both domestic and interstate strife.

One way to answer the question is to focus instead on how things are developing rather than in an absolute sense. It is possible to be cautiously optimistic about religion at a global level. Consider the long-term evolution of the Catholic Church, noted above, in the direction of active peace-building. Examples of mediation efforts from within Christianity also can be cited. Moreover, religious pluralism is being promoted by both states and NGOs. Perhaps these efforts will crystallize, with enough time, into a clear trend toward religion as a force for peace and social justice.

Overall, the jury is still out on religion. NGOs and some governments work toward a better world, but other governments and religious extremists continue to engage in oppression and acts of violence. Peace-oriented agendas are moving forward to the extent that theology, NGOs, and governments come together in the right way.

This discussion leads naturally into the question of how religion and global governance relate to each other in a general way. Recall from chapter 1 that global governance is an encompassing concept. It is more than just how governments interact with their people or each other. Instead, global governance refers to institutions, mechanisms, relationships, and processes to manage interests, rights, and obligations (Thakur 2006; Thakur and Weiss forthcoming). While it might seem arbitrary, a focus on each of the first four concepts, in turn, should permit a relatively complete treatment of global governance.[1]

Consider institutions. Religion is a double-edged sword here. It can grant extraordinary levels of legitimacy to institutions, which then makes them more powerful forces – for better or worse. The message here, as elsewhere in this volume, seems to favour pluralism. State religious exclusivism, taken to extremes, may encourage international conflict and even warlikeness. At the same time, consider highly inclusive institutions such as the Alliance of Civilizations, built under the auspices of the UN. Perhaps it could be said that, at this stage of human history, most institutions with a religious character lean toward the exclusive end of the scale, but with some discernible movement in the other direction. An optimistic but not unrealistic reading of human history would suggest that learning on this subject, like others, is not only possible but probable.

Mechanisms of global governance with potentially positive effects come through clearly from this study. One example is mediation. Another to consider is dispute resolution based on religious principles, although the immediate instance from this volume met with mixed to negative reactions in what would seem like a hospitable setting. With greater knowledge of religion – or, to be candid, lower levels of ignorance among the public – a more accepting environment for governance incorporating religious principles might be expected to emerge in the increasingly multicultural and diverse societies that make up the world of today. This does *not* mean embracing theocracy – that would take us back to exclusivism – but instead a willingness to consider a wider range of value systems, some of which have origins in religion, for governance within and even beyond the level of the state.

Encouraging are stories told in this volume about relationships that involve religious entities. One example is the coordination of religious NGOs and middle powers to achieve more together than either could separately in meeting UN development goals. Since an obligation to assist those in need forms a part of all religions with significant numbers of adherents, this bodes well for global governance.

What about processes of global governance? A process leading to more responsiveness of governments to the vision of human rights held by their own citizens – not necessarily the ideas purveyed by the West – would be most welcome in the Islamic and especially Arab world. Islamists, it becomes interesting to note, are engaged with a discourse on human rights and may even find some common cause with their governments regarding self-determination – a key difference with Western states, highlighted during the colonial era, on what is meant by human rights in a more encompassing sense. Another process, perhaps weakly underway as a delayed reaction to 9/11, is a more accepting attitude toward religion among residents of technologically advanced states. Noted already in this volume are the tendencies in academe and the popular media to ignore or even ridicule religion. This will not help leaders engage the vast majority of the world's population, which *is* religious and unlikely to abandon such inclinations. More informed foreign policies, which take into account religious identity in shaping political allegiances, would improve global governance.

Religion and Leadership in Foreign Policy

How might governments in general, and especially the international system-leading United States, reconsider their foreign and domestic policies in light of religious resurgence around the world? In particular, what is the legacy of the Bush Doctrine and what should come next?

The first of these questions answers itself to some degree in that virtually everything underway now in the domain of policy should be reconsidered in light of a more realistic view of religion. A military confrontation writ large with religion is not the way forward and the monolithic portrayal of Islam, in particular, misses so much of the inherent ambivalence within the great religions (Appleby 2000). Appleby, to cite one example, emphasizes education among religious communities to stimulate their thinking about the more peaceful aspects of doctrine already in place. Education and the value of greater knowledge is a priority that comes back again, below, in an even more encompassing way.

One basic problem with existing foreign policy is clear after reading chapters 2 and 3 of this volume: lack of knowledge creates bias and hostility to religion among academics who advise national leaders, and decision-makers themselves. Consider the low levels of awareness about Islam in particular from the poll results reported in those chapters. In addition, chapter 4 describes a role for Islam in promotion of human rights that may well surprise many readers. Add the shocking effect of 9/11 to low levels of understanding and it is easy to end up with sub-optimal policies toward religion in world politics.

U.S. and other decision-makers, as urged by chapter 5, need to look at religion and religiously motivated actors on the world stage more objectively. Imputing irrationality and even evil intent to those with a religious agenda can only lead to policies that produce more disappointing results. Some general recommendations either appear in or are implied by respective chapters from this volume:[2]

- Be more sceptical about the assumption that religion is behind a given conflict and that it must play a negative role in politics (chapters 3, 4, 7).
- Coordinate with FBOs to achieve community enhancement at home and abroad (chapter 2).

- Move further away from the War on Terror discourse, as per initial steps of the Obama Administration, to avoid isolating and possibly radicalizing natural allies among Muslims and Islamic NGOs in development of civil society (chapter 6).
- Encourage interfaith organizations and religious pluralism (chapters 5, 6, 14).
- Encourage faith-based conflict management and mediation (chapters 10–11).
- Show greater willingness to work with NGOs, who may have complementary goals and appears less threatening in many settings (chapters 12–14).
- Make an effort to integrate Muslims into civil society (chapter 9).
- For the United States in particular, as related to Iraq, recognize that religious organizations can and must be part of any viable effort toward political stabilization (chapter 8).

This list leads into two more encompassing observations.

First, much can be done to improve the role of religion in the world and take advantage of what it can offer rather than simply assuming it out of existence or treating faith as an obstacle to human progress. It is time to move beyond secularization in theory and practice. This is not a call for any particular person or group to adopt religious beliefs. Instead, the message is to accept religion as a part of this world and address it constructively.

Second, this volume's ideas, evidence, and practice converge exceptionally well on a pragmatic and viable set of recommendations that follow from the first point above. Enhanced knowledge about religion, cooperation with NGOs, and interfaith dialogue would be a welcome change from what exists now. Lack of knowledge about religion accounts for many of the problems besetting the world today. The slow progress in Iraq is merely the most high-profile example of what can happen when religion is assumed to be epiphenomenal and destined for the trash bin of history.

This observation returns to a point of curiosity from the outset of the volume: what about the Bush Doctrine? While chapter 1 established it as something other than a religious statement, matters of faith come to the forefront in its assessment. The Bush Doctrine reflected a one-dimensional and highly militarized national security policy. This mindset did not start with Bush, but it did intensify after 9/11. Notable is the absence of a nuanced sense of what role religion in general and

Islam in particular might play in policy implementation. President Bush created a discourse, summed up as the War on Terror, that created a sense of 'good' versus 'bad' Muslims and greatly distorted relations with the Islamic world and, most regrettably in the immediate term, religious factions in Iraq. Islam as well as Islamism are multifaceted in their sense of belonging, and a 'black-and-white' division is not helpful in interacting with the products of these belief systems. Perhaps the best legacy of the U.S. experience with the Bush Doctrine in action, if it transpires, would be a less monolithic sense of encompassing belief systems such as Islam. This could facilitate an improved performance in U.S. foreign policy across the board.

Even John Paul II, with all of his disposition against the use of military force, realized that in some instances it still could be justified. Thus the message here is *not* that any and all military actions are wrong, with religion as the basis for holding that belief. Instead, a greater balance needs to be achieved by the United States, the likely system leader for decades to come, between military and other implements of foreign policy. Ironically, some of the best ideas about 'how' might be right next door – in Canada, where debates about peaceful management of multicultural realities have been underway for decades. If the diversity of the world's great religions can be comprehended more fully, the worst by-products of policy made out of lack of knowledge may be averted.

Final Thoughts

This volume started out with three sets of questions. The answers provided in this chapter, of course, lead to new questions. If religion is real, what are the causal mechanisms that lead from faith to either cooperation or conflict? Given that religion can be used to promote peace and well-being in some contexts, how can those conditions be encouraged around the globe? Finally, if governments (most notably the United States) need to reorient their policies to take religion more seriously, how can that be encouraged to happen? These and many other questions will continue to preoccupy the study of religion, identity, and global governance for years to come.

NOTES

1 It is understood that the concepts overlap with each other in some ways,

so this path is followed to facilitate a summary rather than offer a rigorous scheme of organization.

2 It is quite possible that additional chapters imply a given recommendation on the list, but those noted are deemed sufficient to make the point.

REFERENCES

Almond, Gabriel A., R. Scott Appleby, and Emannual Sivan. 2003. *Strong religion: The rise of fundamentalisms around the world*. Chicago: University of Chicago Press.

Appleby, R. Scott. 2000. *The ambivalence of the sacred: Religion, violence, and reconciliation*. Lanham, MD: Rowman & Littlefield.

Fox, Jonathan, and Shmuel Sandler. 2004. *Bringing religion into international relations*. New York: Palgrave Macmillan.

Murphy, Craig N. 2000. Global governance: Poorly done and poorly understood. *International Affairs* 76:789–803.

Thakur, Ramesh. 2006. Enhancing global governance through regional integration. *Global Governance* 12:233–40.

Thakur, Ramesh, and Thomas G. Weiss. (forthcoming). *The UN and global governance: An idea and its prospects*. Bloomington: Indiana University Press.

Contributors

Yasemin Akbaba is an assistant professor at Gettysburg College. Her research focuses on mobilization of ethnic and religious groups and the effects of religious discrimination on ethnic and religious conflict. Her publications have appeared in journals such as *Civil Wars* and *International Interactions*.

Anthony Chase is associate professor of diplomacy and world affairs at Occidental College. Previous works include *Human Rights in the Arab World: Independent Voices*, a range of peer-reviewed articles, and guest editorship of a Muslim World Journal of Human Rights special volume, 'The Transnational Muslim World, Human Rights, and the Rights of Women and Sexual Minorities.' He is working on a book entitled *Human Rights Debates in the Muslim World*.

Jonathan Fox is an associate professor of political studies at Bar Ilan University in Ramat Gan, Israel, and director of the Religion and State project. He has written extensively on the intersection of religion with politics, conflict, and international relations. His most recent book is *A World Survey of Religion and the State* (Cambridge University Press, 2008).

Patricia M. Goff is associate professor of political science at Wilfrid Laurier University in Waterloo, Ontario. She is co-editor with Kevin C. Dunn of *Identity and Global Politics* (Palgrave Macmillan, 2004) and author of *Limits to Liberalization: Local Culture in a Global Marketplace* (Cornell University Press, 2007).

Ron E. Hassner is an assistant professor of political science at U.C. Berkeley. His research revolves around symbolic and emotive aspects of international security with particular attention to religious violence, Middle Eastern politics, and territorial disputes. His book *War on Sacred Grounds* (Cornell University Press, 2009) examines the causes and characteristics of conflicts over holy places.

James L. Heft is a Marianist priest and the Alton Brooks Professor of Religion at the University of Southern California and the president of the Institute for Advanced Catholic Studies. Author and editor of nine books and over 160 articles, his latest edited work to which he contributed a chapter is *Learned Ignorance: An Inquiry into Intellectual Humility in the Abrahamic Religions* to be published by Oxford University Press.

Patrick James is professor and director of the Center for International Studies at the University of Southern California. He is the author or editor of seventeen books, along with over one hundred other articles and book chapters. James recently served as vice-president of the International Studies Association and president of the Association for Canadian Studies in the United States.

Steven L. Lamy is a professor in the University of Southern California's School of International Relations and vice-dean for academic programs in the college. He earned his PhD in international relations from the Graduate School of International Studies at the University of Denver in 1980. His areas of research and teaching include international relations theory, foreign policy analysis, European security, human security, and global governance.

Robert B. Lloyd is associate professor of international relations at Pepperdine University and heads its International Studies Program. He received his PhD from Johns Hopkins University's Paul H. Nitze School of Advanced International Studies in Washington, DC. His areas of research include international conflict management and negotiation and Africa.

Cecelia Lynch is professor of political science and director of the Center for Global Peace and Conflict Studies, University of California, Irvine. Her expertise, publications, and teaching concern the role of religion and ethics, humanitarianism, social movements, and civil society in international politics.

Manus I. Midlarsky is the Moses and Annuta Back Professor of International Peace and Conflict Resolution at Rutgers University, New Brunswick. His latest books are *The Killing Trap: Genocide in the Twentieth Century* (Cambridge University Press, 2005), *Origins of Political Extremism: Mass Violence in the 20th Century and Beyond* (Cambridge University Press, forthcoming 2011), and the edited volume, *Handbook of War Studies III* (University of Michigan Press, 2009).

Evan H. Potter is associate professor of communications at the University of Ottawa, Ontario. He writes frequently on nation-branding and is the author of *Branding Canada: Projecting Canada's Soft Power through Public Diplomacy* (McGill-Queen's University Press, 2009).

Nukhet Sandal is a Visiting Fellow at the Watson Institute for International Studies, Brown University. Her research interests include religion and international affairs, politics of divided societies, and international relations theory.

Chris Seiple is the president of the Institute for Global Engagement (www.globalengage.org), a Virginia-based, research, educational, and diplomatic 'think-and-do-tank' that builds sustainable religious freedom worldwide through local partnerships – one relationship at a time. He is the founder of *The Review of Faith & International Affairs* (www.rfiaonline.org).

John F. Stack Jr is director of the School of International and Public Affairs and professor of politics, international relations, and law at Florida International University. His book, *The New Deal in South Florida*, co-edited with John A. Stuart, won the silver medallion in the 2009 Florida Book Awards for non-fiction.

Zeynep Taydas is an assistant professor at Clemson University. Her research focuses on causes of civil conflicts, third-party interventions in ethnic conflict, and Turkish politics. She is co-author of the book (with David Carment and Patrick James) *Who Intervenes? Ethnic Conflict and Interstate Crisis* (Ohio State University Press, 2006), and her articles have appeared in *International Interactions* and *International Studies Review*.

Index

Abu-Lughod, Lila, 109–10, 124n1
Abu-Nimer, M., 162
Accatolli, Luigi, 214
Accounting for Fundamentalisms (Marty and Appleby), 54n10
Acheson, Dean, 287n1
Action by Churches Together, 124n5
Adler, E., 188
Afghanistan, 213, 281, 285
AFSC (American Friends Service Committee), 262
Aga Khan, 11, 282
Air India bombing, 277
Akbaba, Yasemin, 8–9, 159–86, 325
Al-Qaeda. *See* al-Qa'ida
al-Qa'ida, 72–3, 175. *See also* terrorism
Albright, Madeleine, 221, 293
Alexander VII (pope), 227
Alliance of Civilizations (AoC) project, 297–8, 307n6, 319
American Friends Service Committee (AFSC), 262
American Jewish World Service (AJWS), 256–7
Amnesty International, 194–5

Anabaptists, 226, 228T, 236–7, 236T
Anderson, L., 167
anger, 130, 133–4
Annan, Kofi, 298
Appleby, R. Scott, 44–5, 54n10, 97, 218, 223, 241n4, 313, 321
Aquinas, Thomas (saint), 245
Arbitration Act (Ontario), 9, 188–90, 195
Aristotle, 132
Arjomand, Homa, 195
Artists beyond Borders (Keck and Sikkink), 250
Asad, Talal, 113
Atatürk, Kemal, 136, 137
Atlantic Monthly, 302
Augustine (saint), 204, 224
Aurangzeb (king), 135
authoritarianism, 133
authority space: of Indian Muslims, 137, 138F; of Jaffna Tamils, 148–51, 152F; of Sunnis, 170, 172–3, 180n5; theory of, 8, 129–32, 130F
Axworthy, Lloyd, 255, 279

Baath, 167–9, 175
Badawi, Zaki, 136

Badr Brigades, 176
Ban Ki-moon, 298
al-Banna, Hassan, 71
Baptists, 228T, 229
Beagle Channel dispute, 228, 234
Ben-Dor, G., 84
El Bendary, Ahmad, 124n8
Benedict XVI (pope), 215. *See also* Ratzinger, Joseph
biculturalism, 274
Biddle, S., 174
bin Laden, Osama, 133, 143
Black Tigers, 153
Boyd commission, 189–90, 192, 193
Breaking the Spell (Dennett), 53n3
Bremer, Paul, 172, 301
Bringing Religion into International Relations (Fox and Sandler), 48
British Empire, 147–8
broad approach, 5, 37, 43, 44, 46–8, 46F
Bromke, A., 289n13
Bryant, Michael, 189
Buckley, D., 245, 246
Buddhism: and non-governmental organizations, 252; in Sri Lanka, 94, 148–9, 179; and state religious exclusivity, 89; teachings of, 139, 246. *See also* Sri Lanka
Bueno de Mesquita, B., 82
Bush administration: on Muslim world, 57; use of human rights language, 65. *See also* United States (foreign policy)
Bush doctrine: and crisis, 83; defined, 13; foreign perceptions of, 285, 286, 288nn20–21; Iraq invasion, 177; and John Paul II, 217; legacy of, 14, 322–3; and national security, 303; as response to terrorism, 31–3. *See also* United States (foreign policy)
Bush, George H.W., 212
Bush, George W., 83, 300, 303

Cairo Trilogy (Mahfouz), 71–2
Callières, François de, 220
Calvin, John, 51, 225
Canada: Canadian Charter of Rights and Freedoms, 193, 194, 195, 274; immigration to, 190–1, 276; Kissinger on, 271, 287n1; media outlets in, 283; minority rights in, 275, 288nn6–8; multiculturalism in, 190–1, 272, 277–83, 283–4. *See also* faith-based arbitration
'Canada and the Holy See,' 287n3
Canada (foreign relations): Canadian International Development Agency (CIDA), 280; diplomatic brand of, 275, 288n5; Global Centre for Pluralism, 11, 282–3, 318; international reputation of, 275, 288n5; and statecraft, 11, 273–7, 284; and United States, 284–6; and Vatican, 287n3
Canada (organizations): Canadian Catholic Organization for Development and Peace, 261; Canadian Council of Churches, 257; Canadian Council of Muslim Women (CCMW), 195–6; Canadian office of the Council on American-Islamic Relations (CAIR-CAN), 193–4; International Commission on Intervention and State Sovereignty, 244–5, 255–6; MCC Canada, 280–1; Mines Action Canada, 280
Caritas Internationalis, 124n5, 260–1
Caritas Report, 253

Carlson, Jeffrey, 124n3
Carr, E.H., 25, 294
Carter doctrine, 13
Carter, Jimmy, 228T, 229, 231, 234, 237, 238
Casanova, José, 112–13
The Case for Democracy (Sharansky), 14
Cassin, Rene, 66, 76n4
Catechism of the Catholic Church, 215, 216
Catholic. *See* Roman Catholic
'Catholic Contributions to International Peace,' 241n2
Center on Faith & International Affairs, 304
Centesimus annus (John Paul II), 209–10, 212, 216, 227
'The Challenge of Peace,' 211
Charest, Jean, 275
Charter of Rights and Freedoms. *See under* Canada
Chase, Anthony, 6, 57–77, 325
Cheney, Dick, 14
China, 14–15, 252
Chrétien, Jean, 255
Christian churches and organizations: Actions by Churches Together, 124n5; American Friends Service Organization, 262; Canadian Catholic Organization for Development and Peace, 261; Canadian Council of Churches, 257; Caritas Internationalis, 124n5, 260–1; Catholic Relief Services (CRS), 261; Center of Faith & International Affairs, 304; Church of Sweden, 265; Coast Interfaith Council of Clerics, 120; Ecumenical Earth Program, 252; Grow Climate Justice, 261; Institute for Global Engagement (IGE), 12, 221, 236, 297, 303–4; Lutheran World Federation, 124n5; MCC Canada, 280–1; Mennonite Central Committee, 11, 280–1; My Sister's Keeper, 259–60; Norwegian Church Aid, 265–6; Project Ploughshares, 257–8; Quaker United Nations Office, 261; Religious Society of Friends (Quakers), 261–2. *See also* Islamic organizations
Christian-Muslim Relations in Africa (PROCMURA), 120
Christianity: and Canadian foreign policy, 279–81, 289nn12–16; Christian mediator (term), 223; Evangelical Christianity, 13–14, 119–20, 295–6; liberation theology, 254; missionary activity, 148; and non-governmental organizations (NGOs), 295; Social Gospel movement, 253–5; and social responsibility, 245, 257–63, 265–6; traditions of, 223–7; and war, 203–6. *See also* John Paul II (pope); papacy; religion
Christianity and the Social Crisis (Rauschenbusch), 254
Christiansen, Drew, 209
Cibamo (priest), 260
The City of God (St Augustine), 224
Clash of Civilizations and the Remaking of World Order (Huntington), 44, 84
Clinton, Bill, 237, 238
Coalition Provisional Authority (CPA), 172
Coast Interfaith Council of Clerics (CICC), 120

Cold War, 12, 115, 300
Cole, J., 167, 177, 179–80n4
'A Common Word' (Benedict XVI), 215
The Compendium of the Social Doctrine of the Church, 217
Comte, Auguste, 22
Condorcet, Jean-Antoine-Nicolas de Caritat, 22
conflict: conflict resolution process, 230T; conflict transformation, 231
Connor, W., 30
Cooper, A., 248
Council on American-Islamic Relations, 193–4
counterinsurgency manual, 302
Cox, Robert, 26, 249
crisis: and religion, 83–7, 93–9; state religious exclusivity, 6–7, 87–9, 94T, 95T, 96–8; study of, 81–3; variables in, 82, 99n2. *See also* international relations (IR)
Cross-Cultural Roundtable on Security, 283
culture: biculturalism, 274; cultural mistreatment, 173, 180n5; and ethnic strife, 30
Culture and Religion in International Relations (Lapid), 48

Dalai Lama, 246
Davies, G.A., 82
Dawkins, Richard, 39
de Chastelain, John, 288n5
De Silva, K.M., 147–8
de Waal, Alex, 115
death penalty, 215–16
deep approach, 5, 37, 43, 44–7, 46F
democracy: and crisis, 82; and human rights, 63–4, 76n4; in India, 134, 139, 140; and religious regimes, 124n4
Dennett, Daniel, 53n3
A Dialogue on Foreign Policy, 280
diplomacy. *See* international relations (IR)
Dispute Resolution in Family Law: Protecting Choice, Promoting Inclusion, 189–90
diversionary theory, 7, 82–3, 85
'Do Muslim Women Really Need Saving?' (Abu-Lughod), 109–10, 124n1
Dodge, T., 171–2, 180
Dorfman, Aaron, 256
Durkheim, Emile, 22
Durrani, Akram Khan, 305

Eastern Europe, 26, 207–11
eastern religions. *See* Buddhism; Hinduism
Eberstadt, Ferdinand, 299–300
Eck, Diana L., 286
Economist, 151
Ecumenical Earth Program, 252
education: and pluralism, 281–2; and religion, 293, 304, 321; in Sri Lanka, 148
Eelam People's Revolution Liberation Front, 150
Egyptian Organization of Human Rights (EOHR), 60–1, 70–1, 74
Eickelman, D.F., 20–1
Eisenhower Administration, 307–8n9
Eisenstein, M.A., 84
emotional reaction: anger, 130, 133–4; fear, 133; loss, 129–34, 141, 152–3; xenophobia, 191
The End of Faith (Harris), 39

Engineer, Asghar 'Ali, 137–9
the Enlightenment, 22, 113
Enterline, A.J., 82
ethical guidelines, 110–11
ethnicity: and blame, 132; ethnic conflict, 161; and identity, 29–30; impact of secularization, 112–13; in Iraq, 166–9, 171–3, 174–7, 178; security dilemma, 164–5; in Sri Lanka, 146–51, 316
Evangelical Christianity, 13–14, 119–20, 295–6
Evangelium vitae (John Paul II), 216
Evans, Gareth, 248

faith-based arbitration: Arbitration Act, 9, 188–90; and identity, 187, 194–5; Islamic law, 189–97
faith-based diplomacy, 221, 281, 289n17
Faith-Based Diplomacy: Trumping Realpolitik (Johnston), 220–1
Faith campaign (*al-Hamlah al-Immaniyah*), 169
Finkel, D., 84
Fontan, V., 170, 172
Ford, John, 205
foreign aid, 280
forensic theology, 302
Forrestal, James, 300
Fossum, J.E., 247, 249
Fox, Jonathan, 7, 27, 48, 81–107, 83, 84, 164, 325
Freedberg, S.J., Jr, 293
Freud, Sigmund, 22
Friedman, Thomas, 295
Frijda, Nico H., 130, 132
Frost, Robert, 31
Fuchs, M.H., 245, 246
functionalism, 96

Fundamentalism Project (Marty and Appleby), 4, 44–5, 54n10

Gadhafi, Moammar, 228
Gandhi, Mahatma, 39, 136
Gandhi, Rajiv, 128, 154
Gaudium et spes, 206, 208, 218n1
Geertz, Clifford, 30–1, 49
Gelpi, C., 82
gender: gender equality, 64, 67, 195–6; Muslim women, 109–10; non-governmental organizations, 259–60
Gerson, Michael, 13
Gill, A.J., 163–4
Girard, Rene, 50
Glazer, N., 23–4
Gleditsch, K.S., 82
Global Centre for Pluralism, 11, 282–3
global governance (defined), 15n1
The Global Resurgence of Religion and the Transformation of International Relations (Thomas), 48
globalization: global infosphere, 277–8; and human rights, 68–73; and identity, 197; impact of, 20; and religion, 295, 306
Globe and Mail, 194
Goff, Patricia M., 9, 187–200, 325
Gonçalves, Jaime, 228
Good Samaritan states, 11, 244, 246–7, 247–50
Gopin, M., 97, 98, 278
Gorbachev, Mikhail, 209
Gordon, Milton, 23
group identity. *See* identity
guide states, 11, 247, 249
Gulf war, 212
Gurr, T.R., 168

Haidt, J., 132
Hammarskjöld, Dag, 225, 237
Harris, Sam, 39, 53n3
Hasenclever, A., 84
Hassan, Bahey el-Din, 60, 70, 74
Hassner, Ron E., 5–6, 37–56, 325–6
Heft, James L., 9–10, 203–19, 326
Hehir, Bryan, 212–13
Higgot, R.A., 248
Hinduism: in India, 8, 134–6, 139–41, 143–5; religious conflict, 128–9, 145–6; in Sri Lanka, 94, 179; state religious exclusivity, 89. *See also* Sri Lanka
Hitchens, Christopher, 39
Hoffmann, S., 25
homosexuality, 64
Hoon, Geoff, 171
Hullander, Edwin, 117
human rights: Canadian foreign policy, 278–9; categorization of, 67–8; and democracy, 63–4, 76n4; Egyptian Organization of Human Rights, 60–1; faith-based law, 194–5, 196; and globalization, 68–73; and international relations, 296–9; in Iraq, 169; and John Paul II, 210; in Muslim world, 6, 57–68, 70–6, 318, 320; treaties, 66–8, 70–1, 76n3
humanitarianism: government suspicion of, 7, 116–18, 124n7, 316; humanitarian intervention, 115, 255–7; interfaith groups, 120–2, 125n11; post–9/11, 115; post–Cold War, 114–15. *See also* non-governmental organizations (NGOs)
humiliation, 172–3, 180n5
Huntington, Samuel, 44–5, 48, 84, 246

Hurd, E.S., 98
al-Hussainī, Karīm (aga khan), 11, 282
Hussein, Saddam, 8, 159, 160, 165, 166–9
Hyun-Kyung, Chung, 124n3

identity: dimensions of, 28–31; and globalization, 197; and immigration, 187; rebuilding of, 303; social imaginary, 9, 191–3, 198
identity (religious): definitiveness of, 168–9; faith-based arbitration, 187, 194–5; influence of, 84, 162; interaction with other identities, 110–11, 124n3; and politics, 86, 99n5, 142, 173, 313–15
immigration: to Canada, 190–1, 276; and identity, 187; and Islam, 198; minority rights, 275, 288nn6–8; reasonable accommodation, 271, 287n2
India: extremism in, 134–5; Muslim intellectuals in, 137–43, 315–16; pre–Independence India, 135–7; and Sri Lanka, 128, 153–4; violence in, 8, 126
Indonesia, 281
information politics, 251
Inglehart, Ronald, 24–5, 48, 64
Institute for Global Engagement (IGE), 12, 221, 236, 297, 303–4
Institutes (Calvin), 51
insurgent forces: in Iraq, 165–6, 167, 169–73, 174–7; in Sri Lanka, 150–4
Inter Caetera, 227
Inter-Faith Action for Peace in Africa (IFAPA), 121
International Action Network on Small Arms (IANSA), 258

international affairs. *See* international relations (IR)
International Campaign against Shari'a Courts in Canada, 195
International Commission on Intervention and State Sovereignty (ICISS), 244–5, 255–6
International Covenant on Civil and Political Rights (ICCPR), 66–8, 76n3
International Covenant on Economic, Social, and Cultural Rights (ICESCR), 66–8, 76n3
international crisis. *See* crisis
international relations (IR): faith-based diplomacy, 221, 281, 289n17; global infosphere, 277–8; Good Samaritan states, 244, 246–55; guide states, 247, 249; and human rights, 65, 75, 296–9; internationalism, 273, 287–8n4; middle powers, 247–50; and Muslim world, 188; and pluralism, 277–83, 283–4; publications about, 38–41, 53nn1–2, 54n7; relational diplomacy, 304; and religion, 292, 307n5, 321; and secularization theory, 293–4. *See also* crisis
international relations (IR) (study of): approaches to, 25–6, 37–8, 40–1, 47–8, 49; and religion, 25–7; theories of, 294, 298, 307n6
International Religious Freedom Act (US), 119–20
internationalism, 273, 287–8n4
Interreligious Coordinating Council, 122
IR (international relations). *See* international relations (IR)
Iran, 60, 72

Iraq: ethnic groups, 166–9; human rights, 67; insurgent forces in, 165–6, 167, 169–73, 174–7; invasion of, 65, 165–6, 170–4, 300–1, 302, 308n10; and John Paul II, 211; and religion, 8–9, 163–4; Saddam Hussein, 166–9, 170; security dilemma, 165–6, 170–4, 177–9
Isaacs, H.R., 28–9, 30
Islam: faith-based arbitration, 189–97; and global security, 304; human rights in Muslim world, 57–68, 70–3, 73–6, 318; in India, 134, 135, 137–43, 315–16; Ismaili Muslims, 11; militant Islam, 301–2, 308n11; Muslim politics, 20–1; and papacy, 215; perception of, 31–3, 118–19, 142, 276, 297, 321; and politics, 136, 162; publications about, 38–40, 53–4n6, 53nn4–5; public/private distinction, 114; and Saddam Hussein, 169; social responsibility, 245–6, 267, 268n1; and terrorism, 84; in Uzbekistan, 294; in western societies, 137, 187–8, 198, 276, 284, 288nn7–8, 299. *See also* religion
Islamic organizations: Canadian Council of Muslim Women, 195–6; Canadian office of the Council on American-Islamic Relations, 193–4; Coast Interfaith Council of Clerics, 120; government suspicion of, 7, 116–18, 124–5n10, 124nn7–9, 316; Holy Land Foundation, 124n10; International Campaign against Shari'a Courts in Canada, 195; Islamic Center of Southern California, 125n11; Islamic Institute of Civil Justice (IICJ), 189,

192; Islamic Jihad, 228–9; Islamic Relief, 267; Islamic Society of North America (ISNA), 194; Muslim Aid, 119; Muslim brotherhood, 71–2; Muslim Communities Working Group (MCWG), 11, 282–3; non-governmental organizations, 59, 62–3, 115–16. *See also* Christian churches and organizations

Islamists: beliefs of, 76–7n5; and human rights, 59–61, 70–3, 74–5, 320; insurgent groups, 175, 176–7

Jama'at-i Islami, 141
James, Patrick, 3–16, 313–24, 326, 327
Jaruzelski, Wojciech, 209
Jervis, R., 177
Jinnah, Mohammad Ali, 136
John Paul II (pope): *Centesimus annus*, 209–11, 227; and Eastern Europe, 207–11, 287; on himself, 205; and just war theory, 9–10, 203, 204, 213–14, 216–18; and Middle East, 211–13, 214, 215; papacy of, 204, 206–7, 213, 215–16; and United States, 217, 237. *See also* Christianity; papacy
Johnson, D.M., 278
Johnston, D., 220–1
Judaism and Jewish peoples, 214, 245, 256–7. *See also* religion
Juergensmeyer, Mark, 19, 21, 38, 50, 52, 161
just war theory: Gulf war as just, 212; and John Paul II, 9–10, 203, 204, 213–14, 216–18; theology of, 215–16, 316. *See also* war

Keating, T., 287–8n4
Keck, M., 250, 258, 263

Keller, J.W., 82
Kengor, Paul, 13
Kennan, George F., 300
Kennedy, John F., 303, 307n9
Kenya, 118–19
Khan, Maulana Wahiduddin, 141–2
Khan, Sayyed Ahmad, 137
Kharazi, Kamal, 59–60
Khatami, Mohammad, 60, 298
Khilafat movement, 143
Khomeini, Ruhollah (ayatollah), 71, 72
Kiernan, B., 20
King, Martin Luther, 39
Kirkpatrick, L.A., 84
Kissinger, Henry, 271, 287n1
Kuo, David, 14
Kurds, 167–9
Kutty, Ahmad, 194
Kymlicka, W., 190, 197–8, 274–5

Laborem exercens (John Paul II), 208
Laghi, Pio, 211
Lalman, D., 82
Lamy, Steven L., 11, 244–70, 326
Lapid, Yosef, 48
Larson, E.J., 41
Laustsen, C.B., 86
Lawler, P., 244, 247
Laythe, B., 84
Lederach, John Paul, 231, 236–7
legitimacy, 85, 163–4, 319
Lerner, J.S., 130
Letter to a Christian Nation (Harris), 53n3
Leuba, James L., 41
Levant, Ezra, 289n19
leverage politics, 251–3
LeVine, M., 114
Lexis-Nexis database, 53n4, 53–4n6

liberal expectancy. *See* secularization theory
liberalism, 197–8
liberation theology, 254
Liberation Tigers of Tamil Eelam (LTTE), 146, 149–54
Library of Congress subject searches, 38, 53nn1–2
Lloyd, Robert B., 10, 52, 220–43, 326
Loewenstein, G., 130
loss: and anger, 133–4; emotional reaction to, 129–34; and Indian Muslims, 141; and Jaffna Tamils, 152–3
Lubac, Henri de, 208
Lumsdaine, D.H., 247–8
Luther, Martin, 51, 225
Luttwak, E., 98
Lynch, Cecelia, 7, 108–27, 326

MacIntyre, A., 224
magisterial reformation, 225, 236
Mahdi Army, 176
Mahfouz, Naguib, 71–2
manipulator (term), 233, 234
Markings (Hammarskjöld), 225
Marty, Martin, 44–5, 54n10, 215
Marx, Karl, 22
material leverage strategies, 252
Matthews, Robert, 279, 289n12
Maududi, Maulana Sayyed Abul 'Ala, 140, 141
Mayaram, Shail, 146
Mbillah, Johnson, 120
MCC Canada, 280–1
McCormick, Richard, 207
McDougall, Walter, 303
McGuinty, Dalton, 189, 190, 196
McLuhan, Marshall, 277
Mearsheimer, J., 26

media: bias of, 37; in Canada, 283; Danish cartoon controversy, 283, 289n19; influence of, 70; and international relations, 278; and Islam, 276; and multiculturalism, 288nn7–8; non-governmental organizations, 251–3; publication statistics, 38–40, 53n1–5, 53–4n6, 54n7; secularization theory in, 39, 42, 53n3
media (outlets): *Atlantic Monthly*, 302; *Economist*, 151; *Globe and Mail*, 194; *New York Times*, 37, 39, 53n6; newspapers, 39–40, 53nn4–5, 53–4n6; On Faith (online forum), 39, 53n5; *Time*, 207; *Toronto Star*, 288n8; *Washington Post*, 39; *Western Standard*, 289n19
mediation: benefits of religion, 97–8, 220–1; characteristics of Christian mediation, 10, 229–37, 314; Christian involvement in, 221–2; Christian mediator (term), 223; Christian traditions, 223–9; conclusions about, 239–41; conflict resolution process, 230T; faith-based arbitration, 187–97; motivation for, 223; niche diplomacy, 248; religious ideologies, 86–7, 88, 97, 100n12; responses to, 237–9, 317, 320; roles of, 232–3
Mennonites, 11, 228T, 236–7, 280–1
Metzger, Yona (chief rabbi), 203
Meyer, Jane, 14
Middle East, 211–13
middle powers, 11, 247–50, 264–5, 318
Midlarsky, Manus I., 8, 128–58, 327
The Mighty & The Almighty (Albright), 221

Miles, Jack, 19, 21, 217
Millennium Development Goals (MDGs), 263–5, 267T
Miller, A.S., 84
Miller, R.A., 82
Mills, C. Wright, 23
missionary activity, 148
modernization, 85, 138, 161
moral leveraging, 252
Morgenthau, Hans, 25–6
Moynihan, Daniel, 23–4, 26–7
Mozambique, 228, 233, 235, 238, 240
Mughal empire, 135, 137, 138F
Muhammad (prophet), 141–2
multiculturalism: backlash against, 275–6, 288nn7–8; and Canada, 190–1, 272, 273–83, 283–4, 284–6; and identity, 198; liberal multiculturalism, 197–8; and Muslim intellectuals, 138–9
Mumtaz Ali, Syed, 192
Munton, D., 287–8n4
Muravchik, Joshua, 14
Murphy, Craig, 318
Muslim Aid, 119
Muslim brotherhood, 71–2
Muslim Communities Working Group (MCWG), 11, 282–3
Muslims. *See* Islam
My Sister's Keeper, 259–60

Nader Shah, 135
Nadwi, Sayyed Abul Hasan 'Ali, 139–41
Nasr, Vali, 45
Nasserists, 60
neo-realism, 26. *See also* realism
the Netherlands, 249
New York Times, 37, 39
news industry. *See* media

newspapers. *See* media (outlets)
NGOs. *See* non-governmental organizations (NGOs)
niche diplomacy, 248
Nicholson, James, 211
'No Peace without Justice, No Justice without Forgiveness' (John Paul II), 213
non-governmental organizations (NGOs): actions of, 245, 317; and Christianity, 295; Code of Conduct, 115, 124n5; government suspicion of, 116–18, 122–3, 124–5n10, 124nn7–9; and middle powers, 249, 250; in Muslim world, 59, 62–3, 115–16, 267; in Nordic countries, 265–6; and politics, 11, 250–5, 314–15; and Responsibility to Protect Doctrine (R2P), 255–63. *See also* humanitarianism; religious organizations
Norris, Pippa, 24–5, 48, 64
Northern Ireland, 19
Norwegian Church Aid, 265–6
Nossal, K., 248, 289n13
Novak, Michael, 208, 211

O Canada: Armed and Ready, 281
Obama, Barack, 33
Okumu, Washington, 233
Omar, Mohammed (mullah), 143
On Faith (online forum), 39, 53n5
One Campaign, 253
Ontario, 188–97, 314
Organization of Economic Development (OECD), 263

pacifism: and Anabaptists, 226; in Canada, 281; and Christianity, 204, 317; and John Paul II, 208–9, 212–

13; Project Ploughshares, 257–8; Quakers, 261–2. *See also* war
Pakistan, 136–7, 140, 143–4, 305
Palestinian Academic Society for the Study of International Affairs (PASSIA), 121–2
papacy: and Canada, 287n3; and politics, 205–6; and repentance, 213. *See also* Christianity; John Paul II (pope); Vatican
Patriot Act, 116–17, 124n7
Paul VI (pope), 206, 260
Paulston, C., 274
Peace of Westphalia, 21–2, 33, 293, 307n1
Pearson, Lester B., 287n4
Pedahzur, A., 84
Peebles, P., 146, 148–9
People's Liberation Organization for Tamil Eelam, 150
Perle, Richard, 14
permeable societies, 250
Philpott, Daniel, 19, 21, 27, 33, 38, 50–1
Piscatori, J., 20–1
pluralism. *See* multiculturalism
pluralism (religious), 111
policy formation, 250–5, 273–7, 284
politics: accountability politics, 252–3; global campaigns, 253; and identity, 173; information politics, 251; in Islamic states, 59–60; Islamic theology of, 136; leverage politics, 251–3; and papacy, 205–6; political extremism, 129; political prisoners, 60; political scientists, 42–3; publications about, 38–40, 53n1–2; and religion, 161; symbolic politics, 251
population growth, 23–4

Portuguese empire, 147
Posen, B., 164, 170
positivist approach, 45–6, 46F
post-modern states, 277, 289n11
Potter, Evan H., 11, 271–91, 327
Prabhakaran, Velupillai, 153
Praeger series (Lapid), 48
Pratt, C., 244
Prejean, Helen, 216
Project Ploughshares, 257–8
prospect theory, 131–2
Protestant Reformation, 50–1
Prothero, Stephen, 40
psychological needs, 86, 163, 168
Pupatello, Sandra, 189

Qadhafi, Moammar, 228
al-Qa'ida, 72–3, 175
Qibla, Ayaz, 306
Quaker United Nations Office, 261
Quebec, 191, 275, 288nn6–8

radical reformers, 226, 236
Ratzinger, Joseph, 214, 216
Rauschenbusch, Walter, 254
Reagan doctrine, 13
realism: critique of, 294; and John Paul II, 210; and religious beliefs, 25–7. *See also* neo-realism
reasonable accommodation, 271, 287n2
reconciliation, 231
reflexivity, 250
the Reformation, 225–6
Reformed tradition, 228–9, 228T, 235–6, 236T
regime, 88. *See also* state sovereignty
relational diplomacy, 304
religion: and Canadian government, 273–4; as cover factor, 96, 315; and

crisis, 83–7, 93–9; current status of, 23–4; and diplomacy, 278; and education, 293, 304; and globalization, 295, 306; ideology, 295; influence of, 20, 33–4n1, 292; and legitimacy, 85, 163–4; and liberalism, 197–8; nature of, 30–1; and politics, 160–2, 313; practice vs. doctrine, 110; as private, 113–14; psychological needs, 86, 163, 168; publications about, 38–41, 53n1–5, 53–4n6, 54n7; relevancy of, 27–9; religious communities, 273; religious extremism, 111; religious hybridity, 111–12, 124n2; religious literacy, 40, 321–2; state religious exclusivity, 6–7, 87–9, 94T, 95T, 96–8, 315, 319; and terrorism, 83–4, 318; in United States, 20, 23–4, 32–3, 98; ways of life, 295–6. *See also* Christianity; identity (religious); Islam; Judaism and Jewish peoples; theology

Religion: The Missing Dimension of Statecraft (Johnston), 220–1

religion (study of): in academia, 41–3, 108, 320; approaches to, 5, 37–8, 40–1, 43–52, 46F, 109–12; and international relations, 25–7; Muslim intellectuals, 137–43; reasons for, 112–14. *See also* secularization theory; theology

religious violence: and crisis, 83; eastern religions, 179; and extremism, 84; Huntington's *Clash of Civilizations*, 44; increase in, 160–1; as intrinsic to religion, 84–5, 99n4; in Iraq, 167–9, 173, 174–7, 178; in Northern Ireland, 19; and secularization, 21–2, 112–13; and South Asia, 128–9; and terrorism, 19, 96; and thick religion, 50, 52. *See also* wars

respect, 296–9

Responsibility to Protect Doctrine (R2P), 245, 248, 255–63

Review of Faith & International Affairs, 304

Revolutions in Sovereignty (Philpott), 38, 50–1

Reychler, L., 164

Reynal-Querol, M., 161

Rhetoric (Aristotle), 132

Rice, Condoleezza, 302

riots, 143–5

Rittberger, V., 84

Robertson, Colin, 287n1

Robinson, Rowena, 144

Roe, Anne, 41

Roman Catholic Church: and Canada, 287n3; *Catechism of the Catholic Church*, 215, 216; history of, 22, 224, 224–7; and mediation, 227–8, 228T, 234, 235, 236T, 237–8, 240; and social responsibility, 260–1; Vatican II, 204, 206, 218n1. *See also* Christianity; papacy; Sant' Egídio (community of)

Roman Empire, 204, 224

Roosevelt, Eleanor, 66, 76n4

Rubin, B., 98

Rudolph, S.H., 28

Sacred and Secular (Norris and Inglehart), 48

Sadr movement, 176–7

al-Sadr, Muhammad Sadiq (ayatollah), 176

al-Sadr, Muqtada, 176, 314

Sahnoun, Mohamed, 255

Saideman, S.M., 165
Salvatore, A., 114
Sampaio, Jorge, 298–9, 303
Sandal, Nukhet, 7, 81–107, 327
Sandler, Shmuel, 48
Sant' Egídio (community of), 228, 228T, 233–4, 235, 237, 238, 240. *See also* Roman Catholic Church
Saudi Arabia, 66, 67–8
secularization theory: development of, 22–4; influence of, 4, 39, 41, 42, 53n3, 81; and international relations, 293–4; liberal expectancy, 4, 23, 26; and secular values, 112–13. *See also* religion
security dilemma, 9, 164–6, 170–4, 177–9, 256
Seiple, Chris, 12, 236, 292–310, 327
Seul, J.R., 86
shaming campaigns, 252
Shaping the 21st Century, 263
Sharansky, Natan, 14
sharia law, 9, 189–90, 193–4, 199, 314
Shia, 71, 72, 289n18
The Shia Revival (Nasr), 45
Shiites: and invasion of Iraq, 170, 176–7; and Saddam Hussein, 167–9, 179–80n4; study of Shi'ism, 45
Sikhs, 275, 288n6
Sikkink, K., 250, 258, 263
Sinhalese. *See* Sri Lanka
al-Sistani, Sayyid Ali al-Husayni (grand ayatollah), 301
'Six Principles of Political Realism' (Morgenthau), 26
Snyder, J., 177
Social Gospel movement, 253–5
social imaginary, 9, 191–3, 198
social responsibility: and Christianity, 257–63, 265–6; foreign aid, 280; Islam, 245–6, 267, 268n1; Judaism, 245, 256–7
social sciences, 22–4, 41–2
social sins, 254–5
Somalia, 119
South Africa, 233
South Asia, 128–9. *See also* India; Sri Lanka
Spenser, Herbert, 22
Sri Lanka: ethnic conflict in, 146–51, 316; Indian intervention in, 128, 153–4; LTTE activity in, 149–53; pre-Independence, 147–9; Sri Lankan Army (SLA), 151–4; violence in, 8
Stack, John F., Jr, 4–5, 19–36, 327
Stansfield, G., 167
state sovereignty: ethno-religious cleansing, 113; humanitarian intervention, 255–7; and international relations, 27; and legitimacy, 163–4, 319; and Peace of Westphalia, 21–2, 33; post-modern states, 277, 289n11; and Protestant Reformation, 51–2; security dilemma, 164–5; state religious exclusivity, 6–7, 87–9, 94T, 95T, 96–8, 315, 319; weakening of, 161–2
Stenner, K., 133
Stokke, O., 244
Strong Religion (Almond, Appleby, and Sivan), 276
subject searches, 38–9, 53–4n6, 53nn1–2, 54n7
suicide bombers, 96, 146, 152–3, 154
Sulcz, Tad, 209
Sunnis: as insurgents, 170, 172–3, 174–6; perception of, 71; and Saddam Hussein, 168–9, 174–5

Svensson, I., 100n12
Sweden, 249, 265
symbolic politics, 251
Syria, 63

Taft, Robert A., 299
Tamils: authority space of, 148–51, 152F; Liberation Tigers of Tamil Elam (LTTE), 146, 149–54; Tamil Eelam Liberation Organization, 150; Tamil United Liberation Front (TULF), 151. *See also* Sri Lanka
Tanzim al-Qa'idat al-Jihad fi Bilad al-Rafidayn, 175
Taydas, Zeynep, 8–9, 159–86, 327
Taylor, C., 191–2, 198
Terror in the Mind of God (Juergensmeyer), 38
terrorism: Air India bombing, 277; American policy, 301; and Bush doctrine, 31–3; funding of, 115–18; publications about, 40; and religion, 83–4; and religious violence, 19; suicide bombers, 96, 146, 152–3, 154; and thick religion, 50, 52. *See also* al-Qa'ida
Tessler, M., 76n5
Thakur, Ramesh, 15n1
Thalheimer, Fred, 41–2
theology: forensic theology, 302; importance of, 317; Islamic theology of politics, 136; of just war theory, 215–16, 316; liberation theology, 254. *See also* religion
thick religion, 5, 38, 46F, 47–9, 50–2
Thomas, Scott M., 48
tikkum olam, 245, 256
Time, 207
Toft, M.D., 84, 163
tolerance, 286, 288n5, 296

Toronto Star, 288n8
The Tragedy of the Great Powers (Mearsheimer), 26
Treaty of Tordesillas, 227
Treaty of Westphalia. *See* Peace of Westphalia

United Nations: Alliance of Civilizations project, 297–8, 307n6, 319; Millennium Development Goals, 263–5, 267T; Quaker United Nations Office, 261; Responsibility to Protect Doctrine (R2P), 245; Universal Declaration of Human Rights, 58–9, 66, 68, 76n2
United States: counterinsurgency manual, 302; and religion, 20, 23–4, 32–3, 111; Republican Party, 15n3; United States Institute of Peace, 221, 241n2; as world power, 12–14
United States (foreign policy): cultural approach to international relations, 25–6, 293; Eastern Europe, 26; faith-based diplomacy, 221; foreign perceptions of, 285, 286, 288nn20–21; funding of terrorist networks, 116–18; invasion of Iraq, 165–6, 170–4, 180nn6–8; Iraqi perception of, 167; and John Paul II, 211–13; national security policy, 299–303, 307–8n9; political thought of, 19; and religion, 12, 13, 98, 119–20. *See also* Bush administration; Bush doctrine
Universal Declaration of Human Rights (UDHR), 58–9, 66, 68, 76n2
us-them syndrome, 30, 44, 133
Uzbekistan, 294

Varshney, A., 143, 145

Vatican II, 204, 206, 218n1
violence, 143–5. *See also* religious violence; terrorism
Voltaire, 22

Waever, O., 25, 86
Waite, Terry, 228–9, 238, 240
Wald, K., 42
Walker, Liz, 259
Waltz, K.N., 26
Waltz, Susan, 66
war: publications about, 38–40; and religion, 39; as social sin, 254–5; War on Terror, 115–23, 125n11. *See also* just war theory; pacifism; religious violence
Washington Post, 39
Weber, Max, 22
Wee, Paul, 229
Weigel, George, 208
Weisman, S.R., 308n10
Weiss, Thomas G., 15n1
Wentz, R., 86
Western Standard, 289n19
Westphalia (Peace of). *See* Peace of Westphalia

White-Hammond, Gloria, 259
Wilcox, C., 42
Williams, Rowan, 199
Witham, L., 41
Witte, K., 133
Wojtyla, Karol, 206, 208. *See also* John Paul II (pope)
Wolfowitz, Paul, 14
women. *See* gender
Women of the Book, 122
Woodward, Bob, 14
World Concern, 119
World Conference of Religions for Peace, 121
World Council of Churches (WCC), 252
World Day of Peace message (John Paul II), 212, 213, 218n2
world politics, and religion, 28
World Vision International, 119, 266
Wyszynski, Stefan, 217, 218n3

xenophobia, 191

al-Zarqawi, Abu Musad, 175–6
Zartman, I.W., 230